BOOK OF HEROES

DATE DUE

Lest We Forget

of Southwestern Michigan

VOLUME 3

Stories from:
Revolutionary War
Civil War
World War I
World War II
Korea
Vietnam
Middle East

Edited by
Teresa LaPlante

Designed by
Marlena Andvik / Teresa LaPlante

Lest We Forget Project Managers
Don Alsbro / Robert Hatch

The stories contained within this book are the personal recollections and perspectives of participating individuals. They are not intended as a substitute for an official history or record of military service. *Lest We Forget of Southwestern Michigan* does not verify the accuracy of the accounts described by participants and/or their family members.

Library of Congress Cataloging-in-Publication Data
Book of Heroes, Compiled by Lest We Forget of Southwestern Michigan, Volume 3: Stories from Revolutionary War, Civil War, World War I, World War II, Korean War, Vietnam War, the Middle East, and Patriotic stories/ poems.

This book is third in a series, following Wartime Memoirs of Southwestern Michigan Veterans, Volumes 1 and 2.

p. cm.

ISBN: 978-0-9711114-1-7

INTRODUCTION

This book of veteran's stories is a project of _Lest We Forget_, a non-profit organization in Southwestern Michigan that was formed in 2006 to preserve and disseminate the memories of the men and women who fought for the freedoms we sometimes take for granted! Unfortunately, patriotism is not being taught in our schools and the wars such as WWII, Korea, and Vietnam don't rate more than a page or two in their school history textbooks with no questions on the state tests.

Someone, in talking about memories, once said, _"When a veteran dies without writing his or her story, it is like a library burning down."_ What you have in your hands are the memories of veterans who, fortunately, did put their stories to print before their libraries burned down. This is _Lest We Forget's_ third book of veterans' stories. The first one, written in 2008, contains 83 WWII stories, and I venture to say that during this period (2008-2012) at least a quarter of the 83 veterans have passed on. Fortunately, they put their thoughts to paper before their library burned down. Their children, grandchildren and great-grandchildren are the benefactors.

With this third book, we now have recorded over 250 veterans' stories that have been preserved. _Lest We Forget_ is not trying to glorify the horrors of war. Rather, it is our passionate desire that through our educational programs such as WWII re-enactments, WWII, Korea and Vietnam Long Distance TV Learning Panels, Vietnam Travelling Wall, tribute to the Korean veterans and our veterans story books that we have "brightened the future by illuminating the past!" We are a free nation because of our veterans!

This book is a departure from the first two books which were stories of only Berrien County veterans. This book contains the stories of local veterans, but it also contains stories of individuals who have meant a lot to _Lest We Forget_. Bob Heft was a high school student in 1958 who designed our current 50-star American flag that has flown over our country for 62 years. Bob made at least eight visits to our _LWF_ events before his untimely death in 2009. Likewise, there are stories by WWII Medal of Honor recipient Hershel Williams and Korean Medal of Honor recipient Ron Rosser who have both made several visits to our LWF events. In that same regard, _LWF_ made four visits to the West Virginia home of Frank Buckles, the "last living American WWI veteran." Our fifth visit was to Arlington cemetery in March 2010 for Frank's funeral. A dozen members of _LWF_ were privileged to say that they spoke with this man.

We also have stories about Dr. Bassett Brown and his professional, athletic and military accomplishments during WWII; Ted Tees, the recipient of not one, but two Silver Stars for heroism during the Vietnam War; Ron Robaska's riveting story "Agent Death is Killing Me;" and Cheryl Lane Walberg not knowing for years whether her husband who was shot down in Vietnam was dead or alive. This is just a snapshot of the stories that await you in this book. Thanks to everyone who took the time to write their memoirs or to gather memoirs from others.

I hope that you will enjoy reading these stories and that it will motivate you to make sure your family members write their stories.

Don Alsbro, COL, US Army (ret)

President, _Lest We Forget_

LestWeForgetUSA.org

ACKNOWLEDGEMENTS

<u>HOW I WANTED TO STAY OUT OF THE WAR</u> - I would like to thank Rhonda Payne for all of her help in being introduced to veterans like Mr. Strasser. As Physical Activity Director at the convalescent center, she spends a great deal of time taking care of   the patients there, including all of our veterans. I appreciate her assistance. --Gary C. Lulenski, M.D.

<u>A MEDIC IN THE BATTLE OF THE BULGE</u> - *Lest We Forget* would like to thank Karen and Dale Freehling. They were of invaluable help in gathering the information for this story. Karen actually brought written material about the 75th division that she has kept all of this time, since Zach returned home in 1945. We very much appreciated their assistance.

<u>PHOTOS FROM ABOVE</u> - *Lest We Forget* would like to sincerely thank Barrie Chapman for providing most of the information and actually spending time during the interviewing process so that this veteran's story could be put together. Without his help it really would not have been possible to produce the story.

<u>CAPTURE OF THE GERMAN SUBMARINE U505</u> - *Lest We Forget* would like to thank Evelyn Clifford who helped to establish the invaluable memoirs of this story.

<u>SERVING IN THE COAST GUARD</u> - It is clear from Veteran Wood's story that he has an excellent memory and really did not need much help from the interviewer to complete his memoirs. His wife, Margaret as well as his daughter, Mary Lou Dickey, were helpful in refreshing his memory and were interested in his story. They were actually present in all of the interviewing. It was truly a delight to spend time with this colorful and somewhat witty gentlemen. —Gary C. Lulenski, M.D.

<u>THE LAST HORSE CAVALRY TROOP</u> - This veteran's story was compiled from a series of interviews, as he was not able to write it down on his own. The assistance of his wife, Katie, and his son and daughter-in-law, Terry & Maggie James, were invaluable in putting this story together. They helped with the chronology and with the editing of the manuscript, as well as, provided a picture book, which helped Veteran James to remember a great deal about his time in the service. This was a fascinating story for all of us and I hope you enjoy reading it.—Interviewer: Gary C. Lulenski, MD

BELATED ACKNOWLEDGEMENT

The following stories of deceased veterans in Book One, Wartime Memoirs,
were researched and written by Robert Hatch:

Edward Dwan	Eber Van Brocklin	William Hood
George Jones	Erwin Kriel	*(co-written with daughter)*
Robert McMullen		

CONTRIBUTORS/CREDITS:

Ruthe Bomberger
Jimmy Butt
Richard Grom
Robert Hatch
Sharon Haynes, Program Director,
      Berrien Springs Parent Partnership
Dr. Gary Lulenski
Phil Manni
Lila Megna
Jim O'Malley
Loren Patterson
Ellen Marshall
Jennifer Scally
Ron Schadler
Raymond Sreboth
Cristine Timmons
Cheryl Walberg

TABLE OF CONTENTS

TABLE OF CONTENTS

TABLE OF CONTENTS

TABLE OF CONTENTS

CONTENTS OF CD

These are the expanded versions of the print stories

To read the stories on the CD, you will need to have an Adobe Reader program on your computer. You can download this for free at www.adobe.com.

STORIES FROM PRE-CIVIL WAR

Revolutionary War
War of 1812

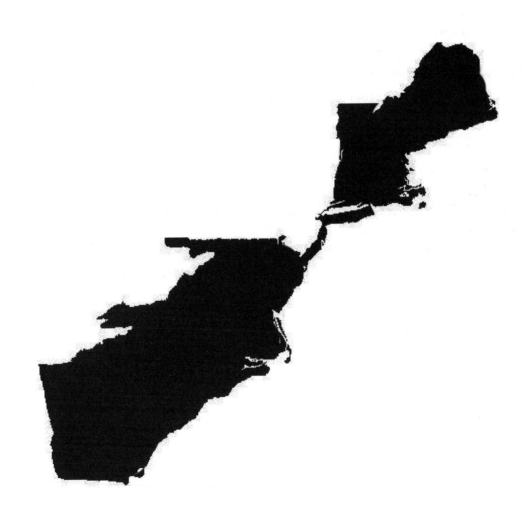

SIKES/PARREN REVOLUTIONARY WAR HISTORY

Abner Sikes

Ludlow, Mass.

Abner Sikes, Ludlow, Private Capt Ruben Nunn's Company. Nicholas Dike's Regiment; pay abstract for mileage dated Roxbury, Sept. 17, 1776, also same company and regiment, pay abstract for mileage, etc., dated Boston, Nov. 26, 1776, mileage for 92 miles allowed said Sikes. Also, Captain Aaron Graves' Company Col. David Leonard's Regiment, entered service May 8, 1777; discharged July 8, 1777, service 2 months, 10 days at the Northward including 10 days (206 miles) travel from camp to home.

Also, Captain Ephraim Chapin's Company, Col Ruggles Woodbridge's Regiment; enlisted Aug. 12 (also given Aug 23) 1777; discharged Nov 30 (also given Nov. 20) 1777; service 3 months 26 days (also given 3 months 14 days) under General Gatesin Northern Department, including 7 days (146 miles) travel home order for payment amount of roll dated at Springfield and signed by Captain Chapin.

Mrs. Zenas Sikes, Grandfather, Samuel Janes, 11, had a remarkable 'soldiers' family. It appears that all four of his sons were in the Revolutionary War and were in it at such an advanced age:

Samuel was 53 and 55 years old

Jonathan was 51 years old

Obediah was 49 years old

Elisha was 43 years old

These four brothers have their graves in East Street Cemetery, Easthampton, marked with Revolutionary Soldiers markers and their names are on the Memorial Tablet at Memorial Hall in Northhampton.

Samuel and Jonathan were soldiers in the French & Indian War, and were at the fall of Louisburg. Samuel, Jr. is said to have lived after the war in the eastern part of the state and was probably buried there.

There were 16 soldiers in the Revolutionary War from Massachusetts by the name of Sikes. All but two or three were from Springfield and its surrounding towns and probably were descendents of Richard Sikes.

READ MUCH MORE OF THIS FAMILY HISTORY ON OUR CD

STORIES FROM THE CIVIL WAR

1860 - 1865

A country divided. . .

THE GOD OF PEACE SHALL BE WITH YOU

John Akin

1st Michigan Cavalry Co. M

Written by Etta Akin Perham - 1968

"The God of Peace shall be with you." Phil. 4:9

John Akin was born in Scotland in 1843, came to Canada with his mother, Mary Ann Akin, at the age of four years. His father had died and his mother was brought to Kingston, Canada, with his uncle who was captain on the big ship upon which they sailed.

There were John and his mother and sister, Agnes Akin, who left their native home to be near her brother in Canada. A short time after coming to Canada, Mary Ann gave birth to a second daughter, Mary Ann, who was always called Ann. John, as I remember them telling later, went to live with his uncle who lived in New York state. I remember him telling of Albany, and how he used to skate on the Erie Canal. His uncle was a blacksmith as I remember. Pa used to tell of things that happened but children don't listen as they should.

Later, Grandma Akins married a man by the name of Vickerman, and they owned the place where the Thomas Glavin family live, the same house, only remodeled. Vickerman died, and later Grandma went to Watervliet, Michigan, to live with Aunt Agnes and Uncle Pete Heffner. Grandma was a little short scotch woman with a brogue.

LaEtta Elizabeth Stener was born near Niles, July 19, 18--, but I can't make out the rest of that year. She was the daughter of John & Mary Staner. Her mother, who was the former Mary Hinchman, died when LaEtta was nine years old, and she helped care for her two sisters, Ora and Ellen. They also had a brother, William Staner. John Staner married three times, all wives named Mary. The last one outlived him. This last Mary was an aunt of Mamie Parren. Grandpa and this Mary had two children, Lillian and Charley, they were much younger than the other children. Ma said the second Mary was an angel, but the last one made it hot for them. After Pa and Ma were married, they came to Harbert to live and, after living in a few places, they bought out old farm and built a home there. Just got it finished when I was born.

Pa was a Civil War veteran and served from '61 to '65 with the First Michigan Cavalry Company M. He used to tell us how they went hungry and when they would go through a farm, they would kill a pig and almost eat it raw. How I wish I had been old enough to ask and write down different things!

Pa built our farmhouse using logs for the underpinning and small poles for rafters, and I am quite sure had lumber sawed for siding and roofing. But we had fun. In our house, it was open to everyone and we had a big family, but always had others there with us. We didn't have much money, but always plenty to eat, enough to wear and a warm house--that was something in those days.

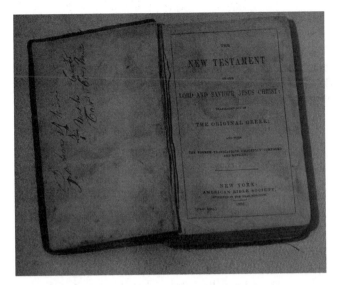

Most of the fun was young and old getting together and singing and dancing, hayride parties, skating parties, and in the summer we had all Lake Michigan to play in, walk two miles to get there and swim, walk home in the dirty sand and bathe again.

All of us kids attend the Harbert school, and on Sunday, the Sunday School was held in the schoolhouse. Larry Sizer's mother and father used to be the head ones to keep the Sunday School going. I remember Larry's grandparents—he was an old man then and played the Fife. They owned property near the lake bought for possibly one or two dollars an acre, now it would be that much a cup full. Larry's aunt Olie took sick and died after skating on the ice. She was a wonderful girl and ma helped care for her when she was so bad. Ma was a practical nurse and for years brought all the babies around there.

We was at your grandpa Parren's when Grandma Parren died, and dressed her for burial. Grandma Vickerman was with your grandma Parren when your father was born, and Ma was with Agnes when Mildred was born. These are just extra things I know and throw them into other dates. Now of all our sisters and brothers I am all that is left.

I think you have your grandfather's old powder horn and the New Testament he had in his pocket when a bullet grazed the book which saved his life. I have some things like a hat band, badge which I feel that Mark should have as he is the only great-grandson and it will mean more to him in years to come.

[Transcription] **Donated by Mrs. Huey Parren**

This [*above*] testament was given to John Akin, 1st Michigan Cavalry Co. M, Civil War, by his sister, Ann Abernathy, to carry in his vest pocket over his heart.

While in action, his horse was shot from under him. You will notice where one of the bullets grazed the Testament and by doing so saved his life.

CIVIL WAR STORY

Homer Lowell Bacon (b.1842, d.1923)

Private, Company K, 21st Wisconsin, Oshkosh, Wisconsin
Discharged 17 February 1864. Surgeon's Certificate of Disability signed by R.D. Lynder, Surgeon, US
Army, General Hospital No. 2, Nashville, TN. Grandfather of JoAnne Jeffers
Transcribed by Lila Megna

In 1995, JoAnne Bacon Jeffers (husband, Dale Jeffers) found notes regarding the Civil War record of her grandfather, Homer Lowell Bacon. At an unknown date, one of Homer's six children made some notes. What follows is the "best guess" interpretation of those notes.

On August 15, 1862, Homer Lowell Bacon of Oshkosh, Wisconsin, enlisted for three years in a Manitowoc Unit. He was 20 years old. After spending about two weeks at the First Regimental encampment at Oshkosh, he went to Cincinnati. His first battle was the Battle of Perryville on October 8, 1962. Thereafter his regiment went south following General Bragg. They got as far as Lebanon. At that point Homer developed a fever and was hospitalized at Bowling Green. His mother visited him in the hospital. He was there for three months. Diagnosis: Typhoid.

Homer rejoined his regiment at Murfreesboro. He fought in battles at several Cumberland Mountain locations, including Chickamauga.

On September 19, 1863, east of, or on, Kelly's Field, Homer's brigade was supporting a battery line that had been driven back by General Bragg's Rebels. Shortly, the brigade was alone and an orderly gave orders to retreat. Homer was wounded just as he got up to retreat. Two hours after he was wounded, a surgeon came around and Homer asked him to do something. The surgeon replied that he was not much used to this kind of work and Homer better wait until others came along. Nothing was done for him except the cloth that had been driven in was taken out. He laid on the battle field near Snodgrass Hill for nine days. Rebels drove the line back about two miles and then the Union drove the Rebels back. Homer protected himself behind a battery horse, crawling on one side or the other.

The wounded were taken back to a field hospital. The Rebels drove Union soldiers back again, so the wounded lay in a Rebel line. Rations while in the field hospital consisted of a fruit cup of thin corn gruel without salt three times a day. Homer traded a jack knife with a Confederate soldier who was guarding them for pieces of meat, pieces of corn bread and a piece of wheat bread. The same soldier wanted to trade canteens with him—an old style slave canteen from Revolutionary time—for Homer's that was a regular Army canteen of galvanized tin covered with green felt. Homer was taken into Chattanooga on parole where he laid without surgical attention and existed on quarter rations from October 1, 1863, to the middle of November when a siege was raised.

On December 1, 1863, he was sent to a hospital in downtown Nashville. After about two weeks, Smallpox broke out and the wounded were moved out on what was called College Hill in an old college building that was made into a hospital.

Homer was mustered out in the hospital on February 17, 1864, and got home February 23, 1864. Surgeon's Certificate of Disability was signed by R.D. Lynder, Surgeon of the Army. General Hospital No. 2, Nashville, Tennessee.

A FAMILY IN THE CIVIL WAR

Pvt. John Boone, Infantry
Spencer Welsh
Edward Easling
Written by Russell Wainright

In the years before the Civil War, America was getting ready to boil over on the issue of slavery. Most people felt that the presidential election in the fall of 1860 would be a major turning point for the United States. My 3-great-grandfather, James Boone, who had immigrated from Somersetshire, England, in 1856 with his wife, Louisa, and eight children, was strongly antislavery, for Great Britain had abolished slavery in 1834. James became a Republican, and supported Abraham Lincoln in the election. When James' next son was born on Lincoln's Inauguration Day, March 4, 1861, there was no indecision, the sixth son just had to be named Lincoln Boone. James voted straight Republican the rest of his life.

On April 12, 1861, the South fired on Ft. Sumter and the Civil War had begun. When the war started, James had 6 sons, but only the oldest son, John, was old enough to enlist, but an accident as a child resulted in John being nearly blind in his right eye, so he was turned down. On the 4th of July 1861, 19 year old John married a young lady by the name of Almira. In 1863, when the army was desperate for men, John volunteered again; this time he was accepted by the infantry. James' youngest son, George, also enlisted in the 11th Michigan Infantry as soon as he reached the age of 17. However, the war ended less than 4 months later while George was still in training.

During the Civil War, Michigan furnished almost 100,000 soldiers to the Union armed forces. About 3,000 Michigan men were killed in action, about 1,300 died of their wounds, and over 10,000 men died of disease. Even greater numbers of soldiers had major wounds that would affect them throughout life, such as the loss of limbs, vision or hearing, head injuries and mental impairments. Thousands more contracted chronic incurable illnesses, such as TB or malaria.

The farm boys of Michigan did not have the immunities of the men who had lived their lives in crowded urban areas. They were not accustomed to living in the crowded, unhygienic Civil War camps. Disease ran rampant through Michigan camps.

Most men enlisted for 2-3 years. After their enlistment was up the soldier was free to leave. However, the war lasted longer than their enlistments. Most men had enlisted as a group.

John Boone

Therefore, their enlistments all ended at the same time. Even though the war was a horrific experience, most were volunteers and dedicated to the Union. They had come this far, and they wanted to make sure that the job got done. They wanted to be there at the finish. Therefore, many soldiers re-enlisted. A soldier who re-enlisted was called a "Veteran." A company where most men reenlisted was called a "Veteran" company.

A normal company could have anywhere from 40-100 troops, but generally far fewer than 100. In the Civil War, men enlisted to be a part of a specific company, with the company part of a specific regiment. So for example, 100 men from Benton Harbor would enlist as a group and become Company A of the First Michigan Infantry Regiment. When men got sick, captured, wounded or died, they frequently would not be replaced. The company would just get smaller and smaller, until eventually, it could no longer function as a company. Sometimes, after a major battle, there would be only a few men left; some companies literally had no one left. Several of these shattered companies would then combine to form a new company, and the old companies would no longer exist.

The Veteran Reserve Corps (originally called the "Invalid Corps") consisted of soldiers who had become gravely ill or injured and could no longer perform normal duties. They were still able to perform light duty. Many of these men had serious disabilities. Many had chronic diseases such as TB or malaria. Many had lost arms, legs, eyes, or had other severe war injuries. Many members of the Veteran Reserve Corps were severely limited in what they could do. But, by handling duties to the best of their ability, they freed up able-bodied soldiers to serve on the front lines.

Most people, when they picture a Civil War battle, see two huge armies fighting on a southern battlefield. They certainly don't see the fighting taking place in Michigan. But many Confederate sympathizers lived in Canada, having moved there at the start of and prior to the war. In addition, Confederate agents could easily enter Canada, and were free to move about that country. Michigan, since it was on the Canadian border, was continually threatened with invasion and raids by rebels who were living in Canada...

Six of the nine companies defending the Detroit border were Federal troops of the Second Regiment Veteran Reserve Corps. This regiment was created by combining the survivors of ten companies which had been decimated in battle. These six companies were also members of the Veteran Reserve Corps, so they all had disabilities and would not be able to fight as well as an unimpaired soldier.

In 1863-1864, military and civil authorities received tips, and intelligence reports almost daily about planned raids. Rumored terrorism plots included raids on American border cities, burning and destroying villages, and the disruption of shipping on the Great Lakes by capturing and sinking ships. These rumors kept the border area in a continual state of alarm. Many of these rumors were actually true. It was only by constant vigilance and quick action by law enforcement agents and the military that the plans failed. However, authorities were being constantly pressured by the public to do more to protect Southeast Michigan and insure the safety of their homes and businesses.

In November 1863, the U.S. government was notified by the British, that they had information about a plot to invade the United States by Confederate agents who were living in Canada, The Confederate plan was to cross the border into Michigan; hijack some steamboats on Lake Erie; sail the boats to Johnson's Island near Sandusky, which was a Union POW camp; free the rebel prisoners; and then using the freed soldiers to attack Buffalo, New York.

A few months after this report, the Michigan government sent a letter to the U.S. Secretary of State. This letter stated that *"Unless you can suggest some better mode of raising a regiment for service on the [border], I recommend that the authority be given the Governor of Michigan to raise a Volunteer Regiment....This additional force is absolutely necessary, and should be organized before the Detroit River is frozen over....The Regiment can be raised at once and the arms, appointments and clothing are now on hand for it. No lesser force can render the frontier of Michigan secure."*

The U.S. Secretary of War authorized Michigan to raise a State Regiment of 10 companies, approximately 1000 volunteers, for this home duty. Regimental headquarters was in Jackson. Recruiting officers traveled throughout southeast Michigan signing up officers and men. Volunteers enlisted for 12 months service to be engaged in frontier duty in Michigan along the Detroit and St. Clair Rivers until June, 1865. The 10 companies were stationed at different points along the Detroit and St. Clair Rivers, and throughout southeastern Michigan.

Almost a year later, on September 19, 1864, the plot to invade the U.S. that was discovered the previous November was put in motion by the Rebels. Four enemies took passage on a passenger ship out of Detroit. Additional enemies boarded the ship at other ports, until there were about thirty on the ship. The enemies overpowered the captain and crew, and the other passengers, and hijacked the ship.

The Rebels sailed the ship across Lake Erie towards Sandusky, Ohio. Johnson Island was about 2 miles off the coast of Sandusky. It was a prisoner of war camp where over 3,200 Confederate soldiers were held prisoner. The Rebels intended to free the prisoners, capture more ships and then start raiding Northern cities.

So far their plan was going well. They landed at another island, where they seized another ship, capturing the captain, crew and 300 unarmed U.S. soldiers who were passengers going home to be mustered out of the army because their enlistments were up. Half the Rebels took control of the second ship and both ships continued toward Sandusky. They got to within 14 miles of Johnson Island.

Johnson Island was guarded by the *USS Michigan* an ironclad warship. Part of the plan was for a prominent Sandusky man (who was also a Confederate spy) to have dinner with the officers of the Michigan. During the dinner, the spy was to drug the officers' wine. The spy would then send a message to the Rebels, who could then easily capture the Michigan. With an ironclad warship and 3,200 troops, they could have wreaked havoc on Great Lakes' shipping and border cities.

The entire plot fell apart when the spy was discovered. When the Rebels failed to get the spy's message, they panicked. They put all their prisoners on the first ship and sunk the second ship. They then sailed back to Canada in the first ship, where they released the prisoners, sunk and burned the ship, and abandoned their mission.

Following this failed plot, the War Department decided to federalize the new State Regiment.

Effective January 9, 1865, it was now the 30th Michigan Infantry Regiment, with Regimental Headquarters in Detroit. The 30th Michigan served until the war ended. On June 30, 1865, the officers and men of the 30th Michigan were mustered out of service, paid off and sent home.

On May 12, 1864, at the age of 22, my great-great-grandfather John Boone enlisted in the army as a Private, He volunteered in Hillsdale, Michigan for a 12-month term of service in Company G of 30th Michigan Volunteer Regiment, a State organization. In January 1865, the unit officially became a Federal unit. So on December 31, 1864, John was officially a member of the Michigan 30th Infantry Regiment.

On May 1, 1865, John was hospitalized in Jackson, Michigan for inflammation of the lungs or as the Army doctors called it, "Typhoid Newmonia." He remained in the hospital until his honorable discharge at the end of the war when on June 17, 1865, he was mustered out of the Army at Jackson. He continued to have lung problems the rest of his life.

John was a member of the organization the "Grand Army of the Republic" (GAR) Post 398. The GAR was a fraternal organization of former members of the U.S. military in the Civil War. They were a politically active group that once had a half million members. They were a major force in the Republican Party, with five of their members becoming U.S. President.

They retained their political power well into the 20th Century. They worked hard for veteran's rights and the establishment of pensions for veterans. In addition, in what was unusual for the times, the GAR recognized and respected the contribution of the millions of black soldiers in the Civil War. The GAR was an integrated organization, with huge numbers of black members. The GAR worked hard promoting the right of black veterans to vote. In 1868, the GAR was the first to designate May 30 as Decoration Day (later called Memorial Day) as the day to honor dead veterans by putting flowers and flags on their graves.

As John grew older his lung condition continued to worsen and he filed several pension applications. He was finally approved and he received a pension of $2.00 a month. The amount increased over the years and he was getting $27.00 a month at the time of his death from bronchitis in 1913 at the age of 71.

His wife, Almira, died on March 5, 1926, at the age of 84, of a cerebral hemorrhage. Her granddaughter, Pearl remembered Almira fondly (Pearl was in her 20s at the time of Almira's death). Pearl loved to stay with her grandmother in the summertime. She said that her grandmother loved to sit on the front porch during nice weather. She always had time to talk

---

TRIVIA NOTES: The Detroit Light Guard was a very popular, well-known and respected military unit in Detroit, before, during and after the Civil War. They called themselves the "Tigers". In the 1880s, a professional baseball team was created in Detroit as part of the National Baseball League. They called themselves the Detroit Wolverines. In the 1890s, when the Wolverines decided to become part of the newly created American League, they decided to change their nickname to the Detroit Tigers, to profit from the Detroit Light Guard's popularity. After receiving formal permission from the Light Guard to use their trademark, the baseball team officially became the "Tigers."

Another interesting fact: The commander of the Scott Guard was Col. August Goebel, who after the war founded the Goebel Brewery. Goebel beer was a popular drink in Michigan from 1873 until 1964.

with friends and neighbors who came by. Almira would sit in her rocking chair and rock, all the while puffing on her corncob pipe.

Spencer Welsh

Another soldier in the Boone family was Spencer Welch. Spencer was born in Fulton, Ohio in 1844. At the age of 19, Spencer joined the Army as a private, enlisting in a State Regiment of Michigan Volunteers on July 12, 1863 in Hudson, Michigan, which is near the Ohio border in Southeast Michigan. For the next 5 months, Spencer and other new recruits learned the basics of how to be an artilleryman. On December 7, 1863, the volunteers were federalized and became part of the Union Army. Spencer began his Federal service in Battery F of the First Michigan Light Artillery Regiment.

The Union Army mandated that the State of Michigan furnish one Artillery Regiment. The First Michigan Light Artillery Regiment consisted of 12 Batteries, with each Battery having six guns. Battery F was originally organized at Coldwater in January 1862 and they were sent South in March.

Battery F's first action was near Richmond, Kentucky in August of 1862. Unfortunately, their first action was almost their last. Their infantry support was pushed back; the Battery was cut off; all the men had to retreat without their guns; and all their guns were captured. For the next year, being without guns, Battery F was placed on detached service at various outposts on garrison duty (basically just being a military presence in the area).

In December 1863, Battery F became artillery again. Spencer joined Battery F just in time to march across the Cumberland Mountains from Kentucky to Knoxville, Tennessee. The Battery arrived in Knoxville on January 22, 1864. It was a terrible march through the mountains, during severe winter conditions. The men and horses suffered greatly from the extreme cold. There was little food for the men or forage for the horses.

During the march, Spencer became very ill and had to be sent to the military hospital at Camp Nelson. Camp Nelson is about 20 miles south of Knoxville and today is a National Civil War Heritage Park and National Cemetery. The doctors at Camp Nelson gave Spencer the diagnosis of "typhoid malarial fever". As soon as Spencer was able to travel, he received a furlough and was sent home to recover. Military hospitals were crowded. There were few nurses. Hospitals got the soldier well enough to travel; then they sent them home, leaving the job of long-term nursing care to the soldier's family...

Upon his recovery, Spencer returned to his unit and was reequipped, refitted and assigned to General Sherman's Army, who was just starting his Georgia Campaign.

Battery F left Knoxville at 9 o'clock on the morning of April 28, 1864, heading for Charleston, Tennessee. This was a 70 mile march and they reached Charleston on Sunday, May 1. They rested there until Tuesday morning May 3, and then marched until they reached Sherman's Army the following afternoon.

Battery F was very active in Sherman's campaign, with almost daily skirmishes during the famous "March across Georgia." They participated in many engagements, including the Battle of Kennesaw Mountain in June. The Confederates had strong defensive positions on and around Kennesaw Mountain. They were protecting the city of Atlanta, which was less than 20 miles away. Starting in mid-June 1864, Sherman's Army and Battery F were fighting daily, often at close range, jockeying for position as they tried to force the Rebels out of their defenses. There were frequent artillery duels with the Confederates. Battery F lost many soldiers, horses, and guns. ..

On March 10, after three more months of marching and fighting, Battery F participated in the Battle of Wyse Forks in North Carolina. Battery F lost more men during this battle, in addition to the many sick and wounded. Battery F was becoming low on men. On April 8, 1865, they were ordered to New Bern, North Carolina to refit for field service. The war ended on April 9th. The battery eventually arrived back in Jackson, Michigan on June 24, and was mustered out of service on July 1, 1865. Thirty-three men of Battery F died during the war, with many more carrying the effects of disease or wounds for the rest of their lives.

Spencer Welch continued to have occasional bouts of malaria throughout the war. In early May, Spencer had another bout of malaria and was hospitalized for three weeks. By the time he was released, the rest of the Battery was already on their way back to Michigan, so Spencer did not return to his Battery. Instead, he was sent to David's Island in New York Harbor, where on June 10, 1865, he was mustered out of the army.

Spencer, now 21 years old, returned to Michigan, where he met 15 year old Anna Boone. Anna was James Boone's second daughter. Two years later, Spencer and Anna were married. After the war, Spencer was a life-long farmer. He was a member of the GAR Post 111 in Eaton Rapids, Michigan. Bouts of malaria plagued him for the rest of his life, and he received a partial "Invalid Pension". However, the government did not consider him totally disabled until he turned 80. Spencer lived until the age of 81.

Edward Easling

Another brother-in-law of John Boone was Edward Easling. Edward Easling was born on Valentine's Day, 1838 in Yates County, New York, where he grew up on his family's farm. On September 21, 1861, at the age of 23, Edward enlisted as a Private. He was given a $100 bonus to enlist, which was a large amount of money at that time. He joined Company A, 8th New York Cavalry Regiment on October 9, 1861. Edward was the perfect size for a cavalryman, 5 foot 5 and a solid 175 pounds. He loved horses and worked with horses throughout his life.

Company A was organized at Rochester, New York. Most, if not all, of Company A were from Rochester and surrounding farms. The regiment left Rochester on November 29, 1861, and served in the defenses of Washington, D.C. through December. On March 15, Company A was transferred to the Department of the Shenandoah, where they conducted cavalry operations throughout the Shenandoah Valley until June 17. Then they were transferred to the Army of the Potomac under General McClellan, where they remained for the rest of the war...

There is little rest for cavalry. They are meant to be in continuous motion. They are the eyes and ears of an army. While other branches are in camp, cavalry is out riding, scouting, guarding, gathering information, and keeping a lookout. The cavalry is hard work. They are almost continuously "on duty". However, the cavalryman would have it no other way. They'd do almost anything rather than walk a half mile.

Unfortunately, the frequent battles and skirmishes, the loss of sleep, and short rations, took a heavy toll on both men and horses. In addition, a job with horses under war conditions is particularly physically demanding. Horses can function on poor food for only so long. They can survive on grass, but they require richer food, like corn and especially oats, to work at the high pace of war. These demands, along with battle losses and the difficulty in finding enough quality horses with the stamina, skills and temperament needed for cavalry, frequently led to a shortage of horses. Dismounted cavalry were not doing their job as cavalry. At times there were hundreds of skilled troopers literally standing around, because of the lack of horses.

The Union Army continued sparring with Lee. On Nov. 16, 1862, Edward was shot again. He was shot in the arm. His horse was also shot. The horse fell, landing on Edward and breaking his leg. From that point on, Edward was never again able to lift his arm above his shoulder. Once again, Edward was sent home on a 30-day furlough to heal. However, the wound and his leg did not heal quickly.

Because of this, he was not able to return to his unit until August, over seven months late. He discovered that he had been listed as a deserter. After this was resolved, Edward was sent, on September 9, 1863, to Culpepper, Virginia, to continue his recovery with a light duty assignment. He was assigned to Company K, 23rd Regiment, U.S. Veteran Reserve Corps. On April 6, 1864, after seven months, Edward recovered enough to be sent back to Company A....

In early June, Company A fought at Cold Harbor, followed by heavy fighting in front of Petersburg. On June 29, 1864, south of Petersburg, Virginia, Company A was on a raid near Stony Creek. Company A got caught in an ambush, and Edward was shot in the left hand and captured. He was sent to the infamous prisoner of war camp at Andersonville, where he was imprisoned for five months. During the course of the war, almost 13,000 of the approximately 45,000 Union prisoners died there. Andersonville was a hell hole of starvation, malnutrition, disease, and abuse from its guards.

Edward received little medical care, small amounts of bad food, and drank the same swampy water the prisoners polluted daily with their waste. Prisoners slept on the open, bare ground, with little or no cover. During the time Edward was there, over one third of the Union prisoners died from scurvy, malnutrition, dysentery and exposure. They were then buried in mass graves.

Edward started the war at 175 pounds. After five months at Andersonville, he weighed only 77 pounds. When he was released, he was suffering from scurvy, eye problems, and severe intestinal ailments. Edward never fully recovered.

After Edward's release on a prisoner exchange, he was sent to a military hospital. When he finally recovered enough, and it looked like he would probably survive, he was sent back home to Rochester, New York. There, on February 15, 1865, he was mustered out of the army.

In Edward's application for a pension, his wife, Sarah, wrote of the effects of malnourishment: "his mouth and gums and throat were so affected that he could only speak in a whisper. It was three months before he could speak a loud word." Edward wrote: "[My] mouth became sore ... my jaws, head and face swelled up and pieces of jaw bones with flesh attached to it came out. From that time on, I kept losing my teeth until there are only five left." In addition to the effects of his malnutrition and scurvy, Edward continued to have vision problems, and he would never read or write again... He died of stomach cancer on May 11, 1918 at the age of 80. Edward was an active member of the GAR and was given a full GAR funeral ceremony.

—READ MUCH MORE ON OUR CD—

OVERCOMING FEAR
Junius Hopkins Hatch Jr

Transcribed by Robert Hatch, grand-nephew of Junius Hopkins Hatch, Jr.

CIVIL WAR LETTER FROM JUNIUS HATCH, JR.
(On the field of Hanover near Richmond, Virginia. May 28, 1862)

Junius Hopkins Hatch, Jr

Dear Dad,

We had a fight, a severe one, the 414th suffered severely. We lost many brave men—but we stood our ground and were victorious. We fought against superior numbers at first and for two hours it was a desperate fight, but reinforcements coming up, the enemy were scattered and ran like hounds, leaving us in possession of the field where we still had two men killed on each side of me—but I am unhurt. A ball grazed my hand and a second one struck my arm but only made a slight bruise. My gun was disabled after firing a few rounds and I took a gun which lay beside a dead man and the rest of my cartridges. I cannot give a correct account of the fight elsewhere than in my immediate vicinity. I paid no attention to anything else than to lay low and to load and fire at them as quick as possible. This is a diagram of the field and scene of action where we were. [diagram below]

We were ordered to deploy as skirmishing in the woods to the right when the enemy were supposed to be concealed in force their object was, evidently, to surround our flank while we were deploying in the woods. Firing commenced from the woods on our right, we then rallied and formed a line of battle in the field and near the ravine. We had scarcely done this when they opened on us from behind trees and our men being in full range and unprotected by cover began to drop, so we lay down and returned their fire with interest but we were too crowded so we dropped back a few feet to the road and stood there—whenever the enemy showed themselves or attempted to take our guns (which were nearly silenced at one time) we made it too hot for them, they dare not come out and we had not sufficient force to render it prudent to advance and drive them out of the woods where they had the advantage of position and numbers. So we fired away as fast as possible men falling on all sides and 'til I thought they would silence or fire; from 4 o'clock 'til near sundown the fight raged—our flag was riddled with holes and once shot down it in an instant was up again a fair target for the skulking devils who kept close in their hiding places and never showed their rage, at length reinforcement s came we hailed them with cheers, and while we gave them thunder in front the fresh troops took them on the flank and they retreated and ran leaving their dead and wounded we took more than a hundred prisoners and quantities of arms and equipment &c.

I write this on a piece of paper picked up on the field, the best I can get so excuse its appearance.

Hope to date [the letter] from Richmond soon. I am all right, give my respects to all and write soon. Why don't some of my friends write once in awhile?

I don't want to see another fight like that of yesterday twas too desperate & unnecessarily so. I think.

Reinforcements should have been nearer, in which case we would have made short work and much less loss of life. I am thankful my life was spared & and hope & trust I shall live through it.

(My 1st battle letter to Vosburg—May 28th 1862)

Junius, Jr., the firstborn son of his father, Junius Sr., was born April 5, 1837, at Monroe, Michigan.

Lieutenant Junius was a Civil War Veteran and a volunteer with Ellsworth's Avengers. The history of this regiment stands out in the annals as exceptional because of the high quality of the men who composed it. This elite body of soldiers were members of the 44th, New York volunteers whose early efforts under General McClelland were ill-starred.

Junius was credited with firing the first shot at Yorktown. He is also credited with being among those who fired the last shots of the war before Lee's surrender.

During his long career with the Army of the Potomac, he participated in most of the major battles of the Civil War. He was hit by a spent bullet at Gettysburg (Little Round Top) and followed Lee's troop to the Potomac. There they crossed below Harper's Ferry to Warrenton. He was also involved in the Rapahannock Station Battle, Mine Run, Weldon Railroad fight and Gravelly Run fight.

On the sixth of April, 1865, he was wounded at Five Forks in the left wrist, the bullet passing completely through his wrist and partially disabling him for life. He had to walk eight miles to the Fifth Corps Hospital at City Point, Virginia to be treated.

Finally on June 15, he was honorably discharged and released to return to civilian life. The Washington correspondent of the <u>New York Tribune</u>, writing on the occasion when the Ellsworth Avengers passed through the capital to the front said: *"Used as we are to marching regiments, there is nothing that can compare with this one. It is the finest body ever enlisted on the Continent."*

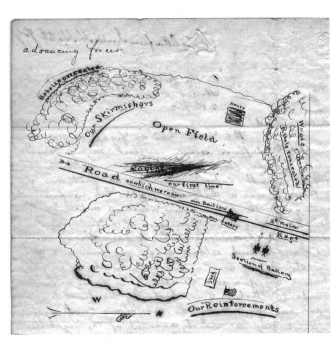

map of battlefield

After his service. Junius moved to St. Joseph where he became active in local affairs. In 1877 he served as clerk for St. Joseph Township. He practised law and was appointed as Justice of the Peace. Later he moved to Lansing, Michigan and accepted a position with the Auditor General's Office where he stayed until his retirement. His firstborn, Junius H. III, was born in 1873 and died in 1882. He is buried in the City Cemetery on Lakeview Avenue in St. Joseph, Michigan. Junius II died March 15, 1921 and is buried near a large carved boulder bearing the Hatch name in Mount Hope Cemetery in Lansing, Michigan.

Follows is his own account of his service 50 years after...

"Now nearly half a century after those stirring events which welded contending sections in the fiery furnace of war & made us a Nation—and acting by request of your Committee—I will endeavor to relate some things which I saw & took part in, and which even at this late date may not be uninteresting...especially to those who were similarly occupied & had like experiences.

If I use the personal pronoun frequently, my excuse is that these are personal recollections.

I enlisted from Buffalo N.Y. in Co A. 44th N.Y. (Ellsworth Avengers) or Peoples Ellsworth Regt – Aug 8, 1861 – Went into camp of instruction at Albany N.Y. & thence to Camp in the field Hulls Hill, Va –

We were in Butterfields Brigade 3 Div, 3 Brigade, 5 Corp, Army of the Potomac – served with 44th N.Y. 'till August, '64 & was then commissioned & assigned to 94th N.Y. in which Regt I served as 1st Lieut Comd'g Cos D. & I. till the end of the war – was wounded at Five Forks - & finally dischg'd June 15, 1865.

I was in the following actions (*see battle card*).

I held successively the following positions: high private in the rear rank – Sergt, 1st Sergt – in 44 N.Y; & 1st Lieut in 94 N.Y.

We first smelt Rebel Gunpowder at the siege of Yorktown, where the spade proved mightier than the sword, & one fine morning we marched into their deserted forts, the rebs having "skipped out by the light of moon," to meet & greet us later on – Then came in due time many hard fought battles.

Our 1st Battle - Hanover Court House gave us great confidence in our staying power. We were fired on suddenly from a concealed force in the woods - in fact taken by surprise – we returned their fire & held our position till relieved by reinforcements. My personal recollection of that fight is that at 1st I felt pretty shaky, but gradually regained nerve – got quite excited & loaded & fired as fast as possible. I remember a remark of one of our officers – "Cowards die many times – brave men but once" – but don't remember that I was at all desirous for that final "once. " I had no desire to be a dead hero.

At Gettysburg our Brigade held a position on Little Round Top – we got there just in time & stayed there. What would have happened if we had not got there in time or had been driven back can only be conjectured – we helped make history there.

Our Army of the Potomac had a very difficult task, a well nigh impossible one. We were most of the time between Lee's Army & Washington & were called on to protect the one & crush t'other, & not until Grant took command did we begin to see an end to the war – before that, we were in the habit of making an advance, getting repulsed, acting on the defensive or being ordered back to cover Washington – if we made a favored move in the direction of the Confederate Capitol, something would occur to make it expedient to retire or change our base.

We had an exciting experience at Harrisons Landing – a night attack from Rebel batteries across the James river, shells exploding in & over our camp at midnight. Next day, our Brigade crossed the river & put a stop to that kind of entertainment during the balance of our stay there – While before Petersburg, later on, there were several occurrences of this kind— trying ordeals, the sudden boom of Cannon & sound of bursting shells, startling us out of sound sleep. Darkness, uncertainty & the confusion of moving out in the night to face an unseen & unknown danger made it extremely disagreeable -

Burnside Mud March – was another episode of Army life not soon to be forgotten by those who were in it. It commenced raining soon after we started out gunning for the enemy on that occasion, the farther we marched, the harder it rained. It seemed as if in the olden time that the "wonders of heaven were opened" & the only consolation we got was from the fact that the same rain was soaking the enemy –

We were horse, foot, artillery & baggage literally "stuck in the mud." - an army of mud socks, soaked shivering & swearing - & by nightfall, having had full rations of Commissary Whiskey dealt out by the Pail full, many of the Army of the Potomac were disrespectably drunk & disorderly. Had it been possible for "the Johnnies" to get at us or we to them, we would've put up a great fight—we couldn't run & were full enough to be ugly & dangerous –

Panic sometimes occurs even among the most reliable troops. On the change of base, as it was called, from the Chickahoming to Harrisons landing – our Brigade (with others) was thrown into confusion, broken & ran into the woods, pell mell every man for himself & the Devil take the hindmost – The only cause "a big noise in the night," a mule team runaway came tearing down the road we were on. Someone hollered, "a Cavalry Charge" & off we went like scared cats –

We, Dan Butterfield's pets - who had met Stonewall Jackson's men & held them back, the reserves of the Army of the Potomac - always to be depended on - put to flight & routed by 4 Army mules –

The charge on Maryes Hgts at Fredricksburg was a never to be forgotten bad place for us - it was, as all know, unsuccessful & useless, a sacrifice & slaughter for us. Brigade after Brigade had charged & been repulsed. Our turn came; we were ordered forward, & forward we went as far as possible & lay down under fire until darkness – then retreated –

Another experience which "rises before me like a dream" was at Chancellorsville; we put in there to cover a retreat there, 11th Corps had been broken & we the 5th filled the gap. Night came; the woods were on fire Occasional volleys of Musketry & Artillery kept us on the alert. The cries of wounded between the lines, the wailing notes of Whippoorwill – all tho the weary watches, made it a most memorable experience.

At Five Forks - my final battle - things came our way. The rebs, their communications by rail having been broken, were forced to come out of their Petersburg fortifications & meet us in the open - or stay there & starve – Sheridan at Dunwiddie Court House had met & found them too strong for his Cavalry to drive back – we the (5th) Corps were sent to his support. When all was ready, a charge was made, led by Phil himself. It was hot work, but soon over. As I was leaving the field, wounded, it seemed to me that most of the Confed Army were prisoners, we had cut thru' their lines – our Cavalry were in their reach. This was my last view of war –

The Surrender at Appomattox followed soon after...

And finally in one his letters (and perhaps the reason my grand-uncle came safely through 29 battles) was what he wrote, in part, in one of his early letters:

"*...on the Subject—I've got one thing to do, that is, obey orders & I don't care about the consequences—If it's my fate to come out all right—why then I shall be all right unless I should allow myself to feel scared & then I would lose my good name & everything else worth living for. This is the way I reason & you dont know how much better a person feels who has overcome fear—and is not to be intimidated by any danger—I believe I have, almost done this & if I ever return, you will see a different person than the J Hatch who went away last August to join the P.E. Regt—*"

I am unable to Muster Out as I expected — they have filled the Reg't up with Recruits — & will not Muster Out the Officers. I shall however get a leave of absence very soon —

The Paymaster made us a visit last week. I drew 3½ Months Pay $430.00

Deduct (Income Tax 5 pct.)	21.50	
" Mess account	90.00 for (Hard Tack & Coffee)
" Cigars & Tobacco	20.00	
" Clothing	75.00	
" (Subscriptions)	10.00	
Hospitality & Conviviality	10.00	
Expenses for 3½ Months	$226.50	
Balance on hand	$203.50	

Pretty good you see but very expensive living —

I shall not send any money by mail

Junius Hatch's letter upon mustering out

as there have been extensive robberies perpetrated upon Soldiers letters of late. & I shall probably be able to go North on leave in a few days — Give my love to all & hoping to see you soon. I remain

Your Affectionate
Grandson
Junius —

17th March /65

STORIES FROM WORLD WAR I

1914 – 1918

WWI

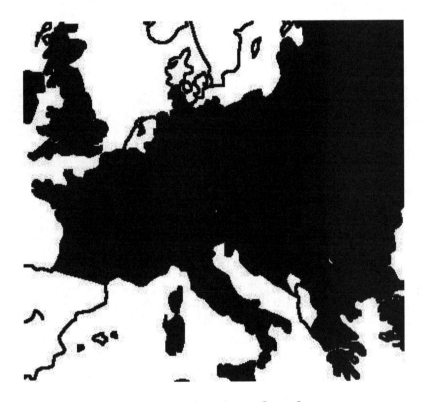

Territories involved:
Europe,
Africa,
Middle East,
Pacific Islands,
China and
off the coast of South and North America

FRANK BUCKLES – AMERICA'S LAST WWI PATRIOT

Frank Buckles

Written by Don Alsbro, Dan Stice, Bob Heft, Gust Anton, Ray Damaske, and Kenneth Stice

Foreword
by Don Alsbro

Lest We Forget had the privilege of making four visits to Frank's farm in Charles Town, WV and the fifth visit was Mar. 15, 2011, for his funeral at Arlington National Cemetery. A total of 12 LWF members made at least one of these visits and four of us—Dan Stice, Gust Anton, Dale Hemphill and myself—made all four visits.

The first trip was made January 29-February 1, 2009, in commemoration of Frank's 108th birthday on February 1, 2009. This trip was the result of a suggestion by Dan Stice at one of our meetings that we needed to visit the last living American WWI veteran who would be 108-years-old on February 1, 2009. At that time there were four living WWI living veterans; the others were located in England, France and Australia.

It took considerable research and phone calls to gain access to the Buckles family. Finally, Dale Hemphill was able to talk to Frank's daughter, Susannah Buckles Flanagan. Dale explained that LWF wanted to honor her dad by bringing an American flag signed by Bob Heft, who designed our 50-star American flag as a high school junior in 1958. He told her that Bob would be coming with us. *(NOTE: Bob's story is also featured in this book.)* Dale also told her that as designer of the "Spirit" flag he would also be bringing a flag to fly with the American flag.

Frank "saluting" LWF in appreciation for raising the flag at his farm.

Susannah told Dale that "Poppa" would appreciate the flags, but that they didn't have a flagpole. It was around January 20 when Dale told me that they did not have a flagpole. I looked through my patriotic catalogs to see if I could locate a company that could get the flag pole to the Buckles farmstead ASAP.

I called one very well-known flag company (who will go unnamed) and after explaining that the flag pole was for Frank Buckles, the last living American WWI veteran, I asked if they could get it to his residence by next week. They said they could, and that the price would be around $350 which was the list price. I asked if they understood that their flagpole would be receiving some national attention and couldn't they give us a discount. She said no, and, after speaking to the supervisor who said the same thing, I resolved that I wouldn't deal with this company again.

I then remembered that I had purchased for our home several years ago a 20-ft flag pole from Uncommon USA flag company located in Chicago. I called them and after telling them who the flagpole was for, they wanted the shipping address. I asked the price they said there would be no charge. They were honored to recognize Frank. When we arrived a week later at Frank's residence the flagpole was waiting for us.

There were six of us who went on the first visit: Gust Anton, Jim Heyn, Ken McKeown, Dan Stice, Dale Hemphill and myself. We made the trip in Dale's Spirit of America van that is highly decorated with the Spirit flag; truck drivers on the Indiana, Ohio and Pennsylvania Toll Roads gave us salutes as we passed them. These trips became a neat bonding experience for us.

Bob Heft came from Saginaw, Michigan, and was driven by his nephew, Eddie. On Friday morning, January 30, after breakfast, we drove out to the Buckles farm which is on State Route 9, about 3 miles south of Charles Town. Charles Town, West Virginia, is about 45 miles from Washington DC and 45 miles from Hagerstown, Maryland. At breakfast we were asked by the waitress what we were doing in town and when we said that we'd come to visit Frank Buckles, she wanted to know who Frank Buckles was? The interesting thing is that on our first visit to Frank, we discovered that there were a lot of people in the Charles Town area that didn't know who he was, but on our third and fourth visits we noticed that he had a lot more name recognition.

After locating the farm outside of Charles Town on Route 9 we drove about five miles east to Harper's Ferry as Dan who is a Civil War history buff told us that it was a precursor to the Civil War (aka John Brown's Body). We found it to be a very delightful site to visit. The village of Harper's Ferry has been restored to what it was like in the 1860s, on a smaller scale to how Greenfield Village in Dearborn, Michigan, has been restored.

There is so much history in the Charles Town area. In one direction is Harper's Ferry and 15 miles to the north is Antietam, the Civil War battlefield that saw the largest number of American casualties for a one day battle.

"Old Glory" and Spirit of America flags flying proudly from the flagpole at Frank's house, outside his bedroom. (l to r): Gust Anton, Dale Hemphill, Dan Stice, Don Alsbro, Ken McKeown, Jim Heyn

Frank's Life Story
by Don Alsbro

Before we talk about the visits it is important to bring the reader up to date on Frank Buckles' background. Frank was born February 1, 1901, on his father's farm in Harrison County, north of Bethany, Missouri. When he was a teenager, the family moved to Dewey County in Oklahoma. As a teenager he was inspired by patriotic posters he saw in the tiny town of Oakwood, Oklahoma. At only 16 years, he walked into a Marine Corps recruiting office in Wichita, Kansas, and said he was 18. The recruiter didn't believe him and sent him away. The Navy rejected him as flat-footed. Finally, an Army recruiter in Oklahoma City accepted him, but only after Buckles insisted that the only proof of his age was in a family Bible back in Missouri. He claimed that Missouri didn't issue birth certificates in those days. Frank once told a reporter, "A 15-year old boy is not scared of anything."

When he joined the Army on August 14, 1917, he was in a hurry to get to the front. A sergeant told him to join the Army ambulance corps as the French, our ally were "begging for ambulances." At Fort Riley, Kansas, he learned how to use his belt to cinch a wounded soldier to his back and carry him from a trench.

In December 1917, he sailed from Hoboken, New Jersey, on the _RMS Carpathia_, the ship that had rescued survivors of the _Titanic_ after it sank in 1912. Frank says he passed the time listening to the crew's accounts of the rescue. While in England, the young corporal drove dignitaries around. He eventually got to France, "close enough to battle to see the results , but not close enough to pull anyone from a trench." He stayed in Europe to escort POWs back to Germany.

After the war, Frank would go on to spend most of the next 20 years working on cargo and passenger ships in South America and other foreign destinations. He worked mostly as a ship's purser and freight expediter on the White Star Line before making a fateful decision to take a steady job as a freight expediter with the American President Lines in the Philippines in 1940. Frank was in Manila on December 7 when the Japanese bombed Pearl Harbor. He went to the Army HQ to enlist and was told to wait. In early 1942 he was captured by the Japanese and endured 39 months in two notorious POW camps: Santo Tomas and Los Banos. These were camps from which few survived their captivity. In the camps he went from 140 lbs to 75 lbs by the time he was liberated in February 1945. He routinely gave his food to the children in the camp.

A couple of prisoners escaped from Los Banos prison camp in February 1945 and reached a detachment of the 11th Airborne Division to warn them that the Japanese planned to execute all of the remaining prisoners because they had run out of food. The 11th Airborne parachuted in the morning of February 23 as the Japanese soldiers did calisthenics in their loincloths. All 2,000 prisoners were rescued without a single loss. Buckles returned to his burning barracks to get the starched shirt, shorts and polished shoes he'd kept ready for his liberation. The burning building collapsed moments after he left.

After the war he returned to the US and in 1946 he married Audrey Mayo whom he'd met in California before the war. They lived in San Francisco for a few years and in January 1954 they bought Gap View Farm, a 330-acre West Virginia cattle farm. Frank told a reporter in 2007 that "I'd been bouncing around from one place to another for years at sea. It was time to settle down in one place."

In 1955 his daughter, Susannah, was born. In the dining room of the Buckles homestead is a picture of Audrey in a hunt seat equitation suit on a beautiful hunt horse. Susannah said that her mother loved to ride.

Settle down he did, as he lived on the farm from 1954 to his death in 2011—fifty seven years. It is reported that he drove a car until he was 103 and the farm tractor until he was 106. In his later years he was taken care of by his daughter, Susannah Buckles Flanagan, and her husband, Michael Flanagan. On all four of our visits to the farm, Susannah and Mike were either working or had just quit working when we arrived. On our first visit in 2009 they had over 200 head of cattle to tend.

Susannah and her father, Frank Buckles

In 2009 Buckles visited DC and urged a Senate committee to refurbish an existing WWI memorial to Washington DC troops and re-dedicate it as a national tribute. By then Frank had become the last living American WWI veteran and he readily assumed the role of honorary Chairman of the National WWI Memorial Committee. His comment was "I knew that I would be among those who are the last, but I never realized that I would be the one." Sadly, he died February 28, 2011, before seeing the completion of this project.

My Recollections of Corporal Frank Buckles, SN 15577
by Don Alsbro

Each of us that went to visit Frank had different reasons for making the visit. Besides the obvious one of honoring him for his patriotism, my reason was very personal. My dad died in 1950 when I was nine-years-old. I knew that he'd been in the Army, but didn't know the extent of his involvement. In 1982 when my mother passed away, I discovered pictures of him in an Army uniform sitting in the cockpit of an Army plane and pictures of him on an Army cot in a large military tent. There was no date or indication where these pictures had been taken. I later learned that they must have been taken in the Los Angeles, California, area of Mount Wilson.

Frank Buckles & Don Alsbro

I became interested in the origin of these pictures and a few years ago I sent a request to the Army Archives in St. Louis asking for his service record. I received a one sentence reply: "All of the records of Army personnel who served prior to 1932 were destroyed in the fire of 1972." A couple of years later I was attending a Plymouth High School reunion in Plymouth, Michigan, and went to the city library where I found some very helpful information.

In going through the yearbooks I came across a picture of the 1917 PHS Football team. Next to the season record there was the wording, "Our team

Don Alsbro presenting an honorary LWF membership placque to Frank

captain Oscar Alsbro quit school after the third game of the season to join the Army Air Corps." I looked in the 1918 yearbook and there was nothing for my dad, however, in the 1919 yearbook there was his senior picture. I'm guessing here, but it would appear that he never shipped overseas, as the war ended on Nov. 11, 1917.

Every time I spoke with Frank I could imagine that it was my dad that was speaking. How I wish that I knew his complete story! This is the reason that I strongly encourage every veteran to write his/her story so that future generations won't have to guess. My favorite saying is, "When a veteran dies without writing his story, a library burns."

Some Quotes by Frank

One of the first things he said to us on our first visit was, "I appreciate you coming. It is a long way from Michigan."

On one occasion Frank was asked by a reporter why he lied to get into the Army. He answered, "I didn't lie!" he said with a smile. "Nobody calls me a liar, I may have increased my age."

Frank was aware of his place in history. "I always knew I'd be one of the last because I was one of the youngest when I joined," Buckles told the New York Daily News after he became the last survivor. "But I never thought I'd be the last one."

"I was never actually looking for adventure," Buckles once said. "It just came to me." In addition to his WWI ambulance driving, international ship's purser and freight expediter and WWII prison camp survivor, he survived the Spanish flu pandemic, witnessed black U.S. track and field star Jesse Owens win four gold medals in the 1936 Berlin Olympics, and bumped into Adolf Hitler on the stairs of a Berlin hotel during the dictator's rise to power.

Bob Heft and Frank Buckles

I will always remember our first visit in Jan. 2009 and the picture of Bob Heft showing Frank the original flag that he created in 1958. Bob was a high school junior in Ohio when he designed our current 50-star American flag. This flag is the longest flying flag in the history of our country. Bob made many trips to Southwestern Michigan in support of *Lest We Forget* and he once told me that he had been a visitor many times to the White House and to presidential functions, but the two things he held the highest was the opportunity to talk to Frank and the association he enjoyed with LWF.

George Washington

After our first visit to Frank I came across a 1975 issue of the National Geographic and on the cover were the words: "The Beautiful Shenandoah Valley." I looked at the article and in the first paragraph, the author said, "I'm standing at the mailbox of this beautiful farm and I'm talking to Frank Buckles. He has informed me that I'm standing on the land that was surveyed by the teenage George Washington in 1746 and was purchased by a member of the Washington family."

On our second visit to see Frank, I showed the article to Susannah. She told me that she was a teenager and remembered standing with her father talking to the reporter at the mailbox, but had never seen the article. She was very appreciative of it.

Description of the Farm

The farm is located several miles east of Charles Town, WV on WV Hwy 9. To the east of the farm a few miles is Harpers Ferry and a few miles north is the Antietam battlefield. The farm is still a working farm with over 300 acres and 200 head of cattle. Every time we visited Frank (four times) Susannah and her husband Mike were busy feeding the cattle, working on the farm equipment and other duties that come with a large farm.

Visiting Frank Buckles (l to r): Ray Damaske, Dan Stice, Frank, Don Alsbro, Gust Anton, Dale Hemphill (Frank in center, front)

LWF Trips to the Buckles Farm

The first trip on February 1, 2009, was to honor Frank for his 108th birthday, to plant a flagpole in his yard next to his den and to raise the American flag and the Spirit flag. It was a cold and windy day! We drove thru an ice storm to get to Charles Town. On the way we stopped in Fremont, Ohio, to honor our WWII hero Arthur Jibilian. Jibby was the WWII radio operator who brought in the planes to rescue the "Forgotten 500" airmen trapped in Yugoslavia. Another True Patriot. (NOTE: The story is told in the book *Forgotten 500* by Gregory A. Freeman. Read about Jibby, too, in this book.)

What an honor it was to place the flagpole outside of Frank's den and bedroom. It is situated about 15 yards from the house. I've been told that the stone portion of the farmhouse dates back to the 1700s. The house sits on a flat hilltop with a 360-degree view of the countryside. I can see why George Washington was so taken by the location.

The second trip was in November 2009 to replace the flags and to place a plaque next to the flagpole to let people know that LWF had put in the flag pole. We also presented Frank with a letter from U.S. representative Fred Upton stating that he had signed on as a co sponsor of the bill to create a national WWI monument in D.C. It was on this trip that we brought with us a WWI gas mask and steel helmet. Susannah saw the helmet and she said "Papa I want to see what

you look like in the helmet," and with that we had a classic picture of Frank wearing the helmet. While we were out replacing the flags, Frank's nurse bundled him up in blankets and brought him outside on the porch to watch the flag being raised. When we completed the flag raising, Frank gave us a salute that was another classic. What memories!

The third trip was in March 2010 to replace the flags and wish him a belated 109th birthday. We were able to spend much quality time with Frank since the media wasn't around.

Presenting Frank Buckles with gifts (l to r): Don Alsbro, Gust Anton, Frank, Ray Damaske, Dale Hemphill, Dan Stice

The fourth trip was in November 2010 to present Frank with a "Lest We Forget Honorary Membership" plaque and to replace the flags (the wind is always blowing and a flag does not last very long).

Sadly, the fifth trip was not to Frank's home but to Arlington cemetery, March 15, 2011, to honor the life of this American Patriot.

Susannah Buckles Flanagan and Frank wearing the WWI helmet.

General John (Black Jack) Pershing

I remember Frank telling us that he attended a meeting that General Pershing was speaking. Frank was the only one in the audience wearing a WWI uniform and Pershing picked him out immediately. He told his aide that he wanted to speak with "the soldier in the uniform" and after the presentation, they had a nice one-to-one chat. He learned that he and Pershing were both born in Missouri, "43 miles apart as the crow flies." Frank said that "he [Pershing] noticed the six stripes on my sleeve cuffs and thanked me for my overseas tour." (NOTE: enlisted soldiers receive one stripe for every 6 months served overseas). Frank recalled, "He asked where I'd served. He noticed that my uniform was of a higher quality than the Army-issued uniforms and I told him that I'd purchased my own uniform."

Experiences as a POW

On our last visit, Susannah gave several of us a detailed description of Frank's experiences as a POW. She showed us a small picture of her mother that Frank was allowed to keep, along with a tin cup that he used to drink his tea and soup out of, and a clean pair of clothes that he kept to wear when he was released. That shows how optimistic Frank was. He was in the POW camps of Santo Tomas and Los Bonas, both camps known for Japanese atrocities. Frank had been told by the Japanese that they would never leave the island alive. Every day they had to line up in formation morning and evening for roll call and usually there were only a couple of Japanese guards with rifles. Then on February 23, 1945, at Los Bonas, while lining up Frank noticed that all the guards had rifles and he knew that this was the end. However, suddenly the sky was filled with paratroopers and tanks were rumbling in. It was the famous aerial and ground assault by the 11th Airborne Division. Frank stated that if the American troops would've been a few minutes later he wouldn't have survived. He went into the shelter and put on his clean clothes. Just as he left the shelter erupted in flames. Another close call!

I don't know if this is true or not, but at the funeral home during the visitation, I was talking to one of Frank's distant relative from Portland, Oregon. He said that Frank told him that the reason he wanted to stay in Manila and not leave when he had the chance, was that he was secretly letting the U.S. undercover know the whereabouts of the Japanese. This was the reason that he was taken POW, because they discovered his informant role. I don't know how true this is, but because of Frank's patriotism it makes sense. In one of our visits, Frank told us that he came from a military family and that patriotism runs strong among its members, including him.

Importance of Exercise and Physical Fitness

Frank said he liked the Army right off because he enjoyed calisthenics. We LWF members can attest to his enjoyment of physical fitness as on one of our visits we had to wait a few minutes before we could get in to see him as he was finishing his morning exercises. He kept 3 and 4 pound weights close to his living room chair, and at various times in his life he taught calisthenics. Matter of fact, during his 3.5 years as a WWII prisoner of war in the Philippines he led the other prisoners in exercises. In an article in the November 2008 American Legion Magazine the statement is made, "Although he is slowed and bent by age, Buckles does 50 push-ups in bed to keep in shape before preparing to meet the many visitors he receives almost daily in his home."

WWI National Spokesman

It is a sad fact that 4.7 million Americans served in the military during WWI, 117,486 American soldiers killed and 205,690 wounded, yet there is NO national WWI monument in Washington D.C. There is a WWI monument, but it was dedicated in 1931 by President Herbert Hoover to recognize the Washington D.C. citizens who fought in the "Great War." Since then, national monuments have been dedicated in honor of those who served in WWII, Korea and Vietnam.

David DeJonge, a portrait photographer who lives in Grand Rapids, MI has served for the past few years as the family spokesman for the Buckles family. David became acquainted with the Buckles family when he produced a book with photographs of the last living American WWI veterans. When Frank became the last living American WWI veteran, David made Frank the honorary president of the National World War I Memorial Foundation. In March 2008

Frank made a trip to the Pentagon to participate in a ceremony honoring him as the last living American WWI veteran. While in Washington David said that Frank saw the memorials for WWII, Korea, and Vietnam and thought that there was a gap. In 2009 Frank appeared before a Senate committee and urged them to refurbish an existing WWI memorial to Washington D.C. troops and rededicate it as a national tribute. On Feb. 1, 2011, Frank's 110th birthday, Senators Jay Rockefeller of WV and Jim Webb of VA introduced a bill to accomplish this renaming and work is presently underway in D.C. to honor the WWI veterans – an honor that is long overdue!

This move had been sought by Frank and was wholeheartedly supported by him. Work is presently underway to make this happen. It is too bad that Frank will not be able to be present, but his spirit will be! On our last visit, we asked Frank about his advice concerning WWI and he answered: "It was important... Don't forget about WWI!" **It is Lest We Forget's fervent desire that we not forget about Frank Buckles and the WWI monument that is so richly deserved by all those Americans who fought in the "Great War."**

Arlington Funeral and Burial

Frank died on Sunday February 27, 2011, but unfortunately he was not laid to rest until Tuesday, March 15, over two weeks later. This late burial was the result of a "Congressional scuffle" that broke out.

In June 2010 when David DeJonge exhibited his photography at our Vietnam Traveling Wall, he indicated that the groundwork had been laid for Frank's funeral. He would receive full military honors and lie in repose in the Capitol Rotunda. This supposedly was the agreement that David and West Virginia's two senators had with the Congressional leadership. The honor of lying in the Capitol Rotunda requires congressional approval. The bodies of prominent citizens have been displayed in the Rotunda on 30 occasions, starting in 1852 with Henry Clay, a KY senator and congressman. Others include President Abraham Lincoln and Ronald Reagan, unknown soldiers from America's wars and civil rights hero Rosa Parks.

Susannah, Buckles' daughter, wanted her father to lie in repose in the US Capitol Rotunda to represent the 4.7 million Americans who served during WWI, but Congress did not muster support. It should be recognized that France and England both honored their last living WWI veteran with this ceremonial honor. As the son of a WWI veteran, I deeply feel the pain of this rejection by our Congressional leaders: Rep John Boehner of Ohio and Harry Reid of Nevada. It is sad that both in real life and posthumously Frank was rebuffed in his desire to raise awareness for the "American Doughboy."

Finally, it was decided that Frank would be buried Tuesday, Mar. 15 (over two weeks since his death) with full military honors at Arlington National Cemetery with visitation on Sunday and Monday at a funeral home in Washington D.C. On Tuesday morning he would lie in repose at the Cemetery's Memorial Amphitheater, which is located at the site that the "changing of the guard" occurs. A slow stream of mourners filed through to pay their respects. A soldier stood guard at his casket throughout.

We left Mishawaka, IN about 5 pm on Sunday evening and after driving through the night we made it to the funeral home at 11:30 am. Since visitation was scheduled for noon we decided

(l-r): Dan Stice, Don Alsbro, Gust Anton, Dale Hemphill stand at the casket. Rob Kesterke is taking the picture.

to go in and we were surprised that for quite some time we were the only ones in the funeral parlor. Finally around 12:30 visitors started arriving. It was interesting talking to several of the family members who had stories about Frank when he was younger. We left the funeral home around 2 pm and proceeded to Fort Belvoir where we stayed overnight.

In the morning, we proceeded to Arlington where we toured the cemetery, noting where the famous military leaders were buried. Very inspiring!! At 2pm the public viewing at the Amphitheater was ended and there was a large crowd gathered across the street from the amphitheater. Around 3 pm a large procession of limousines, led by motorcycle policemen pulled up to the amphitheater. There were at least eight limousines and the crowd surmised that in one of them was probably President Obama. We later found out that both Obama and Vice President Biden were in the limousines.

At 4pm Frank was taken in a horse drawn caisson from the amphitheater to his burial site, near the grave of Gen. Pershing. The news reports stated that a "crowd of nearly 200 family, friends and mourners gathered at Buckles gravesite for the burial service." What an insult to Frank! There were at least 1,000 mourners.

At the gravesite, Susannah was presented with the flag that draped her father's casket. A 7 person rifle team performed a three volley salute. A lone bugler played taps and a military band closed the ceremony with "America the Beautiful." The Army Chief of Staff, General Casey and SGT MAJ of the Army, along with the Secretary of the Army, the Secretary of Veterans Affairs and the senators from WV attended the service. All in all, it was a "beautiful service."

We proceeded to get in Dale's "Spirit of America" van at 5 pm, and after again driving through the night we arrived in St. Joseph around 8 am on Wednesday morning. It was a tiring journey, but one that I'll never forget! In burying Frank, the nation said goodbye to its last "Doughboy," BUT hopefully the final chapter will be the creation of the National WWI Memorial in Washington D.C.!

Meeting and Knowing Frank Buckles
by Dan Stice

The first time I went to visit Frank at his home in West Virginia was when we placed a flagpole with Old Glory and Spirit of America Flags in his backyard. This was probably the most awesome experience I have ever had. The trip out there with Don, Dale, Gust, Jim, and Ken was a "comedy of errors"—getting lost and finally finding our way was a most memorable and humorous adventure. We took the "scenic route," that's for sure.

Once there, I had the distinct honor of meeting Frank Buckles and Bob Heft—both great Americans—for the first time. I can remember walking into Frank's parlor where he was sitting in a winged-back chair, conversing with Bob. I was overcome by the honor of it all, standing there with, not one, but two absolute living legends. The hair literally stood up on my arms—I was in the presence of greatness.

To see Frank at 108-years-old looking spry and speaking so eloquently was simply hard to believe. When I got to shake his hand and felt his strong firm grip, I could only say "It is truly an honor to meet you sir." Then I closed my mouth and let him speak. He was being asked many questions by the crowd of *Lest We Forget* members and the media, cameras flashing and videos recording the whole time. I remember he spoke very softly, and held such a wonderful conversation with the group—answering each question directly and specifically.

Someone in the crowd asked him if he ever had any vices such as smoking or drinking, and he stated he had smoked cigars in the past and could still stand a little drink of whiskey now and then. At that point I asked what was his favorite food and he stated: "I've always been a steak-and-potatoes man myself." He went on telling us that he had driven a car up until he was 103 and was still doing farm work on and off the tractor until he was 106.

The best laugh we all got was when one of the reporters asked him about his meeting with President Bush at the White House the year before. Frank pointed to the photograph on his wall of him with President Bush. Frank told us that when the president came into the Oval Office, he was not sure who this fellow was until he sat down next to him, shook his hand and started talking. He said the president was a very personable man and his visit with him was very pleasant. Then someone shouted out "were you a Bush supporter?" and Frank replied "Now you know better than to ask me a personal question like that—because you don't know what I might say!!!!" Perhaps he was not a supporter of President Bush—we will never know.

Our second visit to Frank's was when we replaced the faded flags and put the dedication plaque at the base of his flagpole. At this meeting we all had more

Dan Stice rendering a final salute.

42

private time with him. I gave Frank a small antique framed lithograph picture of George Washington as a personal gift to him – knowing his high regard for him, and the ties to Washington through his ancestry. The photo of me giving this small gift to Frank was the one the local newspaper put on the front page of their Sunday edition. All the LWF guys asked "who did you pay off to get this done?"

My reply was "no such thing—they just used the best looking fellow in the bunch."

I was able to hear Frank tell the stories of his attempt to join the military in 1917 and being turned down by the Marines for being too young – then going to the Army recruiter and "exaggerating" his age to enlist—claiming that he had no birth certificate to show them because Missouri did not make those documents back then. He also said the proof was in his mother's family Bible, but he would have to walk all the way back home to get this very fragile old Bible and bring it back to the recruiter. The Senior Recruiting Sergeant in charge there finally said, "that's okay—no need for all that, just sign here." Frank was in!!!!

ABOVE: Showing Frank Dale Hemphill's Spirit of America Flag (l to r): Don Alsbro, Frank, Dale Hemphill, Dan Stice, Ray Damaske

BELOW: On the front steps of the Buckles Farm. (l-r): Gust Anton, Dan Stice, Don Alsbro, Susannah, Dale Hemphill, Ken McKeown

He told the story of traveling with his Army unit across the Atlantic aboard the _Carpathia_, which had picked up the survivors from _RMS Titanic_ just five years earlier. Regarding his war service, he stated that even though he was not fighting right up on the front lines, he was driving ambulance for the U.S. Army in France and "was in the thick of it all."

He told the story of meeting General John J. (Black Jack) Pershing just after the war. Frank said the General was traveling around the USA, getting his name and picture in all the newspapers (perhaps Pershing had political aspirations at that time?). Frank was wearing his Army uniform at one of the events, so the General took time to single him out of the crowd and talk with him. Frank said "I gave him a snappy salute and called him 'Sir.'" Pershing noticed Frank's Missouri accent and said "where were you born?" Frank told him that he was from Bethany Missouri, and Pershing stated, "why that's just 43 miles as the crow flies from where I was born." Frank became a lifelong admirer of the General. In fact, the bolo tie medallion Frank almost always wore had the image of Pershing in uniform on it.

Frank talked about his years as a Japanese POW during WW II. I recall him saying "I really never went looking for adventure—it just seemed to find me." He again showed us the old tin cup he saved from his POW days, stating that he ate, drank, and washed using this old cup. It was pretty much the only piece of Western civilization he had to hold on to during his entire time in captivity.

Someone asked Frank at what point in time he knew he would be the very last WWI Veteran. He stated that he had known for some time that he was among the last of the World War I Veterans, but never expected to be the last one—proudly calling himself "The Last Man Standing." I recall him saying "someone had to be the last one, so it might as well be me."

At our third visit, I gave Frank a reprint of Bannerman's War Surplus Catalog of 1929 as a 109th birthday gift. It is a fully-illustrated sales catalog of all war surplus items from weapons to uniforms to military medals – dating from before and during the Civil War up through WWI. In it, the current Army regulation items were all contemporary to his time in the Army, so, knowing he was an avid reader, I thought it would be interesting for him to browse through. While I was showing him all the different sections in the book, he asked me about an award (pin) he had received upon discharge. His words were: "we all got one whether we wanted it or not."

Well guess what… about a week after we got back home, I got a phone call from his daughter, Susannah. She said that Frank had spotted the U.S. Soldier's WWI Victory pin in the catalog and wanted to know how to order one out of the catalog, because he had misplaced his awhile back. We both had a good laugh when I told her that Bannermans has been out of business since 1952.

However, I told Susannah that I could get him an original one from a dealer friend of mine and I would be more than happy to send it to Frank in the mail as a gift. Within two weeks, I was able to get the pin and mail it to Frank. Susannah then called about a month later, stating she received the pin and had given it to Frank, and he was proudly wearing it as we spoke. She also confided that he really had not lost his in the first place. It had ended up in her jewelry box somehow, and she did not know what it was until I sent this one. No harm done though, now she would proudly wear one on her collar too any time her and her "papa" were in the public eye.

Our fourth visit with Frank was especially exciting to me because my son, Major Kenneth Stice (active USAR/ARNG) went with us. We all got to see Ken's uniform from his 2003-04 tour in Iraq at the National Guard Museum in DC. I can't tell you how proud I am of him. Then at the visit with Frank, again we had lots of quiet time with him to just listen to his wonderful stories. Ken told Frank that he was still in the active military and had been on missions to Japan, Iraq, and Afghanistan. Frank replied "You young soldiers really get around these days." Ken's profound statement after meeting and talking with Frank was: "Just meeting him, I'm leaving here a better person."

We made Frank an Honorary Life Member of *Lest We Forget* at this visit.

Again, our visit with Frank was featured in the Sunday edition of the local newspaper. The photo used in the article—front page, above the fold—was that of my son Ken "a current member of the

U.S. Army meeting our last WWI Veteran." Again I was asked by the other LWF guys "What's up with the Stices always getting front page press?" And again I replied: "Must be our good looks!"

This was the last time we got to see Frank. It was fortunate that we came with a large group this time, including my boy Ken, Harvey Ross, Marv Abbott, and T.W. Lane, in addition to the regulars of Don, Dale, Gust and I. We told Susannah and Frank we would come back to see him shortly after his 110th birthday—probably in March of 2011, depending on the winter driving conditions. They told us we would be welcome to come and they would look forward to our next visit.

BACK ROW: Ken Stice, Dan Stice, Dale Hemphill, Harvey Ross, Marv Abbott, Gust Anton

FRONT ROW: T.W. Lane, Frank Buckles, Dan Stice

It was not meant to be. Frank passed away 26 days after his 110th birthday. Our LWF delegation then had the distinct honor of attending his funeral at Arlington with Full Military Honors. This was an awesome, beautiful, and solemn event. It is hard to be sad about Frank passing, because he lived to be 110 with no aches & pains, and died peacefully in his sleep, in his own bed at home with his loving family.

In retrospect, I am glad that I was the one who suggested we visit Frank as the last living WWI Vet, way back in 2008. The LWF membership agreed, and it evolved into a bi-annual pilgrimage out to his home in Charles Town, West Virginia. The LWF delegation changed a few times and included Ray Damaske and Rob Kesterke, as well as the others previously mentioned. We all became as close as brothers during our trips out to Frank's place. We also took in many of the wonderful historic sites out there—Washington DC with all the presidential and war memorials on the mall, the Smithsonian, Arlington, The National Guard Museum, The National Archives, Library of Congress, The USMC Museum, The VA Hospital, Harper's Ferry, Antietam Battle Field, Fort Belvoir, and the Shenandoah Valley.

I will treasure the photos of these places and the pictures of each of us with Frank and his family. As an old man, I will be able to sit my great-great-grandchildren on my lap and show them the pictures of me with Frank... a link to the long-passed generation of our US WWI Doughboys.

A few days after we got back from our visit, I emailed my son, Ken, and told him that "Now that you and I have had the honor of meeting and conversing with our last WWI Veteran, we need to make it our goal (as father and son veterans) to go and visit with the last WWII veteran when the U.S. is down to only the last one. The way I figure it, giving the vet the benefit of doubt that he or she lives —let's say to be 112 yrs old—I will be 91 years old and you, Ken will be 70... so I will let you do all the driving." Ken's response was: "Sounds like a plan to me, Pop – let's do it!"

This gives me and Ken something really spectacular to look forward to. And I, too, am a better person for having gone on all these trips and having made all these close friendships.

Recollections
By Bob Heft

Designer of our current 50-star American flag

NOTE: This is an email that Bob Heft sent me on Sunday, February 1, 2009, after our trip to Frank Buckles' house to put the American and Spirit Flags in his yard. Bob and Frank had a discussion about the importance of the flag and Bob showed him the original flag that he created in 1958. --Don Alsbro

Dear Patriot Don:

I have been moved and impressed by many things that I have participated in over nearly a half century, including

Bob Heft, designer of American flag in 1960, showing original flag to Frank (2/1/2009)

fourteen visits to nine Presidents at the White House, but none has been any more meaningful than our visit to Mr. Frank Buckles farm in rural Charles Town, WV.

He is an alert and charming gentleman of 108 (as of today). As he recited a portion of his life, it was clear that he is a man of great pride in what he stood for during WWI and his love of country. As Mr. Buckles and myself watched the first raising of the flag, he looked at me and said "that is a beautiful sight."

On that cold and blustery day, both Mr. Buckles and I enjoyed the view from his den in a quiet reflection of pride of this historic event. He requested of me that as the visitors came in, to make sure that they signed his guest book, as he often reads the book. He stated, that he relives the occasions and cherishes those who visit him.

What a warm and friendly human being. His family truly made us feel very welcome and we enjoyed our visit to a True American Icon. God Bless Mr. Buckles! I am proud that you are now able to view "Old Glory" with each sunrise over the hills of Charles Town.

Bob Heft, Designer of America's 50 star flag

Recollections of Frank
by Gust Anton

"The 108th Birthday of Frank W. Buckles" – Visitation by Six Veterans of Berrien County Michigan

February 1, 2009

What an exciting visit it was. Everyone clamored to hear the words of wisdom that this young man would evoke. He sat in his favorite easy chair with people clamoring to talk and shake the hand of this humble man. He can salute just like a raw recruit of our present day soldiers. He is the last living soldier of WWI. I was proud to be in the presence of this centurion, plus eight years. He is intelligent, spry, witty and 108 years old. I asked him what made him live as long as he has? He said, "You've got to want to live every day as long as you can!"

Frank Woodruff Buckles has a 330 acre farm and he drove his tractor until he was 106 years old and worked around the farm until he couldn't walk anymore. He has a daughter, Susannah, who is as capable as her dad and works the farm of feeder cattle. She has the work ethic of her father, out feeding her 200 plus cattle and doing the daily chores that have to be done around the farm each day and taking care of Dad, although she says he doesn't need much help. Don't stand in her way when she's doing chores. Her husband Mike is a real helpmate, what Susannah can't do, he does.

This visit was prompted by Don Alsbro and Dale Hemphill. I'm glad they asked me to accompany them. I wouldn't have missed it for the world. This man is an icon, a positive example of a real soldier.

Frank is a Shriner

On all of my four visits I spoke with Frank about being a Shriner. Frank belonged to the OSIRIS Shrine Center in Wheeling, WV. He was proud to be a Shriner. Frank took many trips to the Shrine hospitals to see these children with various disabilities. He and I had this in common because we know how well the children are treated in the 22 Shrine hospitals in the U.S. The pay we receive in seeing the wonderful care given to these children is all that we need. He was interested in helping children who had a disability and wanted to make sure that they would not go through life with a problem that we could treat. We've seen many wonderful miracles performed at our Shrine hospitals.

Recollections of Frank
by Ray Damaske

Frank in his soft voice whispered to me that "God has already blessed me" when I held his hand and gave him my departing words: "May God bless and keep you." His eyes twinkled when he told me that. Somehow he knew that his day was near to meet the Lord. When departing (I was the last to leave the room with him) I gave him the farewell of my fatherland, "Auf Wiedersehen" in German and he said it verbatim back to me with a smile. He, of all people, remembered the strife America had with Germany and Japan during the Great War and WWII.

It gave me goose bumps when I finally realized the span of time this man—a true American patriot, and the oldest one alive at that time—bid me "Until we meet again" phrase used so often during the war years.

Frank loved those of us that took the time to go see him and his great family in Charles Town. Here's a guy that met many U.S. presidents and notoriety's over the many decades of his life. I'm sure that we humble folk, meant just as much as the celebs and leaders, because he knew we loved him enough and wanted to share time with him.

I don't know if any of the other guys recall Frank's reaction to the gas mask of WWI vintage that we brought with us, but I remember his comment that, "WE were ALL issued one of these masks, whether we wanted it or not!" (I think what he was trying to say is that even if it was a "pain in the ass" to wear in combat, that it was a necessity for life; and the choice between life and death. This is what I got out of it, anyway.)

Don, thank you for making the effort to collect our accounts and conversations with Frank. Mr. Buckles has passed on, just like Bob Heft and Art Jibilian. We only have our memory now and maybe others can enjoy these great American's thoughts as we share them. At the time we thought we would have numerous other visits and memories to enjoy... but, like the old saying goes, "You never know what you have, until it's gone."

Meeting and Knowing Frank Buckles
by Major Kenneth Stice

Ken (left) and Dan Stice visit with Frank Buckles

It was November 2010 that I departed on a journey that has provided me with many amazing memories. I flew to South Bend, Indiana, and headed to Dan Stice's house (my father). The next morning dad and I met up with other members of the *Lest We Forget* (LWF) organization. We loaded up our vehicles and began the long drive to West Virginia where America's last surviving WWI Veteran still lived on his farm.

The day of the scheduled vist, I had the honor of giving the LWF members a tour of the Army National Guard Museum in Washington DC. Many of the LWF members were retired active duty soldiers. They were a little surprised to see how much history the National Guard really has, going all the way back to 1636. And at the end of the tour, we found my dad standing next to my uniform I wore in Iraq during Operation: Iraqi Freedom (2003-04). You could not have removed his smile with a 40-pound hammer! I know he is proud of me, but I'm just proud to be able to serve.

After the visit at the museum, it was time—the moment I was waiting for—time to go see Mr. Frank W. Buckles! I'm sure my dad forgot to mention this in his notes, but we did get lost on the way to his farm. I was a bit surprised as this was their fourth visit. We did manage to get back on track and made it to the Buckles farm just in time for our appointment.

As soon as the van pulled up, Mr. Buckles' daughter, Susannah, met us outside. What an amazing person. She has a wonderful heart and was just beaming with joy to see some of the familiar LWF faces. All received big hugs from her, even those of us that were there for the first time. Susannah was such a gracious hostess, allowing all of us to enter her home to meet with her father.

When we walked into the dining room, there he was. Mr. Buckles was wrapped warmly in his chair, caressing a small hand warmer. Susannah stood behind her father and proceeded to give us a little background on him and a little history of the farm. Mr. Buckles sat patiently, knowing he was going to have to entertain a group of men anxious to ask him many questions he had answered before. I'll never forget though, that during Susannah's talk, Mr. Buckles piped up and said "Is that Suzie?" I know it does not seem like much, but I did get a little chuckle out of that.

When Susannah was done talking, the members of LWF and I had the chance to personally meet and shake Mr. Buckles' hand. I have to be honest. When I shook his hand, I was expecting a frail little grip from Mr. Buckles. Boy, was I wrong! For 109 years, 10 months old, the man still had a firm grip. We all asked two or three questions, and then Susannah brought out the cup Mr. Buckles had as a POW in WWII. This REALLY interested the other LWF members, and they all followed Susannah into the kitchen to see some other items. The only people that stayed behind were me, my dad and T. W. Lane.

No offense to the other LWF members, but I did not fly and drive from Arizona to see artifacts/memorabilia. I came out to see Mr. Buckles. With the other members in the other room, I had the golden opportunity to kneel down right next to Mr. Buckles and talk one-on-one for a good 20 minutes! I was in awe. There is no other way to explain it. Mr. Buckles told me about being at Camp Riley (now Fort Riley) Kansas for training. And then he was shipped (literally) to Europe on the *RMS Carpathia*. I asked him if the crew were on the ship the night they pulled survivors and bodies out of the water after the *RMS Titanic* sank. He said YES! He stated that the stories the crew told him still bother him today. It was then that it really hit me. This man has seen SO many things during his life.

Ken Stice —the youngest of our group and a veteran of Iraq and Afghanistan—talking to WWI veteran, Frank Buckles

After Mr. Buckles spoke to me for a bit, I told him that I too did some training at Fort Riley, and that I have done two tours in the War on Terrorism (one in Iraq and one in Afghanistan). He looked me straight in the eyes and said "Boy, you soldiers sure do get around a lot these days!"

My one-on-one time with Mr. Buckles ended when the other LWF members came back into the dining room. Before I stood back up to move to the back of the room, I once again shook Mr.

Buckles hand, thanked him for his service and for being an amazing American. I then saluted him, gave a subtle nod, and he saluted back. I will NEVER forget that moment.

A bit later it was time to leave. I was full of mixed emotions as I was still on the adrenalin rush of getting to meet Mr. Buckles, but sad that our time together came to an end. It was an amazing trip to say the least. Of course, Susannah walked us out to our van and wished us safe travels. I cannot say enough about her. I wish I would have had time to chat with her one-on-one as I'm sure she has some amazing stories/memories as well.

They say that it is important that soldiers have good family ties and support to keep their mind focused overseas. I'm sure Mr. Buckles had that support during WWI. More importantly though, I feel that his family's love and support, especially Susannah's, over the past 60+ years is what has kept him in such good health and alive for so long. So, Susannah, thank you and your family for loving and caring for this wonderful man! He will truly be missed by those whose lives he touched. I'm grateful and honored that you allowed me into your home to get a once-in-a-lifetime visit with one of our American heroes.

Frank Buckles lying in state at Arlington Cemetery.

STORIES FROM WORLD WAR II

1939 – 1945

Territories involved:
Europe, Pacific, Atlantic, South-East Asia, China,
Middle East, Mediterranean and Africa,
and briefly, North America

D-DAY WITH THE 299TH

Joe Amorelli

I was inducted into the service in March 1943, and trained to be a combat engineer, serving in Company A, 299th Combat Engineers, 1st Infantry Division. We were sent by ship to Southampton, England, with assault landing training at Bristol Bay. That is where we were told about the invasion we would be making at Normandy, France.

Six other fellows and I were going to be on a rubber raft loaded with explosives in order to blow up obstacles on the beach. We would be the first ones off the assault craft to land on Omaha beach, to set our explosives to clear the way for the landing in our section. This was to take place on June 6, 1944.

It turned out that Omaha Beach was the worst one to land on. On June 5, we started across the English Channel to France. About two hours out, our landing craft sprang a leak, causing us to abandon it and make a hazardous switch to a different craft. One of our men was swept out to sea, along with four tanks.

We were to land twenty minutes before H hour, when the rest of the GIs were to arrive. We immediately ran into heavy gunfire from well-hidden Germans. As soon as our craft hit the beach, we were shelled and strafed about 50 yards offshore. We had to wade into shore in about 2-3 feet of water, with the first seven of us pulling and pushing the raft ashore. As we got near the shore, the seven of us were instantly hit by gunfire. The craft we had just left was blown out of the water, along with about 42 men who hadn't made it off yet.

I got hit as soon as I got off the landing craft. As the demolitions man, I had two bags of explosives tied to my back and front. I was in about one foot of water when I got hit in the leg. With all the equipment I had on me, I started to be pulled back out to sea. I was going under when one of my buddies, Frank Morabito, got behind me and pushed me ashore. He dragged me across the beach to a line of low hills about a hundred yards in. He didn't know it at the time, but he put me down next to a landmine; I had to move over next to a dead GI.

If you saw the movie, "Saving Private Ryan," that was the closest movie to show how it was on Omaha Beach. Almost everyone in our battalion got hit or killed. The whole length of the dunes was lined with dead GIs. Later I learned there

Joe and pals

were 85% casualties, most happening within about the first fifteen minutes. All around me, GIs were getting shot. I was sure we would be pushed back into the channel, but the line held. Other GIs finally pushed inland.

My right upper leg had been blown open. A couple of medics patched me up, so I didn't bleed to death. When they moved away from me, they both got shot.

My rifle jammed with sand in it, so it wouldn't fire. Germans were shooting everywhere. I popped my head up, and a German was aiming right at me; a bullet whizzed by my head. I picked up the dead GI's rifle and shot him before he could get a second shot. It was a luck-shot and the first German I knowingly killed.

Shortly after that, another wounded GI helped me to crawl to the high cliff, about 100 yards away, out of the shooting below. Until about 10am, we didn't know what was happening. I never saw that GI again.

Sometime later, when it was safe to leave the area, all of us wounded were carried to a landing craft and put on a boat to take me back to Southampton, England. There, I was kept in a hospital for three months. It looked like I would lose my leg, but the doctors finally decided it could be saved.

After they got me aboard, they dressed my wounds and gave me a shot to calm me down. I don't remember too much about the trip to Southampton, but was told that I went crazy and it took two guys to hold me down until I got another shot, which put me out. I had many nightmares about the German I shot.

I spent three months in the hospital and a month in rehabilitation before I went back to another Engineer outfit. I was sent to Belgium just before we were to hit the German Siegfried line. Our combat demolition unit was to go out before our troops and blow out some road blocks and bridges before the rest of the troops could advance.

Luckily, I was not injured in any subsequent battles, including the Battle of the Bulge.

In January 1945, our patrol group came across some GIs who were digging out the bodies from under the snow near Malmedy, Belgium. A month earlier, the

Frank Morabito   Joseph Amorelli
Omaha Beach, D-Day, First Wave

"This picture is a not-so-good shot of me hitting the ground after I was shot. The guy bending over me was Frank Morabito, who dragged me up the beach to the dune line. He saved my life. This picture has been shown on the History Channel many times."
- Joe Amorelli

53

Germans had trapped dozens of our men in the infamous Massacre of Malmedy. They had shot and killed 84 of them, although a few did manage to either feign death or escape. Our GIs found the bodies frozen in the snow some weeks earlier, and took the bodies away for burial in a local cemetery. When we saw the grim sight, it was decided there would be no more German prisoners taken for awhile.

I was in Malmedy until VE Day; sometimes my time in service was scary, sometimes it was funny. I was discharged November 5, 1945. I could never figure out why I made it, and I still don't know.

After leaving the service, I returned home and worked at the Main Post Office in Niagara Falls, New York. I married, was the father of two daughters and one son, and was widowed. After retirement, I moved to Indiana to be near my eldest daughter, where I married again

DOING MY PART
Alice Jeanne (Nesman) Atwood

Jeanne Atwood - 1944

I entered Michigan State College in East Lansing, Michigan, in 1942 at 16-years-old. In 1944, when I was 18, during the three month summer vacation between my sophomore and junior years, I took a job on the night shift (11pm-7am) at the Oldsmobile plant. The factory was going "big time" (three shifts in 24 hours) doing war work. I had to screw up courage to take the bus for the 2-mile trip to the plant in Lansing, because I had to stand on the corner--a single girl in the dark night waiting for the 10:30pm bus.

I trained on several machines, so I could move to any machine where parts were in demand to meet production. For a time, I worked on a 6-spindle drill making barrel bolts for B-29s. I had to put my feminine feelings on hold because I was up to my elbows in oil on this machine. On several weekends, I was desperate to get back to my college room and scrub away the factory oil "perfume" in case my boyfriend could escape from his dental school studies in the Army ASTP program at the University of Michigan. Usually, though, I could take a nap before he would be able to hitch hike to Lansing. We would have a couple of 5-cent Cokes and a free sock dance at the Union building, and then back to the war work.

Jeanne Atwood - 2012

The plant was not air-conditioned and often it was 90 degrees inside. Large doors were always open for ventilation but that didn't cool the air.

We had a brief break to eat. I carried a small lunch. At times the inspectors were drunk. This being the case, I took my job seriously and made certain my machined parts met the required specs. Several times that summer the shop foreman had some of the college co-eds sell government Liberty bonds.

Besides the good feeling of knowing that I was helping with the American war effort, I earned enough money to buy a raincoat and pay some of my college expenses.

HONORING A VETERAN
Gertrude Baldwin

Written by Richard Grom

Overview by Hospice at Home

Over 1,800 Veterans die every day. One in every four deaths is that of a Veteran. There were an estimated 670,000 Veteran deaths in the United States in 2010. Approximately 75% of Veterans do not receive care through the Veteran's Administration Health Care System. Instead, their care is received within their own communities. Most Veterans who are enrolled in the VA Health Care System still die in the community, approximately 4% of Veterans deaths occur in a VA facility.

As a Veteran approaches the end of life, he/she presents end-of-life cares and concerns that are unique to Veterans, as well as those end of life concerns typical of most people. We are caring for three War Eras of Veterans who are approaching end of life – WWII, Korean, and Vietnam. Each has different Veteran stories which impact their quality of life and dying. There are an estimated 8 million Vietnam era Veterans and their numbers are fading. The number of Vietnam Veteran deaths has nearly doubled since 2001 – 103,890 in 2010, approaching 300 a day.

Honoring our Veterans and honoring our Veterans preferences for care through the end of life is the right thing to do. At Hospice at Home we have launched a multi-faceted effort to reach and care for our Veterans.

Arden Pridgeon (WWII) and Velma Ripsco (WWII), surrounded by the Baldwin family, present a Veteran Certificate of Appreciation to Gertrude Baldwin

The Story of Gertrude Baldwin

"We often take for granted the very things that most deserve our gratitude." - Cynthia Ozick

On Saturday, September 10, 2011, *Hospice At Home* (HAH) honored a Veteran patient of ours, WWII Nurse Gertrude Baldwin. The event was well attended by family members and other residents of the assisted living facility where she resides.

Presenting the Certificate of Appreciation from HAH and the Proclamation of the event was Mr. Arden Pridgeon, a WWII Veteran, and Mrs. Velma Ripsco, herself a WWII nurse. Gertrude was visibly moved by the celebration, and stated often that she was "so undeserving of the honor."

Gertrude deserves this honor, and so much more. She served her country as WWII was coming to an end, and helped to establish a branch of the *Blue Star Mothers* in this area. *Blue Star Mothers* provide support for active duty service personnel, promote patriotism, assist Veterans organizations, and are available to assist in homeland volunteer efforts to help our country remain strong. Gertrude still has an active presence with this organization and is passionate about the good works they provide. (For more information on *Blue Star Mothers*, visit their website at bluestarmothers.org.)

We are honored to recognize the service that Gertrude has provided to her country, and are thrilled that the presentation of the Certificate of Appreciation meant so much to her and her family. Below are a few words from her son, Thomas:

"The day was very special to Mom and you will never know the happiness our family felt to see her so excited. Thank you to Hospice at Home *and thank you to* Lest We Forget *for your efforts to make the last the days of my mom's life so good."*

NOTE: Gertrude Baldwin passed away in November, 2011. In the "Volume Two, Wartime Memoirs by Southwestern Michigan Veterans" published in 2010 by Lest We Forget of Southwestern Michigan, Gertrude penned the story "Okinawa: Charles Baldwin," about how she met and married WWII veteran Charles Baldwin in 1946.

Charles was born in Benton Harbor in 1924 and after basic training at Ft. Custer and F.t Rucker he fought in the Pacific Theater of WWII, participating in the island battles of Pelelieu, Anayar, Leyte and Okinawa with the 96th Infantry Division. On an assault on a hill at Okinawa, he was hit by enemy mortar fire. After being treated in the Army hospitals of Guam and Hawaii, he was sent to Percy Jones Hospital in Battle Creek for recovery and rehabilitation. While at the hospital he met and married Gertrude who was a cadet nurse. In her story, Gertrude relates how they married in secret, since she was not allowed to marry while a student nurse.

After his discharge, they returned to Benton Harbor, which was Charles' home. Charles was a member of the Disabled American Veterans and Veterans of Foreign Wars until he passed in April 2001.

After September 11, 2001, Gertrude became concerned over the fact that she saw no blue stars. She said, "During WWII every house had someone in the service and they had a blue star or several in their windows. After 9/11 I saw no blue stars so I started making them and giving them to people whose kids served in the military. That is how the Charles Baldwin Chapter of the *Blue Star Mothers* evolved." This organization has done a terrific job in recognizing the sacrifices of the current generation in the Iraq and Afghanistan conflicts.

NOTE: The preceding story was obtained from the "Lines of Hope," Winter, 2011-2012, published by Hospice at Home, St. Joseph, MI.

ARMY AIR CORP PILOT IN WWII
Thair Best

NOTE: *The above is an interview on WNIT Public TV (South Bend, IN) on May 17. 2007*

Transcribed by Cheryl Walberg

QUESTION: Where were you when you found out about Pearl Harbor?

Thair Best

I was a senior in college ready to take final exams. As soon as Pearl Harbor happened, I went down to enlist. It took me a couple of sessions to get involved in the Army Air Corp, as it was called at that time. By enlisting in the Reserves they said I could finish college before I was called into service. I thought that was a great idea because I only had winter quarter to start and spring quarter and I would have graduated. In February, they decided they needed us in the military more than they needed us in college, so I went into the military with all the college seniors. They didn't know what to do with us after they got us there so they sent us to Oshkosh, Wisconsin, to a junior college for about a month until they had an opening at the pre-flight school in California.

After pre-flight in California we went to Thunderbird Field #1 in Glendale, Arizona, where we were taught how to fly. We soloed in a single-engine two-passenger open cockpit biplane. From primary flight school you go to Basic Training where you are supposed to fly the BT-13. I never sat in a BT-13. I went right into the AAT-6, an advanced trainer. At that time, I only had 75 hours flight time. We learned how to fly planes with retractable gear and flaps and adjustable props at Basic. From there we went to Advanced Training where we went into night flying in stripped down P-38's. We had to sit in the cockpits blindfolded and memorize all the instruments that were there so we could touch them as the instructor called them out.

I did get one piggyback ride with a pilot as he told me to fly it. We were flying out of Williams field in Arizona about 35 miles south of Phoenix which was off limits to us, but I did manage to get it up in the air. I got the wheels up, the props up and I looked down, and I was 35 miles away right over Phoenix. That was a big charge and I didn't have wings at that time, for I hadn't graduated. After that we went for training in Oklahoma City at Will Rogers Field where they taught us how to operate cameras and assigned us targets to fly to out of Oklahoma City for practice.

I graduated in March of 1944, and we were overseas and ready to fly combat by June. The month of June 1944, I joined the squadron in England. We were in the middle of the Atlantic Ocean when they invaded France on D-Day. So I did not fly any missions out of England.

We immediately transferred the whole squadron as soon as they had a place carved out for us in Rheims, France. We landed in an airfield that still had bomb craters on it. We had more pilots than airplanes so I had to fly with two other guys in a trainer with all our gear to fly over France and then we stated flying missions as soon as we got to France and we would move across France and follow the front lines.

From June to January, we moved four times to four different fields to stay close to the front lines. We did bomb damage appraisal for the 9th Air Force and we did mapping studies for Patton's 3rd Army. He would have an officer in our headquarters, and we would have a pilot in Patton's office to interpret the pictures we took. Most of our work was done from above 20,000 feet but occasionally we had to go in at low altitude. It was our squadron that photographed all the beaches in France before the invasion. I didn't join the unit until that was finished. We lost over one third of the pilots photographing the beaches of France flying these low altitude missions. But that was before my time.

It was that same kind of mission that I was on when I was shot down. It was my 45th mission. When people ask me how many missions I flew I say 44 ½ because I went out and I never came back from it. My assigned altitude over the target was less than 50 feet and I flew for probably a mile or two looking up at the telephone poles watching the tracers going up over the top of me. I was so low they couldn't shoot at me or they would have been shooting at each other. Eventually I had to bank to turn and they hit my left engine and it caught fire immediately and started filling up with smoke. I did get the engine shut down and got the props feathered. I flew on a single engine until I came to a hill and got up above a low layer of clouds.

I had to go in at such a low altitude because they needed the pictures of the equipment that the Germans were assembling to make an attack on Bastogne and we couldn't do it at a high altitude above the clouds, so it was a low altitude mission. It was also a volunteer mission, I didn't have to take it but when my turn came, I said I would go, even though I could have turned it down. When I finally did bail out, I went into the clouds upside down and pushed with my feet. Another plane showed up next to me. I don't know where he came from. He did not see a parachute, so he went back and reported that I crashed with the airplane. My parents were notified that I was killed in action and they had no word from me until after we were liberated from a POW camp in Germany.

I was a POW for 99 days and I lost over a third of my body weight. I went from 155 pounds to 100 pounds. When I was liberated in the later part of April, I was still wearing the same clothes that I had been wearing when I bailed out over Germany in January. I borrowed a leather jacket from my roommate before I went on my last mission. I still have that leather jacket today.

QUESTION: Tell us what happened as you were coming down with your parachute.

Coming down I kept hoping the soldiers would not use me for target practice. I landed in about twenty inches of snow. There was no wind so the parachute just settled down over the top of me. I dug out from under the parachute and all I could see were gun barrels pointing at me. A heavy-set sergeant was in charge. The rest of them were very young. Germany was getting down to the bottom of people to keep in the army. The airplane crashed and landed long before I came down in the parachute. It was burning around 500 feet away from where I landed. The sergeant pointed over to the airplane and said "Machine kaput!"

A couple days later they got me to a train to Frankfort and then up to an interrogation camp which was north of Frankfort. I was put in solitary confinement in a 6x9' room painted white with one window with bars and frosted over so I couldn't see out. During that time I was only given bread and water. They took me in for interrogation every day and wanted to know who I was. I found out they knew more about my squadron than I did. The interrogation officer had been an officer in the Luftwaffe and had been injured. He spoke English very well. Because I wanted to get out of there, I had stayed awake one night and memorized all the names of the pilots that had been killed in action. So when the officer wanted names, those were the names I gave. That seemed to satisfy him, but then he wanted to know the name of my Flight Officer and I told him it was Captain Garner. He looked at me and asked me if I was sure he was still a captain. I said the last time I saw him he was. Mind you, we are in a prison camp inside of Germany and the man looked at me and said he got his captain bars in England in April, 1943, by now he should be at least a major. He knew even more. He told me the name of my Flight Officer's sister and his hometown in Texas. That was German intelligence.

I finally got out of there after about ten days of bread and water and was taken to a camp in Nuremberg with close to 10,000 Air Force officers from all over the world. There were English, French, American, Indian, New Zealand, and Canadian officers. We were kept sort of segregated by our countries. We were given very little food to eat. We were in this camp when the American Air Force bombed Nuremburg off the map. When we were sent to the second camp in Mooseberg, we saw what was left and it looked like a pile of bricks.

It took us about ten days to walk down to the Mooseburg camp where they had a tent city set up for us. It was temporary housing – they wanted to keep their hands on as many prisoners as they could to use as a bargaining agent. At the Mooseburg camp, most of our guards had been injured at some time during the war. Some had lost an arm or a leg but they treated us the best they could. When Patton's army was pressing in close, they surrendered the camp to the POWs and they stayed in the prisoner barracks. We had American and English guards in the gun towers guarding the gates. They didn't want the prisoners running out all over Germany.

When the Germans came back through and found that their guards had surrendered to us, they threw hand grenades into the barracks and killed their own guards. Shortly after that, Patton's army arrived and it took several days before they could fly us all out to a hospital base in France where we got deloused, debugged, showered and were given clean clothes. They kept us on a very limited diet. They fed us very small amounts about four or five times a day until we could get used to food again. We could not eat a normal full size meal without getting sick. One day, I went into town and some GIs gave me a candy bar and a shot of brandy. I was sick for two days.

While I was at the hospital in France my very good friend Jack Walden flew down to see me before I flew out of Germany to France. I told Jack that I wanted to fly a P-38 that he flew. Jack said that I couldn't because I didn't have a crew chief. I said "You be my crew chief." We started it up and after taking off, I buzzed that runway so low that no one was left standing. That was the first and only time I flew in a P-38.

I came back on a hospital ship. When we arrived in the US we were interrogated and then we received sixty days recuperative leave to go home. That is when I got married to a young lady I'd met in Oklahoma City. We are still married. This year we are celebrating our 62nd wedding anniversary.

We were sent back to Luke AFB in Arizona where we flew four hours a month so that we could continue to receive flight pay. Flight pay was a big bonus – fifty percent over base pay. One day, coming out of an officer's club I happened to pass a major who called me to attention for not saluting him. "Did you not get to the courtesy meeting this morning?" I replied, "No sir, my car wouldn't start." He told me that from now on when I met any senior officer on that base, I was to recognize them with a salute. I said "Yes sir," turned around, walked down to headquarters and told them I wanted out. I was gone two days later because I had more than enough points to get me out of the service.

QUESTION: Tell us about going back to Luxemburg.

About four-and-a-half years ago, I had a message on my answering machine from a man named John who had a German accent. He said he was calling for a Lt. Thair Best whose airplane crashed in the German-Luxembourg border, January 22, 1945. I knew he had to be for real because he had the exact date that I crashed. He called back the next day and we must've talked for thirty minutes. He wanted me to help identify the airplane. They had found the crash site years ago and he knew from German records and archives, and from a farmer nearby, that a pilot had been taken as a prisoner of war. It took him over four years to track me down to the States and to get a phone number for me. We had several conversations and we also started emailing back and forth.

One day I mentioned to John that my wife had wanted me to take her to Paris. I told John that I wasn't too happy with the French, but I wouldn't mind going back to Luxemburg. He told me that if I came to Luxemburg he would be my host. On Fathers Day, 2006, my son Bruce called and told me that he would go with me to Luxemburg. He even arranged for his younger brother to come and stay with my wife for the week that we would be gone. So in 2006 my son flew from Madison, Wisconsin, and I flew from South Bend, Indiana, to meet in Detroit, Michigan, where we flew on to Amsterdam and caught a shuttle to Luxemburg.

I didn't realize it, but the country of Luxemburg is actually two small countries: Luxemburg City and Grand Duchy. The total area is about the size of two counties in Indiana. The size is about 35 miles long and 20 miles wide with a population of about 400,000. When we arrived at Luxemburg, we used my son's Hilton card and got a nice big room at the Luxemburg Airport. I called John and told him that we'd arrived but since we hadn't slept for over a day, we needed a good night's rest and would meet him in the morning. John said that he would be over in the morning to pick us up in his Jeep. I could see him showing up in a WWII jeep. Was I surprised when he pulled up in his Mercedes full size SUV with TV monitor in front and back!

We then went to the American military cemetery in Luxemburg City. We were met by a television crew and the local newspaper was there to interview us. I had my picture taken at the grave of General Patton. From there we went to the George Patton museum where I was presented with a medal for coming back to visit Luxemburg. We then went to the Air Force Aviation museum where they had two pieces of my airplane on display. They also had an engine on display from a B-17. I told them that the engine was made in my hometown of South Bend. The nametag was still on the engine: Studebaker Corporation.

I then asked John to find us a typical Luxemburg hotel room, which he did. I mentioned to my son that the bedroom was almost as big as our bathroom last night in the Hilton Hotel. However, it was a nice, clean room. John picked us up the next day and we went to see the mayor of Hosingen. The mayor showed us pictures of what the city looked like after a WWII battle of German and American tanks. The mayor didn't speak English, but John served as our interpreter. I was presented with a nice plaque.

We drove out to the crash site and we could still find the hole in the ground which was about six feet in diameter and about 25 inches deep. A television crew and a man with a metal detector came out, too. They would dig down and bring up little pieces of metal from the plane that had crashed there over 60 years ago. I was able to bring small metal pieces of my plane back with me. We also went to Bastogne and visited the memorial to the American Armed Forces. We were very much involved with Bastogne. When Bastogne was encircled, we would photograph the whole area and drop the pictures inside of Bastogne. It was quite a treat to go back to Bastogne.

QUESTION: What did your service mean to you?

I was very proud to be in the service. You couldn't buy what I went through for a million dollars, but I wouldn't give you a dollar to go through it again. It was a very rewarding experience. I did what I wanted to do. It is so much different than the war we are in right now against Iraq and Afghanistan. You don't even know who your enemy is over there. People are fighting each other and we're in the middle. We knew who we were fighting. They fought by the rules and they treated us as we should be treated as POWs. I am very proud that I did serve.

CAUGHT IN THE MIDDLE
John Bettig

John Bettig

I was born on April 7, 1930, in Poland. My name was Jan. In our home, we spoke Ukrainian, and in school, we were educated in the Polish language. Under the Soviet regime, my name was Ivan and in school, we were educated in the Russian language. When we came to Germany, we had to learn German in school and my name was Johann Bettich. When I became an American citizen, my name was changed to John Bettig. In Russia and the Ukraine, I was best known by the name Ivan Romanovich Bettig.

Before I was drafted to the US Army in October 1953 *(see my experiences in the Korean section)*, I experienced two different parts of World War II: the Polish war in 1939 and the Russian war in 1941. During the Polish war, we experienced the German blitzkrieg with immense bombing. It was an extremely dangerous situation. The Polish authorities arrested most German men and many of them were murdered. A Polish man informed my dad of his impending arrest and told him to hide. My dad followed his advice and was spared.

In 1939, Germany attacked Poland from the west and the Russians attacked from the east. We were caught in the tug of war between Germany and Russia. Since we lived close to the Russian border, we saw many Russian soldiers. Polish and Jewish citizens may have preferred a Soviet regime to the Germans, but the Soviets soon proved as hostile and destructive towards the Polish people and their culture as the Nazis. They began confiscating, nationalizing and redistributing all private and state-owned Polish property. They arrested many Polish citizens, mostly civilians, and deported them. Many of them died.

During the Soviet occupation, nobody knew who would be arrested next or for what reason. People did not talk to each other out of fear of being accused of a crime for something they did or said. We, as children, attended Russian school to learn the Russian language. We were reminded that there is no God. To be a good student and make good grades, we should report what our parents did and said in our home to our teachers. Some children sold out their parents. Anyone suspected of anti-Soviet activities was detained, sent to labor camps, prison, or executed. Some parents were shot in front of their children. Other parents were taken from their children and never seen again.

Since my Dad was of German descent, we were among those who resettled in Germany. We had to leave almost everything behind. We only took what we could carry, and that was not much since most of the children were too small to carry much. The first 16 months in Germany, we were in 12 different refugee camps. Shortly before the war with Russia began, we were released from the camp and settled in the eastern part of Germany. In 1944 as we celebrated Christmas Eve and the peace that should come to all men, we heard in the far distance the thundering of heavy artillery. We knew the Russians were coming and they were very near. The question was, what should we do: flee with the rest of the people to the west or go hide in the forest? We knew of many times those fleeing from the Russians were surprised by Russian planes and killed. My father had worked in the forest and knew some places where we could hide from the Russians. He decided we would go into the forest and hide.

My father, my brother-in-law, Anton, and Paul Opalko, went deep into the forest to build a shelter. The shelter was 24x12,' more than six feet deep and completely camouflaged. The night before the people of the village had to leave their homes, we three families also left ours—to go into our shelter and hope the first troops would soon pass so we could return to the village. We were so wrong.

After a few days in the shelter, we heard activity of war far in the distance and we felt safe. We waited and waited but instead of the Russians coming, the Germans found us. They were surprised to find us in such a place, saying, "What are you doing here? Don't you know you should go to the west of the Neisse River? You better go and go fast before the Russians catch you." We did not have a horse to pull our wagon, only an ox. We put our belongings, which were few, on the wagon with the small children and headed for the west side of the Neisse River.

As we moved along, the German soldiers were laying mines on the road behind us, preparing for the Russians. We had to go through the forest at least six miles before we reached the village where we would cross the river. As we entered the village, there were no civilians anywhere to be seen. We only found one man who invited us to stay with him. During the night, the noise was unbearable and nobody could sleep. The German army moved across the river to the western side. There they positioned themselves ready to fight the Russians. The next morning I took my bicycle and went across the river to the city of Rothenberg in search of food.

As I arrived at the bridge, I noticed some Germans scurrying about. I stopped to ask them what was happening. Their reply was, "Boy, what are you doing here? The Russians are here! We will blow up the bridge any moment. You better go and hide somewhere."

Heavy artillery began to pound that hill. I hurried back to the house, a half mile away, as fast as my feet could pedal. I think it was the fastest bike ride of my life. When I arrived at the house, I found my family and friends lined up with their hands raised. Six Russian soldiers with fixed bayonets were interrogating them. All we knew and could tell them was that the Germans were on the other side of the river. They took valuables, like watches, from us, and told us to get away from the front line.

Our poor ox was so frightened from all the artillery explosions on every side that he would not pull the wagon. We blindfolded him and finally, with great effort, made it up the hill behind the cemetery heading back to the shelter in the forest. We traveled on a different road this time and weren't at all sure how to get back. Besides, we knew of mines on the roads making us more cautious as we went along. As we reached the forest, we moved forward carefully, trying to use the protection of the trees, seeking our shelter. We weren't familiar with the area because the sky was so very, very red from the continuous pounding of heavy weapons and planes. After awhile, Russian troops filled the forest and there was no place to hide from them.

As they had done the first time they stopped us, they searched our wagon, taking most of our food and all of our bicycles except one. They told us to follow them to a dirt road full of

Russian troops marching west on either side. We were ordered to go east in the middle of that same road. The first chance available to us, we turned into the forest leaving the enemy behind. The search for shelter continued.

Finally, we found a place we felt was safe enough to spread blankets on the ground for the children to lay down and sleep. My dad took the only bicycle remaining and went looking for a familiar place, hoping to find the shelter. He found a beet that had fallen off the broken wagon as a load was being transported earlier to the shelter. This beet was a road sign for Dad. He now knew instinctively where he was and what direction to go. We arrived at the shelter late that night. What a relief to be back! We stayed approximately four weeks, always hearing the heavy pounding by the artillery in the background. The trees all around us were stripped of their bark as the fighting between the Germans and Russians came closer. Several times shells hit close causing the entrance to our shelter to cave in.

We did not starve during this hard time. Our neighbor had planned to hide with us in the forest. He buried canned goods and potatoes ahead of time, and only my dad knew the location. When the time came to go, our good neighbor changed his mind, deciding to go west with the rest of the refugees. The food he left behind saved our lives.

We don't know how long we would have remained in the shelter if it hadn't been for one wrong move. We ran out of dry wood needed for cooking. Dry wood gives off less smoke than damp wood. We didn't want anyone to find us. My dad, Anton, and Mr. Opalko went looking for dry firewood. Dad knew where some piled wood could be found. Anton decided to pile three logs on his shoulder, the other two each took two thick logs and off they went. Anton couldn't keep up and soon lagged behind. Assuming he was following in the right direction, he actually became lost and didn't know it. When he heard sounds, he assumed the men were already chopping wood, and he followed the sound to go "home."

Suddenly, someone shouted, "*rooky vyerch*," which in Russian means, "hands up." Too late, he realized it was a Russian army post. He dropped the wood and stood before several Russian soldiers pointing their guns at him. He immediately spoke with them in Russian, telling them his family was in the forest. Perhaps thinking he was a deserter or a spy, they didn't know what to do with him. Anton offered to lead the soldiers to the shelter, but he was not sure which way to go. Finally, four soldiers agreed to go with him, ready with automatic weapons for an ambush.

In the meantime, we were waiting for Anton, but he didn't come. We heard shooting in one direction and wondered if he was killed. We decided to look for him in the direction of the woodpiles. There, we saw in the far distance several men walking in the other direction. We started running toward them and quickly recognized Anton walking in front of the soldiers pointing their guns at him. When they saw us, we put our hands up. After they searched us, they knew Anton had been telling the truth. They followed us to the shelter, finding many children. They searched us for weapons. The only thing that looked suspicious to them was a map from our area under the mattress in a child's buggy. The officer in the group said: "Now I know who you are, you are spies. You took your family as a cover-up to your spying activity. You will not get away with this." With these remarks, he ordered the other soldiers to kill us.

My parents and others in the group started to explain that we weren't spies, for we had neither telephone nor radio. We told them the Germans were close, over the Neisse River, and that we were running from them. We assured them we were refugees. We begged them not to kill us. The children began to cry, others began to pray. We could not see any escape. Then God did something unexpected. The soldiers walked away a short distance in order for us not to hear their discussion. They came back and said, "You get ready; we will go and return with a truck to pick you up." All four of them took off and left us alone.

As quickly as possible, we put our few things and small children on our wagon, put the ox in front and off we went in the opposite direction. Again, we trusted God. We don't know if the Russian soldiers returned and searched for us. They could have easily sent the truck after us, and we assume they did, but perhaps in the wrong direction. I believe our Lord blinded their eyes so they could not see us.

—READ MUCH MORE ON OUR CD—

FRENCHY
Dean W. Betz

It was in a muddy, shell-torn orchard in Normandy where I first saw Frenchy. About 30-40 others like myself had been sent up to this particular infantry company as replacements. The losses had been heavy in the hedgerows and Company K had not been spared. As I lay in the Norman mud I looked up at the torn and twisted apparition above me which at one time had been a lovely apple tree. Machine gun and rifle fire continued unabated while mortar shells dropped spasmodically around us. Rain dripped from the mangled tree as I examined the deep well-spaced foxholes dug into the hedgerow in front of me. A few grimy haggard spectators watched us as we lay there. I concluded that they were all that was left of the company command post.

These spectators, who peered at us, seemed very inquisitive as though we were from a different world. They inquired as to our number and asked what part of the States we were from. However, they never ventured from their holes, but merely stared at us with blank and pitiful expressions on their faces. We were lying in the mud and rain waiting to be assigned to a platoon. Twice, a mud-caked GI came and took about half of our number. Then from a narrow hole in the hedge came a bearded, hunched figure. He approached our group and selected about a dozen of us and then introduced himself: "My name is Frenchy. I'm your platoon sergeant – second platoon. Follow me through this hole in the hedge at a ten-yard interval. Keep low and move fast. As soon as you find an empty hole, hit it and remember to keep low cause Jerry has our whole area covered and knows we're bringing up replacements. After things quiet down, I'll come and talk to each of you personally. Let's go."

I was off on the greatest adventure of my life as I followed the man in front of me through the hole in the hedge. I dashed for a vacant hole that was half full of water, but it provided a welcomed covering from the fierce firing of the enemy. Later I became better acquainted with Frenchy and from that time on was a keen observer and worshipper of the most courageous and indomitable person I have ever known.

Dean W. Betz

In that first lonely and strange night of combat, I was overwhelmed with a terrible case of nervousness and jitters like most newcomers to the front lines. I had been standing guard behind a thick protective hedgerow for perhaps a half-hour while a steady barrage of shelling continued from both sides. Now and then a German plane droned lazily overhead discharging flares, which illuminated the countryside. Up and down the line from me, grenades could be heard exploding while I stood peering out into the inky blackness ahead of me. Then, from behind, I heard someone moving about. It was Frenchy, checking the guard.

He approached me and began talking in a low voice. "Try to relax, kid. This is nothing compared to Africa. We had to pull guard all night long by ourselves. We had to dig in out in front of our lines and sit there all night with fixed bayonets. Sometimes we had to pull the pin out of a grenade and sit there and hold it to keep from falling asleep."

He also told me that our outfit would be relieved soon and we would go back to the rear for a few days where we could sleep and eat all we wanted. I found out later that all rookies were given this false information to boost their morale. So you see, Frenchy was not only a master tactician but a psychologist as well. A few minutes later he snuck off to another position and left me standing there behind the hedgerow alone and wondering how, with all the horror around me, Africa could not have been worse.

On the second day of the titanic battle for St. Lo, after meeting fanatical enemy resistance, Frenchy was hit. He got "his" while in the process of clearing out a machine gun position over in the far corner of the hedge. After being knocked down by the blast, he rose to his feet and tried to continue the job that he had started. Instead, he collapsed at the feet of our medic, who hurried over to give him aid. I found out later that shell fragments had torn through both his legs. Afterwards, it was rumored that both legs would have to be amputated. Like hundreds of others that horrible day, he was sent back to the hospital and was never expected to be seen again.

After Frenchy left the outfit, many legends concerning his adventures began to circulate. In Africa and Sicily, he accompanied the battalion commander on secret patrols at night behind the enemy lines. He walked up in the middle of a street just after D-day firing his Browning automatic rifle and slaughtered at least a dozen of the enemy. He brought about the surrender of an entire German company. After his old comrades had either been killed or wounded, Frenchy fought on. (Losing one's close friends, watching them "get theirs" and going on for a great length of time unscathed is one of the mysterious and heart-rending factors of war.)

In November, to everyone's surprise, the invincible Frenchy returned to the outfit. We discovered later that he had escaped from the hospital in England and had somehow made his way back to our Division. Was love of war so strong in him that he would deliberately rejoin his outfit where death and destruction early awaited him? Was he out of his mind? I came to the conclusion that it was probably the atmosphere of close comradeship and understanding, the mutual aims and unity of effort that drew him back. Something that couldn't be found anywhere else. Whatever it was, he was given a hardy welcome. Once again the company had that extra spark of superb leadership given by Sergeant Frenchy.

By July, however, things had changed. There were new faces and new surroundings. No longer were we in the hedgerows but instead we were now situated in the wooded and rolling country of the Ardennes near the German town of Munchow in the Siegfried line. One quiet afternoon, after renewing my acquaintance with Frenchy, I sat and talked with him about old times. We talked about the big air show at St. Lo, the bombardment and about how terribly hot it was that day. We joked about some of the incidents that happened and then Frenchy began telling me how it had felt when he got hit.

Motioning to his legs, he proudly said, "Feel the lead in my legs, here below the knees. They didn't get it all out." I felt, and sure enough there were hard lumps under the skin of both legs. He told me they were planning on taking it out just before he left the hospital. *What was he trying to prove? Why didn't he remain in the hospital and let them take the rest of it out? Why, he might even have been sent home.* These were some of the thoughts that ran through my mind as I sat there on the edge of the hole talking to him. Then he began to tell me all about his brother who was in high school back in New Jersey. He had sort of a fanatical but remorseful look in his eyes as he talked. His greatest ambition was that his brother would never get mixed up in the war. He was always thinking about someone else and never himself. He was funny that way.

He told me how he despised killing Germans but went on because he could do the job just as well as the next guy. "Why brush a dirty, lousy job like this off on somebody else when you can do it yourself?" he said. I nodded my head in agreement, but at the same time wondered if other people could even begin to realize just what kind of hell some men were going through for them. Here was a man who had been in the thick bitter fighting for two whole years but hadn't given up. Here was a man with almost supernatural courage and strength. Here was the personification of the ideal American soldier.

The next day I saw Frenchy for the last time as I was sent back to the hospital. Sometimes I wonder if he lived through the war or if his brother ever got involved in the conflict. Sometimes I close my eyes and think of all the other "Frenchys" who fought in all parts of the world. Sometimes I wonder where we would all be today without all those "Frenchys."

—READ TWO MORE OF BETZ' STORIES ON OUR CD—

WWII

"RADAR O'REILLY" OF WWII
Donald F. Briney

Interviewed and written by Phil Manni

United States Army, WORLD WAR II, US Army 36455797

Donald F. Briney

I was born in Coloma, Michigan, on December 5, 1915, and graduated from Coloma High School in 1933. Prior to entering the service, I spent most of my time working on the family farm. My first job was at a gas station in Coloma, basically doing any odd job that needed to be done. I made $10 a week and this was not a 5-day week. I worked there seven days a week—long days—and was glad to have this job. I also worked at I&M for a year-and-a-half before Uncle Sam came calling. I married Alice Schultz on September 15, 1940, and we began our life together.

I was asked to join Uncle Sam in March 1942, but at the time, my wife was hospitalized and I inquired on whether I could get an extension until I could get my wife home from the hospital and settled. The extension was granted, but when I was to report, the Draft Board office in Benton Harbor came under some scrutiny, as it seemed as though there was a young lady that worked there that was giving out draft deferments to some of her friends and, of course, this was frowned upon. Once all the dust was settled from this incident, I was drafted into the US Army on March 10, 1943.

The other draftees and I were taken by train to Camp Grant, in Rockford, Illinois. There, we were outfitted with clothes, given the necessary shots, and completed paperwork as we were prepared to leave for Basic Training. I served two months Basic Training in Atlantic City, New Jersey. From there, I was sent to Huntsville, Texas, a small college town, where I attended Tech School and received training to become a Company Clerk. For those of you that were fans of the popular 1970s television show, *M*A*S*H*; that's right—I was trained to be a 1943 version of Radar O'Reilly.

My first assignment was at Selfridge Field, where I was assigned to the 1309th Signal Pigeon Company. This Company trained homing pigeons which were used when it was necessary to maintain radio silence during troop movements and intelligence gathering. These birds were used to fly messages between Commanding Officers on the front lines and those officers that directed movements from the rearward positions. These birds and their missions were invaluable when it was necessary to keep the radio "chatter" to a minimum.

My Signal Company got overseas orders and traveled by barge from Fort Kilmer, New Jersey to Long Island, and then by ship to England. Because of the speed of our ship and the submarine traffic in the North Atlantic, we traveled in an unescorted, zigzag pattern eastbound, to prevent our ship from being intercepted or allowing enemy submarines from plotting our course, and because of this, our crossing took 14 days. We landed in Liverpool on the 15th of August, 1944.

We then traveled by train to the west coast of England to the town of Cardiff. We stayed there for a month, sleeping on cots and homemade sleeping bags. Days and nights were very cold and we struggled to stay warm. We then drove cross-country to South Hampton and boarded an LST landing on Omaha Beach September 20, 1944. The weather caused us much grief as it was a constant, steady rain for the first month. We settled near the Channel, approximately 14 miles inland, and our encampment was in a series of hedgerows. The winter of 1945 was very snowy and once again caused us many problems due to the cold and snow. The Commanders kept us on alert as they were told that we would be moving up (forward), but this never did happen.

A typical day for me included payroll processing, setting up necessary filing systems, and always making four copies of any report I had to make, which ended up with me throwing three of those away. I also distributed the mail we received, which usually took about a month to find its way to us across the Atlantic. The system used in securing our mail was known as V-Mail.

We never did move forward, so I was not in any battles, but I did pick up some notoriety on one of those *extra* jobs that I was given. I was dispatched to pick up a Chaplain at a station hospital when he arrived in the country. I went to the motor pool to secure transportation and proceeded on my journey. As I drove to the pick-up point, I found the route took me past a coke pile that had been abandoned by a German work crew repairing roads. Coal was used to heat tar which was used as a repair material. This coke pile was a by-product of coal, which I knew because of my days on the farm back home. I picked up the Chaplain and proceeded to take him back to our Company. After I was sure he was settled in, I went back to the motor pool and exchanged my jeep for a 3/4-ton truck. I then proceeded back along the route I had just been on and picked up as much of the coke pile that I could carry. I took it back to our tents and this coke provided much needed heat, which made me quite popular back in camp. Our 1st Sergeant thought that this was a tremendous boost to our morale as it sure made the cold, rainy days a little more tolerable.

I served nine months in Normandy and was then issued orders to return back to the States. We boarded the ship at LeHarve and headed westbound back across the Atlantic. The trip back to the USA was faster, but much more turbulent, as far as the Atlantic was concerned. I remember looking out over the bow and seeing 30-50 foot waves crash over the ship and felt many times that we might not make it through the trip. I can't begin to explain how I felt as we sailed by the Statue of Liberty and ported in New York harbor. I (as well as all of the others) was so glad to be back in the greatest country in the world.

As we disembarked the ship, there was a WAC band playing the song *"Rum and Coke"* and they sure made us feel very welcome. It was great to be home. I completed in-processing and then boarded a train and traveled to my next duty station, Fort Hamilton in New York. During the trip, we were given steak dinners with all the trimmings and I can't remember a meal that tasted as good.

Upon leaving Fort Hamilton, I was sent to my separation center at Fort Sheridan, Illinois, where I was granted a 30-day leave at home. It was then, that I first met my new daughter, who was born while I was traveling by train box car across France to board the ship at LeHarve. With my 30-day leave complete, I reported to Fort Jackson, South Carolina, in preparation for my next assignment. While there, the atomic bombs were dropped on the islands of Hiroshima and Nagasaki, bringing an end to the war with Japan.

I received the Good Conduct medal, as well as, the European Theatre medal and was discharged as a Corporal, on October 5, 1945, from Fort Jackson, South Carolina. I traveled back home eager to return to civilian life and my wife.

Upon discharge, I was employed by my brother-in-law for a number of years. In 1966, I opened my own roofing and siding business, which I ran until my retirement in 1985.We were blessed with two wonderful daughters, one living in Stevensville, Michigan, and the other resides in Jerome, Michigan.

I currently reside in St.Joseph, Michigan, and with the exception of arthritis, have been living a comfortable retirement and still live unassisted in my home. Reflecting over the time I spent in the service, I wouldn't change anything. I went in a boy, and came back a man.

—READ MUCH MORE ON OUR CD—

A HERO IN MANY WAYS
Dr. Bassett Brown

Written by Cristine Timmons

Bassett Brown

NOTE: Dr. Brown was an active member of "Lest We Forget" up to his death on February 6 , 2012. Cristine was asked to put together a tribute to this true patriot.

We often think of heroism as it relates to war. Bassett Brown was a hero during World War II, but he was also a hero after the war. He was a champion of the underprivileged, an idol to both children and adults and a winner at life in a time when racial discrimination penetrated deeply into the American culture.

After speaking with many of Dr. Brown's friends, it became obvious that the central part of his biography was his close and loving family. WWII, education, career, basketball, religion and civic duty helped define him, but it was his family who instilled a sense of altruism that was at the core of Bassett Brown.

Bassett was the second of three children born to Wilbert and Ada (Grant) Brown. His brother, Paul, was born in 1921 in Mercer, Pennsylvania. Bassett and his sister, Delores (b. 1926) was born in Benton Harbor, Michigan. Charles Bassett Brown arrived two days before Christmas in 1923.

The family lived on the near east side of Benton Harbor on Burton Street, close to Business I-94 (Main Street) and M-139 (Martin Luther King Drive). "Bassett's parent's were down-to-earth wonderful people," recalls Roy Shoemaker, retired from Heath-Zenith. "They welcomed everyone…it was the place we all gathered." Shoemaker recalled that Bassett's dad started a basketball team with the local kids and recruited local sponsors as support. They played other YMCA teams. It was also Bassett's dad who drove the neighborhood kids to social and sporting functions according to Shoemaker.

This generous spirit passed from Wilbert and Ada to their children. According to a Herald-Palladium story published February 8, 2012, Sammie Smith, retired public housing director for Benton Harbor and Benton Township remembered growing up across the street from the Brown family. "He's (Bassett) the first one that taught me about football, he and his brother Paul." Smith said Bassett always had time to work with neighborhood youth on his trips home from college. Smith also recalled that Bassett pledged that when he finished his schooling, he would fix the cleft palate of a girl he knew for free. "That's the first thing he did," recalled Smith.

The rest of Bassett's life would mirror Wilbert and Ada's commitment to the children of Benton Harbor. Brown's numerous lifetime friends have many stories recounting Bassett's generosity, some of which will be shared throughout this biography.

EDUCATION

The Brown children attended St. John's High School in Benton Harbor. (In 1969, St. John's merged with St. Joseph Catholic High School to become Lake Michigan Catholic). Bassett took his studies seriously and was already thinking of a career in medicine. He was also active in sports and lettered in track, football and basketball at St. Johns.

After graduating from high school in 1941, Bassett worked in a factory and his father's barber shop to save money for college.

In 1942, Brown started his freshman year at Western Michigan University. "When I arrived at Western, I found that blacks were not allowed to live in VanderCook Hall, the only men's dormitory on campus. So I wound up in a rooming house." (*Kalamzoo Gazette*, February 14, 1997) Brown handled this insult as a minor inconvenience. He was there for pre-med and to play basketball.

But WWII was changing everybody's lives and Brown's college career was cut short as soon as it had begun. Brown must have felt his world would be changing soon. He had already said goodbye to guys he had graduated with from St. Johns. Now it was his turn to fight overseas. At least he had completed his freshman year of college.

Brown made it through the war and returned to Western Michigan University to continue his academic career and play on the varsity basketball team as the first African-American starter for the Broncos. Encouragement from teachers made a huge difference in how Brown was to see himself. "Because of the high expectations of Frank Hinds, my biology instructor, Charles Smith, my English professor, and Robert Moss, from the basketball staff, had of me, I elevated my own goals from mediocrity to being the very best I could be." (Dr. Brown quote for the *Westerner*, Fall 1992)

During the summer break, Brown continued to work at his father's barbershop on Colfax to make money for his next year at school. According to Perla Torlentino, Dr. Brown's best friend of 40 years, Bassett and his parents paid for his Bachelor's degree and he used the G.I. Bill to earn his Master's.

After completing his B.S. degree at Western in 1948, Brown attended graduate school at Fisk University, and again, mixed his scholarship with basketball. From Fisk, Brown was admitted to Meharry Medical College School of Dentistry in Nashville, Tennessee where he served as president of his class and of the pre-alumni council of the dentistry, medicine, nursing, and graduate schools.

When Brown graduated in 1953 from Meharry, he became the first African American to intern in the oral and maxillo-facial unit at Metropolitan Hospital in New York City. After his one-year internship at Metropolitan Hospital York, Brown continued his study of oral and maxillo-facial surgery at Northwestern University in Chicago, where he graduated with a Master of Science degree in Dentistry (MSD). Brown completed a two-year residency at Cook County Hospital in Chicago, yet another first for an African-American. He then spent one year as chief of anesthesia and "senior attending" in the Department of Oral and Maxillo-facial Surgery. (*Westerner*, Fall 1992) (Kappa Alpha Psi, Fraternity Inc.; *African Americans Who Blazed the Trail*)

Dr. Brown's office manager recalled that after he opened his practice, he took his DDS and MSD degrees to a high school teacher who long ago, told him he would not succeed. Dr. Brown credited many of the teachers at St. John's for helping him achieve his goals, but acknowledged that the negative feedback also served to ignite his passion to succeed.

SERVICE

(The following is excerpted from Bassett Brown's recollections in Vol. 2 of Wartime Memoirs by Southwestern Michigan Veterans)

"At the end of my freshman year I was drafted into the Army and on June 23, 1943, I was sent to Ft. Custer, Battle Creek, Michigan for basic training as a medic. Upon completion of basic training I was placed in the Army Special Training Program (ASTP) and spent one semester at the University of Nebraska and one semester at Wilberforce University in Ohio learning medical procedures.

"In April 1944, after graduating from the ASTP program, I was assigned to the first black combat unit, the 92nd Infantry Division which was training at Ft. Huachuca, Arizona. I was assigned to the 2nd Battalion, 370th Regiment. After limited training the unit shipped out in June for the European Theater, specifically Italy. We arrived in Italy on July 15th, 1944.

"In Italy the 92nd fought in the Po Valley, Arno, Rome, Naples, Foggia and the Apennines. There were 13,000 of us that went over there and only 5,000 of us came back. All of the enlisted were black, including the non-commissioned officers, but the officers were mixed white and black.

"As a medic, my job was to go out under machine gun fire and find the wounded soldiers and somehow get them back behind our lines, so that they could be evacuated to the rear for medical treatment. It is very stressful as you're trying to keep them alive, while at the same time you're receiving fire from the enemy.

"One significant action that comes to mind is the action around Lucca on November 13, 1944 for which I received the Bronze Star Medal."

NOTE: Quoted here is the Citation that awarded him the medal for heroism:

HQ, 92nd Inf Div, Order #AG200.6-G, dated 26 Dec 1944: "Technician Fourth Grade BROWN, upon learning of a severely wounded man lying helpless in an area under heavy enemy fire, immediately volunteered to go forward with three other men to rescue the wounded soldier. BROWN was required to crawl six hundred yards under sniper and machine gun fire to reach the wounded man and drag him back three hundred yards under the same hazards. During the remaining three hundred yards, he was subjected to three enemy mortar barrages all of which failed to halt the successful accomplishment of his mission. His bravery and courage inspired all the men of his organization."

Dr. Bassett Brown with one of his medals

Dr. Brown didn't mention in the interview that he later received a second Bronze Star for heroism in the battlefield rescue of another injured soldier. This information was obtained from his Discharge Certificate. (DD Form 214)'

The paragraph above was included in Vol. 2 of *Wartime Memoirs*. In addition to that, the following is typed under Decorations and Citations of the Military History section of the ENLISTED RECORD AND REPORT OF SEPARATION HONORABLE DISCHARGE:

EAME Theater Ribbon w/4 Bronze Stars; Good Conduct Ribbon; Bronze Star PerGO #8 w/1 Oak Leaf Cluster; World War II Victory Medal

Dr. Brown continues his interview:

"I had played freshman basketball at Western Michigan, at basic training and at the Army Specialized Training Program and some guys who were in the 92nd had seen me play. The Fifth Army tournament was held in Florence, Italy during the winter of 1945. Victory was about far more than winning a trophy. If you lost the game you had to go back on the front line. We were playing for real! We ended up staying for a month in Florence and winning the tournament. I've always felt that the tournament saved my life because during the month I was gone, the unit was under intense fire and suffered a large number of casualties."

This ends the excerpt from Vol. 2 of *Wartime Memoirs*.

According to the SEPARATION QUALIFICATION RECORD, Private Brown served three months in Basic Training, Med 657; Pfc Brown served three months as Ward Attendant 657; T/4 Brown served 10 months as Surgical Technician 861; and T/4 Brown served five months as Athletic Instructor 283.

The description for Surgical Technician reads: Worked in aid station of medical detachment of Infantry Division in Italy. Gave first aid. Treated and dressed wounds. Gave blood plasma and other injections. Gave vaccinations. Set up and operated forward aid stations. Worked in postoperative hospital wards in United States. Previously was ward attendant.

Another record from Dr. Brown's service shows that he (Tec 4) and another African-American enlistee (Tec 5) were recommended for appointment as 'Second Lieutenants, MAC, in the Army of the United States', but were denied 'in view of the fact that no Tables of Organization vacancies exist to which colored personnel may be assigned, papers are returned with no further action taken.' *(see figure 1 below)*

Soldiers, as well as citizens of color, faced racial discrimination on a regular basis. In part 1 of a two-part series published by the *Herald-Palladium* on February 5, 1995, Niles resident and WWII GI, Robert Love noted, "The day my friends and I were drafted, five of us were in downtown Niles and were refused service at a local restaurant." The *H-P* story continued, 'The segregation that existed in US civilian life since emancipation extended into every aspect of the military during World War II. Black soldiers and sailors served in segregated units, lived in separate barracks from whites, and often were relegated to mundane duties associated with construction, transportation or the Quartermaster Corps. The vast majority of blacks in World War II served in the Army or Army Air Corps. At the start of the war, the Navy had no black officers, while the Marine Corps prohibited blacks from serving entirely until a presidential order in 1942 opened all branches of the service to minorities.'

From the same article, "Blacks went out and distinguished themselves even when things weren't right here at home," said Dr. C. Bassett Brown of Benton Township. "We were glad to fight. We wanted to demonstrate to the people of the United States that we were going to do our part." Dr. Brown continued, "Blacks have contributed quite a bit, and you don't know how much more they could have if the playing field had been equal. But you won't hear any sour grapes from me. The more impediments I faced, the harder I fought."

While Dr. Brown attested to the racial indignities and discrimination that existed in and out of the service, he bore the insults with a grace and dignity that only added strength and dimension to his character.

CAREER AND CIVIC WORK

Dr. Brown could have stayed in Chicago or gone back to New York City to begin his practice in oral and maxillo-facial surgery, but he remembered a promise he had made to himself to fix a little girl's smile.

In 1957, Dr. Brown, known as "Doc" Brown by many, returned home to open his practice at 407 S. Fair in Benton Harbor. On the wall, he put the mission statement that he had written at Meharry Medical College: *"Mine is a mission of service, competence, and compassion that is focused on the disadvantaged, the indigent, the poor, the minorities, the elderly, and the forgotten of our inner cities."* His office manager, Darlene Hawkins said that Dr. Brown lived by those words, and added that he never charged policemen or firemen. "It was his way of thanking them for their service," Hawkins said.

Hawkins started working the first day Dr. Brown opened his practice until the day in 1991 when Dr. Brown retired. "For the first five years it was just the two of us. I was his assistant and office manager in those days, but we became family and have been close ever since."

Hawkins fondly recalled a ritual that was never spoken of. She said there was a cross on the wall at the end of the hall by the surgery room. "Every time we went to perform a procedure, both of us would stop by the cross and say a silent prayer. We never talked about it, it was just something we both did."

Dr. Brown loved his work and felt it very gratifying to be able to fix something that was very visible and gave the patient a sense of pride. There were not many practitioners when he started and he was the only oral and maxillo-facial surgeon in the area. Still, racial discrimination kept some patients away. Hawkins remembered a white male who balked when he saw that she was African-American. "He asked if the Dr. was black too, and walked out when he got his answer."

WWII

CITATION

"CHARLES B. BROWN, Technician Fourth Grade, 16088417, Medical Department, 370th Infantry Regiment. For meritorious service in combat, on 13 November 1944, in Italy. Technician Fourth Grade BROWN, upon learning of a severely wounded man lying helpless in an area under heavy enemy fire, immediately volunteered to go forward with three other men to rescue the wounded soldier. Technician Fourth Grade BROWN was required to crawl six hundred yards under sniper and machine gun fire to reach the wounded man and drag him back three hundred yards under the same hazards. During the remaining three hundred yards, he was subjected to three enemy mortar barrages all of which failed to halt the successful accomplishment of his mission. His bravery and courage inspired all the men of his organization. Entered military service from Kalamazoo, Michigan".

E. M. ALMOND,
Major General, U. S. Army,
Commanding.

"After we'd been open about a year, Dr. Brown went to Switzerland for six weeks to attend a course on left-handed surgery," Hawkins said. He continued to learn about new techniques and also practiced two days/week at Cook County Hospital in Chicago for four years.

According to a story in the _Herald-Palladium_, on December 25, 1991, Dr. Brown worked with the Health Volunteers Overseas program. "I've been volunteering my services down there (Mexico) a couple of weeks a year for a number of years," says Dr. Brown. "I operate on young kids with cleft palate."

Fluent in Spanish, Hawkins said that Dr. Brown would get calls from local medical providers for assistance in translation with Hispanic patients.

Darlene Hawkins and Perla Torlentino, both recalled that Dr. Brown had sent medical equipment to Haiti and planned on going there to teach, but something happened in Haiti that prevented him from going.

Dr. Brown continued to help the youth of Benton Harbor. Hawkins said that Dr. Brown tutored teenage boys at The Loft (St. Johns) in the late 80s and early 90s. Gladys Peeples-Burks, retired educator and community leader, said that in the late 1950s and early 1960s, Dr. Brown spearheaded the drive to add a pool to the YMCA on the corner of Crystal and Britain Ave. "He was always looking after the youth."

The February 16, 2012, obituary of Dr. Brown of the Benton-Michiana Spirit Community Newspaper states that the "Benton Harbor chapter of Kappa Alpha Psi dedicated and named their youth development building The C. Bassett Brown Youth Development Center in appreciation of his tireless efforts on their behalf."

Dr. Brown's accomplishments speak volumes. (The following from, _African-Americans Who Blazed the Trail_, Kappa Alpha Psi, Fraternity Inc.) In 1960, Dr. Brown was the fifth African-American to be certified as a Diplomat of the American Board of Oral and Maxillo-Facial Surgery in the United States. He was the first to practice Maxillo-Facial Surgery in Illinois & Michigan. He served as chairperson of the Benton Harbor Federal Housing Commission and was a member of the Governor's Comprehensive State Health Planning Advisory Council.

In 2010, Dr. Brown was honored in the category of health by Iota Iota Omega chapter of Alpha Kappa Alpha sorority at event called "AKA Salute to Excellence—Honoring African-American Men in the Community." Jackie Baker, organizer of the event, said the men were chosen on the basis of six criteria: leadership, the ability to be a team player, creativity, dependability, a good work ethic, and a commitment to whatever they're doing, whether that's a job or a community organization.

He was an active member of the WMU and Meharry Alumni Associations' Board of Directors, the Meharry Foundation Board of Directors and was a member of both Universities' President Clubs. He was designated Distinguished Alumnus of the Year in 1970 for Meharry Medical College and received the same award in 1992 from Western Michigan University. In 2006, Dr. Brown was inducted into the Catholic Heritage Athletic Hall of Fame.

"Brown has been an active member of numerous professional organizations, has been a frequent guest lecturer at both national and international conferences, and has written more than fifty articles for various professional publications." (_Westerner_, Fall 1992)

Dr. Brown was an active member of his fraternity, Kappa Alpha Psi, which works to help young black men prepare for college. Between 1967 and 2010, the fraternity helped 800 young men get a college education. Dr. Brown believed that by helping the young men achieve their college goals, they would, in turn, pass along their experiences and help others achieve their dreams. (*Herald-Palladium* on January 4, 2010)

He was a member of the WMU Alumni Association Board of Directors, served for eight years on the WMU Foundation Board of Directors and has been a member of the University's President's Club since 1980. (*Westerner*, Fall 1992)

Dr. Brown was a witness to history, sometimes making it himself. He was at the Lincoln Monument in Washington D.C. on August 28, 1963, when Dr. Martin Luther King Jr. delivered his famed, "I Have a Dream" speech. "I realized the significance of the event," he said. "We were right down in front, close enough to almost touch him. It's a great memory." (*Herald-Palladium* in September 8th, 1991)

Then came Dr. Martin Luther King's funeral. The memory would be strong, but the feelings of exhilaration and empowerment were replaced by a somber despair. Dr. Brown marched solemnly near the front of the procession and brought home a rope that was used on the wagon that carried King's casket.

Dr. Brown was a life member of the NAACP and was Chairperson of the Education Committee of the Twin Cities branch. In King's tradition, Dr. Brown fought for integration and equalization of resources in the Benton Harbor School System in the late 1960s.

"It was just obvious that those little kids were getting short-changed in those all-black schools," said Brown, recalling that even chalk and erasers were more plentiful at predominately white schools. (*Herald-Palladium* Sept. 8, 1991)

BASKETBALL

Basketball was an unbroken thread that ran through "Doc" Brown's life. From playing roundball on the team his father started, (he believed his brother Paul was the better player) to playing pick-up games with his buddies at the YMCA, basketball helped Dr. Brown stay active well into retirement.

In 1942, Brown played freshman basketball at Western Michigan University under Clayton Maus. He is quoted from the *Kalamazoo Gazette*, October 14, 1992, "I knew it wouldn't be easy because I wasn't anywhere near as good as Davage Minor. But Clayton Maus made it comfortable for me and I had a rewarding season with the freshman team." [NOTE: Minor was an excellent African-American player. H.W. (Buck) Read, Broncos head coach at the time, was not about to start a black basketball player. Minor ended up completing his career at UCLA.]

After WWII, Brown returned to Western. "Read was the coach," he said, "and I fully expected to be cut from the team. But the other players were very supportive of me, and Read could see that. They spoke to him on my behalf before an important game with Central Michigan. Buck apparently figured a win was more important than some other things and gave me a starting assignment. I made good on the opportunity, hitting all seven shots I took and adding a free throw as we won." (*Kalamazoo Gazette*, October 14, 1992)

A quote from Dr. Brown in a *Herald-Palladium* story from September 8, 1991, shows why young Bassett was ready for his golden opportunity. "Like my father said, if you've got your bat ready, when somebody throws you a strike you've got a chance to hit the ball."

Brown went on to play basketball for Fisk University, traveling the South in the days of Jim Crow laws. In a question and answer interview with the _Herald-Palladium_, published January 4, 2010, Dr. Brown was asked what it was like going to college in the segregated South.

Dr. Brown answered that they were kept isolated, even when traveling for basketball, and didn't run into much trouble. He did recall an incident while playing Ball State University where he was told he couldn't stay at a hotel. But the check-in lady changed her mind when, "......my coach told her that I was Puerto Rican." These kinds of slights were a regular occurrence. Dr. Brown said he felt very fortunate that he never ran into a truly dangerous racial situation.

In 1948, Brown got the chance to advance his game and experience the thrill of playing with a star team. Brown played 6 games with the Harlem Globetrotters as a stand-in.

As years passed and Brown became Dr. Brown, he never gave up his love for basketball. After all, he truly believed it had saved his life in WWII by taking him out of some of the deadliest battles to play a game that gave our soldiers a sense of normalcy in a very abnormal situation. Dr. Brown entered his practice and continued to play ball at the YMCA and engage area youth with basketball.

As Dr. Brown neared retirement, his old friend George Gaunder, now retired from Whirlpool, approached him with an offer her couldn't refuse, even though he tried at first. But before we look at the two friends, now in their late 60s, let's visit them back in the late 1920s.

"We started 1st grade at St. John's together and played sports (through the years)." Gaunder also said that his grandparents lived kitty-corner to the Browns. "We used to play marbles when we were kids," Gaunder said.

The marbles turned into roundball and by high school, Doc and George were playing some serious basketball. According to a _Herald-Palladium_ story published on December 25, 1991, Gaunder (guard) and Dr. Brown (center) were starters on St. John's team during their senior year (1941). Gaunder said they had a very good team that season, winning the first eight games, including two to Stevensville. Unfortunately, they lost to Stevensville in the districts and Stevensville went on to win the state title that year.

Now it was 1989 and Gaunder had taken on the role of head boys basketball coach at Lake Michigan Catholic. He needed an assistant and he knew the perfect man for the job.

"He didn't want to do it at first," Gaunder said, "but he came around once he was there with the kids." According to the _H-P_ story from December 1991, Dr. Brown said, "I came over to beg off, but once I met the kids, I changed my mind. The old bug bit me." He added, "...George knows how to handle kids. He's always encouraging them and never puts them down."

Gaunder was quoted as saying, "They look up to and respect Bassett (Dr. Brown). I don't know how many we'll win or lose. But when the season is over, these kids will know there is more to life than playing basketball. Right now we're having a lot of fun, and I know the kids are, too."

The coaching alliance lasted three years. Looking back Gaunder said, "We really enjoyed this time together."

Dr. Brown continued playing basketball as he aged. YMCA Director, Mike Ahearn said Dr. Brown played with the "over-40 group", but did not shy away from playing with the younger players. He remembers Dr. Brown, Reverend Don Atkins and Sam Watson as being part of the group who played pick-up games on Mondays, Wednesdays and Fridays at noon.

In basketball, as in the service, and in fact, all of life, Bassett Brown knew that the key to victory was to keep your eye on the ball, work as a team, and use incoming racial discrimination to fuel success, not defeat.

PERSONAL

Many of Bassett's life-long friends were interviewed for this biography. Unfortunately, not all their stories will be included, as space has run out. Here are a few highlights of the people and events of C. Bassett Brown's life:

Bassett Brown's life was made up of bold moves: from his rare career choice to his vibrant clothing choices, from his classic cars to his classic moves on the basketball court and the dance floor, from his heroism on the battlefield to his heroic handling of racial discrimination.

He's often defined as soft-spoken, but I don't think anyone would deny that his demeanor also included steely determination. Generous, gentle, religious, engaging, humorous, compassionate, entertaining, knowledgable. These are all words that come up again and again by Bassett's many life-long friends.

Doc had a deep infatuation with cars. His first, recycled from his parents, was endearingly known as Ironsides. Then came the pink Chrysler, followed by the yellow Corvette convertible (1955 or 1958), then the green Corvette hard top, the ever-elegant Rolls Royce, and the reliable Ford truck. And then there was the amphibian car.

Doc's lifelong friend, Roy Shoemaker remembers taking his first ride in what he thought was just another car. Shoemaker recalled, "We were driving down Riverside Dr. when Bassett drove the car into the river. I thought he'd lost his marbles, but then we started floating."

The amphibian car put a smile on many faces, until one day in 2002, Doc forgot to put the plug in. Perla was working at the 777 Building on Riverview Drive, when Doc called her. The car had sunk in the same place Bassett had shocked Shoemaker years before. Doc and a buddy made it out of the car before it sank, but the car would never float again.

Perla and Darlene also had a story to tell about the Rolls Royce. Doc had applied for membership at the Berrien Hills Country Club, a place where Bassett told Perla he had caddied when he was young. It didn't seem to matter that he was a well-respected, successful doctor. He was denied membership. "Doc went out and bought the Rolls with money he would have spent at the club," Darlene said. "He didn't let that stuff get to him, he just moved on."

Phyllis (Ash) Seabolt was also a life-long friend of Bassett's. Seabolt told how the teen-age African-Americans from the neighboring communities got together for social gatherings. "Growing up as a minority in Dowagiac was limiting," Seabolt said. She went on to explain that most of her Dowagiac friends were cousins. Getting together with kids from Decatur, Paw Paw, Niles, Benton Harbor and South Haven offered a more interesting social life. Parents would drive and chaperone (Bassett's father was always there) and the kids would enjoy roller skating, dances, picnics and swimming together.

"In the summer we would meet at Eagle Lake for a swimming party," Seabolt said. She explained that it was the only beach the group could go to and feel welcomed and relaxed. While the South had Jim Crow laws to enforce segregation, the North had unwritten standards and behavior. But getting together with friends in different towns somewhat dampened the effects of prejudice.

Seabolt, Torlentino, Hawkins, Peeples-Burks all talked about Bassett's moves on the dance floor. "All the women looked forward to dancing with Bassett," Torlentino said. He was the Fred Astaire of Benton Harbor."

Torlentino met Dr. Brown in 1971. They were both taking a Spanish class and became fast friends. Torlentino and Dr. Brown were together for 40 years and were looking forward to more when Bassett went home to be with his father, mother, brother, Paul, and sister, Delores.

Bassett Brown leaves behind scores of friends, who became his family and a town and community that benefited greatly because of his love, generosity and commitment.

MY COMBAT EXPERIENCE
Lawrence W. Butler

I entered the Military about March of 1941, before Pearl Harbor. I had about nine months in before they declared war. So, then, I was in for the duration, which was nearly five years. I was living in Grand Rapids, Michigan, and working for a wholesale auto supply and machine shop when I entered the service. I tried to join the Air Cadet program, but did not pass the medical test (they said I had too much overbite for my Gs I would get when diving from the plane). So, I just waited for my draft number to come around.

I didn't have to wait long. I figured, "let's get it over with," and went to Fort Custer, Michigan. From Fort Custer, I went down to Fort Knox, Kentucky, for my basic training. They promised about 13 weeks of training, but it turned that they gave us only eight weeks and assigned us to duty. I was assigned to C Company of the 69th Regiment at the medium Tank outfit, and we were part of the First Armored Division. Our Division was made up of a battalion of medium tanks and a couple of battalions of light tanks and artillery ordinance and other units. Around January after Pearl Harbor, we reorganized and we became "I" Company of First Regiment of the First Armored Division. I was probably assigned there because most of my life I had been on the farm and driving tractors, and because of my automotive machine shop experience.

Lawrence W. Butler

In Fort Knox we trained on the care and maintenance of the tanks. We learned the tactics of a fighting team and were constantly cleaning the tanks inside and out. Later, I found out why they were cleaned so well. If a tank was hit by a shell, the energy at the point of contact would set off any oil, padding, or ammunition, and start a fire.

I became qualified as a driver and went on maneuvers in the Southern States, to Ireland, England, North African, and finally to the defeat of Kasserine Pass in North Africa, where I became a tank commander. In Italy, I continued in that position and became a Platoon Sergeant until I returned to the States.

It was easy to make friends while in service, as everyone was lonely. We became close friends as we thought we were the best company in our regiment with great esprit de corps. I lost many good friends in combat. Combat brings the closest of men, which makes it a special family. The trust and love we had for one another went beyond understanding.

After training, we took a ferry boat to New Jersey and to New York City Pier 4 where we loaded on the Thomas H. Barre cruise ship. It held about 5,000 bodies, but they figured they could get about 10,000 on if half were put on the top deck and the other half down in the hold. Twelve hours we would be on top, then go down the stairway for our time below deck. Down in the hold where we were they had bunks three high made out of pipe and canvas, and it was yours for every twelve hours. The only toilet was an enclosed swimming pool with 20 stools. We never saw the toilets upstairs; we finally had to use #10 tin cans for bathrooms, and it made a terrible smell.

For breakfast, we didn't sit down to eat--12-inch planks along the walls held your dishes while you stood to eat. The ship pitches, and there goes the dishes to the right. Some guys would vomit with seasickness as the dishes go by. Then, the ship pitches and the dishes return, along with the vomit. You learned to hold onto your dish and not let it go! The first breakfast was spoiled codfish, gravy and bread. The next few meals were steamed chicken. If the seasickness didn't make you vomit, looking at that chicken could! The third day I was put on KP for a few days. When I went to eat, the cook said, "don't eat that slop; we'll have steak like the officers." Man, was it good!

We were attacked by submarines several times, but lost no ships. The depth charge would rattle the sides of our ship Thomas Barre, and I looked many times to see if our ship was leaking. The convoy was made up of many hundreds of ships that stretched out miles and miles of choppy sea. The command ship was a cruiser. It was off to our right. One toot and everybody went to the left; two toots and they went to the right. We zig-zagged like that all the way up to the coasts of Scotland.

One morning I was in the fog, standing by the rail. One hundred feet away, here comes this cruiser coming right up close to us. Sounding their bell and horns, it moved away. If it had crashed, there could have been 10,000 men drowned all at once.

We remained in Ireland about four months. Then, we went on alert and went down to the beach to load into LSTs at the landing ship tank. When we backed our tanks onto the craft, they did not tell us where we were going, but just took us out into the sea. We supposed we had started out to an invasion, but we did not know where. The Irish Sea was plenty rough that night. The next morning, we were glad to see that we were landing at Liverpool, England. We proceeded to Chester and spent a couple of months there. Then, we went to Cardiff, Wales, and loaded our tanks. We were assembled in a fake convoy. It was days before we were briefed that we were going to North Africa. We were lectured and given a book on the customs of the Arabic Muslim religion.

It being November, the seas were rough. We finally saw the Rock of Gibraltar, and passed through the narrow straits. On another ship, crewmen saw the Germans were outside Gibraltar, and would call for an air attack. Near sundown the torpedo planes flew in just above the water, launching their torpedoes. I was on deck at the time; the ship in front of us was loaded with ammunition. There was a big flash, and there was nothing left. All hands were lost. Four more ships were sunk. We could hear the cries of survivors, but could not stop to save them. They were expendable, although our destroyer escort did save some of them. The next morning, we saw a destroyer go by with a deck full of people they had picked up. We then encountered the worst storm the Mediterranean had seen in many years. I saw 50-foot waves, we'd go down, and not see another ship. Then, all of a sudden, we were on a top of a wave, and the ship would just shudder. The propeller would be out of the water.

Oran Algeria was the main thrust. They got the worst beating, loss of lives and equipment. Although the light tanks rushed to the air field, catching planes on the ground, they had a great time blowing up all the planes. Our landing was just west of Oran, the little port of Arzu. Patton had landed at Rabat, just west of us, with little difficulty. We went into reserve, meaning if there were any big problems, we would be called to action. Since we were stable, we were put up in pup tents. We spent our first Christmas outside of Oran.

We went through Kasserine Pass to Sebatla where we took up positions. Back in the desert, our instructions were to go up left for an outpost and observe. We were several miles out of sight and came through a wadi and deep ditch, and into a tilt that threw the right track off our tank. Our radio was only a receiver, so we could not broadcast the problem to headquarters. After we were there several days, we decided that we'd dig out the left side of it and let the tank settle back, so we could put the track back on. We then set up outside the Fiad Pass. The Germans, of course, controlled that. One day they sent one tank up into the pass. As we got close, they opened fire and sent a plane to bomb us. One bomb made a direct hit on our back deck. It nearly knocked the wind right out of us from the concussion. We were hit in the track and eased down into the valley. General Orlando Ward came out to talk to us and debriefed us on what we saw. It was just a test to see if the Germans would repel us. We saw no Air Force until the African campaign was nearly over on May 15, 1943.

Our unit was relieved from the point in the outpost and taken over by G Company. We moved to the right a mile back, and each morning we'd wake up at 4am, stand to, and start the tanks and be on the alert. Nights we'd stand guard, two hours on guard for each man.

On February 14, 1943, we had our regular alert, but this time there were fireworks. The Germans came pouring out of Fiad Pass. The tanks were followed by foot soldiers. I was the lead tank starting down the road toward G Company and the Germans. Here I thought we should attack while they were busy, but headquarters said, "we're going to feed you in one by one." They hoped only to delay the Germans. In two days, we lost 300 tanks. And as we watched G Company's 17 tanks blow up in flames, it wa a terrifying sight. Platoon 5 tanks went to the right and another platoon went to the left.

We were accurate shooting at 2,000 yards, while the Germans were accurate at about 5,000 yards. They had 88 millimeters. Their shells were about three feet long, and we had little 75s with much less powder charge. Apparently outgunned, we took a lot of direct hits, and we did not get penetrated until after they used high explosives and armor piercing shells. They struck like a sledge hammer, shaking the dust and the smoke on us. One round took off my periscope head, leading me to think I had been blinded. I changed my old periscope and found that everything was okay. My commander Sergeant Pierre got wounded in the right hand and arm. He was bleeding all over the place. He baled out over the side, went for the medics. This kind of cut down our vision, but no matter. There were so many Germans, everywhere. We had all kinds of targets. The Germans outflanked us and they shot my motor out and fire followed. No matter where we were--no matter anyway, because we were out of ammunition by then.

The gunner, C.E. Norris, from Grace, Kentucky, baled out. He was captured and spent three years in a POW camp. The assistant gunner Tekert from Kansas was killed. My assistant driver, Forage, from San Antonio, Texas, stayed with me the rest of the day. We grabbed our submachine guns as we baled out and headed for Citibusin, a small oasis where General Eisenhower had visited our headquarters last night, checking the lines. All the time the Germans' stuka dive bombers were bombing and strafing our air field. Their air field was so close that they could dump their load, refill, refuel, and be back, 10-15 minutes in a turnaround.

I dove into a hole and cried out to God. Not being church affiliated, I did not know how to pray, so I just cried out. I promised I would do anything He wanted me to do if He would just save my life.

I ran over to help the 27th field artillery carry ammunition. We were about to be overrun, so we were ordered to blow up the ammunition and disable the gun. A thermal grenade down the barrel had burned a hole in there and made it unusable. I crawled onto a half track to get out of the German tanks' way. It was kind of cutting off our escape. He fired two rounds at us, missing us, and he raked the sides of the half track with machine gun fire. No one was

TANK CREW, 1944, Italy - Back row (l to r): J.W. O'Nan (KY); C.V. Landrum (MS) Kneeling (l to r): Elmer O'Brien (MI), L.W. Butler (MI); Rolly Hopkins (WV)

hurt. We got to Kasserine Pass where we quickly reassembled. I was one of 16 men of our company to return, the rest were killed, wounded, or captured. . . .

Did the military change my life? Yes. It gave me leadership ability and prepared me for things, but it also did something to my psyche. It was not until 1988 (about 45 years) before I could speak of all that I have told you. Even my wife never knew. But I always heard incoming rounds in my nightmares. The service made a difference all right. It taught me to kill people, and to kill Germans in particular, and its been hard to get over that, trying to forgive them for…they fight to the last man and all of a sudden give up, and you're not to kill them then; it makes you real mad. I'm trying to get over it. You've got to forgive or you're in really big trouble. So, I married a girl who is of German descent. You can't top that, and here I am talking to an interview lady who worked for the German Air Force. And we're getting along pretty good, I think.

The picture of my tank crew are ones that were with me from after Kassurine-Faid Passes, January 14, 1943. Although we lost several tanks, we always escaped. My last action was Casa del Elsia below Pisa. I went home from Rome. I took quite a few pictures, but mostly of the guys as we were too busy when in action.

—READ MUCH MORE ON OUR CD—

PHOTOS FROM ABOVE
Keith Barrie Chapman, Jr.

Interviewed by Gary C. Lulenski, M.D.

It was December 1941 and a lot of people were enlisting after Pearl Harbor. I wanted to sign up with the Air Force and I was fortunate they took me. I had an interest in photography and had taken many pictures of my friends and family before entering the service. I was fortunate the Air Force had a new school at the Lowry Air Force Base near Denver, Colorado. I was fortunate after my basic training in Wichita Falls, Texas to be accepted to that school where I learned about aerial photography and received instructions on how to install cameras into aircraft as well as taking photos. We learned about making filmstrips and how to maintain the equipment in the aircraft. I was also fortunate in being kept on as an instructor after going through the school. Because this was a new aspect of airplane versatility, I was sent to other Air Force bases to teach about the installation of cameras and processing film.

I was even sent to Canada one time and went there by train. It was a memorable trip because there were so many people on the cars I actually could not find a place to sit down so I just sat between two of the cars and ended up sleeping there on the way to an Air Force base in Canada.

After my time at Lowry Field, most of the rest of my Air Force duties were at Chanute Field near Champaign, Illinois, south of Chicago. We continued to teach and learn about maintaining aircraft, specifically the photography components for taking aerial photographs.

Some of the pilots were not so happy with photography because in some planes like the P38 the cameras were put in where the machine guns used to be. The second person in the aircraft who was the machine gunner wasn't to interested in taking cameras without his ordinance. The Air Force let me use the equipment to take family pictures or pictures of the scenery. My son Barry was actually born while I was at Lowry Air Force Base because they had a large hospital, Fitzsimmons Hospital in Denver, Colorado. My daughter was born while I was in Chanute Field in Illinois. I developed a large photographic library and continued to stay interested in photography even after my time in the military.

Although I was trained in photography and its various aspects, I also had to qualify with rifles and machine guns. I never quite understood why that was necessary as I couldn't imagine the switch from installing cameras to shooting a machine gun. I guess that is just the way the military does things. I never did go overseas and I was not involved in any combat. My memories of the time in the Air Force basically are good memories and I met some friends I kept in contact with for years and years. For a long time my wife would send Christmas cards to people I served with during my time in the military.

I came back to Lawrence, Michigan and worked in my father's grocery store that actually had been started up by my grandfather. It was called the Chapman Store and we had a little bit of everything there. I didn't make much money but I was given a home to stay in with my wife and children. I did that for 2 or 3 years and then I moved to Paw Paw, Michigan where I worked at Troy Motor Sales. I became an accountant and parts manager. The management in turn sponsored me to go learn more about bookkeeping, which was paid by the GI bill so I was one of the veterans that really benefited from that part of plusses for veterans after their active military duty. I actually received some further schooling and became a qualified accountant. I went to work for Production Credit, which is a state sponsored organization. I helped to provide loans for farmers in southwest Michigan including Berrien and Cass County.

As I look back over my experience, it was quite surprising to see the investment the military put into the new lab and equipment at the locations where I was stationed, especially Lowry Field. There were really hundreds of photography students that went to the program. I was fortunate to keep a book from the Lowry Field training program and I still have that book, which brings back good memories of my military experience.

I am now in a convalescence center in St. Joseph, Michigan. My son visits regularly as he does not live too far away. I still enjoy looking at the pictures that I took when I was in the military. My son has now put together a book of pictures that I took and also some pictures of myself in uniform and other Air Force enlisted men I served with. It was great to be able to keep my interest in photography during my active duty in the military service and then continue it for many years afterwards.

CAPTURE OF THE GERMAN SUBMARINE U 505
James Clifford

interviewed by Gary C. Lulenski, M.D.

I entered the service in 1943 after attending one year at Notre Dame. I volunteered to join the Navy and was sent to Great Lakes Training Station. I was there several months and was transferred to Norman, Oklahoma where I learned about munitions and qualified to be a machine gun operator with the Navy. I was then sent back to Norfolk and spent most of my time in the military on the Carrier *USS Guadalcanal*.

While serving in the Atlantic on the carrier, our primary job was to escort convoys and assist in searching for German submarines. Not much happened until the first of June 1944.

I was twenty years old and after one semester at Notre Dame, I joined the Navy, finishing my boot camp at Great

James Clifford

Lakes Naval Station. Next came Gunnery School in Norman, Oklahoma, and eventually I was assigned to VC-8 Squadron aboard the Jeep Carrier, "The Card." Our next move was to the "Guadalcanal," an aircraft carrier that accommodated our squadron of six fighter planes and twelve Torpedo Bombers (TBM's) on one of which was my spot as Tail Gunner, or "Aviation Ordnanceman lst Class, USNR."

On that day in June, we were 150 miles out into the Atlantic Ocean off the coast of French West Africa. Our Task Force #223, known as a "hunter-killer" consisted of five destroyer escorts and the flagship Guadalcanal commanded by Captain Daniel Gallery, a Chicago native who had long dared to dream of capturing a U-boat intact. He therefore organized, trained and rehearsed an eight-man boarding party in case such an opportunity presented itself.

There wasn't a cloud in the sky that day on June 4, 1944, and the sea was fairly calm. It was a Sunday morning and not having been scheduled for a "run" that day, I had attended Mass below deck. As I came top side I could hear our "Wildcats" (fighter planes) circling low overhead. The starboard side rail of our ship was lined three-deep with sailors intent on some activity below in the water. I made my way to the rail, but little did I realize that I was about to view history in the making!

A partially-submerged German submarine, the U-505 was being bombarded with depth charges around its perimeter forcing the sub to surface and firing machine guns to mark the sub's location. The German crewmen were popping up out of the conning tower and leaping overboard into the Sea. At the same time our trained Boarding Party had sped to the scene and was boarding the sinking submarine as other boats were circling the Sub picking up the German sailors. By then the sub was surrounded by three of the destroyer escorts, the "Chatelain," the "Pillsbury" and the "Jenks." The Boarding Party scrambled down the hatch of the conning tower not knowing what lay ahead, how much longer would the sub stay afloat, or if it had been booby-trapped. But they did as they had been trained scooping up code books, documents, diaries and records and even the radar system passing them topside. The control room was awash and water was gushing up from one of the uncapped sea strainers. Fortunately, in their haste to abandon ship, the crewmen had tossed the cover nearby which was quickly replaced by the Boarding Party, stopping the flow of water and thus keeping the Sub from sinking further.

All German prisoners were rescued and taken aboard the Guadalcanal and housed in a compartment adjacent to mine (there was but one German fatality). Years later one of the crewmen wrote an article stating how well they were treated during their time here as Prisoners of War.

Eventually the sub was towed by the Guadalcanal 1700 miles to Bermuda arriving there on June 19, 1944, then on to the Navy Yard at Portsmouth, N.H. As it pulled into port, a smokescreen was set off to cover our German prize. Capt. Gallery had ordered the entire task force of 3,000 men to keep secret the capture of the sub. By doing so and with the valuable information they had gathered from the code books and other documents the duration of the War was shortened and many lives were saved.

After the war the fate of the 700-ton Nazi U-Boat was in jeopardy either it would end up as scrap or be towed out to sea and scuttled. By then Admiral Gallery however, came to its rescue and with the help of Arthur Godfrey, a popular radio personality at that time, the public raised $250,000 to bring it to the Museum of Science and Industry in Chicago. Thus the sub began its journey from Portsmouth, New Hampshire, on May 14, 1945, being towed the 3,000 miles via the St. Lawrence Waterway and through three of the Great Lakes, arriving in Chicago a month later.

Being one of about 50 ex-task force men living in the Chicago area, I was invited to take part in the festivities planned for the dedication, the first being the arrival of the sub on June 6, 1954. A large wave had swamped the shoreline that morning however, it did not deter us from meeting off Foster Avenue later that day. Boarding the sub there, we assembled topside and were taken about a mile off shore into Lake Michigan. We then sailed back into the Chicago River under the Michigan Avenue Bridge where we were welcomed by Chicago Mayor Kennelly and many other dignitaries (also my pregnant wife, Evelyn) who were waiting on the Reviewing Stand. The sub remained there while its permanent location was being readied at the museum. Eventually it was towed down Lake Michigan to Jackson Park and then brought overland with much difficulty across Lakeshore Drive and placed adjacent to the museum where it remained until 2005.

Being exposed to Chicago's weather for some fifty years, its exterior began to deteriorate. At great expense it was restored and on June 3, 2005 the sub made its final journey to its new and permanent exhibit completely underground in a temperature-controlled environment inside the Museum of Science & Industry.

The capture of the German U-Boat has its place in history. It was the first capture of an enemy vessel on the high seas during wartime since the War of 1812.

MEDIC & POW
Paul Coen

NOTE: In 2009, Paul Coen (who now lives in Canton, Michigan) came over to St. Joseph to be interviewed by LWF. The story was transcribed by Ellen Marshall.

MEDIC

During World War II, I was in the 29th Infantry Division--the Blue and Grey Division--which was a National Guard Unit made up, primarily, of people from Maryland and Virginia. My highest rank that I attained in the military was Corporal. I was with the 104th Medical company of the 115th Infantry Regiment.

I entered the Military in January of 1943, was trained as a combat medic, and went over to England early in the spring of 1943, and at that time joined the 29th Division.

My battalion, the 3rd Battalion of the 115th Infantry Regiment, was located in Baudman, which was southwest of London, and I was in that area in training with the 29th Division until the middle of May of 1944. While we were in Baudman, we trained usually six or seven days a week, either in maneuvers out on the Baudman Moors or with the British or the American Navy. Our training with the Navy consisted of trial runs of beach assault. They put us on LSTs and we would go out into the channel, then they would drop the landing craft and we would climb over the side and assault the beach. Sometimes we would have two beach assaults a day. The training was probably the toughest experience anyone could ever want to have. Unfortunately we lost a lot people in training. There were members of the 29th Division who were National Guardsmen, and when the unit was activated some of these people were 35-40 years of age and, obviously, 25 mile hikes and beach assaults and all the rest of it didn't sit very well with them. So over a period of time the Division probably became as many new recruits as old timers.

We got along pretty great with the English because, first of all, all of the British troops were out of the country (they were in North Africa or wherever) and one of our assignments was to make sure that the British girls weren't lonely and we worked hard at that, too. I think that the British people were extremely tolerant of the Americans. We didn't get into town as often as we'd have liked to. Every Saturday night there was a dance. There were the British pubs where whiskey and beer was limited because everything was rationed--and because the Americans had a lot of money and had drunk up all the rations. I don't know what the British ever got their hands on. And beyond the dances and the pubs there was the movie house and that was about it.

I can't emphasize enough how tough the training was, but in the long run, it was great because by the time we crossed the Channel into Normandy, I think everybody was in pretty decent shape. I don't think during the training anybody gave a lot of thought to the invasion. We knew that we were one of the units that were going to participate, but nobody sat around at night or over the weekend trying to anticipate what we were going to get into. We didn't know until very late in the game, until just before the invasion, that the 29th Division and the 1st Infantry would be the only two American Divisions that would make the assault on Omaha Beach.

Around the middle of May, we were moved from the camp in Baudman to a camp near Plymouth, England: Fort Tregandal. Fort Tregandal was built to protect the British coast back in the days of Napoleon; that's how old it was. We were there for a few weeks and then the units that were going to be in the initial assault were moved out of Plymouth into a special camp that had been set up for the assault forces—barbed wire enclosure and guards and you couldn't leave the camp. And then around the 28th/29th of May we had our briefings and they had tables set up to replicate the Omaha beach and where gun enforcements would be in the various towns. We went over those for a couple of days and then on the 2nd or 3rd of June we were taken into an area near Plymouth and boarded the assault vehicles that were going to take us across The Channel.

Some of the ships that were used were relatively large. The one we were on was small, it was a landing craft infantry. Landing ship tanks were also used to carry some of the assault troops. And then we were briefed and told that the invasion was going to be on Monday morning, the 5th of June, and that the initial troops who would land from our Division on Omaha Beach would be the 116th Infantry Regiment. Our regiment was supposed to land on Omaha perhaps around noon, we were going to be in the second wave. The 116th would land about 6:30am.

In the briefing, they led us to believe, or they thought they told us, that by the time our unit got on the beach that the 116th would have cleared the Germans. We would simply assemble on the beach and gather in a field on the far side of St. Lawrence Amir and that our first objective would be the town of Longueville. Well, it didn't work out that way. What the Allied forces were not aware of and didn't learn until later (and nobody anticipated) is that the 352nd German Infantry Division had been moved into the area of St. Lo, Villa Amir, St. Lawrence Amir, several weeks before the invasion.

The 116th Regiment did land as planned. Most of them landed on Easy Red and Dog Red beaches on Omaha and suffered tremendous casualties. Alongside of them were people from the 16th Regiment of the 1st Infantry Division. That day those two units lost in excess of 2,500 men. The 116th Regiment of my Division lost over 800. The balance was lost among the 116th from the 1st Division. And although our unit was supposed to be delayed and be in the second wave it became obvious to the generals and colonels that certainly things were not going very well and nobody was getting off the beach, so the decision was made that they would commit our regiment early.

And so I think we probably began to land around 9:30 in the morning. We were supposed to land on Easy Red, but the mortar and artillery, and machine gun and small arms fire on that segment of the beach was so bad that at the last minute they decided they would land us about a thousand yards west of where we were supposed to land on what had been designated as Fox Green Beach. We got off the landing craft pretty well, took some casualties, but the situation on the beach, I guess, was—for lack of a better description—confusion, because everybody realized we were on the wrong beach. We were mixed in with units of the 1st Division and there was chaos and confusion.

Most of the people from my regiment, the 115th and the 3rd Battalion, tried to advance off the beach. There was a marshy area that you had to slog through. And they didn't make a lot of progress initially. As a combat medic we weren't as much concerned with advancing as we were with treating the wounded who were already on the beach and the people in our unit who were beginning to suffer wounds. The entire area had anti-personnel mines and land mines that were inflicting a lot of casualties. I think bit by bit over the following hours they did make headway, and I think that by mid-afternoon, they were able to get up onto the high ground overlooking Omaha.

To the best of my recollection I didn't get off the beach until maybe 7 or 8 o'clock that night, because we stayed there until we had taken care of all the wounded and we were evacuating to a central area close to the beach where they could be put on landing craft and be taken back across the Channel. As it turned out, the 116th Regiment was supposed to be the unit that would drive the Germans out of St. Lawrence Amir, but they lost so many people that sometime during the night, apparently, the decision was made that the 115th would take on the battle for St. Lawrence Amir, and they did. And by mid-afternoon of the 7th they had pushed the Germans out of St. Lawrence Amir.

The reality of it was that even when we did practice assaults there were people who needed medical attention, so our reaction was, "hey, I'm here on the beach and I'm supposed to give first aid and try to save people and that's what I'd better be about." And so that's what you did—and hope that while you were doing it, you wouldn't get hit.

I can remember after we had been on the beach a couple of hours, there was a buddy of mine who was also a medic--kid from Pennsylvania, Joe Dalton--I said to him, "Joe, a couple hundred yards up there, it looks like there's a guy wounded. We oughta go get him." So we grabbed a stretcher and went up. He had lost his left leg below the knee and had put a tourniquet on himself and had given himself a shot of morphine. As we were putting him on the stretcher he said, "Boy you guys are really gutsy for coming up here in the mine field." And I thought, "Geez, I better learn how to fly outta here!" But the reality was you didn't do a lot of thinking, you just reacted--and the funny part about it was, that night about 10:00 we were behind some hedgerows outside of St. Lawrence Amir, dug in for the night, and I remembered I hadn't had anything to eat all day and I got a de-rationed chocolate bar out, and that was dinner.

I don't think anybody deals very well with what we experienced on that beach. Most of the time on the beach, you were trying to make a decision on those that we thought really had a shot at making it and those we felt would not. That's a difficult thing to do: to pick and choose. I don't think anyone could adequately describe the carnage of people who are hit with shrapnel or cut to pieces by machine gunfire. I think the initial scenes of the movie, "*Saving Private Ryan*" probably depicted it the best. What does it take for young men in the face of fire like that to go forward? ...But, they did. And the reality is, how can people who haven't been there empathize with what it was about? It's absolutely impossible.

I don't think that back then (65 years ago) any of us who made the assault on Omaha thought it was a noble cause. The reality was that, until the Allies established a second front and a beachhead in Europe, that war wasn't going to end. My Division, which started out with 15,000 men, suffered 19,000 casualties in less than a year (June 1944-May 1945). In the first six days in Normandy we probably lost 35% of our battalion. Can we find people who would do that again? I'd like to hope so, but, I don't know. Today, we take so much for granted, and maybe that's the way it should be. But, freedom isn't free. During WWII 16 million people put on a uniform and of those people maybe a half a million didn't come home. There are those who went missing and have never been found. And in the Veterans Hospital there are still men who are suffering from their wounds. So we've paid a high price. And I know how lucky I am to have survived.

POW

If I were to describe the first six days after I was captured, I would probably say it was like a Chinese fire drill. The Germans who were defending that area had occupied it for almost four years and they knew the terrain. And although we had been briefed and looked at the maps and everything else, we didn't know the terrain at all. After we captured St. Lawrence Amir, our next goal was to go down and try to sort out was happening near Villa Amir and we almost got to that point and they turned us around and sent us in another direction. And for the next 5 days that was pretty much the routine: we'd chase the Germans and they'd stop and defend a position and then we'd overrun it and they'd fall back, establish another one, and try a counterattack. And all the time both sides taking casualties and the rifle companies in our battalion were getting pretty well depleted. And we were getting reinforcements who came in from England into our Division into our battalion, people we didn't even know. But on the 11th of June the Germans established fortifications along the Yellow River, and we stopped at that point and dug in.

The plan was that the following morning, on the 12th, we'd jump off across the Yellow River after an artillery barrage and try to drag the Germans back. And our rifle companies moved on close along the river and whether it was German artillery or short bursts from our own I don't know, but three of our rifle companies received a tremendous barrage of artillery fire. Those who were still able crossed the river at about four o'clock in the morning. Members of my medical unit spent all morning patching and evacuating the riflemen who had been hurt. And then around 1:00 in the afternoon, a First Lieutenant from the Rangers and a Sergeant came into an area where we were eating rations and said that they had received a message that across the Yellow River there was a group of wounded Americans that needed to be evacuated. And they wanted volunteers to go over and try to get 'em outta there.

We had 8-10 medics and about 20-21 infantrymen, and off we went. I didn't even get to finish my rations--they're probably still there. We crossed the river okay and got about maybe a quarter a mile beyond and by this time I'm sure we were behind the German lines. And the Ranger was leading the patrol, then Sergeant, and then our battalion medical officer, Captain Edwards. I was behind him, and then the others were strung out behind us. There was some automatic rifle fire up ahead and my Captain went around the bend of the road. I didn't see him after that, and he hollered back for me to come up, and I did. He was tending to the Lieutenant who had been shot through the abdomen.

He was trying to patch him up and he said to me, "I think I heard firing up ahead; go and see how the Ranger's doing." So, I went up, and there he was about twenty feet down the road and had been hit. I went down and he had already given himself a shot of morphine. He had taken a round in the thigh and it had come out down in his lower leg.

I said to him, "Just lay there and we'll get a stretcher up." I put a compress bandage on him and hollered back, and two medics came up with a stretcher. As we were going to put him on the stretcher--one of the medics on the far side, another at his feet, and I on the other side with my back to a ditch--I looked up and there was a German on the top of the hedgerow with a machine pistol. I rolled back into the ditch and tried to pull the wounded Ranger with me. The German opened fire and I didn't get a scratch, but he killed all three of the others.

So I laid there for about five minutes trying to crawl up inside my helmet, I guess. Hoping that, perhaps by then, he would think he had killed us all, and left. I heard noises from the direction that I had come in and I thought, wow, what was I worried about, here come the other guys now. So I got up and I checked the two medics and the Ranger and they were gone. And who comes around the bend in the road, but about 18 German infantrymen! I really thought they were going to shoot me because that was what was going on in the early days in Normandy. But they shook me down and made sure I didn't have a weapon , walked me back about 100 yards to what looked like a battalion headquarters with an aid station. I spent the rest of the afternoon treating German wounded. I think getting captured probably saved my life.

My medical skills didn't get me preferential treatment, though. The reality was, I didn't have a lot of choice in providing them medical care. But once I was turned over further down the line, I don't think that made any difference one way or the other. I don't think anybody got any preferential treatment.

Initially I was in three camps in France. In 2007, my wife and I went to a wedding in Allanson, France, just off of Normandy, and that was the first organized camp I had been in: Allanson. The model in Allanson was, "no work no food." So you volunteered. I was assigned to a work detail with 2-4 other fellows that took us every morning into the town of Allanson near the railroad freight yards. We had a German guard, and we'd spend the day uncovering unexploded Allied bombs. Not the best job I've ever had.

We were fortunately only there a couple of weeks and then they moved us to a second camp. All of this time, everything was so uncertain, because you knew when they moved you that you became the target of the Allied Air Forces. I remember a couple of times they were moving us in trucks and here came the 9th Air Force on a strafing run, and we were out of the truck and hiding in a ditch hoping we didn't get hit, because from the air they couldn't recognize who the troops were. All they knew was that those were German Army vehicles.

The rations were skimpy at best. I was in seven different camps (I like to tell everybody they kept moving me around 'cause they wanted me to see a lot of the country). In the first camp I was in, near the Elbe River, the rations weren't bad—a cup of soup a day and three or four pieces of black bread. But then, as the war wore on, the soup disappeared and the rations got skimpier. You had to say to yourself, "it's a day at a time." I was pretty much convinced that once I got to Germany and into organized camps, I would survive, but the starvation diet was tough. I had dysentery in one of the camps and I was really bad. The Germans put me into a German Army hospital. I think if they had not done that, I probably would have died--that's how bad I was. There were people who didn't make it through the camp, there were people who tried to escape and were killed…but I guess it was better than being out on the front lines.

Then, on April 22, 1945, here came the Russians in their Studebaker trucks and all the rest of it. The Germans had all run away. And we thought that the Russians would repatriate us, but they proceeded to tell us that they were going to evacuate us through the city of Odessa on the Black Sea. I had no desire to go to Odessa, so four days after the Russians arrived, four other GIs and I got up at two or three in the morning—they had guards around the camp to keep you from leaving—and made our way across Germany to the Elbe River and the Allied lines.

After we got out of the camp, nobody had a compass or anything. We made our way to a highway, and after we walked along the highway for about an hour, here came a convoy of Russian soldiers who were headed in a northerly direction, apparently going to go to Berlin. They stopped and picked us up. We must have driven with them for at least an hour-and-a-half. and we made it obvious that we wanted to go to the Elbe River. They let us off at a highway, then they went on their way and we went on ours. And, yeah, we were worried about being shot because things were pretty chaotic. There had been no surrender of the German Army and there were still a lot of German troops around with weapons and ammunition. But after we had walked toward the Elbe River 4-6 hours, half a dozen American scout cars came from the direction we had come from. They had been sent out to establish contact with the Russians and were on their way back to the Elbe River, to the Allied lines. We recognized who they were, and jumped out on the road. They picked us up and that night we were back in Allied hands. So, luck was certainly, certainly with us.

Since 2004, the French government has been trying to locate, identify, and honor individuals from WWII. After sorting through paperwork each year, they give the Medal of the French Legion of Honor award to 100 WWII veterans who served in France. One of the requirements to be awarded the French Legion of Honor was that you must have received a significant

93

military honor from your own government during your time in France. I had received the Bronze Star medal for heroism on the 12th of June. I had also received the Bronze Star medal for my service on Omaha Beach on D-Day. And so, I was contacted by the French Console General in Chicago and they asked me to send in some of my WWII records, which I did. On November 2, 2007, three other veterans from Michigan and I received the Legion of Honor from the French government. I view it as a symbolic award. It's France's way of saying "thank you" to all veterans. It is great that I was singled out, and I am so appreciative, but I'd like to think that it's for all of us.

DESCRIPTION OF MEDALS: This is the Bronze Star Medal, and it has the V device which indicates that you were in combat for heroism, and two Oak Leaf Clusters. The first Oak Leaf Cluster is for D-Day and the other Oak Leaf Cluster is for service in Vietnam. The Army Commendation Medal for Korea and for other service. This is a Prisoner of War Medal. This device indicates that I was a combat medic. This was American Campaign. Army Good Conduct. WWII Victory Medal. These medals are associated with Korea. And a Vietnam Campaign Medal. This medal I received from the Republic of South Vietnam. It's their Honor Medal. This is a UN Medal for Korea. And this one from Vietnam as well, Vietnam Service Medal. And this medal is from the Republic of South Korea. Distinguished Unit Badge for WWII and for my Fighter Bomber Group in Korea. Distinguished Unit Badge is from The United States Government. And this one, the Distinguished Unit Citation from the Republic of South Korea. And this was my Army Unit, the Blue and the Grey, the 29th Division. And this was the Unit I served in Vietnam, Military Assistance Command. I served as an Advisor to the Vietnamese Military.

I served in Vietnam in 1965-66, stationed at Bien Hoa.

If we go back to WWII, it really wasn't a case of, "do you wanna be in the military?" Everybody was in the military. If there were 16 million people during that war in uniform, you didn't wanna be on the homefront dressed in civilian clothes, 'cause they knew there must be something wrong with you. I'm glad that I went. I had the experience of serving with some pretty wonderful people. You can't duplicate that kind of comradery. I think I should say, that whether it was WWII or Korea or Vietnam, you often wonder if our civilians understand what it means when people put on the uniform. And it doesn't make any difference whether they're behind a desk, or driving a truck, or carrying a rifle, because when they went in and took the oath they agreed to serve in whatever capacity and put themselves in harm's way, if necessary. So, everybody talks about the "Greatest Generation," but if we think of all of the people who have worn the uniform since WWII, they've done a pretty great job too. I suppose the focus is on WWII Vets because we're becoming a vanishing breed.

I'm sure there would be some people who would throw rocks at me for what I'm going to say, but I think that in the United States we should have some sort of a mechanism, an organization, that allows young people to serve in some type of a government organization for two years before they go on for their education. Whether it's Ameri-Corps or the Peace Corps or the Military or whatever it may be, I think it's part of giving back. I think perhaps I'm in favor of selective service, not that it was always very selective, but at least everybody got a shot at serving their country in one way or another. We shouldn't be engaged in military conflicts that are, in essence, "poor man's wars." I think that young people ought to think about giving back, about doing things that make our country better than it is, and they ought to have a realization that what they enjoy every day has a very high cost. But that's just my opinion.

Paul Coen resides in Canton, Michigan.

MEMORIES OF WWII
Eleanor Dunlop

I was a student nurse at the Lutheran Deaconess Hospital in Chicago Illinois when World War II started. When I came off duty that Sunday afternoon, our House Mother told me Pearl Harbor had been bombed. Right then I decided I would be an Army nurse. My last six months in school I was a Cadet Nurse. We had snappy gray uniforms with red trim and received $30 per month from the government. Street car conductors gave us free rides, just like the service men. (I don't know if they ever wised-up.)

As soon as I was officially a registered nurse, I enlisted in the Army Nurse Corps – my number was N774338. Basic training was at Camp McCoy, Wisconsin. There was a small hospital on base and many nurse recruits. We each had only a few hours of general duty. The only thing I remember about that experience was we had strict orders to not smile at our patients. They were POWs. After basic training I was stationed at Mayo General Hospital in Galesburg, IL in the operating room. I was the scrub nurse for Major Farrington, an excellent orthopedic surgeon. I was privileged to watch him reconstruct GI's shattered arms and legs using bone grafts from their own healthy bones. I was on 'limited service' because I wore glasses and if something happened to them in a combat zone I wouldn't be able to function as needed.

One exciting weekend that summer at Mayo General still sticks in my memory. A beautiful Saturday, many of our patients had passes to go into town. The first clue we had a problem was a call to the MPs to come pick up "drunken GIs." The bus driver put them off the bus on the side of the road because they were vomiting all over. Suddenly it seemed the entire Mayo General population was vomiting. Everyone who had eaten the chicken salad in the GI mess hall had ptomaine poisoning. The officers' mess hall was not infected, so guess who got the duty of cleaning up after the ambulatory patients and enlisted personnel? I was called out to work in Central Sterilizing. In those days we washed all the IV tubing, rinsed thoroughly with distilled water and sterilized it for reuse. We also sterilized the IV solutions. I spent all day Saturday, Saturday night and part of Sunday trying to keep up with the need. Only patients who had blood in vomit or stool received IVs; they pushed oral fluids into the rest. By Monday we were back to normal.

After V-E Day my head nurse called and said I could volunteer for overseas duty in the European Theater if I desired. I jumped at the opportunity. So, December 1945 I was on the high seas bound for Europe. I was not a good sailor. I was only able to stay down in the dining room about 10 minutes before nausea took over and I had to head for fresh air. Soon the steward realized my problem and brought food to me the minute I sat down, kind man. I felt fine on deck and spent lots of time there, playing checkers and backgammon and visiting. GIs gave me all sorts of insignia, even a cigarette wrapped in cellophane which I sewed inside my field jacket. They are still there, but the jacket is a bit tattered. We all had the same mission, to replace war weary veterans ready to go home.

We landed in Bremerhaven, Germany New Years Eve 1945. The nurses were hurried off the ship in short order. We entered an entirely different world. We, and all our gear, were taken to an empty hospital. The room we slept in had a 10 foot ceiling with a dozen cots spaced at intervals filling the room. The bathroom was tiled, about 20 sqf. with one huge tub (only the head of the bather was seen over the edge). About four adults could easily have bathed in it together, but we didn't try that. There were the usual 'foot washing basins' that were all over Europe. Someone finally told me they were actually for ladies douches. Back home on the farm in North Dakota our mother always made us wash our feet before going to bed, and the basins looked perfect for that. Of course the toilets amazed me too, a water box way up in the air and a flat surface john, very strange but very efficient. The next day we were given a tour of Bremen. We visited a church where the water petrified whatever came in contact with it. This was first discovered when a man fell off the roof into a pool of water on the ground. The church was under construction at the time. Workers came the next morning and found the man was petrified. There was a faucet in the church basement, and they showed us petrified cats. They tested the water on small dead animals occasionally. It still has petrifying properties.

From Bremen, the 350 replacement nurses were disbursed throughout the ETO. I was assigned to the operating room of the 50th Field Operating Hospital located just outside Paris in Villesuif. The hospital had been an insane asylum before the US Army took over. We had German POWs doing all the manual labor. They washed, dried and sterilized all the operating room (OR) linen and instruments besides keeping the area scrupulously clean. One day in our operating room we heard a cat meowing. We looked under a supply cupboard where the sound was coming from and found a mother cat with kittens and daylight! The great outdoors.

Since the war was over we did mostly emergency cases. One night we had a German POW with a ruptured appendix. He was terrified of the Americans and was sure we would torture him. He wouldn't report ill until his buddies brought him. After surgery I was to insert a nasal gastric (NG) tube. This was necessary to keep his stomach empty following bowel surgery. The POW fought wildly. The operating room POWs tried to reason with him, but nothing worked until David (my future husband, 6 ft. 7 in. and built like a football player) glared at him and said "You must have it." David inserted the tube. About 30 years later David had to have one himself. He told me that tube was the medical profession's worst (or best) torture invention.

Because the experienced personnel were eligible to go home to the USA we had no medical corpsmen left. The men who volunteered for OR duty were former clerks, machine gunners, etc who had no operating room experience, much less heard about sterile techniques. We nurses had to teach them. They were young and interested, and learned quickly to be "scrub nurses" working with the surgeons during operations.

Paris really has quite a mild climate, which is good because there was very little heat anywhere. The trees in Paris had been severely pruned for firewood without actually chopping them down. When we were off duty, we could go to Special Services and buy tickets to the opera and other entertainments for a very reasonable price. Since there was no heat in the public building we wore as many layers of clothing as we could get on. Our dress uniforms were woolen, which certainly helped. When we saw the actors they were blue with cold, but they ignored it and acted as if there was no problem. The hospital had heat, but our dorm room was cold. We had woolen army blankets to keep us warm.

While stationed at the 50th Field Hospital I was eligible for a two week vacation. I persuaded my two roommates, Gorby and Hayes (we always used our last names, leaving off "lieutenant"), to go with me on a Swiss–Rome tour. It was a bus tour with all accommodations, including meals and entertainment provided. Everywhere I climbed stairs, in Paris the Eiffel Tower and Sacre Coeur (a church) – in Rome St. Peter's Cathedral, and the Leaning Tower of Pisa. In St. Peter's I added my name and address on the yellow stairway wall. All the way up that narrow stairway were the names and addresses of GIs from all over the US. Twenty years later I was so disappointed to see them all painted over. I didn't dare deface that pristine paint job. In Italy we visited the Sistine Chapel, heard the Pope bless the people from his balcony, saw the original painting of the Last Supper and went down into the catacombs.

It snowed only once while I was at the 50th Field Hospital. We got about 4 inches, white and soft. It melted the same day. By December 1946 everything was winding down. Our surgical instruments were given to the French. That disappointed one of my GI friends. He had interrupted his medical education and enlisted in the Medical Corps, so he appropriated a leather kit containing about a dozen surgical instruments. They would be very nice to have in his office or while making house calls. He asked me to put it in my trunk because home-going luggage of GIs was routinely searched by PO personnel and all valuable souvenirs were removed and appropriated by them. (It was called "midnight requisitions".) My trunk arrived home safely, and once back in the US I mailed the kit to him. He wrote to thank me, telling me it was so valuable to a young doctor just starting his practice in Nebraska.

On the ship going home I still wasn't a good sailor. I was so happy to enter New York Harbor and see the Statue of Liberty—home sweet home! My orders gave me transportation to Fort Sheridan, Illinois by train, where I was mustered out. I had enlisted in downtown Chicago. After a Christmas vacation with my family on the farm near Richardton, ND I returned to work at Lutheran Deaconess Hospital. A law passed by Congress guaranteed each returning veteran their civilian job back.

IN THE NAVY
James A. Edwards

I was born in Winslow, Arizona, on November 14, 1922. My family eventually settled in Northwest Pennsylvania where my father made his living as a carpenter. When I was twelve years old, I spent my summers working on neighboring farms to help supplement my family's income. I quit school in the 11th-grade so I could work full time on farms in Pennsylvania, Ohio and New York and send my money back home.

When WWII broke out, my older brother, who was in the National Guard, was inducted into the Army and served with a Tank Calvary Division in France. My younger brother enlisted in the Navy and served aboard the *USS Augusta*—a ship that went down during a battle at Guadalcanal. Fortunately my brother survived.

I enlisted in the Navy in December, 1942, in Buffalo, New York. I traveled by train to Newport, Rhode Island to the induction center where I remember how large the building was, and how I had to give up my civilian clothes, shower, have my hair all cut off and get inspected from my toenails to the top of my head. I remember the shots that were given by pharmacist mates and standing in line to receive uniforms, shoes, a hammock, a mattress, toothpaste, toothbrush, rifles, a rule book, a navigation book and a sea bag that I packed all these things into. They showed us how to fold and roll it into one neat package that could be carried wherever we went. Our first meal was served on stainless steel trays with compartments that they filled with some kind of meat and baked beans for my first meal at the mess hall. This was the start of our boot training at Newport, Rhode Island.

A few weeks later, I left boot camp and was sent to the huge dry docks barracks in South Boston. In dry dock was the biggest ship I had ever seen—the *Queen Mary*—being outfitted for war use.

From there I went to Portland, Maine with twenty-six others that had been farmers. Because we had been farmers we all knew how to splice ropes and wire so we were lent to an outfit called the British Admiralty Net Detail, a part of the British Navy. Our commander was a 4-striper called Captain Curry. During the winter and spring we were putting anti-torpedo nets on liberty ships that were built across the bay at Bath shipyard. Next I was assigned to work on a dock in Boston that was close to old historic ships and Bunker Hill. Right across the slips was Chelsea, Massachusetts, where I would stand guard duty at the Chelsea Naval Hospital. I liked going to Boston because I was berthed ashore.

Spring of 1943 I was ordered to Tampa, Florida, where I was assigned to the *USS Phaon ARB-3* (Battle Damage Repair Ship). As an ex-LST, *ARB-3* had heavier armament, greater deck facilities for cargo handling, and a much longer superstructure deck. The tank deck was covered with lathes, grinders, drills, metal cutters, welding machines and other shop equipment not found on an LST. After shakedown to New Orleans and final outfitting, we headed for Samoa via Guantanamo Bay and the Panama Canal. While going through the locks, I saw the *USS Bunker Hill* which was a brand new aircraft carrier at that time. We anchored in Pago Pago Harbor where we picked up water and supplies. On the island was a squadron of Navy fighter planes who would go out every day looking for Japanese shipping or enemy aircraft. From Samoa we moved to Funafuti in the Ellice Islands, arriving there shortly after the occupation of that island. There, we repaired LCTs, LSTs, pontoon barges, PT boats and restored many craft used in the invasion of Tarawa, Gilbert Islands. This was our first contact with the enemy (Japanese). They would come in every full moon and start bombing and strafing. This went on for a month or two.

James A. Edwards

98

From Funafuti we went to Majuro in the Marshall Islands, and arrived shortly after the invasion. We worked on minelayers, tankers, minesweepers, destroyers, and small boats (LCVPs and LCMs). In March 1944 we went to Eniwetok in the Marshalls, for repair work on small boats, LCTs, and yard minesweepers. In June 1944 a very large fleet was assembled (Task Force 58) and we left Eniwetok for Saipan for the invasion on June 15. Half of the forces were to attack Saipan and the rest was to attack Guam the next week. This never happened because the battle for Saipan took much too long so the rest of the force went to the Philippines. The destroyer *Phelps* (DD-360) came alongside for repairs, as did many other ships. While the *Phelps* was being repaired, she was still firing away at enemy troops and pillboxes.

During an air raid by the Japanese the *Phaon* suffered a near-miss on the starboard side. The damage to the ship was not very serious but the shrapnel fragments killed some men and injured some others. The morning of the Tinian invasion, the destroyer, *Norman Scott* (DD-690) came alongside with numerous dead and wounded officers and men. She had suffered several direct hits but we were able to repair her and the *Norman Scott* pulled away two days later. We also repaired ships for Iwo Jima, Okinawa, and the Philippines.

I was then transferred to the *USS Storm King* and then to the *USS Thomas Jefferson* when the war was declared over. Our ship was involved in an operation called Magic Carpet and we were taking troops as occupying forces from Pearl Harbor to Saipan, the Phillipines, Japan and China. On the way back we would take returning discharged service personnel back to the States. On Thanksgiving Day, 1945, I was assigned to the *USS YMS 374*, a minesweeper. The day the 374 was to go back to the States, I was transferred to the *USS YMS 200* and continued to clean up the mine fields around Japan. We worked in Japanese waters around Hiroshima, Nagasaki, Osaka and Kobe. After that I was sent to Subic Bay P.I. and was attached to the shore base after we decommissioned the 200. The US government was selling decommissioned ships to foreign countries.

I was discharged from service in 1947 at Naval Air Station Alameda, California and arrived home in Pennsylvania with only my mother to welcome me. I was 25 years old.

After the war I worked for a builder for a time, then took a job repairing train cars. I wanted to go to school on the G.I. Bill and signed up for a course in electrical engineering in Detroit, Michigan. After my schooling, a good job was still not easy to find, so I took a job in Michigan working in a foundry (Bohn Aluminum and Brass Company) as an X-ray technician where I x-rayed jet engine parts for Ranger, GE and a couple other small companies. I studied the metal lab procedures and that led to me becoming a metallurgist. I finally moved to South Haven, Michigan as the assistant metallurgist. While working for this foundry I had developed some devices that were used in metal temperature control and handling. I started a company of my own, E-Jay Thermo Products, Inc., to manufacture these products. This I operated for twenty years and then sold it.

I met my wife in South Haven and we were married 30 years ago. I guess this is probably a good place to end this, as it couldn't end on a happier note.

My name is on a brick of the memorial in Richardton, ND, along with members of my family, friends and classmates who served their country with pride and honor. I have always been treated with admiration and respect for having served my country.

NOTE: *Edwards is deceased but his granddaughter wanted his story in the book.*

THREE DAYS IN HELL
William Edwards

William Edwards

My name is William Edwards and I was a private in the United States Army, 4th Infantry Division. During that time I completed three days of complete hell and had an experience no man should have to go through. No love or thought from your fellow human beings, in fact—torture of the worst kind.

It happened in Germany in 1944 while we GI Joes were trudging through the Hüertgen Forest on a forty minute night patrol. I stepped on one of those hidden, but dangerous, mines the Krauts planted to slow our advances. It blew off my right foot. I crumpled in pain and wondered what I should do. I knew I I had to get back to safety and find a medic, but I was in no condition to move.

There were constant artillery barrages sailing overhead with German 88 millimeter shell fragments slamming into my one good leg. I yanked off my belt and wrapped it tightly around my thigh to slow the blood rushing out. Surprisingly, there was very little blood coming out so I loosened it. I learned later that the mine's detonation forced the veins and arteries upward and so, as a matter of fact, sealed off the wound. This was the only good thing that happened during that 3-day ordeal.

As I lay there in constant pain, I thought about my wife and six children back in Hayti, Missouri. I wondered if I would ever see any of them again. I prayed silently that help would come soon, but had to be quiet so as not to draw fire on my buddies. I lay there quietly until dawn. I was afraid to use the little "Cricket" clicker for fear it would bring the enemy.

Finally, after a long night of pain, about 10:30 in the morning, I cautiously called for a medic. I was afraid the enemy might hear me and begin a fresh search. Fortunately the Krauts didn't find me. Soon after a pebble hit my leg and I heard an American medic whisper: "Are you a GI?"

"Hell, yes, I'm a GI," I replied.

"Don't make any noise and we will get you out," the medic whispered. He must have been heard because suddenly a cluster of bullets whizzed toward us, hitting one of the medics in the hand. So, unprotected, they had to drop back. They tried again later, but were again driven back.

As darkness came upon me on the second night, my worst fears were realized. Three Krauts were out beating the undergrowth and they discovered me. They took my field jacket and the five packs of cigs in the pocket. One of them grabbed my canteen, shook it and found it to be half-full. He opened the cap and poured a little in his hand, tasted it and took a big gulp. In spite of my pleas for a drink of "*wasser*," the big Kraut sneered and poured the rest down my front.

One of the other Germans pulled out a pistol and pointed it at my head. The big one put his hand on the gun and said "*Nein.*" Instead they rolled me on my side and placed a land mine under my back, and wired it to my body. I was a human booby trap. I'm sure they figured they would kill more GIs when I was pulled back into the bushes. I was worried that if I fell asleep and I couldn't warn my rescuers, that we'd all be killed. I spent the night and next day restlessly and in pain with that mine jamming into my back—afraid to move for fear of setting it off. Nervous, worried and extremely uncomfortable. It was a night I'll never forget.

I realized that in their frantic search, they had missed a partial pack of cigarettes I had in my shirt pocket. When everything was quiet and there was no rustling in the woods, I cautiously lit a weed and got relief from this simple pleasure.

I was constantly aware that at any minute, the Krauts might return, find the booby trap not working, and finish me off with one of their Lugers. I was resigned to the fact that I would never leave the forest alive.

The Germans must have withdrawn because about 2:00am, two Americans from another company came in to get the wounded. Still conscious, I directed the cutting of the wires to the charge under my back. They carried me away and back to safety. I had lain on the battlefield for 70 hours and was never so happy to see another GI.

Composed by Robert Hatch from 1945 newspaper clippings of Edwards' actual experience.

Kneeling (l to r): C C. Rutter--Mesico, MO.; Eugene Horne--youngstown, OH Standing (l to r): Louis Miller--Benton Harbor; Charles Ringle -- Chicago; Joe Isole--Pelham, NY (Brooklyn)

AN ATHLETE IN THE NAVY

Carl Fiore

Interviewed by Jimmy Butt / Transcribed by Jennifer Scally

Carl Fiore

I was playing minor league baseball in Flint, Mi in 1942 when I decided to volunteer like so many of my close friends. My Dad didn't want me to go, but by the time I got back to my home in Canton, Ohio, I had a notice to report for a physical. About two weeks later I was ordered to report for duty, was sent to Cleveland and then to Great Lakes Naval Center in Chicago. I was 22 at that time. When we checked in the officer in charge asked "Who is the toughest guy here?" I was quiet, but most of the others there, who were also from Canton and knew of my sports background, all pointed at me and said "He is." (At Canton I had played on a state championship football team, was all state in basketball and baseball, and had boxed a little.) So I was appointed Master of Arms for the group.

From Great Lakes I was sent to Bainbridge, Maryland for training with other athletes, about 25 in all. We had been selected for our athletic skills and were being trained to lead recreational programs for troops overseas. I preferred being assigned to a combat unit, but somewhere higher up those in charge felt that we professional athletes were of greater value organizing recreational sports for the combat troops. So we were trained for that purpose. Some of the professional athletes in Maryland with me were: Johnny Mize, N.Y. Yankees; Barney McCosky, Detroit Tigers; John Rigney, White Sox; Joe Grace, Washington Senators; Vern Olsen, Cubs; Fred Schaffer and Leo Nonnenkamp, Red Sox.

Upon completion of this training I was sent to Seattle, Washington, for about two months where I led several exercise classes. Next, I was ordered to San Francisco along with many of the athletes I had trained with for our trip overseas. All were major league players except me. We thought we were going to Hawaii to play ball and that's where most of the major leaguers wound up. But my ship headed for Guadalcanal where intense fighting was underway. Almost everyone got seasick – what a mess! We shipped on a foreign ship, from Hungary, I think, and landed in New Caledonia. I had never heard of the place!

There were three hospitals there and one of our jobs was to help see that the wounded, brought there in ships, were taken to the hospitals. The balance of my time was spent organizing sports and other recreation, seeing that we had equipment, playing fields and such. We organized groups of GI's into teams and leagues to compete in softball, basketball, volleyball, flag football. On weekends we professional athletes would play exhibition baseball games to entertain the troops. I do believe that the diversion the troops received through these games helped their morale, gave them a taste of home, and enabled them to relax before their next assignments. If only I could have gone with them!

Another of our duties was to meet and host the entertainers who visited our base. I recall escorting people such as Bob Hope, Jerry Colonna, Jackie Cooper, Frances Langford, Jack Benny, and Patti Thomas.

"CAN YOU HEAR ME NOW?"
Milton J Fox

Interviewed and written by Phil Manni

US Army 36404200

Milton J Fox

I was born in Scottville, Michigan, on June 30, 1922. My family moved to Benton Harbor when I was 13, and I graduated from Benton Harbor High School in 1941. Following graduation, I was employed by Covel Manufacturing of Benton Harbor, and was taught to run lathes and milling machines used to manufacture the parts necessary to build Covel surface grinders. These grinders were precise machines and would allow surface preparation of metals to within .001 of an inch.

I was drafted into the United States Army on October 12, 1942, through the induction office in Kalamazoo, Michigan. I went through six weeks of Basic training in Sault Ste. Marie, Ontario, and was then sent to Communications School at Camp Tyson, in Tennessee, spending six weeks in training on all aspects of Field communications. I was then assigned to the 582nd Signal Corp and was sent back to Sault Ste. Marie. It was during this assignment that I was exposed to the Barrage Balloon Program. The Soo Locks shipping lanes were very important to the War effort and this Balloon program defended the Locks. At the peak of this program, the US and Britain manufactured approximately 20,000 of these balloons. Approximately one-third of these were in use in Europe. The balloons were tethered to the ground by steel cables, with the idea of being a deterrent to aircraft. There were 54 of these balloons deployed around the locks. When enemy aircraft flew into the Balloon protected areas, they would get entangled in these lines and be destroyed. Many of these aircraft had the wings severed off by the Balloons and these dangling lines. This program, and of course the ground forces, provided valuable protection to the Locks and our shipping lanes.

I received overseas orders and was sent to Fort Bliss, Texas, for overseas deployment training. After 4 weeks, I was deployed to Camp Shelby, Mississippi and began to prepare our equipment for the shipment overseas. This equipment had to be prepared and protected from the salt air that it would be exposed to during the transit to the War Zone. This took us about 1 month and then we began preparing for troop deployment.

On April 5, 1942, we boarded the English ship, the *Rudel Castle*, and began our 12-day voyage to Europe, porting into Glasgow, Scotland, on April 17, 1942. The trip over was smooth and uneventful, just the way we wanted it. We joined a truck convoy and traveled to South Hampton, England where we boarded an LST and sailed to Normandy, France, arriving there on April 20, 1942.

We then set up the Signal Supply Depot which consisted of 200 acres, set up behind the combat lines. My day to day job consisted of overseeing and assisting in the operation of the Depot.

When supplies were needed and the order came through, I would make sure that the soldier that was sent to pick up the order got to the correct area, acquired the needed equipment and signed off the order request. The request could be for any Communication Equipment to include, handsets, telephone poles, anchoring cables and transmission wiring. We also maintained the Depot insuring that we had the necessary supplies. On many occasions, I found it necessary to man a D8 Caterpillar which we manned on 12-hour shifts. This Heavy Equipment was necessary many times because of the hostile weather environment that we were often subjected to. Because of the constant rain that we experienced, many times the vehicles that were dispatched to pick up supplies at our Depot, would get mired down in the mud created by the rains. There were many occasions where the mud was so thick and deep, that we nearly had to use one Caterpillar to pull out another. There were times that these Cats were in mud that covered the top of the treads. We had to take extra care of these vehicles and one of our mechanics designed a maintenance platform upon which we could drive the Cats onto, and thereby, allowing us to service the bearings and tracks of these necessary pieces of hardware.

Occasionally, the Army could always find EXTRA duties for us troops to do. One of the Depot's extra duties was to deliver messages to the front lines. On one occasion, I and another soldier were dispatched to carry a message to a forward position. When we arrived, we were asked the route we had taken to get there. When we explained our route, the commanding officer was very surprised to see us in front of him. He explained to us that his Division was surrounded by the Germans and we had just traveled right through their lines. We had not seen or witnessed any German activity. We returned using the same route and once again, nothing happened. As we reflected over chow that night, we were grateful that we had not been captured.

I had one other, more memorable, encounter while delivering messages. I was dispatched to deliver a message to General Patton with clear instructions that this was personal and was to be hand delivered by me to him, and him alone. When I arrived, I was asked why I was there and explained that I had a message for the General. I was told to surrender it to his aide and he would see the General got it. I explained that I could not do that and must deliver it to the General in person. The aide disappeared and out of nowhere came General Patton.

He approached me and said (and I quote), "What that hell do you want and why are you here?" I told him of the message and he said "Well, give me the damn thing." I did just that, he read it and then told me to "Get the hell out of here and go back to where you came from."

I wasn't all that impressed with this encounter with the General and all I can say is that he was one ornery, tough, old bird.

I left Europe, via Marseilles, France, on December 15, 1945, via ship, arriving in New York Harbor on December 29, 1945. This ride back across the Atlantic was exactly the flipside of my trip over. We encountered many storms and rough seas, and because of these, I never did get my "sea legs." As a matter of fact, I was so seasick at times that I wished I would die and not have to face this uncomfortable ride. After in-processing, we traveled by train to Camp Atterbury, Indiana, and I began out-processing for my discharge. I had attained the rank of Staff Sergeant and was honorably discharged on January 31, 1946.

Although I spent my time behind enemy lines and battles, I was not wounded and did not lose any friends during any conflict that I am aware of. I was awarded the Good Conduct Medal, the European, African, and Middle Eastern campaign ribbon with 3 Bronze Stars, the

American Campaign ribbon, and the World War II Victory Medal for my service in Normandy, Northern France, and Rhineland.

I quickly put my military and civilian training to work as I sought to rejoin the civilian work force. I spent my first five years with three machine shops in Benton Harbor, and developed my skills and trade as a Tool and Die Maker. I then accepted a position with State Tool and Gauge and worked there for 30 years, retiring in 1986.

I married Velma Warsko in 1949; she passed away in 1988. I married Lois Rudduck in 1999 and we reside in Saint Joseph, Michigan and have been in this community for the past 20 years.

In November, 2006, I was honored by the Embassy of France and was presented a "Thank You America" diploma and 2004 Normandy Medal. Those of us receiving were presented this award on behalf of France at a patriotic concert hosted by *Lest We Forget of Southwest Michigan*.

Though many things have changed since my service during World War II—and I don't agree with all that has been or is being done—I still have to say that this is the best country in the world, to live in and I am proud to have served it.

WORKING WITH THE FBI
Charles Frandsen

The year was 1941. Charles Frandsen, a 20-year-old, had settled into a comfortable routine. He worked an eight hour day and attended night classes at Creighton University in his home town, Omaha, Nebraska.

In 1941 most of Europe was engaged in an increasingly bloody war. Germany had defeated the French, Britain was alone. Even though the US was technically neutral the majority supported Britain as did our government. Japan was the military power in the Far East and was challenging the U.S, in the Pacific. In December of '41 they attacked and destroyed the military base in Hawaii. The US was at War—not only with Japan, but with Germany and Italy, as well.

The decision received overwhelming support. Men and women were lining up to volunteer in the military effort. Others served our country in many ways not only in the military but in essential jobs in industry and government—especially in the intelligence services. All contribution to the war effort.

Like most twenty-year-olds at the time I was quick to volunteer. Two close friends and I chose the Army Signal Corps; they were accepted, I was rejected—a heart murmur. During those following four years of government service, I went through two complete physicals at the Bethesda Naval Hospital—no trace of a heart murmur! At the time, the military rejection was devastating, for most of my buddies were on their way to boot camp without me.

Early in '42 I learned The FBI was recruiting. I applied, went through a battery of tests, including a physical, and was offered a job in the Omaha office of the FBI. I was assigned to a night shift. This allowed me to continue my studies at the University. My initial duty was encoding and decoding sensitive reports. Part of my duties when on the 12 to 8 shift was to burn sensitive reports in a furnace every morning.

The downtown office building was located on the busiest intersection surrounded by high rises. One memorable morning I had loaded the furnace and asked the maintenance man to start the gas fire. By mistake he opened a flu and all the contents of the furnace was scattered over the busy streets below. Every employee—agents, stenos and clerks—were sent out on the street to retrieve as much as possible! Fortunately for me, most of what was to be burned turned out to be mostly non-sensitive material (trash). For a while I was blamed, but later vindicated. The maintenance man came to my rescue.

Early in 1944 I was told to report to Washington for additional training; my university studies were put on hold. I was assigned to the SIS Section, the foreign service of the Bureau. After weeks of training, my title was Special Employee (agents had to have a college degree). My new assignment was Mexico City, one of the largest of the foreign offices. I was sent "undercover" as the U.S had reached its quota in the Section. I enrolled as a student in the University of Mexico. I attended classes in the morning and reported back to the Embassy for a 10-hour shift. After 6 months, I was no longer undercover and began working openly on rotating shifts.

One of the biggest cases was the German Microdot case. Germany was losing the war. There was a large German population in Mexico and some were aiding agents that slipped into the country with the intent of sabotaging US industry and transportation systems. These English speaking agents came to the US and Mexico by submarine. Their plots were discovered and aborted—without question saving hundreds, if not thousands of lives.

The places targeted were encoded with small indented dots on cards and letters. As you might expect, Mexico was a popular haven for draft dodgers and deserters. The FBI had developed an extensive network of informants both in the Mexican government and industry and they proved to be invaluable. We met regularly with ONI (Naval Intelligence) and G2 (Army Intelligence) and together made a great contribution to the war effort.

With the end of the war in Europe, every effort was made to locate Nazi military and war criminals who were attempting to flee to havens in Latin America. My duty in Mexico ended and I reported to Washington for the next assignment. It was to be in Manilla. For several weeks I studied everything I could about the Phillipines history, culture. etc. I was all prepared to leave for Manilla (courtesy of Army transport) when I was advised I was going to Caracas, Venezuela. I later learned that Gen MacArthur and Hoover had had a big disagreement over who had authority over FBI personnel. Hoover lost, so he closed the office. There was no Manilla in my future. In a way I was disappointed as one of my volunteer buddies was on MacArthur's staff. The Caracas office was small compared to Mexico, much more of a family feeling.

Relieved of the shooting war, the Soviet Union began sending its agents into Latin America – always a fertile field for communism. Even as allies we had kept a tight surveillance on the

Soviets. With their move into Latin America relations were strained and for us, the Cold War began in early 1946.

Our caseload had doubled in that office when we received orders to close the Caracas office. The new intelligence agency, the CIA, was to handle all foreign intelligence with the FBI in charge of domestic. Several of the larger FBI offices were to remain open (which they still are). Closing that office on such short notice was stressful (an understatement).

I returned to D.C. the first week of September and resigned from the Bureau, then back home to Omaha in time to resume my studies at Creighton, along with a few hundred veterans including my two "volunteer" buddies. We had a great reunion, THANKS TO GOD!!

CRYSTAL NIGHT
Helga Franks

Interviewed by Ruthe Bomberger and Jimmy Butt

I was born on July 15, 1926, in Velbert, Germany, the youngest of five children. My nearest sibling in age was eleven and 3/4 years old. I am told I was terribly spoiled. Though l knew nothing of this, for economic conditions at the time were severe. Germany had lost the first world war and the Allies had imposed severe penalties. Jobs were scarce and paychecks hardly covered expenses. None of this mattered to me. I didn't care if we lived in a cramped apartment or that I didn't have nice clothes. If you wore nice clothes, you had to behave well and take care not to get dirty. I liked to climb trees!

My mother worked hard to keep her large family clothed and fed. My father worked at Yale and Town which was American-owned and the largest plant in town. He was not a happy man.

Helga

He loved music and was a very good pianist, but he would fly into rages over political events. He did not like Hitler. I was learning in school about the wonderful things Hitler was doing for Germany and I couldn't understand my father's hatred of the man.

When Hitler became Reich's Chancellor—the Füerher—in 1936, my father, a beaten man, predicted that this would be the beginning of the most terrible world war the world had ever seen. I was taken aback! How could my father, whom I thought so intelligent, not see how Germany was flourishing under Hitler's rule? Everybody had a job with decent wages. The schools were upgraded and twice a year a team of doctors and nurses came to each school to give the children free medical attention. Actually, though, I hated it when they came to visit our school. I was underweight and was afraid I would be sent to one of Hitler's summer camps for added nourishment.

My sister, Hilde, became engaged and my brother enlisted, thus avoiding the draft. He served with a branch of the military that helped farmers with manual labor and wound up in a mountain troop stationed in Innsbruck and Salzburg in the Alps.

As time went on, my father became increasingly bitter and my mother and I lived in constant fear that he would speak out once too often and we would get a surprise visit from the Gestapo. I was under pressure also. In school, it was mandatory that I join the Hitler Youth Movement and that I buy a uniform. I couldn't ask my father and I didn't want to ask my mother who was already frightened. So I told the leader of the movement that I could not afford to buy the uniform and I was issued one immediately, which I then hid in a friend's house. I felt so guilty. Here I was betraying my father whom I loved and trusted and who loved and trusted me! I couldn't understand his hatred for Hitler. I was ten years old at that time. Looking back, I know now that it was all too much for a ten-year-old to grasp.

In 1938, something happened that shook my belief in the basic goodness of the human race. It was a cold November night. The air was crisp with an icy wind bringing a foretaste of the winter to come. There was a commotion outdoors and suddenly, there was a knock on my door. It was two of my school friends. They said something was happening in town and they wanted me to come with them. I grabbed my coat and raced out of the apartment before my parents could stop me! Every detail of what followed is still etched in my mind!

Most of the retail stores in our town were owned by Jews. There was a small, secondhand store owned by old Abraham and his wife, who were in their late seventies. Though the store was not the cleanest or the nicest smelling, we children liked to go there, because old Abraham and his wife gave us free candy. As we approached the middle of the town, there was total destruction everywhere. The police were standing idly by and not lifting a finger to stop the destruction.

Suddenly we saw smoke coming from the roof of old Abraham's store. I saw two of my brother's friends standing by the store with several pails of cold water standing on the ground beside them. I assumed they were going to help put out the fire. Then I heard a cry, more like a whimper, as old Abraham and his wife, shocked and dazed and unaware of what was happening around them, came out of the store. The young men picked up their pails of water, and to my horror, doused old Abraham and his wife with ice cold water on that cold November night, while their store burned to the ground behind them. Later, that night became "*Chrystal Nacht*" (Crystal Night) and went down in history books as the beginning of Hitler's persecution of the Jews.

I went home greatly troubled. I think that night was the beginning of my doubts of Hitler's idea of the ideal Germany. However, I was 12 years old and by morning I had it all sorted out. I lent a deaf ear to my father's lamenting. Why couldn't he understand the real situation? How could the Füerher know what was happening in our little town? I made all kinds of excuses. Surely punishment would follow! Instead, the next day our teachers told us that the Jews were the cause of the misery our parents had to endure. Finally they were going to get their punishment and they would be eliminated from our country like a cancer. I was confused. I decided the adults would figure it out. I shrugged my shoulders and went on with my life.

In 1939, despite my fears, I was sent to a youth camp, because they said I was undernourished. My parents had no say in this. My poor mother was embarrassed. I knew it was my fault. I was a picky eater and no matter how hard my mother tried, I would only eat what I wanted to eat. I was determined while at this camp, to lose weight. Sure enough, I lost weight rather than gain it and I was scheduled for more drastic measures when the press of events saved me.

On September 1, we were told to assemble in the dining room immediately! We sensed a tension on the part of the camp leaders. We were told that Polish soldiers had been shooting at our soldiers and that last night Germany had declared war on Poland. At first I was overjoyed! It meant I was going home, rather than being sent to another camp. What would war be like? Surely they wouldn't hurt children! Then my father's prediction flashed in my mind. I thought of my brother who was already in the service. Would he be killed? Suddenly I came to my senses. What was I worried about? We were told that we had the best army and Air Force in the whole world, and the best leaders. It was bound to be a short-lived war!

It turned out to really be a short war. Poland surrendered and things began to get back to normal. I was preparing for my graduation from grade school. It was mandatory for every child to work one year on a farm or in a household as a mother's helper. Neither of those options appealed to me and I was glad to be assigned to a family who owned a grocery store, where I sold groceries all day. I was too naive to know that I was being used as cheap labor instead of learning how to run a household!

I was happy to get home from the camp but at the end of that week we learned that my cousin was one of the first casualties of the war. The next blow came when we learned that Russia declared war against Germany. My two brothers were now in combat! When France and Great Britain declared war on Germany, we began to worry but the Füerher gave us all the confidence we needed. There were secret weapons that would blow the enemy away! Our troops were advancing on all fronts.

Even though we were rationed, we had enough to eat and we didn't feel personally threatened. The war would be over soon and Germany would prosper! My only worry was the radio on which my father listened to the British every night, making us all very nervous because this was strictly forbidden. If caught, the penalty was death!

After my graduation from grade school, I received a summons to come to the Rathaus or Town Hall. They had all my school records there and I was informed that I was to undergo training as a secretary, which entailed a four year apprenticeship in an office. The fact that I found office work boring was of no concern to these people, even though I told them I would really like something to do with music or books. I was lucky I wasn't sent to manual labor! I started my job in April, 1941.

The war progressed and we were optimistic. France had surrendered and Russia would follow soon—our troops were approaching Moscow. It would be a cinch to beat England! Our Füerher was right! Germany would emerge as the number one nation in the world! Meanwhile, my father continued to listen to BBC and to hate Hitler. I felt a mixture of love and pity for him.

We were all surprised when America entered the war. We could not understand why they would enter a war that had nothing to with them? We were given answers: the Jews were the cause of it all! They knew with the Füerher in charge, they would lose their financial power and their global influence. They would rather see all humans killed than let that happen!

By now there were no more Jews to be seen in our town. We were sure they had been taken some other place and were being detained. They had to be somewhere! We were sure they were transported to other countries — nobody really knew. We never gave much thought to the right or wrong of it. There were too many other things on our minds. After the war, we thought the accusations about gas chambers and concentration camps were false until it was proven to us.

The war became real to us once the nightly bombing raids began. They increased gradually, eventually becoming an almost nightly occurrence. My father refused to go to the basement for shelter and often I would sleep through the whole thing! Our town of Velbert was not a target, we believed, because it had two large factories owned by Americans. However we could hear and see the bombs as neighboring villages would light up and burn.

Soon all the neighboring towns and villages were in ruins. When bombs fell and the sky lit up over Wuppertal, where my sister lived, we were worried.

Early the next morning we set out for Wuppertal. It was a long walk. I can hardly find the words to describe the death and destruction that we saw everywhere. Fortunately, my sister had escaped unharmed. On the way home, I thought of my father's prediction. Why had I not taken him seriously? Because I had not wanted to believe him. I found it easier to believe what I was taught in school. From that day on, I became a much more critical observer, and I listened more carefully to my father's words. It was 1943 and I was 16.

In time, rations became smaller. Fortunately, my parents were able to supplement our diet with vegetables from the garden they planted.

There was a big empty lot on the outskirts of Velbert that we had to pass on the way to my Aunt Tillie's house. One day, we noticed unusual activity around the place. Soon the whole area was enclosed in barbed wire, followed closely by the building of barracks! Before we knew it, the place was filled with Russians, including women and young girls. We wondered about that! We learned that this was a work camp and that four of the young Russian girls were mistresses of the men in charge of the camp. This huge camp belonged to a nearby factory and all the Russians worked there.

My cousin and I became friends with these four girls. We brought them home with us on weekends. The first thing we had to do was see that they were bathed, since they reeked of a certain antiseptic that everyone knew was used at the camp. They spoke German well, but with an accent that would give them away. We took them everywhere with us. I don't know how we got away with it for so long. My Aunt Tillie deserves a lot of credit. She supplemented rations and other provisions by begging from family and friends, who were in short supply themselves.

In the fall of 1943, my father did speak out once too often. He was given two choices: prison or the front line! He chose the latter. In November of 1943, at the age of 53, he was drafted and sent to the mountains in France. I cannot remember that day without experiencing great pain!

At the end of April 1945, American troops occupied Velbert. They opened the gates of the compound and let the Russians roam free! The four girls were despised by the others and were in danger. I never saw Swetlana or Tanya again. Katya and Lydia made it to the underground and survived. Katya stayed in Germany and later married. Later we learned that Swetlana, along with many others, was executed as a traitor. I believe Tanya met the same fate.

On the day that American troops entered our town, two German soldiers about my age of 17, came to my door. They were hungry and scared, fleeing the oncoming Americans! I fed them, gave them my brother's clothes and his bicycle and sent them on their way!

I had started to date my future husband in 1943. He had once lived in America, but came back because his mother was unhappy there. He spoke excellent English. Now he was a navigator in the German Air Force. His plane was shot down on the border between Germany and East Prussia. When his American captors discovered he once lived in Chicago and could speak English, they made him one of their own.

When my husband got back to Velbert in May, he found conditions severe. There was little food and money didn't go far. We got married in 1946 with no possessions but the clothes on our backs! The American occupation wasn't as bad as we had anticipated, but still, we were always hungry.

I remember standing on the sidewalk as a caravan of trucks loaded with food drove by. One of the trucks loaded with food pulled over to the curb and the driver got out. He was a black man, the first I had ever seen. I was wearing a light summer coat. He asked me to take it off and I complied, wondering what in the world he was going to do with it. He went back to the truck grabbed a sack of potatoes and poured them on my coat, grabbed up the edges of my coat to make a sack, and handed it back to me. He turned on his heel, walked back to the truck and drove off. Not a word was spoken!

A close friend of my husband, whom he grew up with in Chicago and was now a Major, offered him a job! They were going to build an American house that would feature both American and German culture and since my husband had lived in both cultures, he was perfect for the job.

My father came home from Algiers where he had been imprisoned in September, 1946. His prison mates discovered he was a musician and somehow got him an accordian and he had kept them entertained for hours!

My husband and I had two children by now and we decided to come to America! My sister was here already, so we came to St. Joseph and settled down. I gave birth to my third and last child here. I now have 14 great-grandchildren! I am happy to be in America.

WWII

GROWING UP WITH THE MERCHANT MARINES
DK Gaut

DK Gaut

Definition of Merchant Marines: *US Maritime Agency that carried cargo to all fronts during WWII suffered the most casualties in relation to the number of men of any of the US Armed Forces in WWII. The Merchant Marine had to deliver ten tons of cargo space for each person to go overseas in addition to one-and-a-half tons a month to supply him while stationed there.* It was 1942 and the kid had turned sixteen just a few weeks ago. What the hell did he know about being a seaman? Or about the war? Or anything for that matter?

He had sailed a few months that summer as galley boy aboard a passenger liner on the Great Lakes. He had heard the Italian deck hands talk about the "bigga money" being paid to the salt water sailors.

He had made one buddy during those first weeks, Charlie Palermo, older, a real take-over guy. When Charlie said "Let's do it, let's go to New York." Well, what the hell, Charlie knew what he was doing, right?

So in Detroit they changed their Copeland Books (Great Lakes sailing authority) for ocean-going papers, and now he was looking for his first ship. Charlie had been assigned to a tanker carrying gasoline to England. The kid drew a Liberty ship. A Kaiser coffin. Top speed 10 knots. About as fast as a fat man trots.

Now there he stood, not sure if he was at the right pier. Not even sure of what his assignment as mess man entailed. But proud to be a salt water sailor and anxious to get into the war—whatever that meant.

It was the right pier and he found his ship right where the watchman told him, adding, "Good luck, kid." The boy thought that was a funny thing to say.

He really missed Charlie, "Cause Charlie knew stuff, being older." Charlie even had a girl he was going to marry after a couple of trips making "bigga money." But Charlie was somewhere on a tanker which, according to scuttlebutt, was to sail soon.

The youngster who boarded was grudgingly pointed toward a bunk, and the next day began being a mess man. He didn't even have to know how to do the job. But every other man in the crew knew and told him in no uncertain terms that always started and ended with cuss words, given in tones that shut off questions.

Then three weeks later he was a veteran sailor, a combat veteran. His ship torpedoed, but not sunk. A lame duck awaiting a Dutch rescue tug and a tow to Scotland for repairs. A target for German planes that strafed the cripple as they returned from a bombing mission over England.

But by damn, wouldn't he have a story to tell when he caught up with his buddy! Wouldn't Charlie be impressed? He wondered where Charlie sailed to and where Charlie was now.

A few years later, and now a veteran of eight more trips, he happened upon Charlie's girl. "Where is Charlie?" "Did you and Charlie get married?"

Then she told him how Charlie's first ship, the tanker, was torpedoed and blown up—all hands drowned or cooked in a petroleum-fueled hell all within sight of the New York harbor.

Mariners say that the stars are really candles, each burning in memory of a lost seaman. It stays lighted until the one honored is forgotten by everyone.

That war put a lot of stars in the sky—a candle for one out of every 26 Merchant Marines who volunteered to bring food to starving allies and supplies to the Armed Forces.

May the stars burn a long time!

MEMORIES OF AN OLD MARINE
Orvid Harju

Orvid Harju

I, Orvid I. Harju, am an old Marine. I was born in the small town of Wakefield in Michigan's Upper Peninsula on April 21, 1924, the fourth in a family of five children. My father, Alfred, died at age 45 of a strangulated hernia when I was eleven years old. Mother was a strong person who had survived much sadness in her life. For all that she did for me, I am forever thankful.

I was a senior in high school when World War II began, and it seemed to the boys in our senior class that we would be involved in the war by going into military service. We didn't talk about it, but it was understood. Since my mother was a widow and the three older siblings in our family were gone, either married or working elsewhere, I decided to stay home as long as possible with a goal of being home for the Christmas season of 1942. I decided to join the Marine Corps after the New Year. I received my draft notice and was told to report for induction into the armed service on February 7, 1942.

After graduation from boot camp, we were assigned to different places according to our abilities. I was assigned to telephone school which was located on the other end of the Marine Base in San Diego. No one else from my boot camp platoon was assigned there, which meant I had to make all new friends. We were settled in bunk rooms on the base waiting to be assigned to a class, but in the meantime, we were assigned to "mess duty," which meant serving food to the others and cleaning the mess hall after all the men were fed. It also meant getting up early in the morning to ready the area for breakfast.

I was ready to go back to the field telephone school and was looking forward to more experiences with wire communications, but that Monday morning we were ordered to fall out. The sergeant stood facing the ranks and read a list of names, including mine. We were told to gather all our personal belongings in our sea bag and be ready in an hour. We were going overseas.

I was transferred to a place called Camp Catlin, which was between Pearl Harbor and Honolulu. When I arrived, I was assigned to the camp's main switchboard with about five other men. Since I was a newcomer, I was assigned to the late night shift, manning the switchboard. There wasn't much else to do except sleep and go the mess hall to get some food. Soon after arriving at the camp, I was transferred to Battery D of the 15th Defense Battalion, which was stationed at the camp and was training for assignment.

There I met Sergeant Jack Vizard from Grand Rapids, Michigan, who was the wire chief of the Battery which contained four 90-mm anti-aircraft guns. Also on the wire crew of the Battery was Ed Ryan from Oyster Bay, New York, who became the Corporal. Dominic De Masi from the Boston area and George Singer from Perth Amboy, New Jersey, were also part of the crew and were responsible for all the wire communications in the Battery.

Toward the end of January the invasion of Marshall Islands began. The assault troops from the 4th Marine Division landed on the beaches of Roi and Namur with a regimental combat team on each island. The battle lasted about two days until the islands were secured. Our LST landed on the beach on the third day and we began unloading the equipment and moving it to our designated location which was on the eastern shore of the island. We had landed on the western side. There were trails thru the jungle until we got to the shore of our determined location. The guns were placed in position and we began the work of setting up the battery.

Since we were the wire communications, we had to locate the communication center and set up the switchboard then run wires and connect the telephones to each gun, to the detecting device, to the altitude finder, the Battery CEO and the Battalion Headquarters. Digging and filling sand bags was a daily routine until the position was completed. As the months went by, the work on our positions was completed so we were often assigned work on other tasks around the island. Some of the jobs seemed to be wasted effort that didn't accomplish much.

On occasion we were treated to a show put on by a traveling group of entertainers. One of the more notable was a visit by Jack Benny and a group of movie stars. I remember the joke Jack Benny told at the beginning of his show. It went as follows: "During WWI, I joined the Navy with two other men. I was impressed with the Navy as they tried to place men close to what they did in civilian life. The first man was a street sweeper so they put him on a mine sweeper. The second man tore down buildings so he was assigned to a destroyer. How I got assigned to a ferry boat, I'll never know."

Another form of entertainment was something called a "Smoker." It involved pairing a couple of guys who wanted to box. They set up a boxing ring and chose some people according to their size and weight and paired them to box. Those who wanted could go watch the bouts and smokes were handed out free, depending on what you wanted, either cigars or cigarettes. You could sit, watch the fights and smoke. There were not any drugs available, at least I had never heard of any. You could watch without smoking, also.

It was somewhere around September or early October when a replacement battalion was brought to the island. They were black Marines. In those days the blacks were segregated and in their own units. They took over our positions and we were loaded on troop ships and brought back to Oahu and placed in a transit center near Pearl Harbor. While there, we learned the 15th Defense Battalion was being disbanded and we would be assigned elsewhere.

Around late November, I was assigned to Headquarters Company, 1st Battalion, 25th Marines in the 4th Marine Division. I went to the island of Maui where they were stationed and training for a combat operation. We were going on long marches and field problems. Since I had not been doing much on the latter days in the Marshals, I was not in good physical condition so I had to work hard to keep up with the troops.

While at Honolulu harbor, I was able to get an overnight liberty because I had the address of my uncle, Andy Hood who was working at Pearl Harbor. A guy named Frank Radinovic arranged it because he worked at the message center. We visited my uncle and also met a distant relative from Marquette, Michigan by the name of John Osterberg who was a nephew of my grandfather John Harju.

On January 2, the convoy set sail for Saipan, then to Iwo Jima. D-Day on Iwo Jima was early on the 19th of February 1945. We arrived at the island about dawn and we saw the battleships shelling the island. The shells were red hot and left a trail as they shot out of the guns. Some guys had stayed up all night playing poker and were just sitting around. I don't remember how much sleep I was able to get, but with all that going on, I didn't have time to think about it. The time came for us to go down to the tank deck and get into the Gators (the amphibious tractors we would land in). The tractor I was in had a lot of the wire communication gear we needed: telephones, switchboards and wire reels.

Al Kromhaus and I oversaw the equipment. Al was more attuned to this than I was because he had made landings on Saipan and Tinian. There were several others from the wire platoon in the tractor including the Battalion Doctor and some Corpsmen (Medics). The doors on the tank deck opened and the tractors began going into the water. When we first went out, it looked to me like we might sink, but the tractors floated. Once in the water, we began circling around. We were doing this to get organized into a wave. After we circled and were in line, we were waved in at the line of departure by a couple of destroyer escorts with a person on the back waving flags.

Earlier, as we were approaching Iwo Jima, there was an announcement on the P.A. that the Japanese were seen burying barrels along the coast where we were to land. The speculation was that they were filled with a flammable liquid and would be ignited as we were landing. The solution to this was to put a couple extra ponchos in each landing vehicle and as we approached the shore we were to wet them and put them over the troop carriers and the tractor would pass thru the flames. As we approached the shore I saw the Medics getting the ponchos wet and wondered if there were flames on the shore. From where I was sitting I could not see the shoreline but it didn't happen, and thankfully so because it certainly would have complicated matters.

115

After we were waved into the line of departure we began heading for the beach. I was sitting close to the front end of the troop compartment with Al Kromhaus with all the wire communication equipment. They asked for two volunteers to man the machine guns mounted behind steel shields on the front. Two guys immediately got up, Barlow from San Francisco and the other was Freudenberg from Iowa. As we neared the shore, I could hear Japanese bullets hitting the steel shields. It was then that I began to realize that war was about killing. When our tractor reached the shore the ramp on the back of the tractor went down and the troops began running out to get on the beach.

Kromhaus told me he would go out and for me to hand the equipment to him over the side. I would hand an item and he would run with it and put it on the sand and then come back for another. I was alone in the tractor and the driver began to get anxious for me to get out, so he could leave the beach, as the firing was quite heavy. I finally got all the gear out and ran to the shore next to where Kromhaus was. He told me a guy from our outfit named Richard Sturm was killed right on the beach. As I lay there, I was looking up at the sky and saw one of our spotter planes explode in the air. There were no parachutes so I assumed the two men were both killed in the explosion.

Kromhaus said we had to get off the beach because it was so hot with all the shooting. He was concerned about our equipment, so I suggested we leave it there, find more of our men and come back for it. He thought that would work, so we took off running in the volcanic ash that was on the shore. There were terrace-like arrangements so we would run a short distance and then have a bank. Running up the bank was difficult because our feet would slip back on the sand. We ran three or four of the banks before we found some of the men from our outfit. Ted Hubler was on my right and Cullen and Collins were to my right but higher on the bank. The objective of our regiment was to take the first air strip and that was the direction we were headed. I don't know how long we were laying on the side of that bank, but Hubler said he wanted a cigarette but didn't have any matches. I didn't want to try to get the matches out of my backpack so when I saw a Marine thirty yards away I yelled at him for some and he told me he was wounded and couldn't move. I crawled over to him, got his matches, crawled back and lit up a cigarette for Hubler and myself.

Shortly after the Japanese mortar shells began coming in. I saw the first one land in the sand behind us and saw a piece of shrapnel go into the back of Kromhaus' neck. His head went down immediately and I assumed he was dead. When I looked at Hubler, I saw him pushing himself up with his arms, coughing and then suddenly collapsing on the sand. I realized that I needed to improve my cover so I began digging myself deeper in the sand with a canteen I found that had been blown open so I could work it like a scoop. I was kicking sand with my feet wondering what I should do next when another mortar shell landed with a blast and I felt a hot piece of shrapnel go thru my arm and felt the warm blood running down it.

I knew I needed to do something about the wound in my arm. I took off running toward the beach to find a Corpsman and after a short distance I recognized one by the insignia on his garb. He bandaged my arm and gave me a small bottle of brandy that Corpsman carried and asked me if I could see a landing craft coming to the shore. He told me that when it came in I should get in it. When I protested, he said I would not be able to use my arm for a while and I needed more treatment. I ran to it as soon as they unloaded their cargo and just as I got in, an explosion on the side of the craft tipped it to one side. The next thing I knew I was rolling on the bottom. The craft righted itself after the explosion and the boatswain managed to get it off the beach and headed back to the ships.

After we arrived, I was taken on the ship and tended to by some seamen. I was taken to the hold, which was a lower deck where other wounded Marines were bunked. They put me on a bunk and made me as comfortable as possible. The following morning there was some excitement aboard ship as our ship was rammed broadside by another ship. Our first thought was we were hit by a torpedo but when we found out we were rammed by one of our own, our fears were allayed. Then some medics came to our hold to treat our wounds. I got in line and waited for my turn for treatment, but I fainted while standing there, and fell on the deck. I was immediately attended to and was put on a stretcher and brought up to the room where they were doing surgeries. The doctor treated my wound and then looked for more. I told him I didn't have any other wounds and didn't know why I fainted. They took me back to the hold where I was bunked for several days.

One day there was an announcement on the ships P.A. system that Mount Surbachi had been taken and the flag was flying on top of it. After several more days, the ship was loaded with wounded and we left for the island of Guam. Upon arrival we were all placed in a hospital and given cots to sleep on. We were tended by medics and had daily examinations. About a week after arrival, I was discharged and taken to a transit center where I was assigned to a tent and a place to sleep. As I walked into the tent, I saw Sergeant Fink, the wire chief of our unit. We immediately began discussing the people in our unit and sharing our observations. When I told him about Al Kromhaus, he told me that Al had been evacuated ,but had died aboard a hospital ship. I immediately began to feel bad for leaving him. If you asked me why I felt bad, I could not answer. I only knew that I felt inadequate and that I hadn't fulfilled my responsibilities. I would think about the situation and wonder what I could have done to change the outcome. In reality, nothing would have changed it, but I could not get rid of the bad feeling for a long time.

On the way to the transit center I saw a sign indicating an Army unit was located there. The name of the unit sounded very familiar to me because it was part of the address of a childhood friend from Wakefield who I was communicating with. I decided to see if I could get there to check it out while I was at the transit center. One day I walked to the gate and asked the sentry if I could just walk out to the road. He said he could not let me out but pointed to a field that was not guarded and said if I walked out there no one would stop me. I walked across a field and once on the road I began hitchhiking.

A couple guys in a jeep stopped and gave me a ride. When I saw the sign denoting the Army unit, I asked to be let off and walked into the unit. I found the Sergeant Major's tent and asked the person behind the desk if a soldier named Jean Nurmi was a member of the unit. The man told me Jean was in tent number three. I found the tent and walked in and saw him lying on a cot. He was excited to see me. After we talked and the excitement wore off, he took me to the mess hall and we shared some good food. The time came for me to get back to the transit center. My friend, Chinky (his childhood nickname), decided to come back with me. We got a ride with no problem, but when I walked to the gate the sentry would not allow me to enter. Again, he mentioned the unguarded field. After saying good bye, I went back in and Chinky went back to his post.

It wasn't long after that incident that we boarded ship and sailed back to Oahu to another transit center. The trip took about a week or so. I had a bout of nervous tension which affected my ability to sleep. It began when I was thinking about the incidents I experienced on Iwo Jima. I was particularly bothered about leaving Al Kromhaus there thinking he was dead and then discovering that he had been evacuated only to die aboard a hospital ship. I wondered if I could have done something that would have allowed him to survive. It took me a long time to get through that feeling.

When we arrived at Oahu, I went to the sick bay and told the attendant that I couldn't sleep. He arranged for me to go there each evening for a week and take a pill to put me to sleep. I don't know what it was, but it knocked me out and it was the only time in my Marine experience that I missed breakfast chow.

There were only about six Marines in the wire communications unit that had landed on Iwo Jima. Of those, one was a corporal and the rest were PFCs. The corporal was Jim Nabors from Alabama and one PFC was Ray Graves from Massachusetts. Soon, other guys returned after recovering from their wounds. One was Corporal Wellons from the Carolinas and the wire chief, Sergeant Fink returned. John Hovis, a radio operator, returned as well along with others from the radio group. There were quite a few who never returned. A Marine named Rayner from New York was on the same hospital ship as me. He had a small thumb-sized piece of shrapnel in his leg just above his knee. A Marine named Collins returned. I saw him get hit with a serious wound and crawl back to the beach. I have often wondered about their lives and what they were like after the war.

We began getting replacements from the States to build us up to combat strength. We were scheduled to leave Maui for the Philippines the third week of August as that was going to be the staging area for the invasion of Japan. There were rumors as to when the invasion would take place. One was in early November and another was that we would land on the main island near Tokyo in the early spring of 1946. Thankfully none of this came to fruition with the advent of the Atom Bomb.

I was discharged on November 3, 1945, after roughly 33 months in the Marine Corps.

—READ THIS STORY IN FULL ON OUR CD—

THE DIRTY 30TH IN THE 19TH

Arthur Hawkins, Corporal

Military Service - 5 February 1943 - 5 January 1946

MEMBER OF THE AWARD WINNING 19TH BOMB GROUP

A BIT OF HISTORY ON THE DIRTY THIRTIETH

front side of memorial facing north in Memorial Gardens

Whether the sobriquet "Dirty" was applied to the 30th Squadron by a Japanese Propagandist as rumored, or whether it was the figment of a US Air Force Public Relations officer's imagination makes no difference. The appellation has clung to the recounting of the Squadron's exploits and was given renewed impetus at the press releases when the Squadron returned to the US in late 1942.

The 30th traces it lineage back to the First World War when it was organized as an Aero Squadron on June 13, 1917. After service in France during which it overhauled and repaired aircraft engines and apparently saw no combat the Squadron was demobilized in April 1919, then reactivated in June 1932. The 30th was designated a bombardment unit and assigned to the 19th Bomb Group at Rockwell Field in San Diego. When the Army Air Corps was assigned the task of flying airmail in 1934, pilots of the 30th played an important role flying routes in the western states.

In 1937, the 30th was equipped with the new B-18 Douglas bomber, and in 1939 progressed to the first of the famous B-17B Flying Fortress. In May of 1941, under the command of Major David Gibbs, it delivered newer models of the B-17 to Hawaii, and in October of that year the Squadron moved to the Philippines with the 19th group. War with Japan was at hand and, on December 6, the 19th moved two squadrons to Del Monte and the remaining 19 B-17s at Clark Field were under the command of the 30th. All but two of these were destroyed when the Japanese struck on December 8. After the attack, the ground personnel of the 30th remained near Clark carrying out salvage operations and servicing the few remaining B-17s and P-40s that were able to land. When Clark was abandoned on December 24, the 30th personnel were sent to Mindanao and assigned the task of defending the harbor of Bugo on the north coast of the island, armed with rifles and four machine guns salvaged from wrecked airplanes.

In the bombing missions from Del Monte, only four 30th aircrews participated. When the 19th withdrew to Australia in December, some of the 30th flight crews were evacuated but the ground men were left behind to defend the northern approach to Del Monte. These men were surrendered on May 10, 1942, and like other prisoners, suffered the horrors of the POW camps. Few survived to be liberated at the end of the war.

Those of the 30th who got out of the Philippines joined the 19th and performed valiantly in defense of the Dutch East Indies and the operation from Australia after the reorganization of the 19th in March 1942, returning to the US with the 19th in November. Then the 30th remained with the 19th Group in the B-29 operations against Japan in 1944-45. It continued to be a part of the 19th through the Cold War era, flying B-47s under the command of SAC. At last knowledge, the 30th is a squadron within the Thunder Birds.

The short history above was gleaned from "They Fought With What They Had" by John Shaw

To quote from the <u>Tucson Star-Citizen</u> newspaper February 12, 1943:

"Far from the Pacific skies where they slugged it out with the enemy for 12 bloody months, the 19th bomb group receives the Army's salute as the nation's greatest air fighting unit....There is no precedent in the US military history for the honors that come to the 19th, a little bar of blue rimmed in gold leaf signifying heroism in four major actions against the Japanese. Every one of the thousand and more men and officers will be so decorated in the name of the President for battles in the Philippines, Java, Australia, the Coral Sea, Milne Bay, New Guinea, and Guadalcanal."

This high honor, along with other recognitions, has been reaped upon the 19th as noted in the August, 1945 issue of <u>Stars and Stripes</u>:

"Most Honored Outfit...Now it was Aug. 15, 1945, and as they swept down to North Field on Guam they knew it was over. A few minutes earlier and the Saipan radio related the news—the Japs had quit, this raid by 808 B-29's was the last of the war. They pushed into trucks and made for the briefing rooms. They damn well knew there'd be a celebration there because theirs was a special outfit—probably the most famous and honored AAF unit of the Pacific war—the old 19th Bomb Group."

Arthur R. Hawkins is a proud member of that outfit and details how he arrived at that point, as follows:

I was inducted at Fort Hayes, Columbus, Ohio, 5 Feb 1943, Reserves to 12 Feb 1943, and sent to Fort Thomas, Kentucky, Reception Center. 26 Feb 1943 sent by troop train from Cincinnati, Ohio, to St. Petersburg, Florida, for Basic Training. We were housed in apartments and hotels during basic on the beach, through April 1943. May 1943, shipped to 56th Fighter Group, Bartow Army Ordnance. October 1943 to 408th Fighter Bomber Group, 519th Fighter Bomber Squadron (A-36) Aircraft. November 1943 from Drew Field, Tampa, Florida, to Abilene Army Air Base, Texas, by troop train. Was there until April 1944 when 408th was de-activated and I was sent to the Army Air Base at DeRidder, Louisiana. Only one aircraft on Base, an AT-6 Trainer, as the base was closing and again I was transferred to Woodward Army Air Base, Woodward, Oklahoma. Around 25 May 1944, we had P-51 Mustang Aircraft. 2 July 1944 was re-assigned to the famous 19th Bomb Group (B-29s) at Dalhart Army Air Base, Dalhart, TX. I was assigned to 30th Bomb Squadron and moved by troop train to Great Bend Army Air Base, Great Bend, Kansas.

We had our combat training up through November 1944 when we were certified as combat ready for overseas. We were put on alert and departed by troop train around 10 December 1944 to Fort Walton, Seattle, Washington, staging area where we had "abandon ship drill," down rope netting. 16 December 1944 we boarded the Dutch liner and set sail around midnight through Puget Sound to the Pacific. Arrived Pearl Harbor 22 December 1944 and dropped anchor and waited one week for our convoy to arrive. We departed Pearl Harbor on 29 December 1945 and we arrived on Guam on 18 January 1945. We debarked and were transported to northern Guam by truck to North Field. No runways or hardstand. We had no aircraft as of this time, no place to land. We only had pup tents to sleep in. We were assigned to the 314th Bomb Wing, which had four Bomb Groups, consisting of 19th, 29th, 39th, and the 330th Bomb Groups. Each group had 48 B-29 aircraft to a group or 192 planes to a wing and we had three wings in the Marianas Islands of Guam, Tinian, & Saipan.

Our runways were completed in February 1945, and airplanes began to arrive with first missions on the 6th of March over Tokyo, Japan. This kept up the bombing through July into August when the first atom bomb was dropped on August 6th and the second on August 9th, it forced the Japs into an unconditional surrender 14 August 1945. It was officially signed on 2 September 1945 on the *USS Missouri* in Tokyo Bay. This was VJ Day for everyone and General McArthur was our hero. Shortly thereafter personnel were being sent home for discharge. I left Guam around 15 December and arrived at San Pedro Harbor 27 December 1945 and out to Camp Anza, California. Left by troop train and arrived in Camp Atterbury, Columbus, Indiana, and discharged 5 January 1945. This was the end of my Army Air Corp service.

"In Alis Vincimus" - *"On Wings We Conquer"*

Back side of memorial, facing south in Memorial Gardens

NOTE: 19th Bomb Group was most decorated in World War II. 19th Airplanes were B-17s from 1941-1943 at Clarke Field, Philippines to Australia, and back to Rattlesnake Army Air Base, Pyote, Texas, in 1942, November. 19th Trained in B-29s, 1944 and used them up till 1953. B-47 Jet aircraft replaced the B-17 at that time, at the end of the Korean Conflict.

Medals & Ribbons: WWII Service

American Theater Campaign medal Asiatic-Pacific Theater Campaign Medal with two Battle Stars.

Army Good Conduct medal

World War Victory medal

Distinguished Presidential Unit Citation with one Oak Leaf cluster

Philippine Republic Presidential Unit Citation

19th Bomb Group - 6 DUCs and 2 PRPUCs

CLEANLINESS IS NEXT TO GODLINESS
Robert Jackson

Interviewed by Robert Hatch

Robert Jackson

Perhaps it was because I was born on a farm in Eau Claire, Michigan in 1922. Or perhaps after high school it was that I took a Dairy Husbandry short course at Michigan State University and worked as milk inspector that led to my being assigned a MOS120 Veterinarian Technician.

Pearl Harbor in 1941 encouraged many in my age group to volunteer for the draft. This I did September 4, 1942, at Fort Custer where I was sworn in. Two weeks later I was transported by train to Victorville, California, in the Mohave Desert for basic training. There I was assigned to the Medical Corps in the Air Force with the rank of Private First Class.

I received training in mess hall inspections, food preparation inspections and sanitation inspection. We were taught that most of the mess hall personnel were not paying enough attention to the proper cleanliness of the work area. Certainly disease could easily spread throughout the corp., if sanitation was not maintained. This was drummed into us incessantly so that even now when I eat at a restaurant I am tempted to ask the proprietor to see his kitchen first. It is surprising how quickly pots and pans that have not been properly washed and scoured could carry a bacteria buildup. Necessary cleanliness of the kitchen area was a must and it was my duty to see that this was carried out correctly.

Food in the freezer was limited to a life of 36 hours. If it were not used by then, it was dumped. Meat was inspected and dated, eggs were visually inspected before approval. Past due food was incinerated and buried in landfills.

After completion of this training I was transferred to La Junta, Colorado, an advanced B25 training facility. I plied my training and assured my fellow corpsmen that I would be on top of their food inspections. Another transfer took me to Great Falls, Montana, an air transport command facility. Here I was promoted to Corporal. My transfers continued to Presque Isle, Maine to receive preparation to be transferred to Stephenville, Newfoundland. This was an air transport command base, transporting the wounded from Europe. Since I was a medical technician, my training helped in stabilizing the wounded embarking from the planes as well as giving shots to corpsmen. It was also a stopover for refueling before flying to the States. I stayed there longer than my other transfer locations--from August 13, 1945 to February 5, 1946. I felt that my job and the others who protected the cleanliness and sanitation of our mess halls was an important function to keep our men and women fit for duty.

I was discharged at Ft. Sheridan, Illinois on February 12, 1946.

THE LAST HORSE CAVALRY TROOP
Warren James

Warren James

I started my armed service in the fall of 1944 as a draftee. I did not know much about horses, but I was selected to join the Horse Cavalry and was sent to Fort Riley, Kansas, for training. We had a group of about 25 enlisted men. I did learn how to shoot a rifle, as we all needed to know how to handle a weapon, including on the horse, but I never really used my rifle as a Cavalry rider.

I learned how to ride a horse, how to take care of my weapon, plus we all spent even more time learning how to take care of our horses. I got to know my horse, and he got to know me. He knew my voice right away. I could go up to the barn where the horses were kept and, if I whistled a certain song, my horse would recognize that. He would have his head sticking out of the stall, waiting for me, when I arrived.

One of the things we learned to do was to take our horses down the edge of a rocky area. This was called the rim rock. We learned how to get the horses down a hill, which was to let them put their feet together and let the horse slide at his own speed. That way, there was less likelihood a rider would be thrown or the horse would fall.

I remember one highly unusual situation where my horse was unable to clear a ditch and actually got caught in the ditch. Luckily, I jumped off and was not hurt. The horse was not seriously hurt either, but couldn't get out himself. They had to get some belts and a pulley system to lift him up, using a machine somewhat like a crane. They lifted him out and put him on the ground and he seemed to be able to get around, but he just could not get out of that ditch by himself.

After I finished my training in Kansas, I was shipped overseas in the spring of 1945. We went by boat to the Philippines. The horses were also transported, but I am not sure whether they were on the same boat as we were, or not.

In the Philippines we continued to learn how to handle a rifle and be able to recognize our horse and have him recognize us. It was amazing how the horses could learn to do so many things. We continued to rub down or curry each of our horses every night. We would take a brush and damp sponge and wipe down the horse before bed.

I wasn't in the Philippines very long, because the war ended soon after we arrived and I ended up being transferred to Japan. The horses were sent back to the States. I am not sure when or how, but there wasn't any further horse riding for me. I became a jeep driver and we had men on guard duty, so I would drive the jeep and would take four men at a time. There were several jeeps and we would go out and drop the men off, then come back several hours later.

I was actually in Japan for almost two years before I transferred back to the United States. During that period of time I stayed in contact with my family by letters, since we were not allowed to use the telephone. I wrote my wife just about every day. I did not want to leave any unfilled spaces, so it became part of my routine.

A somewhat funny and unusual event happened while I was stationed in Yokohama. While I was talking guard duty one night, I heard someone or something walking through the brush quite a distance from me. It was dark and I couldn't make out what it was, so I yelled out, "Halt!" What it was continued to trample through the brush. I again yelled, "Halt! Show yourself alive" (or something like that). I was alone and I was scared, so I ended up shooting several rounds into the darkness. The noise stopped and I waited until morning for guard change.

Eighth Platoon "I" Troop - 1st Training Regiment. CR.T.C. Fort Riley, Kansas - January 27, 1945

Lt. Henderson, Platoon Leader - Sgt. Hodgins, Platoon Sgt

In the morning, we found a dead water buffalo in the brush. I'm glad he did not say, "I am a water buffalo" when I yelled or I would have probably gone crazy! I was relieved that I hadn't shot a person, though. It was a strange night to remember.

After almost two years, I returned to duty in the United States. There really wasn't any assignment. The war was over; soon, I was discharged.

After the war, I worked for Essex Wire Corporation in Zanesville, Ohio, until I was transferred to Berrien Springs, Michigan, in 1963. I stayed with the company until retirement.

I was also a musician. Before moving to Michigan, I played in a Country & Western band called "Denny Taylor and the Muskingum Valley Boys." We opened shows for all the major touring acts coming through Zanesville, such as, Little Jimmy Dickens, Hank Thompson, Gene Autry, Tex Ritter, and many others. We also had a 30-minute live TV show five nights a week which aired for over five years. My music career ended when we had to choose between life on the road and staying home with our families.

I look back on my military experience as basically a positive time in my life. I liked the idea of being in the Cavalry, because I've always liked horses. However, I didn't much care for the special treatment certain soldiers got back at that time. The actor Mickey Rooney was an officer in my boot camp and was picked up in a fancy car to go wherever and whenever he wanted. The rest of us were restricted as to what we could and couldn't do with our free time. That always bothered me. I remember that I didn't like beer, so when we received some, I would trade mine to other soldiers for their Coke. I was happy to return home and did not have any interest in staying in the Military.

My wife has kept the book of pictures that certainly helped me to remember the time I was in the service. The book has helped me tell the story of my troop, which I later learned was the last Horse Cavalry unit in the Military. The horses were replaced by helicopters and other vehicles.

WORKING AT A SHIPYARD
Norma Aman Jerke

Written by Loren Patterson

Reprinted with permission from <u>Kalamazoo Gazette</u>, May 29, 2011

It was 1944 and I had graduated from Ipswich, South Dakota, High School. I was 17 years old and ready to earn money and face the world.

I went to work for a bakery in Aberdeen, South Dakota, sharing a rented room with a girlfriend. We saw an ad in the paper where the Kaiser shipyard would pay your train fare to Vancouver, Washington, where a job and a room in a dormitory awaited and the fare was slowly taken out of your wages. I was ready for adventure, so we took our physicals and signed-up. My roommate changed her mind, so I took my clothes and guitar, and boarded the train by myself.

The train happened to be a troop train – what fun. I was in a car with all soldiers, sailors, etc. A soldier played my guitar and we sang and enjoyed the trip to Vancouver.

A bus took me to my new home in a girls dorm – Hudson House Dormitories. I shared a room with a girl named Trudy from Springfield, Missouri, who remained a good friend of mine. There was a store with all necessities, post office, etc. Our dorms had house mothers who took care of us and were also good friends we loved. The boys dorms were separate. We got together in the lounges after working hours with our instruments and had a great time singing and playing.

I went to work as a pipe welder earning between $2 and $3 an hour—big wages at that time. We were close enough to the shipyard where we could walk to work. We wore welder hoods, goggles, leather gloves, jackets and pants. I still have a couple of spark scars on my neck. Many times in the ships' bathrooms, we had to weld pipes together in spaces so small our lead man had to push us in and pull us out.

We had to take tests occasionally to make sure our welds didn't leak. My first test weld leaked but we got a second chance to take it over. I remember asking my foreman if I passed. He said, "You had a weld on there that wouldn't leak for 50 years," so I was happy.

We had celebrities who came to launch the ship when it was finished. They would break the bottle of champagne on the bulkhead and name it. Two celebrities I remember were Gypsy Rose Lee and Caesar Romero.

The day they announced the end of the war, a group of us got into a car and drove to watch the ships come in. What a thrill. Sailors ran off the ships into the streets grabbing every girl in sight with hugs and kisses.

The war effort: Norma Aman Jerke stands between her friends Emma, left, and Agatha. They worked at a Kaiser shipyard in Washington during World War II.

I wish now I would have taken my welder's leathers and hood and saved them for memories, but I left them in my locker. I will never forget my shipyard days in 1944 and 1945.

I met many wonderful friends from many states and have happy memories helping build ships for our boys to safely come home.

Norma Aman Jerke resides in Kalamazoo and drove a bus for Comstock schools for many years.

REMEMBERING JIBBY
Arthur "Jibby" Jibilian

Remembering Arthur "Jibby" Jibilian of the Halyard Mission on the Anniversary of his Death, March 21, 2012

OBITUARY FROM FREMONT, OHIO: Arthur "Jibby" Jibilian, 86, of Roselawn Dr., passed away on March 21, 2010 at his home.

He was born on April 30, 1923 in Cleveland, OH and then moved to Toledo, OH as an infant. He was educated in the Toledo Public School District and graduated from DeVilbiss High School.

Arthur was then drafted into the US Navy in 1943. He was trained as a radio operator and then volunteered for the Office of Strategic Services which was the predecessor of the CIA. He was awarded the Silver Star and was recently nominated for the Congressional Medal of Honor for his services behind the lines in Serbia. He returned to the University of Toledo where he met his future wife, Beverly-Jo Williams. They were married on October 27, 1951.

Arthur was employed by Basic Refractories Inc. as Safety Director from 1955 to 1983. He was a Little League Coach and a Boy Scout Leader. He was a former member of the Lions Club and was the president of several other professional organizations. He was a member of the V.F.W., American Legion and the Brainard Masonic Lodge. He enjoyed jogging and running in several 5 and 10K races and networking with his friends on his computer.

He is survived by his wife, Beverly-Jo Jibilian, Fremont; children, Debi Jibilian, Fremont, David Jibilian, Fremont, and Mark Jibilian, Phoenix, AZ; two grandchildren; two great grandchildren; and a wealth of Serbian friends.

His body was donated to the University of Toledo Medical Center for Anatomical Study. His remains were interred in Arlington National Cemetery on May 5, 2011.

Aleksandra's Note: *For me, one of the measures of a man is how deeply the loss is felt in the hearts of those who knew him or, if they didn't know him personally, were affected by his work or*

126

by his existence on this earth in a positive way. OSS radioman Arthur "Jibby" Jibilian was short in stature but a giant of man in the hearts of all of us who were fortunate and privileged enough to know him. He was directly involved in the great Halyard Mission Rescue Operation of 1944 in Nazi-occupied Yugoslavia, both in Serbia and in Bosnia. He was directly responsible for saving the lives of over 500 American airmen stranded on that territory and considered MIA and virtually left for dead for a good length of time before they were rescued.

What was even more impressive was that for Arthur Jibilian, coming home to America didn't mean leaving the past behind. Instead, he made it one of his life goals to vindicate the Serbian commander who made the multiple rescues of the stranded Americans and other Allied airmen possible. Arthur never forgot General Draza Mihailovich, whom he was fortunate enough to meet personally while in Serbia and Bosnia, and gave his heart and soul to seeking justice for the General and righting the wrongs of the historical record. It was a big task. To his dying day, Arthur Jibilian wanted nothing for himself and everything for Mihailovich and the Serbs who had saved the lives of the Americans in the former Yugoslavia during World War II. His efforts were not in vain. The historical record is now a more truthful one, a more just one, because of him.

Arthur "Jibby" Jibilian

When Arthur died on March 21, 2010 I felt the loss in my gut. To this day I continue to feel it in my heart. I selfishly wish he were still here with us, because he was truly such a dear, good man. A good friend. I regret that he did not live to see the Mihailovich Rehabilitation judicial process begin in Belgrade, Serbia in September of 2010. I know that he would have willed himself to live long enough to see justice for the General come to fruition.

I hope Arthur Jibilian is watching and reading and listening. I hope he knows how much he is missed. We have not forgotten.

Below are the sentiments of some people who knew Arthur personally or knew of him that were shared with me back in March of 2010 following his passing. On this second anniversary of his death, these tributes speak to the measure of the man.

Sincerely,

Aleksandra Rebic March 21, 2012

"Last week, (March 2010) I accompanied Don Alsbro and three other 'Lest We Forget' veterans to West Virginia to visit Mr. Frank Buckles, WWI veteran. Along the way, we stopped in Ohio to see Mr. Jibby and his wonderful wife and daughter. We had a nice lunch and spent some time with Jibby and his family.

"I can't tell you how sad I was when I heard the news. Jibby was so gracious when we saw him. He remained strong throughout our visit, but I could tell he was getting tired prior to us leaving. What a soldier! He was totally pleasant and most of all, thankful to all of us for visiting him. I gave him a hug before I left and had a feeling that this would be the last time I would see him. I just never realized that God would take him so soon. I am so thankful that we had the opportunity to see him.

"May God be with you in the coming days.... you must remain strong for Jibby's family... rest assured that we will all see him again, someday!"

Ray Damaske

"Lest We Forget" / Southwest Michigan

"I am so saddened by the news of Jibby's passing. I knew him only months, but his warmth, genuineness and unassuming character made him so loveable and approachable. I can only imagine how much his family and friends will miss him.

American airmen and OSS personnel with General Mihailovich, standing in the center of the photo with his hand over his heart, 1944. Arthur Jibilian is kneeling in the front Row in front of General Mihailovich and Captain Nick Lalich.

I am honored to have met him last June at the "Lest We Forget Forgotten 500 Reunion" in Michigan. He campaigned to the end to vindicate Gen. Mihailovich. We will honor their memory by continuing the campaign to award Jibby the Medal of Honor."

Vecnaja Pamjat.

JoAnne (Musulin) de la Riva, Daughter of Captain George "Guv" Musulin

Commander of the Halyard Mission Rescue Operation 1944

"I wish to offer my condolences to you on the passing of Arthur. I was reminded of his exploits in Yugoslavia and his participation in the Halyard Mission which led to the rescue of over 500 American, British, and Canadian Airmen. I read the entire story of his heroics in a local newspaper. I immediately called him and we discussed our experiences in Yugoslavia. I told him how when he parachuted down near the airfield at Pranjani in August of 1944 and ran up the hill to the airfield, I was one of the first airmen to greet him as he approached with Captain George Musulin and the other member of their team. It took about nine days until Jibilian and the team could set up the rescue. The sick and wounded were flown out on August 9, 1944 and the remaining 200 airmen, including myself, were flown out on August 10, 1944. But Jibilian wasn't through yet. He and the team stayed behind and rescued over 300 additional airmen. They left only when they knew that the airmen had been returned to Allied control.

I thought of that rescue team many times in the years that followed. It took a certain type of person to participate in that kind of mission. Arthur Jibilian was that kind of person... Brave,

Strong, Dedicated, Conscientious, Loyal and Devoted. Thanks, Arthur Jibilian, along with General Mihailovich, the Halyard Team, and the Serbian people for saving my life and the lives of over 500 of our fellow airmen."

With Great Respect,

Milton E. Friend, Lt/Col, USAF (Ret)

One of the "Forgotten 500" Rescued American Airmen WWII of the Halyard Mission 1944

––––––––––––––––––

"Others had their Superman, Captain Marvel, and Green Hornet Super Heroes. I had Nick Lalich, George Vuynovich and Jibby! Rest in Peace, Warrior Arthur Jibilian. Vjecnaja Pamjat.

I admired Jibby as the finest kind of warrior, not only as the brave and gifted WWII O.S.S. radioman, but also in his later years, when he realized there was still another fight to be won.

As a warrior whose thoughts are pure and good, Jibby tried desperately against all odds to tell the true story of General Draza Mihailovich, the Serbs, and the rescue of the 500+ US airmen from behind German-occupied lines in the former Yugoslavia. Throughout these 60+ years, he fought the good fight, defending the honor of General Mihailovich and his Chetniks, in guest appearances on airfields, in Museums, on TV and in interviews for documentary films. Goodbye my friend, Jibby.

To the very end, you were always so helpful to me and so many others. I thank you for your kindness, friendship and love. You were a wonderful part of my life from the time I was seven. Good-bye my special Super Hero!"

Milana "Mim" Bizic / www.babamim.com (Serbian History 101)

––––––––––––––––––

"So sad to hear that Arthur Jibilian has passed away. I knew Mr. Jibilian was seriously ill, but held out the hope that he would be with us awhile longer. May this dear and brave man now rest in peace, and may his memory be eternal. I'm honored to have known him via this electronic medium. Mr. Jibilian was so appreciative and always made himself available to answer any questions or clarifications from me. I will miss his occasional emails. My condolences to his wife and daughter." *Liz Milanovich*

Arthur Jibilian on Ravna Gora with Robert Wilson, Clare Musgrove, & Lt. Col. Charles Davis - 2005

"Was terribly saddened by Jibby's passing..."

Curtis Diles, One of the "Forgotten 500"

Rescued American Airmen WWII of the Halyard Mission Rescue Operation 1944

"This is very sad news. JoAnne said he looked sprite last summer. We do wish these heroes would last forever."

Georgene (Musulin) Murray, Sister of JoAnn (Musulin) de la Riva

Daughter of Captain George "Guv" Musulin, Commander of the Halyard Mission Rescue Operation 1944

"I was stunned. We had lunch with him March 11th (10 days before his death) and while he appeared a little weak, he ate a healthy meal, was jovial and wished us well. 'Lest We Forget' has a mission to 'brighten the future by illuminating the past' and the story of Jibby and how he saved over 500 American airmen during Operation Halyard is a story that must never be forgotten. His heroic story will live on for decades. While small in stature, he was a giant of a man and it was truly an honor to have had the chance to meet him. I never saw Jibby when he didn't have a smile on his face. If there was ever a soldier who deserved the Medal of Honor it is Arthur Jibilian!"

Don Alsbro, President, <u>Lest We Forget of Southwest Michigan</u>

"No doubt Jibby will continue his fight to let the world know the meaning of the name Draza Mihailovich, with even greater effectiveness, from where he is now."

Julia Gorin

"Jibby was a shining example of decency, loyalty and perseverance in defending Draza and his Chetniks. He witnessed the abandonment of Draza by the ruthless Allies while he enjoyed the friendship and sacrifice of the Serbian people, and he felt totally confident moving around Pranjani without restrictions, which he told us he did not experience during his brief exposure to Tito's murderous Communists.

Jibby, you vindicated the perfidy of the US foreign policy and have gained the well deserved admiration of the Serbian people in general and of your Chetnik buddies in particular.

May you rest in peace!"

Sincerely,

Nick D. Petrovich, Mexico City, Mexico

"I met Mr. Jibilian over a year ago during a visit of his to Grand Rapids, MI. He spoke before the Michigan Company of Military Historians and Collectors. During that time, as during his recent on the air interview in my radio program Foreign Policy and You, I met with a man with one of the most gentle smiles I have ever seen.

By the way he told the story of Operation Halyard, in which he was instrumental...never did he give any indication of boasting or bringing attention to himself as he could have done. The word "we" drowned by overwhelming preponderance any allusions to "I."

Volunteering for such a mission to save the lives of others at the risk of his own life was "above and beyond the call of duty." Mr. Jibilian did not receive the honors he deserved while living. Politics got in the way, geopolitics, that is. Our government and our allies decided at one point that it was more expedient to keep that historical event of WWII under covers. It is still not too late."

It was my honor to have conducted his last public interview on March 17. [2010]"

José A. Amorós, "Foreign Policy and You"

Host & Executive Editor, Washington & Marshall Institute

"With the passing of Arthur Jibilian, our country has lost a true American hero. Arthur's brave work in rescuing downed American airmen in World War II must never be forgotten, and I am honored to have known him. He was the quintessential American hero -- humble, modest, quietly proud, but ferocious in seeking justice. I was often struck by how such a pleasant, amiable fellow would suddenly become full of fire and fury when the subject of Draza Mihailovich and the betrayal of the Serbs arose. Art was a man who knew what was right and what was wrong, and he wasn't afraid to speak up for those in the right."

Gregory A. Freeman, Author of The Forgotten 500

"This kind hearted, good humored American Hero that I always called 'Uncle Arthur' will be greatly missed. His soft, calming voice always made you at ease, even when the chips were down. I can see him now, as we speak, still smiling, and saying: 'Sam, this is really not about me, but about Draza Mihailovich and the gallant Serbian people that saved us, and I know that the weight of the Congressional Medal of Honor would add to that cause.'

Rest in Peace Uncle Arthur, we Love You and you will never be forgotten!"

Love,

Sam and Sue Subotich

"To the Jibilian Family: Be strong and brave, because that is how Arthur was all of his life. He did a great service for the Serbs over many years and millions of them will be with you in spirit in remembering Arthur Jibilian, a good man - a wonderful human being."

Rade Rebic, The Rebic Family

"The last of the Halyard Mission operators in the field is no longer with us. Art Jibilian was a brave and courageous man who did not flinch, who unselfishly gave of himself and gave everything to further the cause of justice and freedom and General Mihailovich. More than 500 airmen owe their lives to Jibilian and the Halyard team, and he was the last living connection to those men."

Major George Vuynovich, Chief of Operations, OSS Bari, Italy

Who this year (in 2010) will be 95 years old

"Dear Arthur,

[March 2010] When I talked with you on the phone just a couple of weeks ago, we ended the conversation with my asking you not to die. You assured me that you would try your best not to.

Now, I have another request: When you reunite with all the great ones of Halyard, including the good General, please remember to take lots of pictures.

The memory of you, especially how fully you lived your life these last few years, will inspire me for the rest of my life. I really thought you would live forever.

Thank you for being my friend."

Aleksandra Rebic

MY NAVY MEMOIRS
John G. Johnson

When I graduated from high school in May 1945, World War II in Europe had ended earlier that month with the surrender of Germany. However, the war with Japan was still being fought with fierce intensity. It was thought that the war with Japan would last for a long time. They would surrender only after their homeland had been invaded and completely subjugated. Therefore, the end result was completely unexpected when the atomic bombing of Hiroshima and Nagasaki on August 6 & 9, 1945, caused Japan to agree to the terms of unconditional surrender.

Toward the end of World War II, all young men were subject to being drafted into the Armed Forces when they became 18 years. During my senior year in high school, two of my classmates had become eighteen that fall. They were drafted in December and were unable to complete their senior year of high school. Fortunately, I did not become eighteen until the school year ended, and I immediately enlisted in the Navy.

I reported for duty on June 13, 1945, at Great Lakes Naval Training Station for "Boot Camp." My station was Camp Dewey. The rigorous training which lasted for 10-and-a-half weeks included close order drill, manual of arms, obstacle courses, inspections, and classes.

The rationale of our training program was to instill "physical and mental toughness" in us, so we would be ready for the all out war with Japan. The "scuttlebutt " in camp at the end of training was that we were to be sent to San Pedro, California, for further training as Fleet Marines in preparation for the invasion of Japan.

After boot camp, we were given a five-day leave. While home, I learned of the mass celebration for the end of WWII. All communities had extensive celebrations and churches held special services marking the war's end. In boot camp we had been informed of the end of the Pacific war by radio and newspapers, but I cannot remember any special programs or celebrations. We pretty much stuck to our regular routine in order to be ready for "graduation."

When I returned to Great Lakes after our brief leave, our company was immediately put on a train bound for California, not to San Pedro as we had envisioned, but to San Francisco. The end of the war in the Pacific had changed everything! Suddenly, millions of men and women were not needed for the final agonizing thrust against the Empire of Japan! All plans had to be revised.

When we arrived in San Francisco, there were no barracks available so we were put in hotels until we were able to rent rooms in private homes. We were given the assignment of working in the US Fleet Post Office there. My duty was in the air mail Division where I placed the letters in the boxes of the proper ships.

Since I was a small-town boy from the Midwest, the excitement and beauty of San Francisco was overwhelming. Downtown there were flower vendors on every corner, and the cable cars were unforgettable. Our rooming house was just a few blocks from the beautiful Golden Gate bridge and park. Although my job of sorting mail was not very challenging, the vibrancy of the city compensated for it.

In the immediate aftermath of the end of the war in the Pacific, there was lots of "shuffling around" of those in the service. Those with combat experience and many years of service were eligible for immediate discharge. However, if millions of other service members were discharged all at the same time, it would create an untenable situation in the labor market.

I was transferred to the Fleet Post Office in Pearl Harbor, Hawaii, where I was again assigned to the air mail Division. The total number of workers in that Post Office was over twice the number usually assigned there. Our hours were greatly reduced and we often had every other afternoon off. This extra time allowed us to really become acquainted with the island of Oahu. The city of Honolulu was just a short distance from Pearl Harbor.

The duty in California had been great, but Hawaii was even better! The climate was about perfect with temperatures ranging 68-85 degrees. We were told that the temperature on Oahu had never been colder than 54 degrees or warmer than 92 degrees. The scenery was every bit as fantastic as I had seen in travel books and on picture post cards.

"All good things must come to an end," and my time in Hawaii ended when I received orders to my next assignment on the island of Guam. Guam is an island territory belonging to the United States, and is part of the Mariana Islands. Vital Pacific air and navy bases were located there.

Our transportation to Guam was provided by the aircraft carrier, *USS Point Cruz*. Ironically, although this was a Navy "flat top," there were no planes aboard. This was 1946, peace reigned, and conditions were a direct contrast to what had been happening in the Pacific, just the year before.

The journey from Pearl Harbor to Guam took a very long time. One of the two giant propellers that pushed the ship through the water malfunctioned, and eventually shut down entirely. We could only go half-speed. The ship's captain was ordered to sail to the Bikini Atoll in the Marshall Islands so the propeller could be repaired.

At this time in May 1946, the US government was preparing the Bikini Island area for a nuclear bomb test. Several "junk" ships, and Japanese battleships captured at the end of the war, had been brought in, anchored in place around the island, and were awaiting the test.

While the *USS Point Cruz* was being repaired, we sailors were allowed to go ashore. Bikini was a small, tropical island. All the natives had been evacuated to other islands in preparation for the test.

Our ship was finally repaired and we proceeded at full speed toward our destination, Guam. The journey was uneventful, but I remember marveling at the spectacular sunsets over the Pacific. Guam was greatly damaged during the weeks of warfare when the US was re-taking the island from the Japanese in 1944. The capitol city and most of the island was completely obliterated by the hard-fought battles and the aerial bombing.

I was assigned "general duty" on Guam. I would report for duty each day as a member of a work crew. Because there was so much construction going on, we general duty crews performed a wide variety of jobs, everything from sanding floors to breaking up concrete with an air-hammer. We had arrived during the rainy season and there was mud everywhere. In direct contrast to Hawaii, Guam was quite desolate.

A point system had been established by the Navy, making service people eligible for discharge based on the length of service and the location of service. Overseas service counted double points. I had accumulated enough points to be discharged in July. I was sent back to the United States, and received my honorable discharge at the Great Lakes Training Center.

I feel that my experience of serving in the US Navy was a very good one. Before joining the Navy my travel opportunities had been very limited. I was able to experience a "new world," so different from my first eighteen years. Most importantly, I was able to meet and work with a cross-section of diverse people. This was an excellent preparation for my lifetime experiences.

I took full advantage of the educational benefits of the G.I. Bill, graduating from Indiana University in 1950. I continue to benefit through the prescription drug program of the Office of Veterans Affairs.

WHY I AM THE LUCKY ONE

Richard Kramer

1st Lt Kramer

After graduating from Three Oaks High School in 1937, I worked as an electrician's helper for a couple of years and then decided to go out on my own. I went to Benton Harbor, Michigan, and worked second shift at The New Products Co. I decided shop work was not for me, and my friend, Clare Meyers, and I decided to join the Army.

We enlisted in Benton Harbor. I was okay, but Clare was slightly underweight. The recruiting officer suggested that Clare try eating some bananas to bring up his weight. He did and walked around the block, came back and his weight was okay!

After we enlisted, we were sent by train to Detroit. We were sworn in at the Federal Building by an Army Colonel. I wanted the Army and Clare wanted the Air Force. I was sent to Fort Sheridan, Illinois, by train, and Clare was sent to Elgin Air Force Base in Florida.

Upon arrival at the Fort Sheridan guard house where all recruits checked in, I saw a man standing on his head in a corner. The guard explained that the man was heard to say "I can do the Army hitch standing on my head." The MP in the guard house obliged! What a way to be introduced into the Army! This was in October of 1940.

We stayed in an old Civiliarm Military Training Camp (CMTC) WWI barracks heated by a coal stove at each end. We had been issued woolens so it wasn't too bad. We were there for about two months. On weekends I hitch-hiked home to Three Oaks. Then I was sent to Fort Custer, Michigan, to the 81st Quartermaster battalion, motor maintenance. After a short period I was sent to Quartermaster Motor Mechanics School in Baltimore, Maryland. I was there five months. While there the second week I was doing KP in the mess hall and passed out. They sent me to the base hospital where they drained my sinus with a needle and sent me back to school. At the end of my stay I was sent back to Fort Custer to do maintenance work on trucks. We were readying vehicles of the 1st Infantry Division. Once I worked for 36 hours without sleep. I didn't mind this because I wasn't going to Iceland. I still hitch-hiked home every weekend. I also went through basic training when war was declared with Japan.

Shortly after, one of the company officers approached me asking if I wanted to go to Signal Corps Officer Candidate School because of my interest in radio. I was interviewed and accepted. I was made Corporal and sent to Signal Corps OCS in Red Bank, New Jersey, where I had three months of intensive training. They said it was more difficult than West Point. I graduated and was given 10 days leave at home, and then sent to the 54th Signal Construction Battalion at Pittsburgh, California. From there it was 21 days on a troopship bound for Australia. We landed in Sydney during the time the troopship got jammed in the harbor and we had to disembark over the side on cargo nets. The ship had about a 15-degree tilt.

After a while I decided that construction work, climbing poles, etc., was not for me and I was sent to the 1st Cavalry Division at Camp Strathpine in Rockhampton, Australia. I was made

Signal Corps officer for the Division and was in charge of the Division message center, which routed messages to higher and lower units which enciphered and encoded messages when necessary. After a few months of training the Division packed up and shipped to Oro Bay in the jungles of New Guinea. In a month we were sent to the Island of Manus in the Admiralty group, where the natives ignored us. I set up the signal center with code and cipher machines and trained men in their operation. Communication was mainly by radio, ciphering, and encoding messages. In a few months we shipped out for the Island of Luzon in the Philippines. The 1st Cavalry was the point Division for MacArthur in the Philippines where the 1st Cavalry was the first unit into Manila for the rescue of the prisoners in the Santa Tomas internment camp.

Shortly after the forward unit got to Manila, General MacArthur passed through our headquarters. He wanted to send a message to the forward units and handed it to me for transmission to them. I forwarded it by radio. I remember he signed the message from "Mac A." I tried to get the message afterwards but someone beat me to it! Soon I did get to see the camp in Manila with a few refugees in it. The place around the camp was pretty well shot up.

A few weeks later, I was told that I could go home. I had 33 months in overseas and they figured I had been there long enough. I was sent to a replacement depot and was sent home on the *USS United States* troop ship. On the way home, I laid on the deck, relaxed, and got a real sunburn during my 21-day trip. When the ship was 200 miles from San Francisco, we got word they had dropped the atomic bomb. When we got to San Francisco and disembarked, I did not kiss mother earth although a few did. I was discharged in Camp Atterbury, Indiana, as a 1st Lieutenant. When I got home I was hungry for home-cooked food; I ate six eggs and had fresh tomatoes!

As to why I am lucky: While we were in the Philippines we were told that when we invaded Japan proper on the island of Kyushu, it would be extremely dangerous due to the attitude of the Japanese people which was "Kill all Americans." That is when I finally realized what the two atomic bombs meant. By breaking our coded messages, the Japanese thought we only had one bomb. They never realized we had two. The first one was on target, Hiroshima; the second one was dropped on the naval base at Nagasaki. It was two miles off target. (This was per the Navigator of the Enola Gay who I heard speak recently at the Michigan Lutheran High School.)

An added note: While we were in Sydney, I met Esther Wire who later became my step-mother, after my mother died. She was with Randall Couchman's daughter from Three Oaks at the USO Center. Esther was in the WACs, having enlisted at the age of 37, as we might say "just under the wire!" One year at the Three Oaks Flag Day parade, my father, Mellen Kramer, rode in a car representing WWI and Esther rode in another car representing WWII. They were married at that time.

A WAR REFUGEE'S STORY
By Hedy Liebich

Interviewed by Ruthe Bomberger and Jimmy Butt

Hedy Liebich

I was born in 1921 in Bremerhaven, Germany, the youngest of four children. My mother suffered from epilepsy and my father had to work two jobs to support his family. Conditions in Germany were very difficult at this time. Defeated in World War I, Germany was subject to harsh reparations by the Allies. Inflation was rampant and a paycheck did not cover expenses. It was especially difficult for people in the cities who could not grow their food.

My family's situation grew even more difficult in 1924 when my father died of influenza. I was three years old. Then in 1932, my mother died of malnutrition. My oldest brother, who was 19 assumed our care, so I didn't have to go to an orphanage. He and my older sister worked to support us. I was eleven years old at the time.

When I was 14, I was working as a housekeeper for a family with four children. I learned that my father's brother was living on a farm in Poland and I wrote to him. In response, he invited me to come and stay with him. All I had was his address, but I was determined to get there. I set out with only a sandwich that spoiled before I could eat it. There was no food for sale.

It was an arduous journey. I had to rely on people along the way to get me to the next stop. At one place a kind woman provided me with a bed for the night. At another, a man on the bus gave me chicken soup and directed me to a mill where he said farmers took their grain to be ground and that someone there might know the way to my uncle's farm. Sure enough, someone at the mill knew my uncle and told me how to get nearer my destination. After walking a while I asked a Polish girl for directions and she pointed across the street. I had arrived!

My uncle welcomed me warmly, but his wife did not! So when the mayor of a nearby village asked if I would work for him at his office, I accepted. With two other village girls, I rented a room in the village so that I no longer had to walk three miles to work. And I no longer had to put up with my uncle's wife! I returned to Bremerhaven to visit my sister for Christmas and was advised by friends not to go back to Poland. But a Nazi assured me the Russians were not coming and that it was safe to go back.

Life was going pretty well for me when things changed for the worse. Hitler was forcing Polish people to abandon their homes and move eastward, moving Germans into the vacated space. But in January, 1945, the tide of war changed and the Russians were advancing and causing Germans to flee out of Poland. Everyone was afraid! The Russians were coming!

Finally the order came to evacuate. German troops came to help us. The first part of the journey for me was on a wagon. It was winter and the ground was covered with ice and snow. A

Polish lady who was going to sew my coat gave it back to me the day we left. It was a good thing because it was so cold. We passed abandoned farms where cows had been left behind and they were screaming in pain because they hadn't been milked. Small children and babies were crying because they were hungry and tired. The roads were crowded with frightened people, all fleeing the Russian advance. I later learned that my uncle and friends were searching for me among the dead. And as we traveled through Germany I traded my shoes for food. It was chaotic!

When German troops in jeeps passed us I saw some girls asking the soldiers for a ride. I had an inspiration to do the same. When I approached the first jeep I was turned down. At the next jeep I was told "Don't you see how crowded we are?" I replied "But I want to go home! "He said "Where is home?" When I replied "Bremerhaven" he responded in low German, the language of the country people, and he let me get on his jeep. He was from Bremerhaven!

I can't remember how I got from Posen to Poland, but I had a note of authorization that was given me by a German officer which made things easier. Once as I was standing in line for my ticket, suddenly there were two Red Cross nurses on either side of me. It seems I had fainted! They were very kind and gave me food, but I couldn't eat it! I finally got on the train for Berlin, but the train had to be re–routed because Berlin was being bombed! When I got back on the train it was so crowded there was no room to fall over even if I had fainted again. I finally got to Berlin which was still being bombed. I was able to get another train to Bremer, a city about 35 miles south of Bremerhaven where I had to change trains again. I remember sitting on the train so tired I was unable to stay awake.

Someone helped to get me on the right train to Bremerhaven. Upon arrival I was shocked to see the damage the town endured from the bombings. I had to walk quite a way to my sister's place. When I approached her place, I hoped she was still there. I remembered the secret signal we used to have, so I whistled the tune we used to use. Imagine my joy when I heard her whistle back! What a wonderful reunion!

My sister lived in a 3rd-floor apartment which had suffered some damage from the bombings. The ceiling leaked and we had buckets on the floor to catch the water. There was a nice lady living there who had me over for dinner once a week. She knew someone in the city and could get me a job. However the city was being bombed frequently and I didn't want to work there. We could hear the sirens go off and we would have to run for shelter. Bremerhaven was an important seaport on North Sea. Once I saw a plane shot down and watched it spiral down into the waters of the North Sea. I couldn't tell whose plane it was. I heard about a German ship carrying refugees, mostly women and children, trying to escape the Russians, that was sunk in the Baltic Sea – all aboard were lost.

When the war was over in May of 1945, my younger brother, Joseph, came home. He had been on duty in southern Germany. When he heard the war had ended, he picked up his things and said to his comrades "So long, boys, I'm going home." My older brother, Edmond, was killed in January on the Russian front. He left behind a daughter he had never seen. My sister took Joseph and me into her home. I was happy to realize I was no longer a displaced person, I was a citizen of Bremerhaven!

I got a job at a place that was once a dance hall for American GIs. I don't remember what I did there, but somebody was cooking donuts and making coffee all day long. I would get sick of the smell of donuts frying. I would take leftover donuts home for my sister and brother who devoured them eagerly. But I could eat none of it—I preferred dry, black bread!

After the war I decided to come to America. I worked hard and saved money for the trip. I came through customs in New York City and was sent to Central Station. There, a nice well-dressed lady and friend helped me with my luggage and took me to Traveler's Aid. I arrived in South Bend where I was met by several relatives. I moved into the Eleanor Club in Benton Harbor and later worked at VM Corporation and Heath Company for some 30 years.

I am SO glad to say I am an American.

PARACHUTE
Harold E. Long

In 1942 with the United States fully involved in World War II, I made up my mind to enlist in the Navy. While I waited for my enlistment to go through, I was drafted into the Army Air Corps. After basic training I was assigned to Wright Air Base, now Wright Patterson Airfield, in Dayton, Ohio.

Our assignment was to test equipment installed in various aircraft. The equipment we tested included engine performance devices, navigation equipment and even parachutes.

Fortunately, our tests did not require us to actually jump out of airplanes. We worked at Wright Field and in Washington State. We performed tests on B-17s, B-24s and B-29 bombers, P-51 fighters, and near the end of the war we worked on jets.

It was in Washington State I learned that parachutes could present a danger even on the ground. A supply plane loaded with parachutes for delivery began its take-off roll. The parachutes it was carrying were not properly tied down. As the plane took off and began to gain altitude, the cargo broke loose and shifted all its weight to the rear of the plane. This created a severe imbalance in the plane's altitude and sent it spinning to the ground. With an altitude problem so severe, the plane became aerodynamically similar to an anvil.

I was working on the wing of a bomber in the rear of the hanger when the wounded plane slammed into the hanger doors and exploded. Startled, I looked up and saw flames shooting across the roof of the hanger. I leaped off the wing and hurt my arch, but I escaped the searing flames. I escaped the hanger through the rear doors. I helped to locate five of our crew who were not so fortunate. They lost their lives, the fire being so hot it burned the clothes off their bodies.

When the war ended, I was discharged with the rank of Corporal. I married the love of my life in 1946. We were together for 60 years and raised two fine children. I worked for Indiana Michigan Power Company for 41 years having worked on turbines and as an overhead crane operator. We lived in Northern Indiana and Southwestern Michigan. The memory of my narrow escape from the flames of a crashed aeroplane still returns when I recall the great war.

WAR AT SEA
John Maynard's Story

Interviewed by Ruthe Bomberger

I was drafted into the United States Navy on November 18, 1941. I had been a commercial fisherman on Lake Michigan previously. I was sent to Newport, Rhode Island, for training, and then was detailed to the frigate, the *USS Constellation* which was being refurbished in preparation for designation as an Historic Landmark, honoring it's service in the Revolutionary War.

After serving seven months on the *USS Constellation*, I was assigned to the *Keokuk*, a mine layer. We laid mines around Casablanca and surrounding waters. Casablanca was an important shipping port for the Allies and our job was to keep out German submarines. I remember one occasion when a mine exploded prematurely, creating havoc for us and providing a target for nearby German submarines!

While we were still in port in Portland, Maine, aboard the *Keokuk*, I had an experience I will never forget. I was ordered to launch a small boat to get a replacement part. While I was out in the water, I saw a small white hand come over the edge of the boat! It looked like a human hand! Soon there were two pairs of hands followed by two furry faces! They were sea otters—very friendly fellows! I will always remember them!

The *Keokuk* returned to port in Brooklyn, N.Y., arriving there on October 5th 1943. I was then assigned to the US Smartt, a destroyer escort named after a heroic young flier whose plane crashed into the Pacific. The ship was newly commissioned and was capable of 19 knots with a complement of 55 officers and 183 enlisted men. After its shake-down cruise, the Smartt joined a convoy escorting all sorts of vessels headed for Europe. These ships were carrying a variety of goods such as food, troops, ammunition, even train engines. These were dangerous waters and we had to be alert for German submarines! We sailed through Gibraltar which was under attack! We had to turn around immediately to face German submarines! We were told that a favorite trick of the Germans was to send divers under water to attach bombs to the propellers of ships docked in harbor. When the ship started it's engines the bombs would explode!

Between October, 1943 and April 1944, the *USS. Smartt* escorted three convoys from New York to Casablanca. On one of those occasions we were attacked by German dive bombers— there were 12 of them! Our ship was credited with shooting down three of them at our gun site on this initial run. I was a gunner then. We didn't know whose gun was responsible— bullets were pinging everywhere! Other bombers were shot down on the subsequent raids. The men on our ship received special commendation and we were proud sailors that day!

When we got to back to New York, I spent some time in the Naval Hospital. I was having trouble with my spine and retired from the Navy on February 3, 1945, with the rank of Coxswain.

I was glad to serve my country and I have some wonderful memories, but I also have some bad ones. I remember coming into the harbor at Casablanca and finding it full of dead bodies— casualties of the American invasion.

When I went back to Pentwater, Michigan, I took up my old life as a commercial fisherman and ferry boat wheelsman. Now I sit by beautiful Lake Michigan and I remember.

A MEDIC IN THE BATTLE OF THE BULGE

Zachariah McPherson

Interviewed by Gary C. Lulenski, M.D.

I did not enter military service until I was 29-years-old, and that was in 1944. I had been drafted earlier on two or three occasions. When I went for my physical exam, a hernia was found and I was considered F-4. Therefore, I was turned down for active duty. I am not certain what happened as time went by, but I was again called up in the draft. When I went for a physical at that time, I was told the hernia could be fixed while I was in the military.

I was inducted into the Army and I ended up doing basic training in Augusta, Georgia. While there I was required to do a five-mile hike with a 90-lb. pack and during that march my hernia became quite painful and I was not able to complete the assignment. I again was examined by a physician of some kind and I was told I did not have a hernia and that I was "goldbricking." It was hard for me to understand why I could feel a mass in my groin and I was having such discomfort, but I hoped it could be fixed and, in a short time, the pain went away.

I was in Augusta for about seven months and qualified as a sharpshooter. I learned various Infantry procedures. I learned something important while I was there and that was to stay out of foxholes along the sandy area because if a large truck or piece of equipment came by, sometimes the sides of the foxhole would cave in. That was not a place you wanted to be when there were any big vehicles in the area.

I was assigned to the 75th Infantry Division and our entire battalion was trained at the same location. I was assigned to be a medic and I am not quite certain why that happened. I had not learned much about caring for the wounded, so I was hoping I would learn when I was sent overseas. The entire Division was sent to Europe in the fall of 1944. I cannot quite remember where we started from, but we ended up in Wales and were there for a couple of weeks.

We then rode a ferry across the English Channel to France and transferred to the northern coast of Holland or Belgium. We entered the combat area in January 1945 and were assigned to an area south of Bastogne and actually relieved the 82nd Airborne Division, as they were no longer surrounded by Germans.

We stayed there for about four months. My duties during that time were sort of second echelon. I would help with ID tags for wounded soldiers and help to get them to ambulances where they could be transferred to a field hospital or a dispensary. Occasionally there would be a medic or several wounded and then I would be up on the front line for a short period of time.

Our Division advanced through Belgium and by the end of April we were right at the Rhine River. However, we never did cross the river there, and kind of went back around the area we were in.

During that time, we had an occasion when a wounded German soldier died before we could arrange for some further care. I was involved in making arrangements for him, but I could not find any place that would accept an enemy solider who was no longer alive. Another member of our medical unit and I drove all over, trying to find someplace to have this solider buried. I think we may have ended up in France before we found a place to do that.

My commanding general was General Porter, although I never did meet him. I stayed with the Division until the end of the war and then was transferred to Riems, France, from there to LaHarve. Our captain then volunteered us to do KP, which somehow resulted in the whole battalion being sent to a troop transport and sailing back to England somewhat earlier than we had thought. When we were about 3 days away from New York, we ran into a terrible storm. I really thought we never were going to make it back to the United States. Many soldiers were sick and we had to batten down the hatches and could hardly do anything. The waves went right over the ship. I never saw weather that bad or waves that high in my entire life.

During most of my time in the front, in the combat area, and when we returned to our base in America, I was giving soldiers Penicillin shots. In the combat area I would see 10-15 people everyday. I guess gonorrhea was a big problem at that time. We also had an episode where a soldier was bitten by a dog. We had to consider the dog had rabies so he had to get a shot every three hours for several days to prevent rabies. I volunteered to stay up during the night a couple of nights with this soldier and administer the shots.

I ended up at Fort Atterberry near Indianapolis in 1945 and was discharged from the military there later in the year. I took a bus or a train to South Bend and was able to get a ride to Niles. I stayed at the Four Flags Hotel that is still there. I called my brother-in-law in Benton Harbor and he came and picked me up around midnight and I returned to living in St. Joseph.

Before I went on active duty, I was driving a bus, and when I came back, my job was still there. Someone who was in charge of the bus line told me I might be able to get a better job at the Post Office. I went there and was given a temporary job, but to become a full-time civil servant you had to pass an exam. I had not had much schooling, so I kept putting it off. Finally, someone told me the exam was really not difficult—you just needed to have common sense. I took the exam and became a full-time postal worker. Oftentimes, I would transport mail between Chicago and Detroit. I worked there for 28 years and retired when I was 66-years-old. I have been living here since.

I look back on my military experience as a worthwhile time in my life. I would certainly do it again. I decided not to enter the Reserves when I was discharged and ended up with quite good insurance coverage, so I didn't use the VA care system.

There were several people in my unit who I got to know well. I kept in contact with one buddy who lived in Lacosta, California. After awhile, we lost touch; he passed away many years ago. I still have some of my rememberances from the war and still have my good conduct metal and my sharpshooter badge. I kept a couple of books which showed the front lines of the 75th Infantry Division and one of the books was actually written by General Porter. They called our Division the "Diaper Division" because the drafted soldiers were very young and I was a lot older than most of them. My daughter comes regularly to visit me here at the convalescent center and I still have fairly good memories of my time in the military.

Zachariah McPherson

DON'T TELL EVELYN!
Al Mihalik

Al Mihalik

The first four years of my life was spent in Chicago. My family had a home on the corner of Ridgeway and Archer. Then, wanting to have a farm, my parents purchased a home and land north of Bridgman, Michigan, on Livingston Road. I grew up with siblings, Wally Duchay and Steve, Olga, Bill and Anna Mihalik. I married Evelyn Hendrix on October 3, 1942, and while working at Clark Equipment in Buchanan, I received my draft notice. My choice was the Army Air Corps. My parents, Steve and Anna Mihalik and Evelyn drove me to my training camp at Camp Atterbury in Indiana. It was difficult for my wife and my mother to know that I may be going to war.

During training, we endured days of marching, target practice etc. We lived in barracks and the food was good. I was able to enjoy the USO one time. From Fort Custer, I was transferred to the Army Air Base in New Orleans. My wife, Evelyn, took the train down and was able to stay in a rented room for a month-long visit. The homeowners were helpful, friendly people and we continued to communicate with them for years. I was happy to have my wife there, and I was able to spend a good deal of time with her. We swam in the ocean; my wife was delighted to learn that she could easily lift me in the salt water.

On the day that we were to ship out, my wife realized I had left my dog tags with her. Fortunately, her landlords were able to drive her to the base where she was able to give me the dog tags. How good it was to see her one more time before we were to leave.

The next location we were moved to was Camp Shanks, New York. We spent two weeks there waiting to be taken overseas. During that time, I volunteered to help a farmer on his property. We were all paid individually for our work and were happy to be doing something while we waited to be shipped out.

We took an old military ship for our journey to England. There were three or four bunks stacked in each row. I had the bottom bunk. On the way over we had a storm and were bouncing all over. Men were getting seasick. While I didn't get sick, it wasn't pleasant to be on the bottom bunk.

We had no idea where we were going. I wrote a letter to both my mother and my wife. In my mother's letter, I told her we were being shipped overseas and I added, "Don't tell Evelyn," as I knew Evelyn would worry. Unfortunately, I switched the letters when I placed them in the envelopes and it later became a funny family story. I heard the phrase, "Don't tell Evelyn" many times throughout the years!

In England, we stayed at Kessler Field. We carried our duffle bags off the ship and were transported there by Army trucks. At one point I also stayed in a home the military occupied.

Al and Evelyn Mihalik

On the first night in England, there was an air raid for a buzz bomb being transported by a plane with no pilot. (It would crash when it ran out of gas.) We had to leave our bunks and move to a fallout shelter each time there was an air raid. I can remember one evening when the air raid sirens went off. We were already in our bunks and one of my comrades said, "Al, are you going to the shelter?" I replied, "Yea, yea, I'm going" and then I fell back to sleep. Later my friend said, "Where were you, I thought you were coming!"

I was assigned to the Military Police and also worked on the vehicles. At times, I was assigned to guard duty. We were guarding airplanes and ammo dumps. Our shifts for guard duty were always at night, It was a long 8-hour shift out there alone in the dark. After awhile one started to see things in the darkness. The Officer of the Day would come by in a jeep to make sure we were awake and doing our duty guarding. We would say, "Halt! Who goes there?" The Officer of the Day had to stop and answer us before he could proceed. One time, while the Officer was in my area, conversing with me, the solider guarding down the way from me yelled over saying, "Hey, Al, let me know when the Officer of the Day comes to check on you!" Poor timing on his part. One of the worries was to be caught sleeping while on duty and the punishment was court-martial. A soldier I knew was court-martialed for sleeping and was locked up for a time. During the time he was locked up, he was given boxes of nails. One day he was to spend bending them all and the next day he was to straighten them. The military finally realized that an 8-hour guard duty at night was too long and changed it to a 4-hour shift.

For recreation, we played poker and were able to bet on the horses at the New Market Race Track in England. I also wrote letters home. I would write several letters at one time and then send them out one at a time to my wife. I looked forward to her letters as well. She was a wonderful letter writer and at times mailed packages to me.

A lifelong friendship was formed with a gentleman in our unit from Maryland by the name of John Castagnola. After the war, I took my family to visit him when my children were teenagers and we continued to send cards and call each other until John's passing last year. I valued his friendship.

Two of my brothers were in the war at the same time as myself. My older brother, Steve, served and was shot at, making a dent in his helmet. Luckily he was not touched and continues to live in Sebring, Florida; he celebrated his 96th birthday in January 2012. My brother, Bill, also served, and went on to become Chief of Police in St. Joseph. While we served, my mom would put a blue star in her window for each of us, signifying that she had three sons in the military. How anxious she was for our safe return. During my stay in England, I was able to meet up with my brother, Bill, and my brother-in-law, Bob Hendrix.

Oh happy day when the war ended! We thought we were going to have to go to Japan, but we were sent home instead, on a passenger ship--the *Elizabeth*. It was much nicer than our ship was on the way to England.

Al Mihalik

Al and Evelyn Mihalik

How happy we were to see the Statue of Liberty as we landed in New York, knowing it was also seen by my own parents who came here from Czechoslovakia. There was a bus waiting to transport us to Indianapolis. The military were respected by being able to board the bus first, thus insuring them a seat.

My parents brought my wife to Fort Custer to bring me home at the time of my discharge. How happy we all were to be a family at home in Michigan again. My wife had found a nice apartment for us in St. Joseph. We lived there until we bought a home in Buchanan. Clark Equipment gave all veterans super seniority for the first year back. That gave us first pick of the open positions.

We had our son, Robert, in Buchanan. Longing for a farm, we moved south of Stevensville and purchased a farm in 1950. I switched over to Clark Equipment in Benton Harbor. We planted crops on the farm, bought a dairy cow, chickens, and a horse to ride. In 1959, we built a new home on the same property. The old farm home and a small amount of property were sold. Large gardens were planted every summer and the vineyard kept growing. Grapes were taken to the market, and there were always enough extra to be made into wine.

The farm was a great place to raise our two children. Our son, Bob, became a Michigan State Trooper and married Carol Lauer in 1976. They had two sons, Steve and Scott. Sadly, he was killed while on duty September 9, 1984, at the age of 37. Our daughter, Judith, married Art Schmidt in 1978; they are blessed to have three children: Donna, Kimberly and Brian.

It was a busy time and I became strong with all the hard work. Life is good.

A NOTE FROM HIS DAUGHTER, JUDY: *At the time of this writing, my father has turned 90. He is living in his own home and still plants a garden. My mother and his wife, Evelyn, has gone on, but was cared for by him in their home during her 11-month illness. My dad has always enjoyed sharing his war time stories with us and was fortunately kept away from the horror of it. When he wears his military cap, he appreciates the people who recognize his service. He will always be my biggest hero.*

SUMMARY OF MY NAVY HITCH

George V. Nichols

I enlisted in USNR at Detroit, Michigan on April 11, 1942, then returned home on Inactive duty to finish high school. In June I was called to Active duty and sent to Great Lakes Training Center for training. In August, I was admitted to Great Lakes Hospital with "Cat" fever [a standard diagnosis at Navy medical facilities regardless of the diagnosis. "Cat" was short for "Catarrhal," an inflamation of the mucus membranes]

In September, I was transferred to University of Illinois Diesel School, then to Norfolk, Virginia, in November, and on to Solomons MD. In December, I was transferred to Philadelphia Navy Yard to commission LCIL 29. I requested a transfer to Deck duty.

In January 1943, I was on board *LCIL 29* for shake down cruise, and started down the East Coast Inland Waterway to Charleston, on our way to Panama Canal. We cleared the Canal in March on our way to Pearl Harbor, Fiji Islands, Samoa, and New Caledonia, arriving in Sidney, Australia, in April. We took on Australian troops in Red Cliff, Australia, then headed for the Solomon Islands invasion. As we approached the beach, we took some small arm and mortar fire. In August, we returned to Brisbane to load more troops and encountered small arms fire and mortar fire. I was on the forward 20mm when a round hit the conning tower behind me. I fired a few rounds at the muzzle flashes in the trees. During clean-up, I had two blood spots on my back from shrapnel; we put bandages on them.

We returned to Milne Bat New Guinea for fuel and stores in September, then back to Red Cliff for US Army troops. Then, we headed for invasion at Port Moresby, New Guinea. As we approached Port Moresby, two Japanese "O" (naval ship) came out of the valley at us; two P-51 Fighters came out of the sun and shot them down.

In November, after R&R in Brisbane, I was transferred to a light Destroyer, the *USS Mitchell*. We made a mad dash for Grand Solomon Bay to patrol against a Japanese mine ship they thought was laying mines in the bay. They were right; four days after we started searching, we found one. It was a magnetic-type mine, so we did not pick it up. It got us just forward of the fuel tanks, but almost broke us in half. I was standing on the starboard side next to the conning tower and the concussion blew me off. It was about 0230, so we could not see anything. I started swimming as fast as I could away from the ship, finally stopping and just floating. After what seemed five hours, something very smooth came up against me. I must have jumped four feet out of the sea. After a few minutes, I realized it was a porpoise. It stayed with me until we were picked up late that afternoon. We were very lucky, for there were only two men missing, but many were hurt very badly, so we took off at full speed for a hospital in Brisbane.

Later that month, I was transferred to the Dutch freighter *Bosh Bon Tane* for the States, arriving in San Francisco in January 1944 during a snowstorm. After a survivor's leave, I was transferred to New Orleans, then to Houma, Louisiana, Naval Air Station. I served there until April when I was transferred to McAlester, Oklahoma, Naval Ammunition Depot.

In September, I was transferred to the Great Lakes Naval Depot for mustering out. I was given an honorable discharge on October 8, 1945, with five Battle Stars. I had served three years, four months, and 27 days.

DETERMINED TO SURVIVE
Charles P. "Sully" O'Sullivan

P-38 Fighter Pilot
By Howard Dukes, South Bend Tribune Staff Writer 3/6/08
Reprinted with permission.

Charles P "Sully" O'Sullivan

South Bend Captain Charles P. "Sully" O'Sullivan already had decided how to make his last stand. The Japanese had shot down his P-38 fighter plane in a part of Papua New Guinea controlled by the Japanese. Even worse, some of the natives he encountered were sympathetic to the Japanese, who controlled that part of New Guinea, says Josh Baxter of Hot Springs, Arkansas, who filmed the story of O'Sullivan's ordeal.

His survival came down to three things, O'Sullivan says. "Faith, determination and a little Irish luck," he says, laughing. O'Sullivan survived 30 days in the jungle after his plane crashed on September 20, 1943. Eventually, he stumbled on an Australian commando base behind enemy lines. The story of his survival is told in the recent documentary "*Injury Slight, Please Advise.*" The film's name comes from a portion of the message O'Sullivan sent to his unit, the 39th Fighter Squadron of the 35th Group, after he was rescued.

"I prayed a lot, and I believe in prayer," O'Sullivan, who is 92, says, in looking back on what helped him survive an ordeal that included a harrowing encounter with natives bent on killing him. (Baxter says they were probably from the Gende People of the Madang Province.) "I was very determined that I was going to make it," O'Sullivan says.

First, however, his faith and determination would be severely tested. Very little in O'Sullivan's early life had prepared him for what he would face in the jungles of New Guinea. Like many World War II veterans, O'Sullivan wasn't a professional soldier. He grew up in rural Illinois not far from Peoria, then attended Eureka College, the same school Ronald Reagan attended. "I taught in a country school for a while, but I didn't intend to make teaching a profession." O'Sullivan recalls. O'Sullivan joined the Army Air Force's cadet program on February 11, 1941 – 10 months before the Japanese attacked Pearl Harbor. He and his wife, Mareelee, were married in October.

Although rumors of war were everywhere, it was a time when Americans were focused on getting the country out of the Great Depression and not on sacrificing its young men in another European war. "The Midwest was rather isolationist, and people said 'We don't want to get in the war,'" O'Sullivan says. "I grew up on a farm, and when I applied for the flying cadets, people said, 'Charlie wants to go to war. Let him be a nut.' "That changed quite rapidly after Pearl Harbor." O'Sullivan ended up flying a P-38 Lightning in the South Pacific, where he escorted American bombers on missions to bomb enemy positions. He also engaged in aerial dogfights while trying to intercept Japanese planes that were on missions to attack Allied bases and ships.

It was dangerous work, O'Sullivan recalls. "Our squadron had a complement of 25 pilots, and we had nine shot down," O'Sullivan says. All of the pilots who were shot down were rescued, but a nearby fighter group wasn't as fortunate. "They had twelve shot down and only four came back," O'Sullivan says. He flew 178 combat missions, he says, but encountered enemy planes on only half of them. "A lot of times, the presence (of fighter planes) kept the Japanese planes away," he says. "But this time it didn't."

O'Sullivan was in a group escorting B-24s when the Japanese attacked. When his plane had engine trouble, he attempted to return to base. O'Sullivan didn't notice that a Japanese fighter plane was following him. "I was careless," O'Sullivan recalls. "I was concentrating on a single Japanese plane flying (at a lower altitude). That plane was probably a decoy, and (the other plane) sneaked up on me."

O'Sullivan eventually abandoned his plane after it crash landed. He spent four days walking through the jungle before the natives encountered him. At first they were friendly, O'Sullivan recalls. One of the men gave O'Sullivan some food. The native's friendliness changed when a hostile village elder entered the camp. Soon a power struggle erupted between the villager who helped O'Sullivan and the other man. "I thought they were arguing over weapons, but now I'm sure that they were arguing over what to do with me," O'Sullivan says.

The man who had been O'Sullivan's protector lost the argument. "The friendly (villager) kind of dropped his shoulders a little bit and basically gave up," O'Sullivan recalls. He never saw the man who had befriended and protected him again. "From then on, I knew that I was in trouble," O'Sullivan says. "First they stopped feeding me. That was a bad sign."

Then O'Sullivan noticed all of the women and children had disappeared. He knew the villages planned to kill him and he had to escape. Twice O'Sullivan tried to flee. The first attempt occurred while the village men tried to control a fire they had started in a hut where O'Sullivan was being held captive. O'Sullivan bolted from the room, but the natives caught him before he could use his gun. O'Sullivan's second escape attempt was successful. Some of the villagers surrounded O'Sullivan in a hut, and he brandished his revolver to keep them at bay. Finally, one of the men attacked O'Sullivan by grabbing his arms. O'Sullivan managed to shoot his attacker seconds before another man joined the fight.

"If (the second man) had come at me a second earlier, I wouldn't be here," O'Sullivan says.

As it turned out, the second attacker reached O'Sullivan just as the pilot moved his gun into position to fire again. "He staggered out of the hut and died, and then all hell broke loose," O'Sullivan says.

O'Sullivan escaped into the jungle during the disturbance. He hid in the brush for six hours. During that time, he could hear what was happening in the village. The villagers searched for O'Sullivan and held what he thought were funeral services for the two dead men. He could tell they were angry and knew what would happen if the villagers found him. He was prepared to fight for his life, O'Sullivan says. "I even thought about saving the last bullet for myself," he recalls. But then I thought about my upbringing and my faith. And that's not the way that I was brought up."

Looking back, O'Sullivan knows that he was afraid, and that fear nearly made him consider suicide. "It was just temptation," he says. "It's not a sin to be tempted, but if you give in, that's where sin comes along." The price of giving up would have been high. His wife, who died in December—they shared 66 years of marriage—would have been a widow. His five sons—two of whom went on to become US Air Force pilots—would not have been born.

O'Sullivan was a colonel in the Air Force when he retired in 1968. "I'm proud of my decision," he says. "It was a mental thing, and one of the things I learned is to never give up because there's always hope. "If you're still ticking, then you still have a chance."

ABOARD THE *USS BELLEAU WOOD*
Ed Phelan

Interviewed by J. O'Malley

Ed Phelan

In October of 1941 I married Loretta Arntz, definitely the best decision I ever made. A scant two months later, the Japanese bombed Pearl Harbor and I was faced with another decision: whether to be drafted or enlist. I chose the Navy and in January I left for basic training at Great Lakes Naval Training Station in Illinois. After basic, fondly known as "Boot Camp," I was assigned to a rescue boat based at Corpus Christi, Texas. Our mission was to assist in the rescue of any aviators downed in the Gulf of Mexico. Loretta was able to join me and we shared a small home. I was able to be home two nights of three. While in Texas, we welcomed our first baby.

From Corpus Christi, I was assigned to a small Aircraft Carrier, the *US.S. Belleau Wood*. The *Belleau Wood* was the third CVL, Independence Class carrier constructed on a cruiser hull. These smaller carriers were built to answer an emergency need for carriers in the Pacific.

From The Secretary of the Navy

The President of The United States takes pleasure in presenting the PRESIDENTIAL UNIT CITATION to the *USS BELLEAU WOOD* for participating in the following operations: Tarawa, Wake, Gilberts, Marshalls, Truk, Marianas, Bonins, Palau, Philippines, Ryukus (Okinawa), Formosa, Japan.

"For extraordinary heroism in action against enemy Japanese forces in the air, ashore and afloat in the Pacific War Area from September 18, 1943, to August 15, 1945. Spearheading the concentrated carrier warfare in forward areas, the BELLEAU WOOD and her air groups struck crushing blows toward annihilating Japanese fighting power; they provided air cover for our amphibious forces; they fiercely countered the enemy's aerial attacks and destroyed his planes; and they inflicted terrific losses on the Japanese in Fleet and merchant units sunk or damaged. Daring and dependable in combat, the BELLEAU WOOD with her gallant officers and men rendered loyal service in achieving the ultimate defeat of the Japanese Empire.

For the President

(Signed) James Forrestal

Secretary of the Navy

Our first assignment was to cover the landings at Baker Island, a small island southwest of Hawaii. Our fighters aided in destroying 12 Japanese planes on the ground, earning a "Job Well Done," from the Admiral. As a Bos'n Mate I got my first real action on the landing cable maintenance crew. There are probably more dangerous places than the flight deck of an aircraft carrier during flight operations, but I hope I never see them.

We proceeded to cross the International Date Line. This does not seem to be a noteworthy accomplishment unless it is your first time. We "Pollywogs" were properly initiated, an event I'll never forget, and one I would never want to repeat.

Our next assignment was to join "The Greatest Carrier Task Force Ever Assembled." In addition to our ship were the Lexington, the Yorktown, the Essex, the Independence and the Cowpens. We were to cover the retaking of Wake Island, captured by the Japanese early in the war, after a gallant stand by the Marines. To our surprise, we were never attacked, thanks to our Combat Air Patrol planes who intercepted a group of Japanese planes at a distance of 90 miles and destroyed four Bettys (bombers) and three Zekes (fighters).

Our next mission was to provide air support for the invasion of Tarawa and Makin. Our ship was assigned to the Makin effort. When Makin fell to the Marines a terse message to the bosses simply said "Makin Taken." It was here we had a close call. A Japanese torpedo plane slipped through the outer perimeter headed straight for our bow. It dropped its deadly weapon and flew over our ship masthead high. We executed a hard left turn and held our breaths as the aerial torpedo sliced a mere 10 yards away.

As the Army and Marines battled on the sands, planes from our air group blew up four munitions dumps and sank five Japanese vessels in the lagoon. Our planes also supported the ground offensive by strafing the beaches, clearing the way for our advance. This was a very ticklish operation, attacking the enemy without endangering our fighters.

In the battle for Truk, aircraft from the *Belleau Wood, Essex, Yorktown, Bunker Hill, Cowpens* and *Monterey* engaged the enemy in furious combat, destroying 204 Japanese planes, 127 of them in the air. We suffered the loss of 19 planes. This finished the Japanese air power over Truk.

As we moved on to attack the Marianas we suffered our second narrow escape. One Japanese "Betty" bomber slipped through the withering fire of our screening ships and headed directly for us.. Every ship zeroed in on the hurtling bomber, although burning, it bored on directly for our bridge. Captain Pride swung the ship sharply. The "Betty" skimmed the top of our radar array so close we could see the holes in its fuselage. The plane crashed just off our port beam with a tremendous explosion. The heat from the explosion was so intense, it burned the faces of those on deck.

In about half an hour another "Betty" got through and headed our way.. Our port batteries opened up with everything they had and blew the plane, burning into the sea. Everyone on the *Belleau Wood* owes the Marine gunners aboard our ship for their courage and expertise protecting our vessel from an enemy trying, at all cost, to destroy our ship.

On March 30, 1944, three task groups consisting of 4 carriers each lashed at Palau, sinking 31 Japanese ships and damaging 18 others. The contribution of our planes to this score was 3 enemy planes destroyed, 2 damaged, a medium freighter and a mine layer sunk and a hanger destroyed.

After obliterating the Japanese Air Forces in the Eastern Carolinas, we sailed 1200 miles with our own supplies, equipment and manpower in one of the boldest strikes of the war. After months of staying undercover, the Japanese fleet came out to engage our Task Force. Never before had our radar scopes been so filled with enemy targets. During the morning and afternoon there were 14 Japanese attacks against our fleet. Every one was intercepted by our aircraft and beaten back. By nightfall the enemy was so badly beaten, they could no longer form strike groups.

After a welcome time out in Hawaii and training in Guam we got back into the war in the Philippines and Okinawa. Our aircraft and antiaircraft gunners continued to take a toll against the withering Japanese air defenses. It was near Okinawa that a Kamikaze somehow got through intense fire and crashed into us behind the after elevator. Flames and wreckage shot outward. One of our own planes that was on the flight deck was blown on top of Gun Mount 9, forming a blanket of death. The devastation left 245 casualties including 92 deaths and 54 severely.

After repair refitting and remanning, we got back in the war at Okinawa taking part in the vast offensive. Our planes scored a number of victories against Japanese fighters, bombers and suicide planes.

Our attacks switched to the Japanese homeland. As we steamed toward the enemy homeland our fleet had to dodge mines. This ticklish operation reminded us that, "any Navy ship could be a Minesweeper…ONCE!"

In all, the *Belleau Wood* earned eleven Battle Stars and had sailed 216,682 miles, more than 10 times around the Earth. Our most memorable cruise was in 1945 when we entered Tokyo Bay to serve as an escort for the *USS Missouri* where the Japanese signed the final surrender.

Excerpts from the book "Flight Quarters" by and about the *USS. Belleau Wood.*

THE STORY OF JESSE ROKUSON

Jesse Rokuson

Written by Robert Hatch

Jesse Rokuson

I was born in Brooklyn, New York, on April 17, 1923, and enlisted in the Navy on January 4, 1941.

After receiving basic training I was assigned to the USS Meredith DD434 on March 6th, a training destroyer. This ended on July 14th, 1941 and the next day July 15th I was ordered to report for duty on the *USS Gwin DD433*, another sturdy and dependable destroyer. My rating was Seaman S2.

In November, before the war, around the 15th we left Staten Island, New York, with the first expeditionary force to England. We were to patrol from Iceland to Greenland and await for the balance of our convoy. Our ship got word that the *USS. Destroyer Reubens James* had been sunk. We were accompanying the Coast Guard ship *Alexander Hamilton*. The *Kearney* was also damaged.

We pulled into the harbor in Newfoundland to pick up another convoy. While we were there, we detected a sub on our sonar in the harbor. Knowing it was the enemy, we dropped several depth charges on it. The sub rose to the surface and exploded. Chalk one up for the *Gwin*!

The *Hamilton* was with us when we took radar direction bearings on a Greenland German base. They had been sending transmissions out to the sub. We both closed in until we had pinpointed where the base was. The Coast Guard ship sent in a landing party to capture the base while we patrolled the area giving protection. The landing was a success so we left and crossed the Atlantic, headed for England.

Off the coast of England the English and Canadian destroyers took over. We headed to Londonderry, Ireland. While there, war was declared and we immediately left, re-crossed the Atlantic and headed through the Panama Canal to San Diego, California, to be outfitted for war time. After completing our outfitting we joined the fleet consisting of, among other ships, the Mighty "E,"the famed *Enterprise*.

This Task Force "Mike," under the command of Vice-Admiral William F. Halsey, had left the Hawaiian Islands (April 12) with two carriers (*Hornet* and *Enterprise*) three heavy cruisers, one light cruiser, eight destroyers (*USS Gwin 433*) and two oilers. Their mission was to bomb Tokyo.

After dark on April, 18, aboard the *Hornet* with sixteen B-25s under the command of Col. James H. Doolittle, we joined the convoy.. The after-dark bombing was changed to daylight bombing which was 8:00 am (7:00 am Tokyo time). The take-off flight was about a five-hour flight. We were about 620 miles from Tokyo. My ship, the *USS. Gwin,* was on escort duty.

May 4, 1942, we were under Rear Adm. Fletcher's task force 17. This consisted of the carriers *Lexington* and *Yorktown* and a screen of cruisers and destroyers. We steamed into the Coral Sea looking for trouble. The planes raided the newly arrived Japanese at Tulagi. The battle of the Coral Sea opened on the morning of May 7. Our planes sent the Japanese carrier *Shoho* to the bottom. The opposing task forces finally came to grips on the morning of May 8. By noon the Coral Sea battle was over. The *Lexington* was battered. My ship and other destroyers escorted her out but *Lady Lex* was running out of time. An hour after the attack, fumes from a damaged tank of aviation gasoline ignited. A tremendous explosion shook the ship from stem to stern. In mid-afternoon a second explosion rocked the carrier and fires blazed out of control. The crew was ordered to abandon ship. One of our destroyers put five torpedoes into her to sink her so the Japanese couldn't salvage her.

About 8pm, *Lady Lex* slid under. For the first time in history, a Naval battle had been fought entirely by aircraft carriers. One month later, my ship was in the battle of Midway which was one of the most furious in all history. The battle was fought June 4-7, 1942.

All available ships were sent to defend *Midway*. The task force carriers Enterprise and Hornet along with six cruisers and nine destroyers answered the call. Task Force 16 consisted of the carrier *Yorktown* with two cruisers and five destroyers. Admiral Spruance commanding TF16 flew his flag on the *Enterprise*.

Rear Admiral Fletcher, the overall commander, flew his flag on the *Yorktown*. By the time the battle was over, Japan had been dealt the worst Naval defeat in her history. All four Japanese carriers and a heavy cruiser had been sunk. 250 planes lost, more than 2,000 men killed. We lost the carrier *Yorktown*, one destroyer, the *Hughes* and more than 300 Americans. This marked the end of Japanese dream of Naval domination of the Pacific Ocean. This also cancelled Japan's threat to Hawaii and the west coast. The next six months my ship's homeport was Nomura, New Caledonia.

On August 7, 1942 my ship, the *Gwin*, was in the landing of Guadalcanal. We shelled the Japanese positions on the island. During this time we were with the aircraft carrier *Hornet*. In the battle of Santa Cruz island Oct. 26, she was sunk and the *Enterprise* disabled. September 15 1942 while escorting a transport convoy to Guadalcanal the carrier was torpedoed and sunk by a Japanese sub.

About Nov. 1, 1942 the *Gwin, Porter Walker, Preston*, Battleships *South Dakota* and *Washington* under rear Adm. Willis Ales, engaged a strong Japanese task force. This was the first time sixteen-inch guns aboard a battleship were used.. Two of our destroyers were sunk and two damaged. The *South Dakota* was battered, the *Washington* took on the enemy single-handed and its radar-controlled guns smashed the Japanese battleship *Kirishima* into a ruined hulk.

My ship took some hits mainly in the engine room. We escorted one of the damaged destroyers out with most of her bow missing. We had to sink her and take her crew off.

My tour of duty aboard the *Gwin* ended on Dec. 22, 1943, and I was assigned to the *USS Celeno*. That tour lasted until May 16, 1943, when I was assigned to *USS Solace*, a hospital ship. I was on the *Solace* until July 31, 1943: two months, 14 days.

While on the *Solace* I went into a deep coma. When I woke up, I was in the hospital and strapped to the bed. I was shaking all over which was due to my combat fatigue. My high temperature was diagnosed as left Hydrouephrosis. In 1964, this was changed to Renal TBS after being dormant for about 21 years.

In 1943 they didn't know much about Renal TBS. It will be dormant for the rest of my life and can break out at any time. I must have check-ups once a year. They operated to try to save my left kidney, but it was not successful. A second operation was performed to take out my kidney which was successful. Later my fingernails turned black, my left lung collapsed and I was pronounced dead, but brought back to life.

I was in the US Naval Hospital in Albans, New York, for one month and 13 days—from Dec. 18, 1944 to Feb. I, 1944. On the way home, the scab on my left side broke open and was draining. I was treated with silver nitrate and sent back on duty. I was in a recovery station in New York on Feb. 1, 1944, until the 19th, a total of 19 days.

On February 19, after release, my woes continued. I had an infection on my left side, with a high temperature. The bandages were soiled so they dropped medication in my left side hole and sent me back to duty after 17 days.

I attended Midshipmen's School March 8, 1944, for five days, then back to the Naval hospital again. I was there for two months and 26 days—from June 17 until September 12. Then another try at Midshipman's school for 10 days until Sept. 22, 1944.

Then back to the hospital on September 22, 1944, until Jan. 19, 1945. This time for three months and 28 days. My side opened up, soiled bandages and high temperature. They realized I needed an operation. This operation was performed the right way as the doctor performing it allowed it to heal from the inside out. He told me that it should not have been closed up to form a scab. The crust over the healing would open and infection would set in. Performing my duties, my bandages would get dirty.

They realized I was too weak and ill to perform my duties and I was honorably discharged on Long Island, New York on Jan. 31, 1945.

I was in some of the most notable actions in World War ll and fortunately I came home safely to my family.

—READ THE FULL STORY ON OUR CD—

USS HACKLEBACK SS295
Robert Roloff, Electrician 2nd Class

Interviewed by Robert Hatch

Although we joined the action late, we made up for it by sealing, stamping and handing the Japanese their final naval blow.

I graduated from the Catholic School in St. Joseph in 1943 in the spring, enlisted in the Navy and was called up in the fall. I was sent to Great Lakes for basic training and then to a school in Detroit for training in electricity. After that I was sent to a submarine base in New London, Connecticut. From there we went to Philadelphia and then to the sub base in beautiful Key West. After two more weeks of training at Balboa, Canal Zone, we got our orders to proceed to our next assignment—the Pacific Theatre and Pearl Harbor. We had heard about the Panama Canal since our early schooling, but to go through it was an extraordinary experience.

Our submarine was the *USS Hackleback*. Although a Hackleback is a fresh water sturgeon, she saw the salt water of the Pacific and enjoyed the freedom and expanse it gave her. We set sail 25 January 1945 for Pearl Harbor where we took more training before we left on our first patrol on 6 March 1945 to Bungo Suido, south of Kyoshu.

On April 6, 1945, several Japanese destroyers and mine sweepers appeared on radar, apparently to clear the area for the main Japanese Task Force. Depth charges were dropped over a wide area with one destroyer coming within 700 yards of our position. Our Lt. Comdr. Janney ordered battle stations and silent running that lasted several hours. Soon our sub made full contact with a large task force departing the inland sea location.

Robert Roloff

The Japanese force not only consisted of the largest Japanese battleship Yamato, but many submarines and seven destroyers. We transmitted to HQ Command Submarine Pacific the location, speed and course continuously during radar tracking. We were ordered to just shadow and not attack the fleet. It was a "hands off" order. But we couldn't get within 13,000 yards anyway, because of the protecting destroyers.

We were credited with the first sighting of this task force which led to the sinking of Japan's greatest battleship--the *Yamoto*. Its main battery consisted of nine 460mm (18.1-inch) guns capable of throwing a projectile weighing 3,200 lbs. to a distance of 22 miles within 11 minutes. Its secondary batteries included eight 14-inchers, fourteen 6-inchers, eight 5-inchers, twenty 25-automatic cannons and 150 machine guns. The engines consisted of four turbines generating 150,000 horsepower that translated into a maximum speed of 27 knots with a cruising speed of 25 knots—a real floating powerhouse capable of total destruction of most any fleet!

The next day a search plane from the USS Essex sighted the Japanese armada. Our Task Force of 400 planes commenced bombing and torpedo attacks on them over a period of two hours. Eventually the great battleship, *Yamato*, capsized to port, exploded and sank, leaving behind a towering mushroom cloud. During the rest of our first patrol, we made two gun attacks on small ships but discontinued our engagements when we realized we were being lured closer to shore.

We returned to Midway and prepared for our second patrol. On May 21, we set sail. This time, our primary mission was that of a lifeguard off Saki Shimo Gunto as our carriers pounded the Japanese homeland. On June 22 we picked up a downed carrier pilot, Lt. Comdr C. P. Smith. We also engaged in some shore bombardment. We returned to Guam 12 July.

Sailing for our third patrol on August 14, we were informed that "Tokyo accepts," and two days later we headed for Midway. The long Pacific war had ended and we spent two weeks at Midway and then sailed for home.

We reached San Francisco on September 11. I was discharged at Mare Island and headed back to Michigan.Our sub was decommissioned on March 20, 1946, and sold for scrap 4 December 1968.

That ended my story and our protective war-time shell that carried us half-way around the world and back safely.

MY NAVAL SERVICE
RAY SODEN

This is the story of my naval service. I enlisted in Chicago in March 1942 at the age of 17, with the consent of my parents, and immediately went to Great Lakes Naval Training Station for my boot training, which was quite an experience. We were assigned to barracks and it was the first time in my life I had ever slept in a hammock. Through the night, many of my fellow seamen fell out of their hammocks onto the floor. But after a period of time, we all got used to it and as a consequence I now prefer to sleep in a hammock.

It was very funny because in our boot training, we had to go out into the field and march, and we had broomsticks for rifles. I'm sure the Japanese would have had a hilarious time seeing that action. After boot, I was transferred down to Orange, Texas, which was a typical old Texan town--it had mud streets and wooden sidewalks and the big pastime there was playing Dominoes.

Our ship was built there in Orange, Texas, at the Bath Ironworks. It was a Fletcher-type destroyer, a beautiful ship. I went aboard for the first time and was really awed by the construction of this ship and what it had on it: 45-inch guns, torpedo tubes. It was also equipped with about four 20mm guns. It had enough armament to protect itself and to wreck havoc on others. We went on our breakdown cruise and on to

Ray Soden

156

Guantanamo Bay. Then we went into our shakedown cruise and immediately went on to the east coast of Maine where we joined the flotilla to go over to north Africa for the invasion. It was cold, and I mean cold, as I stood on the bridge. The waves came over and I was just covered with ice. Good thing I had winter gear that covered my face. We encountered German submarine wolpacks in the vicinity but we did make it to north Africa with the loss of only two ships.

After that invasion, we were assigned to the Pacific. We went to Guadalcanal and it was quite a change in temperature and environment. We joined the 7th Fleet and started out on our trip for the invasion of various islands in the Pacific. We had quite an experience in all invasions of the islands. There were seven all together, for which our ship was given seven battle stars, and two Presidential Unit Citations. We got hit by a shore battery in Bougainville, and as a consequence had to go back to Mare Island Naval Yard in California to get our ship repaired, because the entire fan tail was blown apart. After a stayover there, we went back to duty in the Pacific and rejoined the fleet and continued on as we made our various invasions, providing shore fire back-up for the ground forces.

Then we proceeded, after about six invasions, to the last one of them and we were again hit by a kamikaze plane, again in the fan tail, right exactly where my bunk was. A Japanese pilot was blown inside, and went through my bed string. After we finally emptied out the aft-compartment, you could see his skin on my bed string, plus his kamikaze bandana. We lost about 8 men in the aft gun mount because of this incident.

Again we had to go back to New Caledonia to drydock for repairs, and while we were there Tokyo Rose, whom I shall never forget, named our ship, said we were dry-docked and were ready to get underway. It kind of disturbed us—the fact that they knew so much about where we were and who we were and what we were doing.

After being repaired, we went back to duty and proceeded to Okinawa where we had picket duty every day for many hours. The Japanese were making a last effort assault with kamikaze planes and, as a consequence, the Navy suffered its biggest loss of ships because of the kamikazes coming in droves and hitting all of the ships and destroyers. We took a big beating there.

In reflecting back, the scariest time that I had in service was when we were caught in a 200-mile-an-hour typhoon. I had the duty of topside in the bridge, I was on radar and sonar controls. During this time, we were tracking and keeping track of all the ships in the area and, all of a sudden, a ship off our starboard side just disappeared off the screen. It apparently capsized and lost all hands. There was no way we could possibly rescue anyone because of the waves and how big it was. We had to stay on course, heading into the storm.

The biggest night we had was when the announcement came that the war was over. I think every gun on Okinawa, every aircraft gun, every gun on every ship was firing in celebration. As a consequence, we shot down two of our own night fighters, but everyone was so elated that the war was over that the consequences didn't matter much. But I'm sorry for the two pilots that were flying those fighters over Okinawa.

After Okinawa, we went back to the US and went up the Potomac river and into Washington DC to receive our Presidential Unit Citation from the Secretary of the Navy. After that, I awaited my discharge. As a single guy, I had acquired enough points to receive my discharge before many married men. I was happy and elated that I was going home. I was sent back to Chicago, Illinois, where I received my discharge. I was proud of my ship, my fellow shipmates, because of the service they had rendered and how we had survived because we had good men aboard ship and survived all the battles.

The best individual who will remain in my mind for the rest of my life was the Captain I had served with who became famous as Captain Arleigh Burke who commanded our destroyer's squadron and was noted for his maneuvering in the slot in Bougainville. The slot between the islands was a mile wide, and the Japs would come down every night where we were harbored and try to attack us. He would maneuver all the ships, get the ships on their way, and go down the slot at a high speed, which made the Marines on shore real mad because they had their privies built out over the water and as we passed, creating quite a wave, we were knocking some of them out into the water. The Marines got back at us, though. They used to send us some flags that they had made out of parachutes, claiming they were Japanese flags, and we were gullible enough to buy them. They didn't put any kind of signage on them to know if they were Japanese or what they were. That was their retaliation for what we did.

I really revere my service of almost four years aboard one of the finest ships of the Navy, the *USS Charles Claxton DD571*. After the war I found out that she was de-commissioned and sent to the German Navy to join their fleet. After that, she went back to mothballs in the United States. I was hoping and praying that someday I could go back and board her just to re-visit where I had bunked and just see the ol' gal who I am really thankful that, along with all those I served with and the staffers that I had, she brought me home safe and sound.

As a follow-up to this, after discharge, I went back home and joined the Veterans of Foreign Wars (VFW). I started out as a Post Commander and worked my way through the ranks and eventually, in 1973-74, was elected Commander in Chief, or National Commander, of VFW. It's ironic that I appointed Admiral Arleigh Burke to serve on my Veterans Foreign Affairs committee and he came to the conventions with his wife and participated in all the committee meetings and it's a memory that I will carry with me for the rest of my life. He was a great man and I have much respect for him. He eventually became a full Admiral and ended up at the Naval Academy as Director, and later as Chief of Naval Operations, because he was a very intelligent individual and knew his Naval maneuvers and Naval history more than anyone I could ever think of. To this day, I feel indebted to him because he protected us, made sure our fleet was safe. Our destroyer squadron was known as the "Little Beaver" DesRon 23, which made quite a name for itself, as the outstanding destroyer squadron of the Navy in the war.

THE NAVY CAREER OF JOHN SOOS
John Soos

FORWARD from Jimmy Butt - *Below is the Naval career of John Soos as copied directly from his more comprehensive autobiography. Although deferred by his Berrien Springs draft board for being married and having a child, Soos volunteered for service as explained in his story.*

Soos entered service in May 1944 and served for 19 months. He attained the rank of Radioman 2nd Class and was awarded three battle stars for action in the Pacific, including the Okinawa campaign. He was discharged on January 3, 1946.

We drove to the draft board in Berrien Springs where I signed up for voluntary induction. With a short time, I received a letter from the President welcoming me into the service. I took my physical and was given a choice of Army, Navy or Marines. Someone had told me the Navy took their beds and food with them, so I chose the Navy. In May 1944 I was put in charge of the group of inductees and we took a bus to Detroit where we were sworn in.

From there the Navy recruits were sent to Great Lakes for six weeks of "boot camp." It was a great change from civilian life. You didn't have to like what you were told to do, but you did it anyway. There I met men and boys from all walks of life. I was then 28-years-old and older than most of the guys. I just couldn't relax, so I failed the swim test. Several others also failed, and the word was out that unless everyone passed we would have to repeat the six weeks of boot camp. A group of the better swimmers took our towels (everything had our names stenciled on) and went to take the test for us. They floundered around and finally passed, but the instructor caught on and was pretty mad. We all passed boot camp.

I got a week leave and came home. After the leave, I was assigned to Radar School in San Diego. The school was a four-week course, and there were school teachers, college graduates, and all kinds in the class. I was lucky enough to finish at the top of the class. While in San Diego we stayed at the Naval base, but we were unassigned. All we had to do is catch the bus at 8am. After school was out, we had liberty until time to catch the bus the next morning.

After we completed Radar School, we were sent to the Marine base. We had unlimited liberty, and we used it, because if we stayed at the base, we were called out to fight forest fires. From San Diego, I took a train to the amphibious base at Little Creek, Virginia. The "Amphib" training took about three months. While there, I got my first experience with a hurricane. Instead of the rain coming down, it seemed to go crossways. After the completion of the training, half the crew was sent to Baltimore to outfit the ship; the rest of us were sent to the Naval base in Philadelphia. Since there was nothing to do, I requested and received a week's furlough and went home to Michigan.

My closest friends in the crew were the storekeeper, George Joiner, from Albany; Georgia, who was older than I; Bosn's Mate, John Barber, from Kentucky; Charlie Hingel, a nice kid from New Jersey; and Arnie Bartels, the motor machinest from Iowa. I was also friendly with Bill Lynch from New York.

When I returned to Philadelphia from my leave, there was nothing for us to do, so we had unlimited liberty. Our only "must" was to report for muster at 8:00am. Hugo Post was in charge and he was very easy-going. I really liked Philadelphia. Everyone was so friendly. It was easy to understand why they call it the "City of Brotherly Love." One day Lou Vanney and I were assigned to take a case of cigarettes to the crew in Baltimore We were late in catching the train; it was pulling out when we got there. We threw the cigarettes on the train and ran like hell to board. We made it.

When work on the ship was completed, it was sent to Philadelphia to be commissioned. On January 1, 1945, the ship was commissioned LSM 420. The ship had a crew of 50 men and officers. The captain was Ensign George Foster, the exec was Ensign Harry Abel, the engineering officer was Ensign Edgar LeBouf, and the communications officer was Ensign Richard Brown. I was older than all the officers, except for the skipper. After the commissioning, we set out for our "shake down" at Little Creek, Virginia. On the way, we went down a channel at night. I had the radar watch. I picked up an object "dead ahead" at 8,000 yards (4 nautical miles) and reported it to the con. Later I reported it at 4,000 yards, than 2,000 yards, than 1,000, 500, and 250 yards...the closest I could pick up. I then heard someone on the con call out all engines back full, then all engines back flank. There is no all back flank. The con then ordered all engines stopped. The object turned out to be a sunken barge, and the ice had knocked out the warning light. When we stopped, you could have spit on the barge.

Before the incident, the skipper was not a great believer in radar, but after the incident he wanted the radar on even when we were at sea with unlimited visibility.

When the shakedown was completed, we went to Rhode Island where we picked up our cargo, a load of pontoons. From Rhode Island we went back to Little Creek and then to Key West where we had one day of liberty. From there we went to Coco Solo, Panama, where we got another day of liberty. It seemed like every other place in Coco Solo was a bar or a house of prostitution. From Coco Solo we went through the canal to the Pacific Ocean.

While going through the canal, I was in the Pilot House writing a letter when the skipper stopped in. He asked why I wasn't on watch and put me on report. I faced a "Captain's Mast" form of punishment. At the Captain's Mast, I told the skipper the radar was not in operation because we were going through the canal. Even though it would have been my watch, I didn't relieve anyone and no one relieved me, so the charges were dropped and not put in my record.

Once in the Pacific we proceeded to San Diego where we spent two weeks with lots of liberty. That was our last contact with life as we had known it. We headed for Honolulu. The trip took nine days since we could only do 18 knots. We saw Pearl Harbor and lots of ships that were badly damaged in the war in the Pacific. We spent nine days in Pearl Harbor. We learned that we could carry one case of beer for each man. There was no money for the beer, so I bought it all and divided it among the crew. After nine days in Pearl, we left for Eniwetok and then Guam. On the way we learned the war in Germany had ended. Good news.

We spent on day on Eniwetok and then headed for Guam. We were there for one day, then headed for Saipan where we spent two weeks. The fighting in that area was over, but there was still a lot of activity. The island next to Saipan was Tinian where the B-29s were based. Every morning we would watch the bombers take off on their bombing runs. They left in formation but straggled home in the afternoon. Some were shot up. By then, Saipan was used as a supply base. Our storekeeper, George Joiner, would make up a supply order and I would take a work party ashore to pick up the supplies. I instructed the work party that if the order called for two cases, take four. During one of our trips, we saw nine cases of boned turkey and four cases of boned chicken on the dock. We put it on our truck. Usually on Sunday at noon, the cooks served us a chicken dinner, but at night we had cold cuts and cheese. I told Ensign Brown that the crew would rather have turkey for the Sunday evening meal. He said we didn't have enough turkey on board. When I told him about the extra turkey, we were served turkey on Sunday nights.

There was a USO on Saipan where we could go for entertainment. On one occasion I ran into Ed Voelzke who lived across the street from Vivian in Bridgman. I knew him and his family quite well. Small world.

From Saipan we headed for the War Zone, Okinawa. On the way to Okinawa, the ocean was flat as could be when we made a u-turn and headed away from Okinawa. There had been a typhoon warning, and the crew lashed down everything that was moveable. The next morning I got up to take my watch on radar. The officers were in the Pilot House instead of the con. It dawned on me that we were caught in the typhoon. There were 36 ships in the convoy. There were three columns about 200 yards apart. The ships were bouncing like corks. The swells were about 150 feet high. One minute it seemed like we were on the top of a mountain, the next we were down in a valley. Fortunately, our cargo was pontoons, so I doubt that we would have sunk. When the storm settled down, there wasn't another ship in sight.

After the storm, we turned around, regrouped and headed for Okinawa. We unloaded the pontoons, which were being used to build piers. We then anchored in the harbor, about a mile offshore. It was like watching a movie. The planes were dive-bombing the island and the tanks had flame throwers going up and down the mountains. We had a smoke generator, and our job was to make smoke for the battleships and carriers so they couldn't be seen. One evening a "suicide plane" flew over and all the ships, including us, opened fire, trying to shoot the plane down. The plane was hit, but the firing continued until the plane hit the water. While firing at the plane as it was going down, much of the firing was across our own ships. There were casualties caused by "friendly fire." The day after we left Okinawa many suicide planes were shot down.

After 10 days at Okinawa, we headed back to Saipan. From there we went to Tulagi and the Russell Islands, below the equator near Guadalcanal. The thing I remember most about Tulagi was the large billboard on the beach that read, "KILL JAPS, KILL ALL THE YELLOW SONS OF BITCHES," signed Bull Halsey.

Our purpose in the area was to evacuate a Sea Bee base. While in Tulagi some of the crew traded two cases of beer for a jeep. When we left the island, we left the jeep on the beach. The island had lots of coconut trees, so we ate lots of coconut. Never tried the milk.

After 11 days in Tulagi and the Russell Islands, we headed for Eniwetok. We crossed the equator again and arrived in Eniwetock on August 1, 1945. After one day we headed for Guam and then Saipan, arriving there on August 5, 1945. The war with Japan was unofficially over on August 15, 1945. That night in the harbor I saw the greatest fireworks display of my life. Every ship in the harbor shot up flares, lighting up the sky. On August 23, 1945, we left Saipan and headed for Leyte in the Philippines, arriving there on August 28, 1945. The war with Japan officially ended on September 2, 1945. There was much to see in the Philippines, but we only saw the small villages. We also went to Luzon. While there, going to and from the post office, I walked down the road used during the "death march."

We loaded up some Army machinery and about 15 Army personnel and headed for Japan. Most of the Army guys had been oversees for years. I'll never forget the looks on their faces when they saw sunnyside-up eggs for the first time in years. They couldn't believe they could have more than two. We arrived in Wakiyama, Japan. Within a very short time after we hit the beach, the only personnel left on the ship was the gangway watch and the officer of the day. The rest of us went inland to a small town. While there we traded whatever we had for Japanese goods. I remember Bob Buys trading five bags of Sugar for a beautiful Japanese doll in a glass case. He was able to bring it home.

We were able to go ashore in Japan, but we could only take with us one candy bar, one package of cigarettes and one package of gum. We would trade for whatever they had, mostly silks. While in Japan, we made stops at Wakanura, the Kure Naval Base, and Nagoya. Nagoya was one of the bigger cities in Japan. I saw one very large area where the only building left standing had a huge Red Cross pained on it. The rest of the area was all rubble. One of our jobs in Nagoya was hauling Japanese ammunition out to sea and dumping it into the ocean.

One night while in Nagoya I heard a report on the radio saying that if the total points one had acquired, together with the points accumulated during normal travel home, were sufficient, one would be eligible for a discharge. The next morning I went to the skipper's cabin and told him I wanted to go home. That evening there was a message in the radio shack requesting transportation for six men to the United States. I was one of the six. The only others I remember were John Kulka and Bob Buys. We took a train from Nagoya to Yokosuka where we boarded a carrier, the USS Lexington. After being on a small ship, the carrier looked like an island. The carrier had a ship's company of about 2,500. They were also carrying about 2,500 Army personnel headed home for discharge, and 250 Navy men also going home. The Bos'n Mate in charge of the Navy personnel happened to be John Barber who had been with us at Little Creek during our training.

The trip to the States took about 14 days. We were accompanied by another carrier, the USS Intrepid. We arrived at the Naval Base at Treasure Island near San Francisco. There were a great many sailors there waiting to be sent to their respective bases to be discharged. I had not told Vivian I was coming home; I wanted to surprise her. When I saw that I would be delayed, I called her.

While in San Francisco, I shared a room with John Barber. The first night we made the rounds: restaurants, shows and bars. Since I didn't drink, I ordered whatever Barber was drinking and I only drank the coke chasers. He got really smashed. When we got back to our hotel, I put Barber to bed. During the night I heard a scratching on the wall. Barber had fallen out of bed. When it happened again, I put a chair between the bed and the wall. The next morning I went to the lobby, and when I got back, Barber was very upset. When he woke up, he was looking through the slats on the back of the chair. He thought he was in jail looking through the bars of the window. In a few days, Barber got a train home. At the base, I ran into Lou Vanney and we shared the room. It rained almost every day. Two days I went to Bay Meadows Race Track.

It was December 28, 1945, before I got a train to Great Lakes. On New Year's Eve we were on a siding outside Chicago. On January 3, 1946, I was discharged. Vivian picked me up at Great Lakes and my military career was over.

BLACKOUT: CHICAGO 1942

Compiled by Raymond M. Sreboth

Cpl.Ray Sreboth

Preface: Recently, I received a copy of the Chicago Tribune, dated Thursday, July 9, 1942. The newspaper, intact, was discovered during demolition of an old building near Coloma, Michigan, and it was given to me by the owner of the property. On examination I noted an article containing advice as what to do in the event of a Black-Out and reading it prompted the composition below. Older readers may be familiar with the term "Black-Out" and I shall not attempt to explain, since it is described in the following piece:

During the summer of 1942, I was on a break after my first year at what was then Western Michigan College, Kalamazoo, which I had entered the year before after graduation from nearby Hartford High School. The only course in which I had earned an A that first year was Drafting, 101, and it served me well in securing a summer job. Soon after I finished high school in May of 1941, my parents moved from a farm in Hartford to Chicago so I went there to seek work; jobs were available and wages better than in Kalamazoo and I needed money for college education. The huge US Steel plant was located in Chicago on the shores of Lake Michigan, 79th St. the north boundary and the Calumet River at 92nd St., the south and they were hiring. On entering the huge hall of the Employment Office near the 89th St. Gate, I saw several hundred men and women of all shapes, sizes and colors, applying for work in the mill. Soon, it was apparent that many were from the Deep South or perhaps from South of the Border, others conversing in European languages, recent immigrants not familiar with English. Some were illiterate and incapable of filling out application forms. Utilizing lettering skills perfected in Mr. Fred Huff's class, I carefully filled out the form and gave it to the clerk behind the glass partition who in turn delivered to another fellow seated in one of several cubicles in the office. In a short time, another clerk came into the large waiting room paging me and shouting my funny sounding name amidst the contingent of strangers assembled in that smoke filled area. When I stood to be recognized, he approached me and while still in motion, asked: Where did you learn to letter like this? On hearing my response he said, We have job for you!

He explained that I would work in the machine shop of the Maintenance Department but first, I had to purchase steel toed safety shoes to wear on the job. Wearing such safety shoes was required and I bought them in the plant and paid $6.95 for them, an expenditure I could ill afford. My assignment was to be in the machine shop, the largest of several shops in the Department and my work hours, from 3 to 11 P.M. Clustered near that shop were several smaller shops where skilled workers, journeymen, handymen and laborers plying various trades, worked to keep the mill operative, including plumbing, electrical, carpentry, paint shop and a huge foundry as well.

The South Works was one of the largest steel mills in the US, perhaps second only to the Gary, Indiana, plant owned by the same company. In some other business my position might have been considered White Collar, since among all those men and women, who did the hands on dirty work, I was a record keeper with clip board, paper and a pencil, my tools. The data I collected went to time keeping and efficiency experts. In reality, no job in that plant could be described as White Collar. Smoke, fumes, sparks from welding torches, soot and cinders from steam locomotives moving product to rail yards, provided particulates to pollute the air. In a matter of minutes after entering the facility there wasn't anything that could be termed clean, let alone, white.

US Steel South Works

The job was a snap; I was required to visit each man's work station, record his badge number on a paper form, indicate the number of the part on which he was working at the start and the end of the shift. One of the old timers termed my job, easy money, which was also his nick name; any time I inquired as to his work he would respond with that expression! Most of the workers in that shop were Lifers; one old fellow had operated the same massive floor drill press for some 30 years on that same shift! All of this was interesting to me for in college I was preparing to be a teacher of Industrial Arts. On advice from my father, I joined the CIO Steelworker's Union on a temporary basis in order to avoid any hassles with Union members. The wages were eighty five cents per hour and compared to the twenty five cents per hour earned as a part time waiter in Kalamazoo, thus I considered myself very fortunate.

All the foregoing is to set the stage for describing my part in a significant War Time event in Chicago while still a civilian. (I joined the Army in October, 1942, while enrolled for my Sophomore year at Western Michigan College.) In the summer of 1942, National Civil Defense authorities ordered a Black-Out Drill for the Metropolitan area. That drill would be an attempt to turn out all the lights in the City, including shutting down operations in the Mill! There was fear of Axis Bombers, based in Russia, arriving from the north over Lake Michigan, damaging the city especially interrupting production of steel in the Arsenal of Democracy; the glowing blast and open hearth furnaces on the Lake front would be like a beacon to aid in pin-point bombing! The drill was a once in a lifetime occurrence; I do not recall such an attempt taking place before, or after, what I experienced.

Well in advance of the date of the Black-Out, I was instructed as to my duty during the drill; I was to leave the machine shop, proceed to and through the nearby foundry to the carpenter, electrical and plumbing shops to turn out any lights that might have been left on by the skilled tradesman when they departed to make repairs in some other part of the vast complex. The sirens sounded at about 10 P.M. that hot summer night and I began my rounds when the lights were still generally on. Having taken only a few paces into the nearby fume filled foundry, the lights went out! On either side of the narrow path on which I paused, were huge molds on the sand covered floor, being filled from huge caldrons of molten ore. The containers of glowing white hot, molten, metal were slung from chains connected to overhead cranes and they were directly in my path! On either side of the aisle were newly filled molds, or those in the slow process of cooling and solidifying and these lay before me for a hundred yards. At that moment I do not recall if Robert Frost's poem, "The Road Not Taken," came to my mind, but I decided not to take the road I was on! When the place went dark, except for the light given off by the hot metal, I simply sat down on the hot sand and awaited the All-Clear signal in the midst what I imagined Dante had in mind when he wrote _The Inferno_.

All this took place a long time ago, and I do not recall if the Black-Out was considered a success or not; however, if it was faulty because of my failure to turn out some lights at the US Steel plant in Chicago, no one ever informed me of the fact! After all, someone once wrote, Discretion is the better part of valor, and absent judgment on my part resulting in a headlong fall into a mold full of hot metal on the floor, perhaps the management might have found the remains of my steel toed safety shoes in the foundry. Perhaps such artifacts might have been enough to serve as the basis for a funeral at St. George's (Slovenian) Roman Catholic Church on the real East Side at 95th and Ewing Avenue, and interment at St Mary's Cemetery in Evergreen Park, Illinois, where large numbers of deceased members of that Parish, founded by immigrants from Slovenia and Croatia, circa, 1900, are buried. Of course I would hope that the long journey to the cemetery would have been preceded by a good send off by one of the Franciscan Missionary Fathers that staffed the Parish.

—READ MORE OF RAY SREBOTH'S STORIES ON OUR CD—

ANTI TANK CREWMAN
PFC Frank Traficanto
331st Regiment, 83rd Division

Frank Joseph Traficanto was born to Rocco and Dora Traficanto on July 9, 1924 in Scammon, Kansas. His family relocated to Chicago, Illinois in 1941. Frank was seventeen years old when WWII was declared and he remembered thinking that he hoped that the war would be over before he was called to serve. At eighteen he registered for the draft and after graduating from high school worked as a machinist at a war defense plant that made 30-caliber bullets and parts for guns. Frank was drafted into the United States Army on July 10, 1943 at the age of nineteen. He was sent to Camp Walters, Texas, which was an infantry replacement training camp.

Frank Traficanto and wife

165

While at Camp Walters, his mother decided she would play cupid and asked him to write to a young girl named Ruby Jackson. Frank had met Ruby previously at his church youth group. Their correspondence started out very friendly. He would tell her about his army life and she would tell him what was happening at church. During his five-day leave at home before leaving for overseas duty, he spent time with his family and Ruby. Frank knew that he had met his life's companion. Ruby was the only girl he ever dated and he knew that when the war was over, they would be married.

After his leave, Frank reported to Fort Mead, Maryland. From Fort Mead he went to Camp Shanks, New York then an eight-day trip to England on the ship, Ille de France. He was stationed in England from January 1944 until he crossed the channel into France two weeks after D-day. He served as an anti tank crewman in the Normandy Campaign in Northern France and the Rhineland Campaign.

Frank Traficanto receives one of nine service medals presented to him by Congressman Fred Upton during the Veterans Day ceremony on Wednesday. (Lois Jordan photo)

Frank was wounded in Belgium on December 29, 1944, while riding in a weapons carrier pulling an anti-tank gun. The carrier went out of control and broke both of his leg bones between his ankle and knee. He was the only man injured and for him the war was over. He found out later that they were on their way to take part in the Battle of the Bulge. He was evacuated to a field hospital then back to a hospital in England. He was then flown to the United States to a military hospital in Chicago. Using crutches, he was able to go home several times to visit his family. He was then transferred to Percy Jones Rehabilitation Center (now Fort Custer) in Battle Creek, Michigan and was able to come home most weekends. Frank and Ruby decided not to wait until the war was over and married on June 30, 1945. They became the parents of two daughters and were married for sixty-four years until her death in 2009.

After his discharge from the Army on October 17, 1945, he went on with his life that had been put on hold; he never received the medals he had earned. Frank became a minister and served at churches in Illinois and Michigan until his retirement in July 1987.

In November 2009, at a Veterans Day observance in Coloma, Michigan, he was presented with nine service medals by Congressman Fred Upton, which included the Bronze Star and the Purple Heart.

LETTERS & MEMORIES OF WW II
Russell Wainright

Written by Terry Wainright

I am writing this to honor my Dad, Pfc. Russell M. Wainright and his friend and WWII foxhole companion, Cpl. Herman H. Ernst. This is dedicated to all the members of Company C of the 246th Combat Engineer Battalion. It is also dedicated to my mother, Dora, who helped win the war on the Home Front.

Russell died at the age of 90, just before Christmas in 2004. I knew that he had been in the Army in WWII. And while he told me a few stories about his experience, in general he just didn't want to talk about it. After he was gone, I didn't want his story to die with him, so I went on a mission to find out more. In my Dad's effects, I found many letters written by him during WWII

Russell Wainright and wife

to my mother, Dora. I found Battalion and Regimental histories that he had saved. I also found a Christmas letter, addressed to him, from a Herman Ernst.

I wrote Mr. Ernst a letter telling him of my Dad's death. This started five years of correspondence between Mr. Ernst and me, which lasted until his death at the age of 85 in November 2009. I will forever be grateful to Mr. Ernst. Through him, I learned about my Dad and his experiences in WWII. Because of him, I became closer to my Dad. While Herman and I never met face to face, we became friends. Herman sent me other letters and remembrances that he had written. Prior to his death, Herman asked me to share the information that he had given me. I promised Herman that I would write down his story - to honor him, my Dad and the men of the 246th.

Herman Ernst wrote, "I take a long time [to write these letters], because my old memory is faulty. I am 83. Sometimes in the early morning, I see those places and the men who never age. Many things, I can't put on paper, because women might read them.

"One of my friends from the 1st Platoon [about 30-35 men] came from Oregon, to my home in Ludington Michigan. (He needed to talk about the war and he had questions that he had been trying to answer for 60 years.) We talked for 2 hours. Most of the time, he laughed like mad. He died soon after our meeting." [H.E.]

Russell mostly kept his memories inside. When I lived at home, I often heard my Dad yelling out in his sleep, having dreams of those times. My Mother told me that he would awake from those nightmares in a cold sweat, swinging his fists, and still fighting for his life.

My Dad was a PFC (Private First Class) in the 246th Combat Engineer Battalion, Company

C, 3rd Platoon, 1st squad. He was Assistant Squad Leader under Squad Leader, Corporal Herman H. Ernst. Dad earned a Purple Heart for wounds during the Battle for Normandy. Herman got his Purple Heart during the Battle of the Bulge.

The two of them were in almost continuous action, from the Normandy landing to the Elbe River in Germany, when their unit linked with the Russians. The 246th earned a Presidential Unit Citation for their "extraordinary heroism" during the battle to cross the Roer River at Julich. Dad earned five Bronze Campaign Stars for his action in all five major campaigns of Western Europe: Normandy, Northern France, Central Europe, Rhineland, and Ardennes. In addition to those same medals, Herman Ernst earned the Bronze Star, with a V for Valor.

My Grandmother once told me a story: One evening in late 1941, a strange thing happened. In her neighborhood, in East Lansing, Michigan, people were coming out of their houses to look at the evening sky. It was a spectacular sunset. It was amazingly beautiful, but at the same time terrible and horrifying. Grandma said that the entire evening sky was a bright, blood red. She said that the sky looked like it was melting, dripping blood - dripping blood on the Earth. No one else had ever seen anything like it. Grandma had grown up in Germany, in an area where invading armies came frequently. She remembered her childhood and the many times her family had to hide in caves, waiting for the soldiers to leave. Sometimes, during those times, she had seen skies like that. The results were always the same. It was a sign from God that there was to be a terrible, bloody war, which would cover the ground with blood.

Not long after this event, America was at war. Eventually, my Grandma would see all four of her sons and one son-in-law go off to help fight this terrible war. My grandparents were both German immigrants. This made it even more heartbreaking. They still had family living in Germany. Some of Dora's cousins would die during the war, fighting for their homeland, Germany. After the war, my grandparents would send money for Care packages for family members struggling to survive in war devastated Germany.

During WWII, it was customary in America for a family to put a large blue star in the front window of their home whenever a spouse or child was in the military. If the person died in service, the star was changed to gold. Grandma would eventually have 5 blue stars in her window. Fortunately, all 5 came home safely; their stars remained blue. One of those blue stars was for my Dad, Russell Wainright.

Dad was a tall, handsome, muscular, farm boy at 5'10" and a solid 180 pounds. He grew up working hard, plowing fields, walking behind horse drawn plows. He was quiet and shy, more at home outside and in the fields, preferring animals to people. Even though he was quiet, he had a wonderful (but dry) sense of humor. His middle initial was "M". When asked what the "M" stood for, he would always answer with a straight face and a twinkle in his eye, "Mud."

He graduated from Eastern High School in Lansing, Michigan in 1932. In the summer of 1933, Russell and his best friend decided to go to the Chicago World's Fair. The two hitchhiked the 200 plus miles to Chicago. Russell spent one day at the fair, then turned around and hitchhiked home, leaving his friend there. Russ said that it was too crowded, too many people.

A few years later, Russ met Dora. Dora's out-going personality finally overcame Russell's shyness and they had their first date on March 27, 1937. Whenever Russell came to call, Dora's father would entertain the family by loudly announcing, "Hey, Dora! Your butter and eggs man is here to see you." My Mom and Dad were married on Columbus Day in October of 1940.

On December 7, 1941, Russell and my mom, Dora, were spending a quiet Sunday afternoon at home. My Mom's 17 year old brother, Ralph, was spending the afternoon visiting with them. The three of them were sitting at the table, listening to the radio and playing the popular board game, *Monopoly*. Suddenly, the radio program ended and an announcer came on the air. The US naval base at Pearl Harbor had been attacked by the Japanese.

Most Americans had never heard of Pearl Harbor, but they knew that US soldiers and sailors had been attacked - ships had been sunk and Americans had died. That Sunday, war had entered their living room. It was no longer peaceful and quiet. The game was over. They knew that their lives would be forever changed. America was at war, and Americans would be fighting and dying all over the world for the next three and a half years.

My Dad was drafted and inducted into the Army on April 15, 1943, at Ft. Custer in Battle Creek, Michigan and entered into active duty on April 22. At the time he entered the Army, he was already 28 years old and had been married for 2 ½ years. Herman Ernst, at the age of 19, was already married, with two children. Herman and Russell were both sent to Ft. Lewis, Washington for basic training and assigned to the 246th Combat Engineer Battalion.

The 246th was part of the 1104 Engineer Group of the 4th Corps. The 246th had 600 enlisted men and 34 officers. The senior officers and NCOs (sergeants) came from the 32nd Engineer Construction Regiment, which had built the Alcan Highway in Alaska and Canada. The junior officers were recent ROTC graduates. The enlisted men were mainly from Michigan.

Herman wrote, "We were at Ft. Lewis one year - we were well trained. A lot of that time, we were in the wilderness of Oregon. When we started back to the Fort, it was December and the snow in Oregon was 3 feet. We froze!

"The Chief, Clyde Matthews, was a Pima Indian from Arizona. The Pimas, a clan of the Apache Nation, were a tough solitary tribe who wanted to be left alone. But in 1943, Clyde was drafted and ended up in the 3rd Platoon, 246th Combat Engineers. During training, we shared a tent, becoming close friends. In Oregon, he would catch rattlesnakes by the tail and snap their heads off. He did not like the Army, so when they sent him home for a 13-day leave, he stayed for a month." [H.E.]

After 10 months of training, everyone knew that the 246th would soon be going overseas, but details were kept secret from the soldiers. In letters sent home, even speculation about when or where they were going was now forbidden. So when the 246th left Ft. Lewis, family and friends might not learn for weeks or months that their loved one was overseas, possibly never to be seen again. There was no opportunity for farewells - no chance to say goodbye.

On January 2, 1944, a cold, rainy Sunday, the 246th boarded a troop train in Ft. Lewis and headed east. During the long trip, men were not allowed to even leave the train, except for occasional stops for group calisthenics. All communication with the outside world was strictly forbidden: no mailing of letters, no phone calls.

After leaving the Chicago area, the countryside started to look familiar. They were back in Michigan! They were home! The train started going through familiar towns and villages. Many men wrote short letters on penny postcards addressed to their loved ones, telling them that they were going overseas. The men would tie the postcard to a Washington apple and throw it out the window as the train slowly passed through the Michigan villages. They hoped people would find the apples and mail the cards for them.

When the train went through Battle Creek, it was just too much for some of the men. As the train slowed down, passing through town, a number of men jumped from the train and went AWOL. When they were discovered as missing, the MPs knew where to look for them. They were all at home with their families. The MPs rounded them up and took them under guard, to the staging area in Massachusetts, to join their fellow soldiers for the trip overseas.

After six days on the train, they reached Camp Miles Standish, near Boston. Ten days later the 246th was on a former fruit company freighter, now a troop transport called the "Explorer". The "Explorer" sailed the evening of January 19, 1944. It had a Merchant Marine crew of 200 and carried 2,000 troops. The "Explorer" joined a convoy of about 200 transports and supply ships, guarded by a Navy escort of 2 cruisers, 2 aircraft carriers and many destroyers. There were ships as far as the eye could see. The "Explorer" was relatively fast and could run at 22 knots when fully loaded. It had a five inch naval gun, 2 three inch anti-aircraft guns, and several 50 caliber machine guns, all manned by Navy crews. However, Russell and Herman were also assigned to a gun crew.

In England, the 246th got in shape for the fighting to come by taking 25 mile hikes with full field packs. They also learned how to build bridges, clear mine fields, and run all manner of heavy construction equipment. Herman wrote, "We spent four months in England before D-Day. It was pretty good duty, except when you had guard duty. The Ack-ack [slang for anti-aircraft fire] during the air raids fell down on your helmet. You had to remain on your post, because that hot metal can set fires."

Normandy

Once the 246th Combat Engineer Battalion was in France, their mission was to provide engineer support for infantry and armored units, and to fight as infantry, if needed, as a combat unit. The 246th would go on to fight and support other units through campaigns in Normandy, Northern France, Belgium, Holland and Germany.

On June 9, the 246th was trucked to the port of Southampton. During the night of June 9th, the A and B Companies of the 246th crossed the English Channel on the transport "John H. Richardson". They landed on Omaha Beach early in the morning on June 10th (D-Day +4). The 246th were assigned to the XIX Corps whose code name was Tomahawk. The 246th was given the code name "Anvil" and became part of the 1104 Engineer Combat Group assigned to First Army under General Omar Bradley.

The special detachment of 14 engineers rejoined the Battalion. June 10, the following day, the 246th went into action near Carentan. When they reached Carentan, it was still on fire. They were immediately assigned to support the 29th Infantry (who was also a member of the XIX Corps) on the road to St. Lo.

Herman wrote, "As for D-Day, the first members of the 246th that went in were the dozer crews and demolition men. The rest of us landed with dry feet! The beach was full of LSTs and

LSIs ['Landing ships, tanks' and 'Landing ships, infantry'], litter of all kind. [The Allies] lost 6,000 men, the first 6 hours. The hospitals were huge tents, with medical people doing 24 hour stints. LSTs were hauling wounded back to England. Our Air Force controlled the air totally. We have a large cemetery there. Keep writing Terry, it builds my spirits." [H.E.]

From Herman - "It was different when I was a private, happy and content to obey orders. After we hit France, the Captain cornered me and said, 'You're a good soldier, but it's time to get off your ass and take responsibility.' After that, I had the first squad: 10 men, 2 machine guns, 2 bazookas, and a lieutenant who was scared stiff of explosives."

Herman wrote, "Normandy was a huge garbage dump of LSTs, LSIs, floating bodies, and all manner of waste. We lived through it. I don't know how. We kept going. With the breakout, the Germans lost one million men in dead, wounded, or captured. Our Air Force caught the Germans in a gap. And you could walk for 5 miles on smashed and burned tanks and trucks. For the Germans it was a huge tactical error. For us it was a stunning, decisive victory. At one time, we had 4,000 tanks driving ahead of us, the 2nd Armored Division, known as 'Hell on Wheels'. I wish I could forget this, but no dice."

Shortly after landing on Normandy, Company C produced their first enemy casualty. Riding his motorcycle down a lonely country lane, the company messenger was delivering a message to a forward Command Post, when a German sniper fired at him. He stopped his bike, located the sniper, and shot him from his tree.

Herman wrote, "[Your Dad and I] were together 3 years. Eleven months in combat. We were in those muddy holes in Normandy, with German...

—THIS IS JUST THE BEGINNING. READ THE REST OF WAINWRIGHT'S STORY ON OUR CD—

IT DEFINES HIM: THE MEDAL OF HONOR
Hershel "Woody" Williams

WWII Marine, Flamethrower/Demolition Specialist

Iwo Jima Medal of Honor Recipient - Feb 23, 1945

NOTE: The following story was the result of a conversation with "Woody" at the 2011 Medal of Honor Convention in Louisville. We were having lunch and I asked Woody how he became a flame thrower. After he related his story, I asked him if he'd written this story down. He looked at me and said, "you sound like my daughter and the answer is no." "Will you?" I asked him, and the following is the result. —Don Alsbro

With no military background or knowledge of what war really was, I entered the Marine Corps in 1943 for one purpose, to help keep an enemy from taking over America and my freedom. I knew nothing about war. I had no idea what I would be doing or where I would go.

Every Marine is first trained to be a Rifleman. I was no different. When I graduated from "Boot" camp in San Diego in 1943 that is what I was. When I shipped overseas, about all I knew was that I was going to try to capture islands that contained an enemy. I had never seen a Japanese.

Hershel Williams

When I arrived on the island of Guadalcanal, I was assigned as a Browning Automatic Rifle and made a part of a fire team of three Marines: a Team Leader, a Rifleman and a Browning Automatic Rifleman. I was assigned to replace the Browning Automatic Rifleman who was killed on Guam.

The flamethrower was a new weapon that came into play in late 1943. It was to be mainly used to shoot flame down into caves since the enemy used the caves as their hiding place and from which to surprise and attack their enemy. I was "volunteered" or selected to be trained on how to use the Flamethrower and how to use demolition, TNT and a putty like substance called C-2 to blow up things like pillboxes and to close or seal caves.

The flamethrower when full of fuel weighed 70 pounds. We had to learn how to balance it on our back, how to crawl with it, run with it and how to fire it effectively. The first fuel used in it was a jello like substance and we called it phosphorus jell. It would stick to what it hit and continue to burn. It was impossible to brush off and attempting to brush it off only spread it more. The disadvantage was that it was a single stream, like water out of a water hose and most of it was wasted just trying to get on target. The Sergeant in charge thought there was a better way and we started experimenting with gasoline and various other liquids, like diesel, motor oil, and kerosene. The goal was to get something that burned extremely hot, that would cover a larger area even if it was necessary to get closer to the target. The Sergeant finally selected a diesel fuel and high octane air plane gasoline.

The jell like fuel required the flamethrower operator to fire the fuel into the air to reach the target. The liquid required the operator to fire the fuel low to the ground in short 2 or 3 second bursts and roll the flame into the cave or on the target. It also required the operator to get a lot closer to the target, usually no more than 20 to 30 yards, depending on the terrain or ground cover. Once the weapon is fired, it gives off a black smoke because the fuel is oil based and required the operator to immediately change his position since the smoke could be seen from a distance and gave the position away ~ making it an appropriate target for mortars and artillery. Training on using the flamethrower was intense to the point that the operator could function without a lot of thinking and could control his fear.

One of the other duties of the operator or the demolition specialist or someone elected by the operator, was to use what we called "pole" charges to seal a cave or destroy a pillbox or other structures assuring that those person in the target would not be able to attack again. The "pole" charges were an 8 to 10 foot piece of wood, such as a 2x2 with a flat piece of board attached to one end. Explosives were fastened to the board which was placed in the cave or inside the pillboxes assuring the enemy was no longer able to resume fighting.

One of the many concerns of the operator and those doing the supervision was could a bullet penetrate the fuel tanks and cause an explosion? Many tests were accomplished to rule that possibility out. Even if bullets hit the tanks they would not cause an explosion. The danger from the fuel in the tanks was that the reinforced hose carrying the fuel from the tanks to the gun would be damaged or broken and the fuel would somehow ignite. While I had bullets bounce off the flamethrower I was using, I was fortunate that they bounced upward and did not cause any injury. To my knowledge a flamethrower being carried by a Marine never caught on fire or exploded.

A flamethrower, if fired continuously would last about 72 seconds. Using it in 3 or 3 second bursts made it a more useful weapon. Once the fuel is expelled, the operator unbuckles it and retrieves one that is ready to operate. Additional ones ready to operate are located nearby as part of the weapons supply. When conditions prevail, those used are recharged and they can be used over and over. The operators of the flamethrower are still rifleman and when they are not using the flamethrower they perform their regular duty as a rifleman. Operators did not carry the flamethrower unless there was a need for it.

During the taking of Guam back from the enemy, although our unit had the flamethrower weapons with us, there was not an opportunity to use it. The island was mostly jungle and it consisted of a lot of coral rock which made the digging of caves and the building of pillboxes very difficult. The enemy used trees and concealment in the jungle and the flamethrower was not a suitable weapon. I personally never had the opportunity to employ one during that campaign.

When we landed at Iwo Jima, the enemy had many pillboxes and something like 19 miles of tunnel under ground and many caves and holes in the ground. No jungle. At the time we landed, the Gunny and I had 6 operators. We assigned an operator and a demolition Marine to the each Company, A, B, and C. The pillboxes were numerous and those Marines were in constant use. In 3 days, they had become causalties and I was the only one available to the Commander of "C" Company. His Company had encountered a large number of pillboxes and had suffered many casualties and he needed an operator to burn them out and blow them up. I felt it was part of my duty, so I volunteered to use the training I had received to attempt to eliminate some of the pill boxes holding us up and killing so many Marines.

The Citation I received with the Medal of Honor awarded me for the action of February 23, 1945 explains in much better detail the action of that day as written by my fellow Marines than I am able to. I am honored that my Company Commander and Marines in "C" Company believed that I was worthy of receiving such a medal.

In August 1945 while I was stationed on the island of Guam as part of the 3rd Marine Division, we were learning how to respond to street and house fighting. The rumor was we were going to Tokyo. Early in September I was called to the office of the First Sergeant and told "I was being sent back to the States to receive a Medal: The Congressional Medal of Honor." I had never heard of the Medal and had no idea why all this was happening, yet happy to get home after 2 years overseas.

On Oct 5, 1945 I, along with 12 other Marines and Sailors were assembled on the White House lawn. There were 11 Marines and 2 Navy Corpsman. As one who never dreamed of seeing a President, I was called to stand before President Harry Truman and he placed around my neck the Medal of Honor. He said to me as he said to others, "I would rather have this Medal than to be President" My fright at that moment is beyond description. I had no idea the impact that moment would have on my life.

The next day the Marines were ordered to report to Headquarters of the Marine Corps to appear before the Commandant of the Marine Corps. Each of us individually visited his office. Among his words he said to me, was "that Medal does not belong to you, it belongs to all those Marines who never got to come home."

Because of those words and the fact that two Marines gave their lives on February 23, 1945 protecting mine, I have always considered myself as being the "Caretaker of the Medal." I wear it in their honor, and for all Marines who never got to come home. As one of the Medal of Honor recipients said several years ago," it is easier to earn the Medal than to wear it. " Most recipients will quickly say they also wear the Medal for those who made the supreme sacrifice.

In 1985 I was again honored when I was selected by my fellow Recipients to be the Chaplain of the Medal of Honor Society of the United States, At that time there were some 250 of us living. At the time of this writing (Nov, 2011) there are only 85 living, representing WWII, Korea, Vietnam and Afghanistan. I am now Chaplain Emeritus of the Medal of Honor Society. The current Chaplain is a veteran who earned his medal in Vietnam. Time marches on!

The Medal of Honor

The following story on Hershel Williams appeared in the Sunday, West Virginia Gazette, May 27, 2012. The story is written by Sandy Wells and is being used with her permission.

ONA, W.Va. -- It defines him: The Medal of Honor.

The moment President Truman placed that ribbon around his neck, his life, his entire identity, dramatically and irrevocably changed.

He wasn't just Hershel "Woody" Williams anymore. He had new purpose, a new role, an obligation to promote and protect the real meaning behind the prestigious tribute paid to him.

He views the coveted medal as a memorial symbol. He wears it in remembrance of all the soldiers who did not come home -- specifically the two Marines who died saving his life.

The feat that earned him the country's highest citation for valor occurred on Iwo Jima, just hours after AP photographer Joe Rosenthal snapped the iconic picture of the American flag rising on Mount Suribachi.

Hershel Williams

Once rejected by the Marines because he was too short, the plucky 21-year-old farm boy from Fairmont strapped a 70-pound flamethrower on his back and slithered repeatedly across an open field through fierce gunfire to take out seven concrete bunkers shielding Japanese soldiers with machine guns.

Just doing his job, he said.

He spent the rest of his life working in some way as an ambassador for veterans. Sharp and energetic at 88, he still flits from one engagement to another, giving speeches and attending significant military events.

During an emotional and detailed interview, West Virginia's only living Medal of Honor recipient shares his story as a special feature for Memorial Day.

"I was born and raised in a little town called Quiet Dell, just a wide place in the road, right out of Fairmont.

"My dad started a dairy farm when I was about 4. There were 11 in the family. I was the last. Only five of us survived because most were born in the teens and the 1918 flu got them.

"We ended up with about 35 cows, and they all had to be milked twice a day the old-fashioned way. We delivered the milk to town in bottles. When we weren't in school, we kids would go with the milk truck, a Model A Ford.

"My mother was a widow. I was 9 when my father died of a heart condition. My older brother took over the role of dad.

"I started school in a one-room schoolhouse about a mile and a half from the house. When the Work Progress Administration came into play, they built another school with two rooms, one for grades 1 to 4 and the other for grades 5 to 8.

"I rode the milk truck to town to go to high school. I went to East Fairmont one year. It got too difficult. We began losing our customers, so the truck wasn't going as often, and I had no way to get there.

"We very seldom saw a person in uniform. We had two young fellows who didn't like to farm, so they went in the Marine Corps. When they would come home in their Marine dress blues, we kids would gather around them like a magnet. I decided if I ever did go in the military, I wanted to look like one of those guys.

"When the war happened, I was in the Civilian Conservation Corps out in Montana. I had a brother who joined the CCC to make some money. They paid $20 a month.

"We didn't have any money. On Saturday, whenever we couldn't work on the farm, we could go to town. They would give you a dime. The movie was a nickel. An ice cream cone was a nickel. A hot dog was a nickel. So you could go to the movie and have a hot dog or an ice cream cone, but you couldn't do all three.

"My brother would come home on weekends with dollar bills. I seldom saw a dollar bill. I thought I would join the CCC and go where he went, to Pickens up near Elkins. They sent me to Morgantown, then moved that whole group to Montana.

"Our job was to cut pine trees and make them into pine posts they would use to build fences around government property.

"One day, they called us out in formation and announced that America had been bombed. None of us had ever heard of Pearl Harbor. I didn't even know a South Pacific existed.

"They said we could go directly into the Army, because the Army supervised the CCC units. Or they would discharge you for the purpose of going home and going into the military. I told them I wanted to go in the Marine Corps.

"I was still only 17. My mother wouldn't sign the paper authorizing me to go in before my 18th birthday. She said she needed me on the farm. I turned 18 in October. In November of '42, I went to go into the Marine Corps. I handed my paper to the Marine. He just looked at me and shook his head. He said I was too short. The Marine Corps had a requirement of 5-8.

"In early 1943, they removed the height limitation. And they got back to me.

"I was driving a taxi from 6 in the evening until 6 in the morning, waiting on my notice to report to the Marine Corps. Ruby worked in town. Sometimes she had to work over and take a taxi home because the buses had quit running. I enticed her to always call me. We got engaged.

"She had this ring she bought at Murphy's 10-cent store. It had a ruby in it not as big as a pea. A red piece of glass is what it was. She said she wanted me to wear the ring and think of her every time I looked at it. It would turn my finger green, but I wore it all the time I was in the Marine Corps.

"Everybody east of the Mississippi went to Parris Island, S.C., for boot camp. But so many people wanted to get into the war that they didn't have enough drill instructors or housing, so they formed troop trains. They would come through every state and pick up people. They picked up six of us in Charleston and sent us to San Diego. The other Marines called us 'Hollywood Marines.'

"The flamethrower was new to the Marine Corps. When I arrived at Guadalcanal in December 1943, that was first time I had seen a flamethrower. We had just received a shipment of them.

"They said I had been selected to be trained as a flamethrower operator. They also trained us to be demolition people so we could be interchangeable. If we needed to blow up something, we had that ability. If we needed to burn up something, we had that ability.

"The flamethrower had two metal fuel tanks and a compressed air tank that would force the fuel out. The flamethrower weighed 70 pounds and would hold 4 1/2 gallons of fuel.

"They told us we were going to take Guam back. The Japanese had taken it from us in 1942. It was a rough campaign in that it was practically all jungle. The Japanese would hide in that thickness to where you couldn't find them.

"We shipped out for Iwo Jima as a Reserve Division. They told us we probably wouldn't get off the ship. They told us we would be gone about five days. The island was only about 2 1/2 half miles wide and 5 miles long. Intelligence couldn't say it was going to take 36 days to take that tiny island.

"They had no way of telling us that there were 21,000 Japanese on that island or that they had 19 miles of tunnels hollowed out. Frogmen had cleared the beach area. Beyond the beach, we had no idea what was there.

"They decided they were going to need us. We got into a boat to go ashore. We circled all day because the guys on shore hadn't gotten enough territory for us to come in behind them.

"I'd never been seasick until riding those boats all day. Waves were running 12 to 15 feet, so we were constantly bobbing. Everybody got sick. I think I got sick not from rough riding but because someone got sick on me. It was terrible.

"We got back on the ship that night. The next morning, we did get ashore. We had to cross the first airfield to advance. The airfield had no protection. We lost a bunch of Marines.

"Anybody who says he's not scared when somebody is shooting at him is crazy. You have to overcome that fear. If the fear gets the upper hand, you become absolutely useless. I saw lots of Marines become absolutely useless. They could not function.

Hershel Williams in 1985

"I kept constantly repeating to myself, 'I am not going to die. I am not going to die.' I would never let myself think that I was not going to make it. I had to get back to that girl in Fairmont that I wanted to marry. That is what kept me sane.

"The fifth day in, the 23rd of February, was the day the flag went up on Mount Suribachi. The first flag they put up was only about 3 by 5. I didn't even know that happened. When they put the bigger flag up, the Marines around me could see it and sort of went crazy.

"I was about 1,000 yards up. We had been busy trying to break through a whole bunch of pillboxes, or bunkers as we call them today. I was on the beach in a prone position.

"Marines around me starting jumping up and down and firing their weapons and yelling. I got up and saw Old Glory and started firing my weapon, too.

"It was what we needed at the very time we needed it. Morale was very low. The Japanese were in concrete pillboxes with an aperture across the front with weapons sticking out. Anytime we moved, we were in open terrain. You crawled more than you walked.

"Trying to break through the pillboxes, you would lose Marines around you and have to fall back and reorganize and try again. It was a terrible time.

"The company commander's morale was low because he had lost so many men. He called a meeting. A corporal normally doesn't attend those meetings, but I was the last of the group.

"The commander asked if I might be able to do something with those pillboxes with my flamethrower. I said I would try. He gave me four Marines to protect me as I moved across the ground. I just started working, planning what I was going to do with that 70-pound weight on my back.

"You lose track of time. The fuel we were using was a mix of high-octane gasoline and diesel, enough diesel to give it weight so it would move. The high-octane gasoline gave it the heat.

"If you just fired it in the air, it wouldn't go anywhere. Air resistance would hit it, and it would stop. The gunnery sergeant taught us to fire onto the ground and let it roll, and it would turn into a big orange flaming ball, and you could roll it for 6 to 10 yards.

"These four individuals chosen to give me protection, I put two on my left and two on my right so they could have a crossfire into the pillbox. Two of those Marines gave their lives that day protecting me. I never knew who they were. They were just picked out of squads. You don't know guys in other squads.

"I went in there six times and knocked out seven pillboxes over a four-hour period. Even now, it's like a dream. Much of that day, I do not remember. I attribute that a lot to fear. Fear can take memory away.

"Once we were in control, we just kept on going. I was wounded on Iwo on March 6, a leg wound, a little piece of shrapnel. When the corpsman pulled it out, he gave it to me. I still have it.

"He put a tag on my lapel. If a corpsman tagged you, you had to get out of combat because you weren't fit to fight. I pulled off the tag and said, 'I don't have a tag on me.' He just shook his head.

"We left Iwo on April 1, 1945, and went back to Guam.

"We were training to street fight. All us dumb Marines knew we were going to Tokyo. As far as we were concerned, that was all of Japan.

"On Nov. 5, our Division was scheduled to go to Kyushu to take the south end. If that had happened, the estimate is that we would have lost a million people. Instead, we dropped the big bomb. That saved my life.

"On Guam, they called me into the office and said to get into my best khakis because I was going to see the general. Talk about scared. Corporals don't go see generals unless they're in trouble.

"The general congratulated me on being called back to the States to receive a medal. I had never heard of the Medal of Honor. It didn't mean a thing to me.

"I flew to Hawaii. I'd never been on an airplane. They said they would get me to Washington as soon as they could. Prisoners of war had priority. They gave me a flight to the naval air base in San Francisco in the meantime. The seventh day, they finally put me on the plane.

"There is one vision that has always haunted me. The plane was brilliantly lit. There were like 48 individuals on that plane they had just picked up from Japan after being in prison four or five years. Individuals who had weighed 180 pounds now weighed 70 pounds and looked like skeletons. They were the happiest people I've ever seen.

"I asked the guy beside me about his experience. He said, 'You never really know what freedom is until you have lost it.' I will never forget those words.

"At the White House, 13 of us were receiving the Medal of Honor. You do everything alphabetically in the Marine Corps. By the time they got to me, I had built up such nervousness that my body started shaking and would not quit.

"When I walked up to President Truman, I was just quivering. He put the ribbon around my neck, put his left hand on my shoulder and said, 'I'd rather have this medal than be president.' I shook all the way back to my seat.

"The commandant of the Marine Corps is a Medal of Honor recipient from Guadalcanal, A.A. Vandergrift. We had to report to his office the day after receiving medal. He said, 'That medal does not belong to you. It belongs to those Marines who did not get to come home.'

"Truly, it does not belong to me. It belongs specifically to those two Marines who gave their lives protecting mine. What more can you do than give your life to protect somebody else? I don't wear the medal for what I did. I wear it in their honor. All I was doing was my job.

"I came back to Fairmont and married Ruby on Oct. 17. On Veterans Day, they had a big parade. They put me in a red Dodge convertible on the back seat and I rode that way in the parade.

"I'm a country boy. I'm out of my class. Why are they doing all this? Thousands of people were out there. They brought me back to the courthouse and there was Sen. [Matthew] Neely and judges and congressmen.

"A guy says, 'And now may I present Woody Williams for a few remarks.' Nobody told me I was to make remarks. I walked up to the microphone and said three ahs and sat down. Shortest speech in history.

"I spent the rest of my life in veterans work. It's part of the debt I owe. I started working for the VA in January 1946. It was one of best jobs a person could have. I was commandant for the VA home and a counselor and chaplain of the Medal of Honor Society for 35 years.

The President of the United States of America, authorized by Act of Congress, March 3, 1863, has awarded in the name of the Congress the MEDAL OF HONOR to

CORPORAL HERSHEL WOODROW WILLIAMS
UNITED STATES MARINE CORPS RESERVE

for service as set forth in the following

Citation: For conspicuous gallantry and intrepidity at the risk of his life above and beyond the call of duty as demolition sergeant serving with the 21st Marines, 3d Marine Division, in action against enemy Japanese forces on Iwo Jima, Volcano Islands, 23 February 1945. Quick to volunteer his services when our tanks were maneuvering vainly to open a lane for the infantry through the network of reinforced concrete pillboxes, buried mines, and black volcanic sands, Corporal *Williams* daringly went forward alone to attempt the reduction of devastating machinegun fire from the unyielding positions. Covered only by four riflemen, he fought desperately for four hours under terrific enemy small-arms fire and repeatedly returned to his own lines to prepare demolition charges and obtain serviced flamethrowers, struggling back, frequently to the rear of hostile emplacements, to wipe out one position after another. On one occasion, he daringly mounted a pillbox to insert the nozzle of his flamethrower through the air vent, killing the occupants and silencing the gun; on another he grimly charged enemy riflemen who attempted to stop him with bayonets and destroyed them with a burst of flame from his weapon. His unyielding determination and extraordinary heroism in the face of ruthless enemy resistance were directly instrumental in neutralizing one of the most fanatically defended Japanese strong points encountered by his regiment and aided vitally in enabling his company to reach its objective. Corporal *Williams*' aggressive fighting spirit and valiant devotion to duty throughout this fiercely contested action sustain and enhance the highest traditions of the United States Naval Service.

Harry Truman

"When I first became chaplain, we had about 450 Medal of Honor recipients living. Now we have 81.

"I speak to a lot of schools. We talk about the values of America and how fortunate we are to be Americans and have people still willing to give their lives to keep our freedom.

"I was raised in a horse era. Our farm had two teams of horses. I learned to handle horses and work with them and love them. It was one of my goals to do something with horses.

"I planned to retire as early as I could and start a horse training, showing and birthing farm. I began doing that prior to my retirement.

"If I could start all over again, I don't know of anything I would change. My life has been so full and varied and blessed.

"I can't imagine what would have happened to me without that medal. The day I received the medal absolutely changed my whole life. I became a new person. Otherwise, I probably would have been in industry of some kind.

"Sometimes I feel so unworthy. When I get to heaven, one of my questions to God is, 'Why me? Why was I selected when the guy beside me gave his life and wasn't selected?' I don't have the answer."

FACT: OUT OF THE 28 MEDAL OF HONORS FOR IWO JIMA, HERSHEL WILLIAMS IS THE LAST LIVING RECIPIENT.

SERVING IN THE COAST GUARD
Elmer Wood

Interviewed by Gary C. Lulenski, M.D.

It was October 1941 and I got very lucky. When the draft was on, I drew #23. I was in Malcolm County and I was given a choice of doing service in the Navy or in the Coast Guard. I had a friend who was in the Coast Guard so I thought I would do that because he had really enjoyed his active duty. I was inducted on October 2, 1941. I served right on through to October of 1945.

When I signed up in Detroit they gave each of the draftees $20.00 and told us to take the train to New Orleans for basic training. We stopped in St. Louis and changed trains. I was sent to a Camp called Camp Algers. I arrived there with a warm bottle of beer and I got to St. Louis and pretty much without money. There was a long line for dinner and I had not much to eat so I waited and waited and finally got to the serving area. I could not believe it-they were serving liver. I couldn't stand liver but I guess when you are hungry enough you will eat anything. I had it for dinner and I will never forget it. That would not be one of the good memories I had.

We had a group of enlistees and we were trained by a Coast Guard officer called a grinder. We did calisthenics and tried to get as fit as we could. After a while, some advisors told us about the facts of life. He told us how many hospitals were in the area, how many nurses were in town and how many brothels were there. That was our training and new recruits came all of the time. The next day three new recruits came from New Orleans and one from Texas. I got friendly with the soldier from Texas and we kind of stayed together through our training. When we finished we had a choice of stations where to go. Most boys wanted to go to the west coast on a coast guard ship. The unlucky ones got sent to Chicago and I was assigned to the coast guard station at Sturgeon Bay. Our duties there were mostly maintenance of places such as lighthouses and then rescue missions. Most of them were called stiff calls. Those were bodies found floating in the river. It was pretty dreary there. The chief in charge told us we had a telephone that would notify us of an emergency at sea. That telephone would ring once and then someone better answer it. He told us if it rings twice and whoever is on duty is going to be court-marshalled and he meant it. I think there were about 390 men at that station. They renovated an old schoolhouse to put up the extra boys. I was there about 2 years.

I was listed as a yeomen which basically meant I was a paper pusher. I had some experience of typing and that qualified me to take care of a lot of the administrative work at the Coast Guard station. I didn't have to go out on many rescue missions but on December 9th of that first year there was only myself and the maintenance man on duty. We were notified there was a lighthouse station whose light had failed. We had to go out and find out what was wrong. We took an old lighthouse boat and headed across Green Bay. It was pretty lousy weather and the motor conked out but luckily the maintenance man got it fixed and we were able to get back. Another time we had to go about 10 miles out into the lake where a big tanker had gone aground. There was a bad storm that day and the wind was really blowing. It took us better than 4 hours to get there and we kept our lifejackets on all of the way. When we arrived they advised us to go to the leeside of the ship and we took off 2 passengers, the captain and the mate, to take them back to Sturgeon Bay for some equipment they had to get. Later in the afternoon we picked them up and two other people to go back to the ship. I think they finally got it off and we returned to our duty station.

I was transferred after about two years to the east coast and was assigned to a destroyer that was manned by the Coast Guard. We did do gunnery practice with a target that was towed behind a small boat. Our job was to blow it out of the water. I did learn some about how to fire anti-aircraft machine guns. We ended up being assigned to Newfoundland where we were to escort convoys part way across the Atlantic. We would go as far as Iceland and then the Navy would take over for the most dangerous part of the trip over to the British Isle.

We escorted a lot of convoys and there were a lot of women in Newfoundland but they didn't have any teeth. I guess because of the water. We called them goofy, Newfoundens. We continued on that convoy escort duty until April of 1945.

We didn't have any damage or torpedoes coming our way, but there were other ships close to us that did get torpedoed. One of the ships that I knew about was the USS Escanaba; it was hit by a torpedo.

While I was on active duty, I wrote to my wife just about every day. We had met while I was at Sturgeon Bay. We were married before I left to serve on an escort destroyer for the convoys.

I remember a somewhat funny story while I was on active duty and spending most of the time doing administrative work. I was around the officers and the captain quite a bit. I was sick one time with cough and fever and the captain who was a swell guy he offered me his silk bathrobe and told me to keep warm and return it when I was better. He was really like a father and looked after me. He told me early during my career on the Destroyer that I had to turn out the paper. The ship had a paper everyday and that is what a pencil pusher might have to do. He said I had two things I had to do. I had to have a joke in the paper everyday and all of the baseball scores when it was baseball season. I had to get a joke somehow everyday so when I wrote my wife that is one of the main things I told her was to talk to her friends and family and make sure everyone sent any joke they knew because I really was not clever enough to make jokes so I needed their help. By golly, she really did do a great job helping me out.

When the war was over, there really was not much need for all of the servicemen (and that included the Coast Guard), so I was discharged soon after the war and moved back to Sturgeon Bay.

I worked for a truck line as a rig clerk and did office work. The name was Cherryland Transport and we hauled beer and grociers from Milwaukee and places in Wisconsin and other areas. I did that for about eight years. My brother-in-law who worked for the sheriff's bureau in Lansing, Michigan, needed to have someone help with their paperwork, and that is what I did in the service, so they hired me. My experience in the service really did help me get that job, which I kept for a long time.

My wife had relatives in Buchanan, Michigan, so I sought work there. I was hired by Midwest Transport, a trucking company. They would haul goods around Berrien, Cass, and Van Buren County, and often I also went to South Bend, Chicago or LaPorte, Indiana. I worked for them a number of years. The owner was Mr. Oscar Selent; that is where I finished my work after the military.

I view my service in the military as a place to grow up. I worked hard in the office and learned how to handle all kinds of paperwork and got better using the typewriter. I had good commanding officers, and they showed me how to take care of things in the office as well as take care of matters when we were at sea. I was glad to be out of the service but I viewed it as a good time in my life. The fact of the matter is that a lot of officers did not know anything about paperwork so I was in charge, because I knew quite a bit and I learned more. I always felt the Coast Guard was a good place for me and viewed that time as a good experience in my life.

FROM ANZIO TO AUSTRIA

Robert O. Ziebart

I entered active service on June 10, 1943, in St Joseph, Michigan. My 16 weeks of basic training was at Camp Walters, Texas, where I trained with all infantry weapons. A week after the training was completed, my company was shipped out to fight in the Pacific Theater but I was held back. I had the highest score with the M1 rifle in our battalion.

On January 20, 1944, I left the United States from Newport News, Virginia, heading for the European Theater as the first replacement unit for the invasion at Anzio Beach.

We landed at Anzio early in the morning on February 4 and spent the day on the beach. We were given our rifles, ammunition and K rations. Early evening we loaded on trucks to move to the front, walking the last mile until we arrived at a bombed-out and shelled farmhouse.

Our platoon C.P. was in a center room with a candle for light. There were 15 or 20 replacements for the third platoon gathered in the room.

The sergeant informed me that I would be the gunner on the outpost position. I was ordered to turn in my M1 rifle and was issued a sniper rifle. The sergeant then called the name "Joergens" and assigned him as my assistant. Joergens did not have infantry training. The sergeant turned the list over to another sergeant and took the two of us out to the gun position.

As we left the house, the sergeant informed us of our responsibilities and the dangers of that position. We were informed the position had a phone in it so we could communicate with the sergeant. We entered a ravine and crossed a stream of water at the bottom. The gun position was 500 feet up the other side of the ravine. We entered the gun position from the side of the ravine through a hole so we didn't have to expose ourselves on the top. The machine gun was well camouflaged and the hole big enough that we could both stand in it. There also was a well-fortified sandbag hole in the bottom of the ravine where we could rest during the daylight hours.

Robert O Ziebert

The first night was quiet except for the noise from the Germans digging in their positions and the sound of a motorcycle coming and going. Before dawn and in the evening, the Germans would hit the ravine with mortar shells. The first morning, I looked out in front of our position. I could see barbed wire all across the front and looking down the ravine, I saw a bridge crossing the ravine that had not been bombed out or shelled. It was springtime and the grass was getting high. As it got lighter, we crawled out of the hole and went to the bottom of the ravine to the sandbagged hole to rest during the day.

We returned to the gun position in the evening as it began to get dark. It was rather quiet that night except for artillery shells going overhead. I had the last watch in the morning and as I looked out in front of our position, I thought I saw something move. I kept watching and thought I saw a German helmet come out of the grass. The third time I saw it, I fired the machine gun in the area. About five minutes later an 88-shell went over the top of our position and landed on the bank of the other side of the ravine. Joergens got up and we were standing together when a second shell came in our direction. The shell landed on top of the area we had crawled into for refuge. Joergens slumped down; his head and body fell back blocking our entrance hole. The platoon sergeant called; he knew the Germans had spotted our position. I informed him that Joergens was hit. He warned me not to try to crawl out of the hole over the top. he would send a medic right up.

I looked to see where Joergens had been hit. He was breathing hard. When I took off his helmet, I observed a shrapnel wound to his head and I knew he was not going to live. The medic arrived three hours later. We struggled to get him out the back of the hole and onto a stretcher. We carried him through the ravine to a first aid station near the place where we had entered the ravine on the first night. Joergens died shortly after arriving at the first aid station. I am sure he never knew what hit him.

The platoon sergeant never sent a replacement so I went back to the position alone. I stayed in the hole throughout the rest of the day. It was a hard day in which I spent a great deal of time thinking and praying. I began to wonder if I really had seen a German soldier out there in the grass. I knew by firing I had given away our position. Would Joergens still be alive if I had done something differently?

That evening, I crawled back into the gun position. I remained awake, alone, all night. In the morning as the light began to break in the eastern sky, I again noticed movement in the grass out in front of my position, only this time, it was much closer to me than yesterday morning. I soon observed a white handkerchief rise out of the grass. It was a German soldier. I told him to come in with his hands clasped over his head. He got up and I hurried him into the ravine so he would not be killed. I called the platoon sergeant and he sent a soldier to pick up the prisoner. I rested a lot better that day knowing that there was a German soldier out there and I hadn't been seeing things.

From Anzio to Rome

My personal experience during the breakout began on April 23 when I joined the assault group of volunteers who were to spearhead the attack to break out of Anzio. There were six tanks and ten soldiers riding in sleds behind each tank. The tanks were to break through the lines at designated points. We were to jump out of the sleds and hold the positions until the infantry arrived to take over.

Unfortunately, on this May morning (and as is often the case in war), this did not go as planned. Our tanks ran into mine fields and were hit by German artillery knocking out our tanks within 10 minutes. We had no choice but to get away from the tanks. I don't know how many soldiers got hit. Each of us was on his own, but the surge forward had begun.

It took me a day or two until I found my platoon, Company B of the 30th Infantry. The platoon sergeant was glad to see me and suggested I take over one of the squads. The job of being squad leader only lasted about two hours, but a lot happened during that time. We were in an area with dense vegetation making it difficult to see very far in front of us. I placed three of my soldiers along the edge of a small grape patch. They were digging foxholes when one of the soldiers dug up a barrel of sweet wine. The soldier asked me what to do about the barrel. I told him it would be a shame to leave it, so I called the Company Command Post and was instructed someone would come to pick it up.

While the three soldiers waited, they were able to tap the barrel and test the wine. After all, you wouldn't want to send bad wine back to the Command Post. Each soldier carried a canteen cup, which is bigger than your average wine glass, and I am not sure how much was consumed. A jeep arrived a short time later. The barrel was loaded and the driver quickly left the area. When I went to check with the platoon sergeant on something, two German soldiers crawled up and captured three of the soldiers in my squad. It just so happened that the three men captured were the same three who had tested the wine. One of the soldiers escaped later that night and returned to the unit.

Then, Capt. Seaden, our Company Commander, came looking for a soldier named Ziebart. I told him I was Ziebart and he said he wanted me to be his radio man. I explained I didn't know anything about operating the radio but I knew how to use the walkie-talkie or the telephone. He said, "You will be my radio man." I said "Yes Sir." We got into his jeep and the driver took us to the Company Command Post. The radio was easy to operate but I had to learn all the code numbers of everyone involved.

About three days later our company was to make a surprise attack on an area where the Germans were holding us up. I kind of liked this radio man position, because I was in a place to know what was going to happen. That night we were going to attack and drive the Germans out of their position. The plan was to slip up along the front line at dusk. At 8:00pm, our artillery would pound the German position for 15 minutes. At 8:15, we would rush ahead, shooting and hollering, and we would take over the area.

The Captain and I were on the front line ready to go but our artillery fell short of the target. I immediately took the radio off my back, laid it on the ground and I hugged the ground praying. When the artillery stopped, I got to my knees and looked around. It was a dark night and I could not see anything. I decided to pick up my radio and moved back to a hedge a short ways back. I called back to the Company Command Post and Captain Seaden answered the phone. I reported that all was clear up front. A short time later another officer took over his command. We took the area, though I don't know what our losses were. It was a tough week but afterwards, my radio and I had the opportunity to ride the rest of the way to Rome in the jeep.

Once in Rome, the platoon sergeant found me and said I should come back to his platoon. He said the Company Commander had been replaced and he needed me back. We were going to Naples, Italy, to train for the invasion of France. What I didn't know was that I would be replacing the platoon sergeant and be the acting platoon leader throughout the rest of the war.

Three days before the invasion of South France I was asked if I would accept a T-Sergeant rating and be a platoon sergeant. I don't know what happened to Sgt. Brewer. I didn't realize the responsibility that was involved, but my pay increased three times that day. There wasn't an officer assigned to the platoon so I was the acting platoon leader.

On August 14, 1944, we loaded on to LCIs and sailed to the island of Corsica. I had never seen so many military vessels as were following us that day. We arrived about a mile off the coast of Corsica in early evening. Everyone was briefed on what was going to happen the next morning. We did not know where we were landing, only the time our unit would be going in for a morning invasion. Our airplanes and battleships softened the area earlier that morning.

The first soldiers' who landed were to secure the beach and clear an area for us to be able to head up the main road. The Germans did not have heavy artillery, but they covered the beaches with mortar shells. Our unit went in an hour and twenty minutes later. By the time we had gone ashore, we had small armored vehicles and heavy machine guns mounted on jeeps. Our tanks were ashore by mid-day. We ran into resistance only about four times that day and by midnight, we stopped for a rest. The area was hilly and covered with trees. I placed the three squads in our area and guards for the night. My radio man and I laid down to rest when I received a message that the Company Commander wanted to see me.

The messenger took me to the nearby company headquarters, which was a tank off the road with a canvas coming off the side that we crowded under with a candle for light. The captain's message was brief and to the point. I was to take a patrol to a town 10 km (six miles) down the road. They knew there was a German unit in the town. I was to get into town and back by 5:30 the next morning with a report on their size and equipment. The captain laid out a map of the area on the ground. I could see the road going into the town was through the hills and wooded area; the town in a straight line was closer than the road. I chose the road not knowing the area at all. He gave me a soldier from a different platoon who could speak French. I was to pick two from my platoon so there would be four of us. The mission was simple: "get into town and back by 5:30, when the company will be moving out. Don't get into trouble, but if you do, you'll have to shoot it out on your own."

I led, with the rest in line behind me. Each one had to stay close enough to follow the one ahead of him. It was a dark night and I knew I had to go at a fast pace. We got to the edge of town and I could see only one road going in. The houses were two-story, built together with no side yards. I stopped and passed back a message that two of us would get in the doorways on both sides of the street and I would knock on my door.

I knocked on the door. There was a window on the second floor that had a wooden door covering it at night. I didn't hear the door open. A girl looked down and could see a soldier standing in the door below. She screamed, and the door slammed shut. A short time later, the door in front of me opened slowly. I realized it was a man and I said, "American soldiers." He opened the door wide and motioned me to come in. I called to the other three and we went up the stairs to the second floor. The happy Frenchman began pouring glasses of wine for us. We didn't have to use our canteen cups. His wife joined us, then a young women in her late teens came out and sat with her mother.

The man disappeared for about ten minutes and came back with his friends from the town. Each one carried a bottle of wine and was singing French songs. What a party they were having! We got close to an hour's rest and the glass or two of wine helped us to recover. It was around 3:00, and I suggested we head back with the report that the German units had left town as soon as it had gotten dark. We met our tanks and infantry coming up the road before we made it back. They had captured a group of German infantry soldiers in a wood mill shop that we had passed on the road the night before. We advanced through the town and kept going.

Within a week, I had another chance to lead. The Germans had stiffened their resistance by this time. This time the company was expected to make an overnight drive to get into a town before daylight. It was a well-fortified town with three gun positions, well dug in, and plenty of infantry. The Company Commander knew this, but he didn't tell me. Sometimes it was better not to tell the soldiers what to expect. I was again given the choice of how to get there. This time I chose to go through the field with the whole company single file behind my platoon. I held my German compass that I had picked up on Anzio in my left hand—it was easier to read at night than my GI issue.

As soon as it was getting dark, we started out. I knew that we didn't have any time to waste. We pushed forward through fields, orchards, hedgerows and hills. It was getting close to 5 o'clock in the morning and we had not reached the road that was leading into the town. I was getting more concerned and praying now. Moments later, I heard a rooster crow and I knew I wasn't far from the town. I made a half left and soon found the road. The road was raised up with a little ditch on each side. I passed back the message that I wanted soldiers on both sides of the road as we headed to town. I heard German soldiers marching toward us. I stopped and talked to my first scout who could speak German well. I knew most of my platoon heard what I was hearing and something was going to happen. I told Fellbaum, my scout, that when they got close I would jump out of the ditch and stop them. Then it was up to him to tell them to surrender. They got within twenty feet of me when I jumped out of the ditch and hollered "Halt!" using the best German accent I had. The "clup clup" sound came to a dead halt. The officer in charge said in German, "What is wrong?" Fellbaum gave them the message. They threw the weapons they were carrying to the side and folded their hands over their head, and started marching single file back along the route our soldiers were coming. I thanked God that not one shot was fired and all went well.

We were getting ready to head out again when another group of German soldiers came marching toward us. Again, we surprised them and they surrendered in the same manner. We took a third group the same way later that morning, capturing approximately 75 German soldiers in all without firing a shot. Our tanks came up the same road later and found all the gun positions unmanned.

By the end of September 1944, the weather was getting cold and rainy. From the afternoon of the 29th until 2:00 the next morning, we pushed forward to relieve the 141st Infantry. At 7am. the platoon leaders were called by the Company Commander, Standish. He laid out the attack for our company. He said, "Ziebart, your platoon will lead the Company." He added, "You have your scouts out in front of you." I always had the scouts behind me. We all knew this was going to be a real battle. The Germans had built up their positions.

We started out at 8am. I was first, my two scouts behind, in single file. It was a heavily wooded area and we were going down from the top of the mountains toward a city of Le Tholy. The Germans knew we were advancing down the mountain and they threw at us one of the heaviest barrages I had experienced. Word came back for us to return to our overnight position. Being the furthest ahead, I got the message last. As I headed back, a member of my platoon, Bob Nickels, had found a nice German fox hole with plenty of room for both of us. He asked me to jump in the hole with him, so I did. I got down on my knees in the hole and began praying for God to take me home. I couldn't keep going any longer. I was sick to my stomach—I didn't know at that time that I had Celiac disease. God answered my prayer—an artillery shell burst right over our hole and I got splattered with shrapnel. When I came to, there was a soldier from a different platoon standing on the ground above me. He helped me out of the hole. It was then, I saw the soldier from my platoon who had asked me to join him, lying dead on the ground. I don't know how he got there. I think he may have died from shock since only one piece of shrapnel hit him in one leg.

The next day I woke up lying on a stretcher on the ground in a Red Cross tent. They took eight pieces of shrapnel out of me. My right shoulder was hit the worst. There was a piece in my left elbow and one piece through my left foot. The rest were minor spots. I remember being on an airplane and the next day and ended up in the 103rd Station Hospital in Naples, Italy.

The Colmar Area of France

After being released from 103rd Station Hospital, Naples, Italy, I was to go back to Company B, 30th Infantry. We traveled through Italy and France on a military train, mostly cattle cars. I was picked to be the Sergeant of the Guard that was responsible to return GI soldiers who had been picked up by the M.P. Our car was a closed-in box car with one door up front. There were four of us. The prisoners all stayed in the back of the car while we stayed up front by the door. One night three of the prisoners slipped past the guard and escaped. I think the guard had fallen asleep. The next morning when the train stopped, I had to answer to the Lieutenant Colonel as to what happened.

When I arrived back to the Colmar area, I was given the same platoon that I had before, except I only knew about one-third of the guys. Prior to my return, the Company Commander had sent out two patrols but had not heard back from either of them. One of my squads was at an outpost in a house outside of town and there had been no contact with the squad. Within a half-hour of my return, the Company Commander informed me of this and asked me to take a patrol out to find them. About a hundred yards out of town, we found the last patrol that had been sent out, hiding in a field. After sending them back, I decided to go back and take the road out of town to the house my squad was guarding. When we got to the house, the lone squad leader told me a German patrol had slipped up on the house and had captured the first patrol. The squad leader had hid and didn't do anything to help the first patrol. The squad leader was later court-martialed for his inaction....

— IT DOESN'T END HERE. READ MORE ON ZIEBERT'S STORY ON OUR CD—

LE CONSUL GÉNÉRAL

N 1382

Chicago, December 7th, 2010

Dear Mr. Ziebart,

It is a great honor and privilege to present you with the Knight of the Legion of Honor medal. Through this award, the French government pays tribute to the soldiers who did so much for France and Western Europe. More than 65 years ago, you gave your youth to France and the French people. Many of your fellow soldiers did not return, but they remain in our hearts.

Thanks to the courage of these soldiers, to our American Friends and Allies, France has been living in peace for the past 6 decades. They saved us and we will never forget. I want you to know that for us, the French People, they are heroes. Gratitude and remembrance are forever in our souls.

You, Mr. Ziebart, are among these heroes. You enlisted in June 1943 as a Rifleman in Company B of the 30th Infantry Regiment of the 3rd Division. From February 1944 to November 1945, you participated in the Rome-Arno, Southern France, Rhineland, and Central Europe campaigns. For your achievements, the American Government presented you with prestigious awards the Purple Heart Medal with two Oak Leaf Clusters, the European, African, Middle Eastern Theater Ribbon with four Bronze Battle Stars and one Bronze Arrowhead, the Good Conduct Ribbon, the Combat Infantryman Badge, the Distinguished Unit Citation with Oak Leaf Cluster and the WWII Victory Medal.

To show our eternal gratitude, the government of the French Republic has decided to award you the Legion of Honor. Created by Napoleon, it is the highest honor that France can bestow upon those who have achieved remarkable deeds for France.

Thank you for what you did and congratulations,

Sincerely yours,

Graham PAUL
Consul Général de France à Chicago

"...You, Mr. Ziebart, are among these heroes..." Robert O. Ziebart receives Knight of the Legion of Honor medal from the French Consul.

STORIES FROM KOREAN WAR

1950 – 1953

MY SERVICE IN KOREA

John Bettig

NOTE: Read about John Bettig's childhood experiences with German and Russian soldiers in our WWII section.

John Bettig

After I was in the United States for 17 months, I discovered something I never expected. I discovered I had a rich uncle, Uncle Sam. He wrote me a nice letter, congratulating me that I had been chosen to serve in the US Army. I was proud to be chosen to serve the greatest country in the world. I am not sure, but it could have been before I was allowed to immigrate, since I had to sign some documents and one of them was volunteering to be in the US Army. On October 21, 1953, I reported to Detroit. From Detroit, I traveled to Fort Knox, Kentucky. There I received my orientation, equipment and clothing.

As a new recruit, I was taken to Fort Leonard Wood, Missouri. I was given a questionnaire asking what were my first three choices to do in the army. My first choice was to be a cook, the second to be a tank driver and the third, be an interpreter. I had an interview about the cooking. Since I did not have any experience in cooking and weighed only 120 pounds, they thought I would spend more time eating than cooking. I was not accepted. The second interview was about being a tank driver. I was rejected. Finally, I had to take a test in German and Russian. No one knew those languages. I was given a record player that played German and Russian, then they asked me questions. I received several pages of paper with multiple choices of answers and I had to choose the right answer. In several days, I was told "Yes, you qualify to be an interpreter, but we don't have a job for you. We will be training you as a combat engineer." I thought, "Well, I saw some of the world already, now I can see more of it: Korea.

At Fort Leonard Wood I was assigned to "D" Battery, 62nd AFA Battalion. The battery commander was Second Lieutenant William L. Donais. The Commanding General was Major General Arthur W. Pence.

Before I could receive engineering training, I had eight weeks of basic training. That included marching, inspection in ranks, the practice of firing different weapons such as rocket launchers and how to use hand grenades. I had to listening to many different lectures on different military topics. One of the most difficult parts of training was the infiltration course. During the attack course, I was usually the aggressor waiting somewhere in a foxhole, where I would be captured by the attackers.

After the first eight weeks of training, the General congratulated us and I received leave time for Christmas. I went home and gave an engagement ring Christmas present to Alma. She was very much surprised and happy. We were not at all happy with the understanding that I may go to Korea, but we were prepared to accept that situation. We were hoping for the best.

At Fort Leonard Wood, I started engineering training. After completing my engineering training, the Benton Harbor, Michigan, _News Palladium_ wrote, _"Pvt. John Bettig completed engineer basic training at Fort Leonard Wood Missouri, in a unit of the Sixth Armored Division._

Since entering the Army, he received eight weeks of basic training in the fundamentals of army life and the use of infantry weapons and an additional eight weeks engineering training. During engineer basic training at Fort Leonard Wood, Pvt. Bettig was taught the use of power tools, construction of fixed and floating bridges and related subject, besides additional combat skills. At the end of the training cycle with the famed "Super Sixth," men completing training at Fort Leonard Wood are selected either for specialist schools or as replacement for other units."

I was surprised to receive the good news that I was not going to Korea; instead, I would be sent to Germany. That was something that I did not expect. I had not been in the US for even two years and I was on the ship going back to Germany. I arrived in Bremerhaven, Germany on the *USS General Blatchford* on April 23, 1954. I stayed in Germany for 18 months and was able to visit many of my friends and relatives. I had a lot to brag about life in America and to be a proud American soldier.

I was informed that I was chosen for duty assignment to Headquarter Company, 2nd Battalion, 22 Infantry Regiment, S -2 as interpreter to the Intelligence and Security Military Unit. To be part of this unit I had to be an American citizen qualified for top-secret clearance. At that time, I was not an American citizen; as to the clearance, I was investigated by the US government and received clearance to come to America. To become a US citizen, I filled out numerous forms and reported to Frankfurt, Germany with two witnesses, where I was sworn in as a citizen of the United States of America.

I received all kinds of training. I spent certain time on border patrol, which I really enjoyed. During the day, we would travel along the border through villages and towns and enjoy the scenery. We could stop anywhere in a guesthouse and buy a meal for less than a dollar. My favorite meal was, schnitzel with fried potatoes and salad. It was quite cheap because the exchange rate for US $ 1.00 was 4.20 DM.

Survival training was mandatory. This was difficult because we had to stay away from civilization. I would catch fish; find some blueberries in the forest, as well as, mushrooms. Once in awhile I overstepped the rules and went to the store and bought some bread and sausage. Other training was learning how to be behind the enemy lines.

Most of my time was spent in the office with some officer, and that gave me special status. I was not assigned to any kitchen duty or guard duty. I can say that my time in Germany as an American soldier was very important, and valuable. I felt I had a special privilege and honor to be an American soldier. The Army taught me discipline, dedication and determination. A soldier must be courageous, committed to the cause of his calling. I was somebody. When I visited my friends or my relatives, they respected me; I was an American soldier. When I shared with them about the American way of life, they got excited. My brother and two sisters who were married came to America. Six of my friends followed.

In Germany, the recruiting officer tried to persuade me to re-enlist in the Army, promising I would be promoted and receive all the education I wanted. I wrote a letter to my fiancée telling her that I would come home, we would get married, and I would re-enlist and take her with me to Germany. She wrote, "You can do that, but without me." I decided to return and get married.

I received an honorable discharge from Fort Sheridan, Illinois, on October 6, 1955 and remained in the Army Reserve for six years. I was promoted to Pfc. and received the National

Defense Service medal and the Army of Occupation medal (Germany). I am also a member of the American Legion. Three of my brothers also served in the US Armed Forces: Alex served with the Marines in Korea, Erich in the Air Force and Peter served with the Marines as Combat Photographer in Vietnam.

After service, I immediately went back to work at New Products. On November 26, 1955, Alma and I married and started a family.

After settling in America and finishing my education, I was pastor of the Wayside Chapel in Plainwell, Michigan, for four years. In 1970, the Evangelical Free Church of America ordained me. In December that same year, we joined Trans World Radio and moved to Monte Carlo, Monaco. Through TWR, the gospel was brought to the Soviet Union from a radio station that Adolf Hitler built for his propaganda purposes. For five years I worked as a studio technician, editor and announcer. I produced Russian programs and helped in other language program development.

In 1975, we went to West Germany to be representatives for the Russian department, where we developed a relationship with Russian-speaking people who had immigrated to West Germany from the Soviet Union. In the offices of Trans World Radio German National Partner, Evangeliums Rundfunk, we established a Russian department. By 1987 the Russian staff from Monte Carlo, was moved to Germany, merging both entities into one Russian radio ministry. As director of the Russian department, I provided oversight of the production of Russian programs that were aired from Trans World Radio, Monte Carlo, into the formal USSR until 1988 when we returned to the United States, after delegating my responsibilities to the young Russian workers I had trained.

In 1979, the Grand Rapids School of Bible & Music Alumni Association recognized me for a life of dedicated Christian service and consistent Christian testimony. I continued to serve with TWR in banquets, mission conferences, and other church services. I traveled in many foreign countries representing TWR. In December 2000, I was granted an honorary Doctor of Divinity degree from Indianapolis Christian University. After 32 years of service, I retired on December 31, 2002.

In 2004 I founded CIS, "Christian Involvement in Service", a nonprofit mission organization, serving as president until 2009. This involved much traveling to Russia, the Ukraine and Moldova preaching in many national churches. Twelve times, I taught special courses at the Russian Bible School in Samara, Rostov and Moscow Theological Institutes. My wife and I also traveled with church groups from the United States to Ukraine to aid the national believers, in church construction and serving as interpreter.

— READ MORE OF BETTIG'S STORY ON OUR CD—

FLYING IN KOREA & VIETNAM
Weldon Burden

Between semesters in my Junior year at the University of Michigan, I had surgery to remove my appendix. For medical reasons, I could not start the second semester in January 1951, so I lost my draft deferment. I applied for the Naval Cadet Flying program, but there was a large backlog of applicants for flight training. My application was denied. Then, I applied for the Air Force Cadet Flying program, and was placed on a draft deferment until a flying class opened up.

Major Weldon Burden standing in front of a C-5A plane that he was testing.

In June 1951, they cancelled the deferment and gave me two options:

1) enlist as an Airman by June 29, 2951, and wait until the flight class opened up. Once the class opened, they would transfer me to flight school. Or...

2) start the whole process over at a later date, including the written and physical tests.

I decided to take option #1, and enlisted in the Air Force on June 29, 1951. I took Air Force Basic Training at Sampson AFB, Geneva, New York as a Private; on August 17, I was promoted to Private First Class.

In March, 1952, I began basic Flight Training in the T-6G aircraft at Stallings AB, Kingston, N. Carolina. This was a civilian-operated flight school with civilian flight and classroom instructors. Military pilots gave us all check flights and military classes.

In September, I graduated to Advance Flight Training at Vance AFB, Enid, Oklahoma, flying B-25 aircraft. Prior to graduating, I was given the option of going to SAC and fly B-29 aircraft or to TAC and fly C-119 aircraft. On March 16, 1953, I was awarded my wings and was commissioned Second Lieutenant.

I was assigned to the 61st TCS at Ashiya AB, Japan, flying C-119 aircraft into Korea, bases through Japan, Okinawa, and Clark AFB, Phillipines, carrying food, ammunition, paratroopers, military personnel, etc. Once I carried an atomic bomb from Japan to Okinawa. There were a lot of security guards with the bomb (called "Fat Boy"). The Korean War ended in 1953. My last flight into Korea was a *full* load of ping pong balls, boxed and weighing less than 1,000 pounds. I have no idea who used them or what happened to the ping pong balls.

The French were fighting the Viet Minh in Indo-China. The US had loaned both Air Force and Naval aircraft to the French. C-119 aircraft from Japan was loaned to the French. France hired pilots from Civil Air Transport (CAT) to fly the loaned aircraft. The aircraft were flown from Hanoi via Clark AFB for repainting with French markings. In December 1953, the CAT pilots were receiving a lot of ground fire and occuring some damage to the C-119s. The USAF received word that the pilots may quit, so Air Force pilots from Japan were sent to Indo-China as back-up pilots. On Decmeber 29, 1953, I flew a C-119 to Hanoi with a stop at Clark AFB to paint the French markings on the aircraft. There, we were briefed on what our possible role was., our normal script money was replaced by US green currency, and all olive drab (OD) ID was removed from us. Each of us was also issued a .45 caliber pistol. What asked what it was for, we were told if we ever shot down in Indo-China, we were to shoot ourselves before capture.

My stay in Hanoi was 25 days. We lived in straw-roofed, one story concrete buildings where we played a lot of cards. (I learned to play _Bridge_ on these trips to Indo-China.) The US contingent was 5-6 crews, with one senior office in charge. We were primarily off to ourselves, away from the French and CAT aircrews. We did eat our meals with the French and a few times with the French Foreign Legion. Interestingly, we found the French Foreign Legionnairies were made up from men from Poland, Scandinavian countries, Libya, Morocco, Germany... but no French. Perhaps that is why it was "Foreign."

I made my last flight to Indo-China on July 23, 1954. The war between the French and the Viet Minh ended on July 20, 1954 when the fort and airfield at Dinh Binh Phu fell to the Communist forces. We flew the C-119 aircraft from Haiphong to Tourane (now called Danang) south along the east coast of Indo-China. To my knowledge, no US aircrew flew any actual missions for the French.

In June 1956 I applied for and was appointed to "regular" Air Force. Up until that time, I was a Reserve Officer. If a person wanted to make the Air Force a career, he had to be in the regular Air Force to assure staying at least 20 years and be able to retire. After much training and taking courses such as Thermo-dynamics, Caclulus, and Aerodynamics, I received a Bacherlors Degree in Aeronautical Engineering and was promoted to Captain in January 1959.

In September of that year, I applied for and was selected to attend the Air Force Test Pilot School, Edwards AFB, California. I flew T-28, T-34, & T-33 aircraft in flight tests at the school. Future astronauts Jim McDivitt and Ed White were in my class. Future astronaut Tom Stafford was an instructor and checked me out in the T-33.

The Air Force planned to put a lab in space (Skylab) and were working jointly with NASA to establish some tests for selecting astronauts. I was among less than half a dozen classmates who decided to participate in the specialized physical tests. One test was to sit in the altitude chamber and take off our oxygen mask at 100,000 feet to see how long we went before passing out. Another was checking our equilibrium by putting ice water in our ears, and yet another for the heart put our feet in ice. At Wright-Patterson AFB, I was put into a heat chamber at 150-degrees for six hours. Needless to say, I lost 17 lbs during the test. Upon completion of the tests, the Air Force said that I had taken every heart test available in the medical field at that time.

The Air Force dropped the "Skylab" program in 1960. I applied for an astronaut postion in the Gemini program. I was not selected, but was told I was in the top 17 finalists. I later applied for the Apollo program. I was told I was 30 days too old to be eligible. I requested a waiver, but was denied. Thus ended my plans to be an astronaut.

June 1960-May 1966, I was assigned to Cargo Flight Test, Aeronautical Systems Division, Wright-Patterson AFB, Dayton, Ohio. I flew many different aircraft, including JC-54D, JC131B, JC-123, JC-130, C-119C, C-54D, C130A, YC-123H, C-133, C-97, JC-121, HC-130H aircraft and UH-1F AND CH-3C helicopters in tests of aircraft systems, long range communications, zero-G flight, automatic landing systems, de-icing tests, cold weather systems, etc.

In April 1966, my school was changed from RPI to the Institute for Defense Analysis (IDA), Arlington, Virginia, to study Defense Systems Analysis. This was not a degree program. I asked AFIT if I could get a degree while at IDA. They determined I could get a Masters degree in Economics by taking extra courses at the University of Maryland, plus write a thesis. After taking morning classes at IDA, I commuted to College Park for afternoon classes at the University of Maryland. I wrote my thesis, attended classes, plus kept up my flying on weekends at Andrews AFT, all in 13 months. Upon graduation, I was supposed to be assigned to the Pentagon as a Systems Analyst. The Air Force decided I needed a tour of Vietnam first.

In March 1967, I was promoted to Major and went through the Air Force Suvival Course at Fairchild AFB, Washington, followed by Combat Crew Training in C-130E aircraft at Sewart AFB, Smyrna, Tennessee. November 1967-February 1969, I was assigned to the 50th TCS at Ching Chuan Kang AB (CCK), Taiwan. I flew the C-130E aircraft into Okinawa, Vietnam, Thailand, Philippines, Japan, and into other bases in Japan and Korea. I airlefted ammunion, food, support supplies, Army paratroopers, Vietnamese people, and unfortunately, military personnel killed in action (KIA). I foud that the primary reason of flying the C-130 in Vietnam was to show the US government and the American people that we were winning the war. To do that, the tonnage we hauled each day was at a maximum. I don't remember ever flying an empty aircraft in Vietnam.

For example, one time I hauled a load of New York strip steaks (about 20,000 lbs) to a base nearest the DMZ called Quang Tri. When we landed, we told the transportation officer what we had on board. He laughed and said he could not use the steaks since all the troops were out in the field 25 miles away and there were no refrigeration facilities. I called our headquarters in Saigon and was told to leave the load, anyway. The outside temperature was in the 80s and I'm sure the steaks all rotted. The transportation officer did tell us to take 8-9 cases back to our base, Tuy Hoa, and have a cookout on the beach for all the flight crews.

Another example involved a load of *Budweiser* beer. As an instructor pilot, I had the job of checking out new pilots in the theater. On this mission, a new pilot fresh out of a desk job at the Pentagon was flying as I co-piloted. We were taking 28,000 lbs of *Budweiser* to a small airfield on the Laotian border. The Army troops were in an old French fort, 2,000 feet from the airstrip. As we approached, I called them to say we were inbound. They called back, saying they were under a mortar attack and not to land. Again, I called Saigon and was told we had to land and take off our load. The troops asked what we had on board for them. I told them about the beer. They just laughted and said that only seven troops were there with an non-working refrigerator. Because of the mortar attack, we had to land downwind, down a sloping runway. After touchdown, with both of us on the brakes and in maximum reverse, we ended up past the runway, staring at a fence and looking down into a 100-foot ravine. Ten more feet and we would have ended in a heap down the ravine. We off-loaded on the small ramp by unlocking the pallots of beer and, with a burst of thrust, the pallets rolled out onto the ramp. Five days later, one of my fellow pilots picked up the beer and took it back to where I had originally picked it up. As I said, the purpose was to get as much tonnage as possible for reporting purposes.

In June 1971, I retired from the US Air Force at a rank of Major. In my career, 1951-1971, I flew 42 different aircraft, logged a total of 9,800 hours of flight time, flew 165 combat missions and logged 825 hours of combat time.

—READ MORE OF BURDEN'S STORY ON OUR CD—

ABOARD THE MOE
William J. (Bill) Burke

My life began September 14, 1933, in Jackson, Michigan. My father was transferred shortly thereafter to St. Joseph, Michigan, where I completed ten years of school at St. Joseph Catholic. We moved once again, this time to Gary, Indiana, and in 1951 I graduated from Merrillville High School.

I'm sure today, many people are unaware that the draft (as in WW II), was being utilized during the Korean War. My uncle, drafted in the infantry during WW II, spent months in intense combat in Europe when he was 18-years-old. He impressed upon me not to wait and get drafted. With those words of wisdom, I enlisted in the Navy in May of 1952.

Bill Burke

I spent the next 12 weeks in boot camp at the Great Lakes Naval Training Center in Chicago. I was then re-assigned to the Battleship *U.S.S. Missouri* in Norfolk, Virginia. It was quite a shock boarding the *"Moe,"* as I thought growing up as a young boy the largest ships in the world were the *Roosevelt* and *Grand Rapids* docked in Benton Harbor.

A short history on the *U.S.S. Missouri*: It is the most famous ship in the U.S. Navy (per the *Military Channel*). The last four battleships (*Iowa, Wisconsin, New Jersey* and *Missouri*) were built in late 1944, and all saw action toward the end of WW II. *U.S.S. Missouri*'s claim to fame: Japan surrendered to the U.S. aboard the *Missouri* in Tokyo Bay on September 2, 1945, to end the war in the Pacific. General MacArthur signed for the United States, and there is a bronze plaque embedded on the quarter-deck of the Missouri signifying this historic event. Today, the *Missouri* is berthed in Pearl Harbor as a museum near the *U.S.S. Arizona* (start of WW II vs. the end of WW II). The *Missouri*'s armament consisted of: 1) 9-16" guns; 2) 10 dual 5" guns, and 3) 20 – Quad 40mm mounts.

USS Missouri firing her guns

In early September of 1952, we left the U.S. for Korea. This was the second deployment for the *Missouri*, as each of the four battleships were rotated every six months in Korea. The *Missouri* was the first on the scene in September 1950. The *Missouri* was the only battleship *not* mothballed after WW II. (NOTE: Truman was President at that time and—you guessed it—from Missouri.)

My assignment aboard the *Missouri* was as a Fire Control Technician (FT) in the secondary battery division (5" and 40mm) – 80 sailors. Another 50 FTs were responsible for main battery (16") gunfire control systems. Responsibilities included: plotting room computers, radar rooms, directors, and all electronics associated with those systems. During our missions above the 38th parallel, I spent three months in the secondary battery plotting room, and three months as a range finder operator in a 5' director, directing fire on targets of opportunity along the coast of North Korea.

Bill Burke aboard ship in 1952

We arrived in Yokosuka, Japan in September 1952 and relieved the Battleship Iowa. We left immediately for Sasebo, Japan, which was to be our home port during our deployment with the 7th Fleet (Task Force 77). Sasebo was about 170 miles from Pusan, South Korea.

Our firing missions in North Korea were always on the east coast, and lasted 2-3 weeks, then back to Sasebo for a couple of days, and back to North Korea. We operated as far north as Chongjin (30 miles from Vladivostok, Russia). Our most frequent target was Wonsan Harbor where we received counter fire on a few occasions. We always operated with a destroyer, as we had no protection against submarines and there was always a carrier close by. 16" firing was directed by either U.N. forces at or near the front lines, or by one of the two *Missouri* helicopters. During one mission off Wonson, one of the helicopters (pilot and 2 marines spotters) were shot down and lost at sea. During our deployment, the *Missouri* fired 2,861 rounds of 16" and 4,378 rounds of 5" ammunition.

The *Missouri* was relieved by the battleship *New Jersey* in Yokosuka, Japan, and we returned to our home port at Norfolk, Virginia in late April 1953. When we returned to Norfolk, I was selected and sent to Fire Control Technician School (44 weeks) in Washington DC. I returned to the *Missouri* in April of 1954. We immediately got under way for Bremerton, Washington, where the *Missouri* was decommissioned in April of 1955. The *Missouri* was re-fitted and re-commissioned in 1986 for Desert Storm, and later de-commissioned a second time in 1992. In 1998, the *Missouri* ownership was transferred from the Navy to the *U.S.S. Missouri* Memorial Association in Pearl Harbor where the ship now attracts over one million visitors a year.

I spent my last year in the Navy at the Mothball Fleet in Long Beach, California.

Bill & Teresa Burke celebrating 50 years

Upon leaving the Navy in 1956, I used the G.I. bill to attend college, and received a Business Degree from Western Michigan University in 1960. I was not ready for college in 1951, so joining the Navy was probably the best decision of my life. Completing the 44 week Naval Fire Control Technical School gave me the confidence to further my education after being discharged. GO NAVY!

197

The *U.S.S. Missouri* Association was formed in 1974 to promote patriotic ties among former shipmates who served aboard the *U.S.S. Missouri*. We meet each year in a different city. The photo at right was taken at Pearl Harbor (home of the *Missouri* Memorial) in 2003, and was the first time I had been back aboard in 48 years!

I married Teresa McIntosh on August 30, 1958, in Benton Harbor, Michigan. We have two grown daughters (50+ in ages), and two grand dogs. Teresa and I reside in St. Joseph, Michigan, where we have enjoyed 14 years of retirement together (especially vacationing in Arizona). My hobbies include golf.

LETTER TO FOLKS: I FLEW MY FIRST COMBAT MISSION
Richard Edinger

BACKGROUND NOTE: *Upon graduation from Michigan State University and completion of four years in the Air Force ROTC program in 1950, Richard Edinger was commissioned a 2nd Lieutenant. Basic training took place at Wright Patterson AFB, Dayton, Ohio, where Edinger witnessed test flights of the B-36 "super bomber" which never saw active duty, due to the advent of the jet age. Edinger was called to duty in 1951 and assigned to the Information & Education School at Ft. Slocum, NY, and then to headquarters, Strategic Air Command, Omaha, Nebraska, under the command of Gen. Curtis LeMay. He was then transferred to the 58th Fighter Bomber Wing, Taegu, Korea, where he served as Public Information Officer. He was honorably discharged in 1953 with the rank of 1st Lieutenant.*

May 30, 1953, Taegu, Korea

Dear Folks:

Yesterday I flew my first combat mission with the 58th Fighter Bomb Wing. It was quite an experience, and rather unexpected. Several times in the past, I had suggested to headquarters that I would be willing to accompany a combat strike for picture and story coverage. However, they seemed to be lukewarm on the subject. Yesterday, my boss, Colonel Warford, the Wing Commander, was scheduled to fly his 100th mission, completing his combat tour in Korea. The previous day I already had the story written with the details left out as the type of mission hadn't been determined. It was to be a pretty hot item, and I knew I'd have to be on the ball.

Warford was to fly with three other members of the wing command, adding up to a quartet of "bird" colonels which would trump the "Old Man" out in a blaze of glory. News-wise, of course, the angle is only fair, but from the wing command point-of-view, it was to make the Normandy Invasion look like a Harvard shell race. I had, the previous day, briefed my photographer and my sergeant to be on a moment's call the next forenoon, so we could dash right out and snap "wild blue yonder" shots as the returning Colonels stepped from their Thunderjets.

At 8:15 on the morning of the big day, Colonel Davis, the deputy wing commander, called me up at the office and informed me that Colonel Warford, Colonel Nelander, the group commander and Colonel Moody, the deputy group commander were taking off on a close support strike at 0850 and that I was going along and had better get my fanny over to briefing, which was his typically uncouth but well-meaning way of addressing subordinates. This, needless to say, threw the PIO office into a quite but thorough panic. My sergeant scarcely knew which way to turn, my photographer nearly died laughing, being a hopeless cynic, and I dashed off to the barracks to grab my Rolleiflex. Then in a moment of divine inspiration, I ran over to the base photo lab and told them to prepare a movie camera. Dashing off again, I panted into group operations for briefing. I was to fly with the formation of four colonels in a T-33, which is a two seat jet somewhat similar to a Thunderjet, but smaller and with no armament, and is used for training neophyte jet pilots before they go into combat. My pilot was to be Major Davies, a strong silent type with an obvious contempt for Public Information Officer (PIO) activities, particularly when they involved risking his neck in an unarmed airplane over enemy lines.

The four colonels, on the other hand, with well-tuned ears for press releases and who had previously been moved by several of my stories which have appeared in the Pacific Stars and Stripes, were quite clubby. They showed me on the briefing map where we were going, what the target was, and so forth. They told me Major Davies would do whatever I wanted him to do in the line of flying. This added another furrow to the major's already frowning brow. Then, the colonels asked me what I wanted them to do. This took me off balance for a minute, but I quickly regrouped and told them to fly in close formation on the way up so I could get good pictures and then peel off a few times on the way home so I could get pictures of that. They agreed to this and we closed negotiations.

After briefing, with five minutes left before take-off, I ran back to the photo lab and picked up a 16mm movie camera which had been loaded and set by one of their men. The photo officer showed me how to switch it from normal to telephoto lens and that's all I had time for. I went out to the T-33 on the flight line where Major Davies was waiting with a condescending look on his face. He helped me into a parachute, into the cockpit, then proceeded to strap me in with a maze of hooks, locks and buckles to assure my complete paralysis throughout the trip, and to preclude, I suppose, any possible means of my escape. He did, however, show me how to eject. If we were hit, the Major explained, I merely had to pull this switch, turn that knob, grasp this handle, put my feet in those things, my arms in these, and squeeze—don't pull—the trigger. The end result being that I would be catapulted, probably through the closed canopy, into the air. Then, I suppose to short-stop any backtalk or question-and-answer period, he stuck an oxygen mask over my face and a helmet on my head. We were, in a manner of speaking, ready to go. I felt that I was sufficiently equipped to go to the moon, if the need arose.

Being entombed in a jet is an odd sensation. The canopy closed halfway and the engine started with a whining roar, like a completely carried away vacuum cleaner, and the plane seemed to strain at its reins with anxious energy. The intercom was an open connection between the pilot and myself, and couldn't be turned off. The sound of our breathing added to the unearthly quality. Every time we took a breath, it whistled over the intercom like a siren. On the dash was the oxygen counter, a round dial with yellow flaps, or eyelids, on top and bottom, which flipped together every time I took a breah to indicate that oxygen was being inhaled. It looked like a big yellow eye winking at me incessantly. At my left side, down near my feet, there was a little switch the major had shown me, which could be flipped over to give out 100% oxygen. This was to prove valuable later in the trip.

Then the tower started making a lot of noise on our radio and there was much "roger, over, out" type conversation between the major and the tower. I looked down the ramp and saw Colonel Warford start to taxi out. Then the three other colonels began to taxi and we fell in behind them. At this time, I was beginning to get busy with my camera. I had my Rollei strapped around my neck and the movie camera in my lap. We taxied down past the PIO shack on the flight line and I saw my sergeant and photographer waving a fond farewell. It was impossible to get any pictures yet as the jet blast from the plane ahead was blowing hot gasses into our still half-open canopy, nearly blinding me. Finally, we got to the end of the runway and arranged ourselves into take-off position with the colonels paired off up front and PIO bringing up the rear. Then the jet engines exploded into new life. Our plane literally jumped up and down as the jet blasts from the four Thunderjets ahead engulfed us. Major Davies released the brakes on the T-33 and we leaped ahead. I have never felt so much power under me in all my life. It's like someone pushing you violently in a swing, only, unlike a swing, the pushing doesn't stop. I was pinned back into my seat by the acceleration, but managed to shoot a few bursts of movie film at the jets ahead of tearing down the runway. As the jet engine under me reached a screaming crescendo, the plane left the ground, but I was still being pushed back in my seat. The runway disappeared from beneath us and K-2 faded rapidly away. Taegu flashed by under us. Then we went into a turn and I nearly blacked out. When I could see again, we were headed north and climbing. The four Thunderjets were about 50 yards off our left wing tank and flying in what I considered admirable formation, with their thousand pound bombs hanging menacingly from under their wings. Then I remembered my cameras again and started taking pictures like crazy. I would clip off a few feet of movies, then lay it down and fire a shot with my Rollei. The sun was good and there were quite a few cloud formations around for background. Unfortunately, our plane had a radio with a different wave length and we could not communicate with the colonels. However, I worked the fanny off Major Davies.

"All right, Major, let's fly under 'em now—that's good, hold it—now a little to the right—fine—OK now, let's get about 2:00 high so I can shoot back at 'em." Oh, it was great, me telling a real "tiger" how to fly, and a major besides!

Roaring along at 400 miles an hour, the ugly blue ridges and crooked valleys with their crazy quilt patterns of rice paddies sped below us. Thirty minutes melted away as I busily cranked and wound my camera. As we went further north, the peaks became higher and more ugly and the valleys narrower, with the rice paddies missing now. We went into another turn which nearly tore the camera from my hand. Below us was the reservoir, looking just like it did on the briefing map. I knew we didn't have far to go now. In another minute the major croaked excitedly into the intercom, "There she is—the punch bowl." I looked ahead and saw a piece of land that looked somewhat like a moon crater with vegetation. In another few seconds we were over the front lines just west of the punch bowl. It really wasn't something you could pick out and say, "there is the front line," but you could sure tell there was something going on down there. The peaks and ridges weren't like the bleak ones further south. Along the crests of the ridges, I could see the white ribbons of trails, trenches, and paths. And I could see the bunkers tucked away on the safe side of the ridges. In the valleys were good-sized roads over which I could see trucks and supplies moving up toward the peaks like ants trickling home to their anthills with a new found horde of crumbs. But on the enemy side, there was very little activity. I could see a few trenches and bunkers, but no movement. Those boys really had their heads down. Back in the hills on the enemy's side, there were columns of white smoke rising here and there. Probably an artillery barrage or a previous air strike.

"We should be picking up the mosquito any minute now," said the Major. I told you about the mosquito before. He would be the T-6 that would make radio contact with our flight and lead us into the target area. No sooner had he said it when we looked down and saw a small silver speck coming towards us. It was the mosquito. He approached us, then peeled off and streaked toward one of the high peaks below. As he pulled up again, we could see a white cloud of smoke rising from the side of a ridge. That was the rocket fired by the mosquito to mark the target, consisting of a group of Communist personnel shelters, artillery positions and trenches. For the next five minutes I was the busiest PIO in Fifth Air Force. Following the four Thunderjets, we pulled into a wide turn, swept over the enemy lines and dove in on the target from the north. In the meantime, I found out later, the mosquito pilot had gone into a virtual panic about the "fifth airplane" in flight. "Whatthehell,"? he frantically radioed to Colonel Warford, "have you got five airplanes in this flight?"

"He's only an observer," replied Colonel Warford, "and isn't carrying any bombs."

"Jesus," was the mosquito's philosophic reply.

We screamed down toward the ridge and I was blazing away with my movie camera. But at about 4,000 feet, Major Davies apparently felt that publicity can go just so far, and he yanked us into a climbing turn that nearly pulled my ears down to my knees. The nine pound camera suddenly gained about 500 pounds and crashed into my lap as we pulled about four "Gs." My oxygen mask ripped away from my face and I couldn't move a muscle. When we straightened out again, I was feeling nauseated, so I slapped the oxygen mask back on, reached for the switch, and turned it to 100% oxygen. This had a mildly intoxicating effect. So after about three martinis worth, I switched it back off and had that problem licked for the rest of the trip.

We climbed back to about 5,00 feet and orbited the target area, flying violent evasive action while I shot some more pictures. By this time, I could see a great cloud of brown, dirty smoke mushrooming from the side of the ridge. It looked like the boys really worked it over.

By this time, the Thunderjets had come off their bomb runs and were headed home. The major goosed the T-33 and we soon caught up with them. The colonels then obediently went back into tight formation and peeled off three times while I shot pictures of them.

In 25 minutes we were again flashing over K-2. The major put down the dive-brakes and flaps and it felt like we had come to a screeching stop in mid-air, but we were actually only slowing down to a comfortable couple of hundred miles per hour. We all made beautiful landings and taxied up to the waiting throng of well-wishers. While the colonels swilled down the customary quart of champagne, I ran around pushing them into position for pictures.

Later, in Colonel Warford's office, he gave me all the details of the strike. Intelligence reported that the colonels destroyed 16 personnel shelters, two artillery positions, and knocked out 75 yards of trench while setting off two secondary explosions. And all with just eight bombs. Then he laughed a little about the upset mosquito pilot. "You can bet your sweet life they were shooting at you, young man," he summed up, with some degree of pride in his voice.

And so ended my first combat mission. Am enclosing rough draft of story I released on this episode, together with photos and cut lines. Will keep you informed of further happenings on this side of the world.

Love to all,

Rich

SUBMARINES: FROM WWII TO NUCLEAR
Robert Montross

I was born in 1929 and grew up on a ranch in the San Joaquin Valley in California. I joined the Naval Reserve after graduating from high school, followed by an active duty tour on a Desroyer Escort resulting in my selection to the U. S. Naval Academy.

Following my initial assignment to a surface ship (*USS Henrico*, a troop transport) and one WestPac deployment, I volunteered for submarine duty. On completion of submarine school in 1956, I served on three diesel-electric submarines - *USS Razorback* with one WestPac deployment and two Special Operations, *USS Rasher*, and *USS Wahoo*, a post World War II submarine with one WestPac deployment and two Special Operations. Following shore duty as a Test Operator of a developmental deep diving two-man submarine, I was selected for nuclear power where I served on three nuclear submarines which included two attack submarines - Shark, *USS Scamp* with two WestPac tours including multiple Special Opertions, and commanding officer of Fleet Ballistic Missile submarine completing five deterrent patrols in the Pacific.

During WWII, there were three general classifications of submarines: pre-war, 300-foot test depth, and 400-foot test depth. The 300-foot submarine class were built quickly to increase the size of the fleet in response to immediate need resulting from the attack on Pearl Harbor. The 400-foot class was in response to the Japanese knowledge of the 300-foot depth limits in the design of their depth charges. Neither class had the snorkel capability which required offensive submerged operations. In short, they operated as surface ships with a capability to submerge. As such, it was important they could submerge in minimum time should they be detected or attacked—when submerging to periscope depth in less than 50 seconds was of paramount importance. The significant conclusion of offensive actions on the surface is borne out by the fact that all five Medal of Honor recipients were submarine commanding officers for offensive combat performed when on the surface which did not diminish the many successful attacks performed at periscope depth. With today's technology, offensive attacks will most likely be performed below periscope depth.

Historical surface operations came to an end with the installation of the snorkel which permitted running the diesel engines while still submerged.

Today, nuclear power gives submarines unlimited capabilities in underwater warfare in that the only limitation they have is the food supply they can carry on board, resulting in the ability to never having to come to periscope depth to charge batteries. In addition, they have complete control over the internal submarine environment by being able to make unlimited fresh water from the sea, then making their oxygen from the fresh water. They are also in complete control of the internal environment, including oxygen, carbon monoxide/dioxide, and potential cooking odors. Showers are routine and an onboard laundry increases the morale of all on board.

Living on board a nuclear submarine means that the environment one starts out with is the same one ends with. It is not uncommon that the first ten days of any deployment all on board will be exposed to the minor airborne ailments brought on board, followed by no further minor ailments for the remainder of the deployment. While one would believe that those living on a nuclear submarine would be exposed to higher levels of radiation, the truth is that they receive significantly lower doses than those at home, due to both the design of nuclear related components, high standards of operational controls, operator training, and the commitment to maintenance and cleanliness.

—SEE THE CD TO READ MUCH MORE ABOUT SUBMARINES—

AIRPLANE vs. MOUNTAIN
Jim O'Malley USN 1951-1955 VP-22

Jim O'Malley was a Naval Patrol Squadron based on the island of Okinawa, flying patrol on the coast of China. Although we were not in a declared war with China, we were fighting Chinese troops in Korea. It was considered necessary to provide intelligence on movement of Chinese troops and vessels in the straits between the mainland and Formosa, (Taiwan). We were to fly three miles off the coastline, so as not to violate Chinese air space.

In order not to provide gunnery practice for the Chinese YAK and MIG-15 fighter planes with our lumbering Patrol Bomber we flew a good portion of our patrol at night. As a deterrent to our observation by Air Search Radar we had an operational ceiling of 500 feet. This meant we were low enough to get our feet wet, and low enough to be below the overcast so we were rained on when the weather was inclement. In the winter the weather was inclement virtually every day and every night. Since our sturdy craft, a P2V- 5 Neptune leaked everywhere, we got more than our feet wet.

Jim O'Malley

My job was being the radar operator. We had a long range navigational radar, and a short range bombing radar. Since the long range radar could be picked up and tracked by the forces on the ground, we were limited to using it only a few seconds at a time. Since we flew so much of our mission in the dark, our radar was the eyes of our gallant, if fuzzy, aviators.

There were several reasons we were to avoid flying over the Chinese land. We were to avoid provocation, even though we were fighting them face-to-face a few hundred miles away. The Chinese mainland had a great deal of antiaircraft weaponry everywhere. The costal area of China was very mountainous with peaks well over 1000 feet, remember we flew below 500 feet.

So it happened one dark moonless night that an unexpected cross wind along with some questionable navigation, (remember we were only 500 feet off the deck, below the overcast, which made conventional "star shot" navigation impossible.) we found ourselves several miles inland over China.

This was a bad thing for several reasons. If we were spotted by the Chinese anti-aircraft gunners, we stood a good chance of being shot down. Since we were flying at 500 feet and the surrounding mountains were well over 1000 feet we could fly right into a mountain. In every aircraft - mountain collision the mountain always won. In the dark it was literally impossible to see what was in front of you.

Our only hope of survival was to pick our way through the mountains without detection until we were once again over open water. We could not use our powerful navigation radar, since it would be picked up by the Chinese and give away our position. We could not climb to a higher altitude since we would then appear on the enemy air search radar also giving our position. We would have to rely on our weaker, directional bombing radar to guide us out.

The more sophisticated technology that presents topographical information had not yet been invented. Our radar did however show the presence of high altitude mountains. The trained eye could detect a "shadow" behind a land mass indicating that whatever it was, it was higher than you were. Radar is line-of-sight. Our intrepid crew hoped that I possessed such a trained eye.

And so we began our tedious journey back to safety. Staring into the radar screen, I began a litany of course corrections to keep us away from the mountains and on a heading that would take us to the coastline.

All was going pretty well, when our bow gunner in the turret in the nose of the plane reported "Mountain dead ahead !" The pilot asked "O'Malley, what do you see?" I responded after staring so intently at the radar screen that my eye balls practically slammed up against it, "Clear ahead." Minutes later, with panic creeping into his voice, our bow gunner repeated "mountain dead ahead!" Again the pilot asked what I could see.

I repeated that all was clear ahead. The pilot asked if we could veer to the left or right. My response was that if we did, we would indeed hit a mountain. We pressed on.

A third time the bow gunner screamed "MOUNTAIN DEAD AHEAD!!!" Again I assured the pilot we had to continue on our course. Now the bow gunner abandoned his turret and came up on the flight deck and shrieked if I didn't turn the plane he would kill me himself. Just then the plane shuddered and bucked a little. Bow gunner, "What was that?" Pilot, "We just flew through a thundercloud." Me, "I am trying to resist the urge to throw you out of the plane if you don't get away from me."

As our hearts started to beat again, we continued to pick our way, gingerly until I gleefully reported we passed the coastline and we were now over open water, out of range of the foes guns.

To show how this experience desensitized us, we had another mountain experience. Near the duty runway on our home field on the island of Okinawa there is a mountain that rises 1600 feet in the air. We were returning from a patrol on a foggy day when I spotted the familiar "shadow" on the radar screen. We were flying at about 1000 feet. In a rather matter-of-fact voice I reported, "Pilot from radar, there is a mountain dead ahead." The response was, "Radar from pilot, will we go over it or around it?" "Pilot, if we continue this course and altitude, we will go through it!" "What do you recommend." "I recommend an emergency right turn." This prompted the plane standing on its right wing as we lurched to the right and idly watched the mountain as we passed by. All this took place with the intensity of a discussion of what movie was playing at the mess hall.

Fortunately in these instances the final score was Airplane 2, Mountain 0. Otherwise I would probably to this day be a part of the Asian landscape.

ONE OF A BAND OF BROTHERS
Ruben Ramirez

Interview by Jonathon Warren/Sharon Hayes

Wartime service was something the Ramirez family knew well. After watching three of my older brothers fight and return home from battles in the Pacific during WWII, it was my turn to do my part. At 19 and finishing high school, I volunteered to join the Air Force, rather than be drafted. After all, in 1949, I was having a hard time finding a job because of the draft, and my remaining two brothers were also answering the call to serve our country in a "police action" in South Korea.

I was selected to be on a communications team and sent to school in Biloxi, Mississippi, with additional training in San Antonio, Texas. I dealt with radio and code, transmitting from air to ground and vice-versa. In 1950, I was travelling on a troop ship overseas for additional training in Japan. I participated in training with a specialized group of 13 men who were selected to go into South Korea. Our mission would be to perform communication interference. When we landed in Tagu, I noticed the lack of legitimate landing areas. Our fources were using makeshift runways out of whatever materials were available. The field we landed on was little more than a field of dust over girded steel.

I wasn't a typical soldier. I didn't carry any sort of heavy weaponry, but rather I simply carried a sidearm to protect myself. We also carried out a different kind of assignment than most envision. My team and I were involved in communication work behind friendly lines. Instead of fighting on the front lines, we were busy performing important work away from the main front. Although we were away from the front line, we were still faced with the very real possibility of an attack. We couldn't be sure that we were always alone at our base.

We set up our camp at Ewa, a woman's university that had been bombed out during conflict. The facility was sufficient for meeting our needs for operation. We were able to carry out our work, but we were very vulnerable to an attack. The building was void of windows and very dangerous in the event of an enemy attack. At one point in our stay there, we were attacked by snipers who had located us and begun firing upon our facility. We were forced to evacuate.

We were fortunate to secure an escort by the 5th Army, which escorted us to their base of operations. Their base had much higher protection than our previous area. While at this base, I was able to cycle back to Japan for a couple of days in order to recuperate from my activities in South Korea. The base had a very distinct smell of battle about it. It was very strong and recognizable, but I can't put it into words.

The war had a big emotional, as well as a physical, toll on me. One day when I was finished eating, as I was going to discard my leftovers, there were children nearby begging for food. I offered one child my leftover biscuit. I hadn't known that the area was under surveillance and, as a result of my action, I was disciplined. It was a hard moment for me, because war required that I surpress my instinct to help those in need.

This may be my story, but in my family, we were truly a Band of Brothers, serving our country. My oldest brother, Bert, served in both WWII and South Korea. Three others--Joe, Tony, and David--served in WWII, and Richard and I served in South Korea. Miraculously, we all returned home.

If I could offer advice to the younger generation, I would tell them to not forget. Don't forget about the sacrifice that was offered during war. I have lived through the Korean War and seen my family live through other wars. I have seen the devastating effects of war, and I know that many details are forgotten. I believe that these events should not be forgotten by the next generation, and I hope that remembering history can lead the way for a better future.

REVENGE FOR A BROTHER
Ron Rosser, Korean Medal of Honor Recipient

Corporal, US Army Heavy Mortar Company

38th Infantry Regiment, 2nd Infantry Division

Note: This story features the exploits of Ron Rosser who has been a guest of *Lest We Forget* on two occasions. Ron has a story that defies the imagination. His exploits were so heroic that Ted Turner made a movie on it

KOREA

Ron Rosser

Born on October 24, 1929 in Columbus, Ohio Ron was the second oldest of seventeen children. He always looked out for his brothers and sisters. Ron joined the Army right after turning seventeen in 1946 and served for three years. In 1951, he re-enlisted in Crooksville, OH because his kid brother was killed early in the Korean conflict and he was bent on revenge. When he was sent to Japan instead of the Korean combat zone, he complained to his commanding officer and was reassigned to a heavy mortar company in the 38th Infantry Regiment in Korea.

On January 12, 1952 Rosser by then a Corporal was a forward observer with Company L directing U.S. mortar fire while his infantry company assaulted a snow covered hill held by a Chinese battalion near the town of Ponggilli. His unit was under fire from two directions. Seeing hundreds of enemy troops swarming over the area, he called in mortar fire, but the Americans continued to take heavy casualties—by the time they reached a point about a hundred yards below the crest of the hill, only 35 of the 170 who had begun the battle were still able bodied. When the commanding officer, badly wounded, used Rosser's radio to call headquarters for instructions, he was ordered to try once again to take the hill. Seeing that his commander was in no condition to carry out the order, Rosser turned over his radio to his assistant and volunteered to organize the remaining men and lead the charge.

As he made his way up the hill, some of the soldiers who had started with him had already been driven back down; others never followed him at all! Halfway to the Chinese position, he realized that he was alone, but he was determined to make the enemy pay for his brother's death. Armed only with a carbine and grenades, screaming like a wild man, he plowed on through the snow, oblivious to the heavy fire all around him. Reaching a bunker in which nine Communist soldiers were crouching, he shot one of them in the face, then whirled and killed another one who had a machine gun trained on him. He then jumped into the trench and killed five more of the enemy. When two escaped to another bunker, Rosser followed them and threw his grenade inside, he shot both as they emerged from the explosion.

Rosser moved on to another trench line and killed five more Chinese soldiers. His ammunition finally exhausted, he went back down the hill to resupply himself by stripping rifle magazines and grenades of dead and injured GIs, then climbed the hill again. He threw a grenade into the first trench he came to, killing seven more of the enemy, then moved over open ground, firing at every Chinese soldier in sight. When his ammunition was again gone, he repeated his resupply trip down the hill, then returned a third time to continue his one-man battle.

After more than an hour of fighting, Rosser organized a withdrawal of his decimated company, ordering those who could walk to take a dead or wounded comrade with them. While officially Ron was credited with singlehandedly killing 13 of the enemy, he calculated that he personally had killed more than twenty Chinese with grenades and another twenty eight with rifle fire.

Ron Rosser

Rosser returned to the States in May 1952 and announced to his mother that he had avenged his brother's death. After being awarded the Medal of Honor by President Harry Truman on July 7, 1952 he decided to stay in the Army. Ron has a picture of the Rosser family travelling to Washington DC on a school bus to receive the Medal of Honor.

Rosser - 2007

In 1968 he lost another brother, this time in Vietnam. When he requested assignment to the combat zone to even his personal score once again, he was refused. "If something happened to you, even by accident, it would be hard to explain," his commanding officer told him. Rosser retired from the Army soon after.

HOW I WANTED TO STAY OUT OF THE WAR
Don Strasser

Interviewed by Gary C. Lulenski, M.D.

I was born in Chicago during the World's Fair on June 12, 1933. I went to trade school and took college courses and all of the sudden the Korean War came. I thought, *oh man, what am I going to do now. I cannot finish school like I wanted to,* but I decided whatever is going to be is going to be. As the war escalated, it appeared very likely I was going to be drafted. I had to decide whether to go into the Army or the Navy. Out of good fortune, the Navy let me in. They really did not need any more men, but I tried them and got shipped to the Great Lakes in March 1953. I went to boot camp for about three months. We did a lot of things, including physical fitness, at boot camp. I learned how to fight fires and handle ship hawsers and also learned how to do firing on the range.

After we were done with training, the orders were posted where we were going to go. About 150 guys were in the class. When they posted the orders, there was shoving going on as everyone was trying to find out where they were going. A lot of guys got mad as heck.

I said "What are you guys looking at me for?"

"Do you see where you are going?"

I said, "No."

"You are going to the east coast—Newport, Rhode Island."

Don Strasser

I said, "That can't be." I looked at it, and that was right. There was about 18 of us going to that area. At Rhode Island, I did some cooking in the mess hall. I was going back and forth to home while I was at Great Lakes but could not do that anymore from Rhode Island. We got there by going on a train and the Navy really treated us well, as we got a Pullman car. We went to Pittsburgh and then to New York. We switched in Boston to another train.

When I arrived, a lieutenant was telling various enlisted men where they were going to be assigned. He said I was going on the *USS John S. McCain* which was a brand new ship. That was really an honor to go on a Destroyer. I do not know why they chose me. All the time I was on it, which was about 2 years, we were always in the shipyard or on trial runs going back and forth. We had to come in and they had to cut some of the hull underneath to put new generators in and re-do some of the electrical work. We were operating out of Newport and did trial runs up the coast and close to Canada. While we were doing some of those maneuvers, the helmsman was not paying attention and he ran over a lobster trap. The old man really chewed his butt for that.

We never did get to Korea. The war ended and we were still hanging around doing nothing. We went down to Santiago, Cuba, and there were more problems with the ship and we had to go back to the shipyards in Charleston, Massachusetts. Then we went back to Newport and had to go back to Rhode Island for some other problem.

Then we were told the *McCain* was going to the west coast. I didn't really want to do that so I asked if I could stay on the east coast. I had met a girl and was kind of engaged to her. I figured she would follow me if I was on the east coast but not if I was far away. I requested another ship. I was assigned to the *USS Daley*. It was an old WWII Destroyer. Soon after I got on the ship somebody made a mistake and took a plate off the bilge and while he was monkeying around, water started to come in and they had to pump all of the water out. Luckily the ship was tied up at that time.

I had weekends off there some of the time. My girlfriend did move to Boston but finally I was told we were going to ship out. I just had to take that in stride. No one knew where we were going. We were out 100 miles at sea before we found out. They told us we were going to go to Africa and then there was a war going on between Israel and Egypt. I thought, *Jesus, I am never going to get home. This is it.* By the time we got there, the war was over as it was only six days.

With no war there, we ended up patrolling up and down the Suez Canal. During that time we were bumped by another Destroyer and one of our crew had to weld a steel plate on it. It was a small hole fortunately and we continued with our patrol duty. After quite a long time, it was obvious I was getting close to being discharged. I talked with the captain and he said, "yes, we will let you get off the ship," and from there I went to an airforce base and was flown to Pakistan. I stayed in the hotel and met some drunken British soldier who was building bridges there in Pakistan. He asked me, "Hey, mate, do you want a beer." I said, "Yea, ok." He said, "Hey, mate, do you want another beer?" That went on and I kept saying "Yea, yea." By the time I got out of there, man I was really wowed. We were fairly restricted to the Air Force base and did not go into town much. There was no war going on, it was just a place I had to go to where I could catch an Air Force plane either going east or west to California. I did not want to go to California so I decided to take a plane going the other direction. I ended up going to Libya. They had a very fine American airbase there. I stayed for just a short while.

At the time I was trying to get back to the States, they did not fly at nighttime; I didn't know if it was because they didn't know how to use the instruments. There were all Air Force guys there. I was the only sailor trying to get back to the states. I took a lot of ribbing. I thought, "Jesus, get me out of here. These guys are going to hang me."

Finally, we flew to the Azores for a day or so. Then we flew to McGuire Air Force Base. I was pretty sunburned by the time I got there. The guys said, "where has this guy been?" I told them I had to wait around in Africa for awhile. I was able to buy some cigarettes there and I figured the guys at home could use them more than I did. I took a bunch of them back to New Jersey (where it was plenty cold compared to Africa), and gave them to some of the enlisted men there. It was time to be discharged, so I was told I could go to New York or go to Boston. I chose Boston and went to visit my girlfriend. Then I returned to Chicago and my girlfriend came there a week or so later and I was discharged.

Shortly after I returned home things started to happen again. The barracks in Lebanon were blown up and about 300 Marines were killed. I thought to myself, *please, I do not want to go again.* They never did call me back. I was in the Navy about four years and was in the Reserves for awhile, but did not return to duty.

I was a bosun's mate at that time and did a lot of work securing the Destroyer when it came into port and helped take care of maintenance work, such as, painting. There weren't any battles and although there were some ships sunk while we were in the Suez Canal, we didn't have any combat or damage to our ship.

I did meet a fellow I stayed pretty close with from Cleveland. He was a real ladies man. He thought he was God's gift to women. I did not marry the girl I had met. I met another girl in Chicago and married her in October 1962.

I had to look around to try to get a job. Fortunately, one of my family members was a state representative in Illinois. He got me a job with the county highway and that worked out real well.

I was thinking back to unusual episodes that happened while I was on active duty. I remember we had a shell that did not fire when we were in the Suez Canal and so it had to be removed. There were 3 or 4 guys there with heavy gloves on. I was not paying attention and just about grabbed that shell and it would have burned my fingers off. Someone yelled at me and I did not touch it. The sailors with the protective equipment on threw it in the ocean and it did not blow up so no one got hurt.

Another funny memory I had was in basic training. When we were at the receiving station, a guy asked the chief why there was a fence around the compound. The chief said "well, that is to keep the civilians out." Of course, all of the guys roared and roared because that was obviously not correct. I actually had numbers to put on with ink or magic marker that would identify us while we were in boot camp. That was a little bit unexpected.

When I became employed after my duty in Chicago with the city, I worked as a draftsman for about 7-8 years and then I saw an opening in the highway department. I applied for that and again was a draftsman and learned more about engineering. We did highway work and Calculus and all sorts of things. I went to school and learned more about mathematics. Some of the classes were taught by the highway department. I ended up working on part of the Interstate System as that was under construction at that time. My wife was from Michigan and she had friends in New Buffalo that lived on a farm. We ended up moving back to Michigan from Chicago. By that time, I had worked long enough to retire, so I have lived here in Southwestern Michigan since then.

I look back upon my military career as sometimes I hated it and sometimes I enjoyed it quite a bit. We did travel a lot of different places and all in all it was a good experience. I thought about staying in, but decided I was going to get married and would want to settle down and have a regular job.

Another really interesting episode happened when we were being repaired and refitted at the gitmo. Some of the guys had bought bottles of rum and had too much to drink and ended up throwing the bottles into the water. The captain got pretty upset about that. One guy failed to pay attention when the ship was leaving and we were actually under power, but he was able to grab a hawser that was thrown to him and was able to scrabble onto the ship. I knew if he had missed the ship he would have been in big trouble.

All in all, my experience was a time that was interesting and I have mostly good feelings about it. I encourage young people to be thankful for their health as now that I am quite a bit older, my health is not so good. I get good care here at the convalescent center. There are a lot of activities and the people here really treat me well.

It really wasn't that I wanted to stay out of the war, I just couldn't catch up to it.

STORIES FROM VIETNAM WAR

1959 – 1975

VIETNAM

MY LAST MONTHS IN THE AIR FORCE
Dennis Churchill

Air Force Aircraft Mechanic on C-130 / Vietnam service: 1968-69

Dennis Churchill

My permanent base in the Far East was located in Taiwan. Although I was assigned to Taiwan for 15 months, I was transferred to Vietnam for nine months of that time.

The last of my four temporary duty assignments in Vietnam was to Cam Rahn Bay for 90 days. My main job responsibility was to provide maintenance on C-130 cargo planes. I was assigned to a flight line aircraft maintenance ground crew. This base was fairly safe compared to other bases located towards the northern part of Vietnam. Since it was somewhat safe, it was used as a base for incoming replacements troops, outgoing troops (back to the "World") and those that were KIA's (Killed in Action). When the civilian planes would land, we'd stand on top of our planes and watch the new troops come in and also check out the stewardesses that were on the flights.

The stewardesses would only stay for a short time and would leave with the troops going home. All work on the planes stopped when the stewardesses would arrive. A lot of the time the stewardesses would walk across the flight line right past our planes. If we were lucky enough to have our plane parked near the Base Operation building, we would be close enough to say hi to them. They must have had bad flights coming over because they very seldom acknowledged our presence.

Also on board some of the planes were crates of somewhat fresh pineapples for the officers' chow hall. We've been known to break into the 20 bushel crates and sneak a few for ourselves. I'm not sure, but others must have done the same somewhere along the trip. By the time they arrived in Vietnam, the crate was usually only about three-quarters full.

I was transferred back to CCK (Ching Chuan Kang) AB in Taiwan for the last two months of my overseas tour. Since I would be transferring back to the States and only had three months left in the Air Force, I received orders for an early out in June '69 for an August discharge month. I was scheduled to start the out-processing 30 days before my DOS (Date of Separation). Before you were allowed to transfer to another base or discharge, you must be cleared by the dentist, get a physical, go through a psychological exam, process through payroll and personnel which is all part of "out-processing."

I left CCK (Ching Chuan Kang) on a military plane to Taipei, Taiwan. I then had to catch a commercial flight back to the "world" (United States). We stopped in Japan on the way to McCord AFB in the state of Washington where I would be discharged.

When I arrived at McCord AFB in the early evening, I noticed people with signs against the fence, around the perimeter of the flight line. We thought they might be waiting for some dignitary. When we got closer we noticed the signs were referring to us. Signs saying, *"Baby Killer," "No*

More War," "Stop The Killing of Vietnamese," and so on. We didn't know what it all meant.

I processed out of the Air Force the next day and took a commercial flight out that night to Chicago. Before I got on the plane I called my folks and told them what time I'd be arriving in Chicago O'Hare airport. In order to fly military stand-by, I had to wear my uniform on the plane. On the flight home, there were only about 15 people on the plane. It was a large plane, perhaps a 707 and there were a lot of empty seats. I had a stewardess all to myself. She sat with me most of the way home, asking me what it was like being in Vietnam. Didn't talk to her much about that, but we did talk about a lot of other things, like who those people were standing outside the flight line at McCord AFB. That is when I learned about the amount of protesting going on.

I arrived at O'Hare airport in Chicago around 4-5:00am. Hardly a soul was in the airport, nothing like now. I walked around looking for Mom & Dad. I saw a couple of younger people with white robes on and barefoot. They were making comments about me and pointing at me. By the time I got close to them I knew they were talking about me and the fact I was in the military. As they walked up to me, I saw Mom, Dad and sisters coming toward me. My eyes filled with tears and emotion as I ran over to them. It was probably a good thing that I didn't wait to see what the two protesters had to say. On the way home, Dad asked me who those people were. I just told him I didn't know… "Chicago, you just don't know what kind of people you're going to meet up with."

As we drove into Michigan, I knew I was finally home and could leave all the memories behind me at last. I saw the intersection of Napier & I-94, then on to Hillendale Rd. Drove by "Coon's Curve," around that corner then home to Spinks Corners. Turned right on Park, noticed Dad's Garage, Grandpa and Grandma's house, Aunt Marie & Uncle Elmer's house next door and into our driveway. My bedroom downstairs was much the same. It was good to be home.

IA DRANG & AGENT ORANGE

A Vietnamese military maxim states: *"He who controls the Central Highlands controls South Vietnam."*

In late October '65 a large North Vietnamese force had overrun the Special Forces Camp at Plei Mei The First Cavalry Div (Airmobile) was given the mission of searching the area around Plei Mei. On Nov 14, the 1st Battalion, 7th Cavalry (Gerry Owen) was given the mission of air assaulting into the Ia Drang Valley to search and kill the enemy. LTC Hal Moore, was the CO of the Battalion and he had spent several years at Fort Benning, GA developing the Air Mobility concept for the 11th Avn Gp.

The Ia Drang battle was the first and largest battle of the Vietnam War. It actually involved several Battalions, the 1/7th, the 2nd Bn, 7th Cav, 1 Bn, 5th Cav, 2nd Bn 8th Cav, 2nd Bn 12th Cav and numerous aviation, artillery and engineer units. All told there were 306 American KIA, while the enemy had several thousand confirmed KIA's.

LTC Moore (later to become LTG Moore) and Joe Galloway, a civilian reporter for UPI later wrote a book "*We Were Soldiers Once..and Young*." General Moore's book covers the battles at LZ X Ray and LZ Albany. The battles were basically over by Nov 20 (7 days after the initial assault).

Later Mel Gibson produced "*We Were Soldiers*," a very realistic and respectful treatment of the three-day battle of Ia Drang. Many film critics have rated the movie in the top 10 of all war movies. However, the movie does not portray the second phase that took place the following day (Nov 17) at Landing Zone Albany in which, of the approximately 400 Americans who went into battle, 155 were killed and 128 wounded. This one-day action at Albany was the bloodiest of the Vietnam War for US Troops.

REMEMBRANCES OF IA DRANG
John Clark Co A/ 1st of the 7th Cavalry 1965-66=

The following is written by John Clark who at the time of the battle was a Specialist Fourth Class in Company A, 1st Bn, 7th Cavalry. He was a radio operator for CPT Tony Nadal who was Co A's commander. His home town was Buchanan and he now lives in St Joseph, MI.

I was raised in Galien, Michigan, and graduated from high school there. I work and lived in Buchanan, Michigan, for several years and have been self-employed since 1979.

It hardly seems possible that I've been out of Vietnam 46 years, and 47 years from the Ia Drang Valley that was written in the book by General Hal Moore and Joe Galloway, *We Were Solders Once And Young*, and depicted in the movie "*We Were Soldiers*" starring Mel Gibson. The 1st Calvary Division Air Mobile went to Vietnam in July of 1965. I was a member of Company A, 1st Battalion, 7th Cavalry. We operated from Bong Song to Kontum to Pleiku in the central highlands. Our base camp was An Khe which is about 50 miles inland from Qui Nhon.

Over the years I have heard many people offer their opinion on why the battle was fought. In November when we were ordered to pursue the North Vietnamese Army (NVA) we were a little over 400 line people in the battalion, severely under strength, instead of the 750 people we should have had. The NVA was estimated to be 1500 to 3500 soldiers by various accounts (there were 1300 killed in the three day battle body count). I believe the US forces wanted this fight as bad as the NVA wanted this first battle with an American unit. The rest is history and can be read in the book as it was written by Gen Hal Moore and Joe Galloway.

I just returned this past Sunday from a reunion with about 55 of the Ia Drang veterans. Maybe it is my age (71-years-old) and maybe it was a reflection of 50-plus years of considering why we went and whether the losses were worth it. It amazes me that we lost 58,000 young men, never lost a major battle and in 1972 had pulled most of our troops out and left the war to the South Vietnamese to defend the south.

Was it worth it? The generals and politicians say so, but I'm sure I'm not the only combat soldier who has served that has some reservations. So I've adopted the view of not talking too much about the war and the battles, but to go see my friends and enjoy the company of friends that had so much in common. Our lives are fleeting, but there is that attitude that is optimistic about the country and the military. We spent some time this past weekend with some Special Forces guys and some Navy seals. What awesome young men they are and they made me feel that we are in good hands with these guys and the rest of the military we have. It would be well for the politicians to step up.

SANDBAG FOR A MACHINE GUN
Jack P. Smith on the Battle of the Ia Drang Valley and the Legacy of the Vietnam War

NOTE: Jack P. Smith gave this speech on 8 November 2003, at the Ia Drang Survivors Banquet in Crystal City, Virginia

I have pancreatic cancer. If it is Agent Orange, it's not the first time this damned war has tried to kill me. Let me tell you about the first time. In fact, the whole and true story of my journey home from Vietnam. But before I do, let me set the scene for you.

It is November 1965. The Ia Drang Valley. The nearest town, Pleiku, a remote Vietnamese province capital. And west of town, beyond the stilted long-huts of the Montagnards, flat scrub jungle cover the hills by the Cambodian border. A smugglers' haven, and now the infiltration route for the first North Vietnamese regulars to invade South Vietnam.

American regular infantry, the first sent to Vietnam as the war escalates, have come to this border country to hunt the People's Army of Vietnam. They are the men of the First Air Cav, the first Army infantry division to ride into war in helicopters. The leading unit is Lt. Col. Hal Moore's 1st Battalion, 7th Cavalry Regiment. Driving their choppers into a landing zone designated X-Ray, a few miles from the Cambodian border, on the 14th of November, 1965, they land on top of a North Vietnamese Army base. A ferocious battle ensues that lasts three whole days. Hal Moore's battalion several times comes within inches of being overrun. In the end, reinforced to brigade strength, the U.S. troops destroy the better part of a North Vietnamese division at X-Ray. Seventy-nine Americans are killed, 121 wounded, a total of 200 U.S. casualties, the highest toll of the war till then...but there are roughly two thousand North Vietnamese casualties.

I came in on the last day of the battle. I remember the NVA bodies were piled so thick around the foxholes you could walk on them for 100 feet in some places. The American GIs were the same color as the dirt and all had that thousand-yard stare of those newly initiated to combat.

The next day, after a restless night, my battalion, the 2/7, walked away from X-Ray toward another clearing called LZ Albany. Around lunchtime, we were jumped by a North Vietnamese formation. Like us, about 500-strong.

The fighting was hand-to-hand. I was lying so close to a North Vietnamese machine-gunner that I simply stuck out my rifle and blew off his head. It was, I think, the only time during the war that a U.S. battalion was ever overrun. The U.S. casualties for this fourth day of battle: 155 killed, 121 wounded. More dead than wounded. The North Vietnamese suffered a couple of hundred casualties.

The fight at LZ Albany was largely overlooked as an aberration- poor leadership, green troops. In this first encounter between their main force regulars, the two sides focused instead on X-Ray. Interestingly, both drew the same conclusion: that each could win using the tactics of attrition.

The ferocity of the fighting during those four days was appalling. At one point in the awful afternoon at Albany, as my battalion was being cut to pieces, a small group of enemy came upon me, and thinking I had been killed (I was covered in other people's blood), proceeded to use me as a sandbag for their machine gun. I pretended to be dead. I remember the gunner had bony knees that pressed against my sides. He didn't discover I was alive because he was trembling more than I was. He was, like me, just a teenager.

The gunner began firing into the remnants of my company. My buddies began firing back with rifle grenades, M-79s, to those of you who know about them. I remember thinking, "Oh, my God. If I stand up, the North Vietnamese will kill me; and if I stay lying down, my buddies will get me." Before I went completely mad, a volley of grenades exploded on top of me, killing the enemy boy and injuring me.

It went on like this all day and much of the night. I was wounded twice and thought myself dead. My company suffered about 93 percent casualties--93 percent.

This sort of experience leaves scars. I had nightmares. For years afterwards I was sour on life, by turns angry, cynical, and alienated.

Then one day I woke up and saw the world as I believe it really is, a bright and warm place. I looked afresh at my scars and marveled, not at the frailty of human flesh, but at the indomitable strength of the human spirit. This is the miracle of life. Like other Vietnam veterans, I began to put the personal hurt behind me, and I started to examine the war itself and to make sense of it.

When I went back to Vietnam a few years ago, I met Gen. Vo Nguyen Giap, the man who engineered the defeat of the French at Dien Bien Phu and then commanded North Vietnamese forces in the war with South Vietnam and us. He conceded that because of the Ia Drang his plans to cut Vietnam in half and take the capital had been delayed ten years. But then, he chuckled, it didn't make a difference, did it?

We won every battle, but the North Vietnamese in the end took Saigon. What on earth had we been doing there? Was all that pain and suffering worth it, or was it just a terrible waste?

This is why Vietnam veterans often have so much trouble letting go, what sets them apart from veterans of other wars.

Nothing is so precious to a nation as its youth. And so, to squander the lives of the young in a war that, depending on one's point of view, either should never have been fought or we were never prepared to win, seems crazy. Yet, that's exactly what happened in Vietnam. However justified the war seemed in 1964 and 1965, and, remember, almost all Americans then thought it was, it no longer seemed that way after Tet in 1968. And no matter what you may remember of the war, we never really fought it to win.

When I was wounded it caused a minor sensation at home. My father was Howard K. Smith, the anchorman and TV news commentator, who was then at the peak of his career. That the son of a famous person should get shot in Vietnam was, in 1965, news. When I returned to the United States after my tour in Vietnam, President Johnson, who was a friend of my dad's, invited me to a dinner party at the White House. I remember a tall, smiling man who thanked me for my service and sacrifice. I liked him then; I still do today. Yet no one bears as much responsibility for the conduct of the war as he does.

In the Gulf War we took six months to put half a million troops into the war zone. In Vietnam, it took more than six years. We were too timid to carry the fight to the enemy until the end, and we tried, impossibly, to keep the war contained to South Vietnam.

The result was that our enemy, a small country waging total war, that is, using all its resources, saw a super power fighting a limited war and concluded that if it could just sustain the 10-to-1 casualties we were inflicting for a while, then we would tire and leave, and it would win. Of course, Ho Chi Minh was right. The war also changed character. The Sino-Soviet split made it seem less like a war of national liberation and more like a civil war - an internal squabble. After the Tet Offensive in 1968, we quit and began the longest and bloodiest retreat in U.S. history. Dean Rusk, then-Secretary of State, many years later ruefully told me, "They outlasted us."

The fact is, democracies don't fight inconclusive wars for remote goals in distant places for very long. Pham Van Dong, Ho's successor, said that.

Whether the war was right or whether it was wrong, it was fought in such a way it could never really have been brought to a conclusion. That now seems clear with time. What a waste. It's why so many veterans of Vietnam feel bitter.

Well, we finally did get our parades and we finally did build our memorial on the Mall in Washington. These helped. But so many veterans were still haunted by the war, and I was, too.

Fourteen years ago, I watched the Berlin Wall come down and, as an ABC News correspondent, I witnessed first hand the collapse of communism. I remember thinking, "My God, containment worked. We won the Cold War." And however meaningless Vietnam seemed at the time, it contributed to the fall of communism. Hardly justification for what we went through in Vietnam, but at least it was something.

Then ten years ago, an event changed me. An opportunity to go back to Vietnam. With ten other Ia Drang veterans, I traveled back to the jungle in the Central Highlands and for several days walked the battlefield. Did I find the answer to my question? No, I don't know if what we did in the war ultimately was worth it. But what I did find surprised me.

North Vietnam may have conquered the South, but it is losing the peace. A country that three decades ago had the fourth strongest army in the world has squandered its wealth on fighting its neighbors and is poor and bankrupt. You look at Vietnam today and you wonder why they fought the war. Many North Vietnamese wonder, too.

What struck me was the overwhelming peacefulness of the place, even in the clearing where I fought, LZ Albany. I broke down several times. I wanted to bring back some shell casings - some physical manifestation of the battle - to lay at the foot of The Wall here in Washington. But, do you know, search as I did, I could not find any. The forces of nature had simply erased it. And where once the grass had been slippery with blood, there were flowers blooming in that place of death. So I pressed some and brought them back. Flowers...that's all that I could find in that jungle clearing that once held terror and now held beauty.

What I discovered with time may seem obvious, but it had really escaped me all those years on my journey home from Vietnam: The war is over. It certainly is for Vietnam and the Vietnamese. As I said on a Nightline broadcast when I came back, "This land is at peace, and so should we be." For me, Vietnam has become a place again, not a war, and I have begun letting go.

I have discovered that wounds heal. That the friendship of old comrades breathes meaning into life. And that even the most disjointed events can begin to make sense with the passage of time.

This has allowed me, on evenings like this, to step forward and take pride in the service I gave my country. But never to forget what was, and will always be, the worst day of my life. The day I escaped death in the tall grass of the Ia Drang Valley. Thank you.

Note: This speech was given by Jack Smith on Nov 8, 2003 at the Ia Drang Survivors Banquet in Crystal City, VA. He died on April 7, 2004.

THE DAY IT BECAME THE LONGEST WAR
Charles Cooper

From: Cheers & Tears: A Marine's Story of Combat in Peace & War

Author LTG Charles G. Cooper, US Marine Corps (Ret) with Richard E Goodspeed, 2002, Wesley Press, Reno, NV 89533 / ISBN 1-55369-882-7

Forward

LTG Cooper had 35 years in the US Marines (1951-1986). During these years, he experienced combat tours in Korea and Vietnam. During his tour of duty, he developed a "Band of Brothers" philosophy of leadership that has become a trademark for Marine leadership. His book is a primer for any Marine seeking leadership principles. Every leader can gain from the outstanding examples of leadership in Cheers and Tears.

"The President will see you at two o'clock."

It was a beautiful fall day in November of 1965, early in the Vietnam War—too beautiful a day to be what many of us, anticipating it, had been calling "the day of reckoning." We didn't know how accurate that label would be.

The Pentagon is a busy place. Its workday starts early—especially if, as the expression goes, "there's a war on." By seven o'clock, the staff of Admiral David L. McDonald, the Navy's senior admiral and Chief of Naval Operations, had started to work. Shortly after seven, Admiral McDonald arrived and began making final preparations for a meeting with President Lyndon Baines Johnson.

Lt. Gen. Charles G. Cooper

The Vietnam War was in its first year, and its uncertain direction troubled Admiral McDonald and the other service chiefs. They'd had a number of disagreements with Secretary of Defense Robert S. McNamara about strategy, and had finally requested a private meeting with the Commander in Chief—a perfectly legitimate procedure. Now, after many delays, the Joint Chiefs were finally to have that meeting. They hoped it would determine whether the US military would continue its seemingly directionless buildup to fight a protracted ground war, or take bold measure that would bring the war to an early and victorious end. The bold measures they would propose were to apply massive air power to the head of the enemy, Hanoi, and to close North Vietnams' harbors by mining.

The situation was not a simple one, and for several reasons. The most important reason was that North Vietnam's neighbor to the north was communist China. Only 12 years had passed since the Korean War had ended in stalemate. The aggressors in that war had been the North Koreans. When the North Koreans' defeat had appeared to be inevitable, communist China had sent hundreds of thousands of its Peoples' Liberation Army "volunteers" to the rescue.

Now, in this new war, the North Vietnamese aggressor had the logistic support of the Soviet Union and, more to the point, of neighboring communist China. Although we had the air and naval forces with which to paralyze North Vietnam, we had to consider the possible reactions of the Chinese and the Russians.

Both China and the Soviet Union had pledged to support North Vietnam in the "war of national liberation" it was fighting to reunite the divided country, and both had the wherewithal to cause major problems. An important unknown was what the Russians would do if prevented from delivering goods to their communist protégé in Hanoi. A more important question concerned communist China, next-door neighbor to North Vietnam. How would the Chinese react to a massive pummeling of their alley? More specifically, would they enter the war as they had done in North Korea? Or would they let the Vietnamese, for centuries a traditional enemy, fend for themselves? The service chiefs had considered these and similar questions, and had also asked the Central Intelligence Agency for answers and estimates.

The CIA was of little help, though it produced reams of text, executive summaries of the texts, and briefs of the executive summaries –all top secret, all extremely sensitive, and all of

221

little use. The principal conclusion was that it was impossible to predict with any accuracy what the Chinese or Russians might do.

Despite the lack of a clear-cut intelligence estimate, Admiral McDonald and the other Joint Chiefs did what they were paid to do and reached a conclusion. They decided unanimously that the risk of the Chinese or Soviets reacting to massive US measures taken in North Vietnam was acceptably low, but only if we acted without delay. Unfortunately, the Secretary of Defense and his coterie of civilian "whiz kids" did not agree with the Joint Chiefs, and McNamara and his people were the ones who were actually steering military strategy. In the view of the Joint Chiefs, the United States was piling on forces in Vietnam without understanding the consequences. In the view of McNamara and his civilian team, we were doing the right thing. This was the fundamental dispute that had caused the Chiefs to request the seldom-used private audience with the Commander in Chief in order to present their military recommendations directly to him. McNamara had finally granted their request.

The 1965 Joint Chiefs of Staff had ample combat experience. Each was serving in his third war. The Chairman was General Earle Wheeler, US Army, highly regarded by his other members. General Harold Johnson was the Army Chief of Staff. A World War II prisoner of the Japanese, he was a soft-spoken, even-tempered, deeply religious man. General John P. McConnell, Air Force Chief of Staff, was a native of Arkansas and a 1932 graduate of West Point. The Commandant of the Marine Corps was General Wallace M. Greene, Jr., a slim, short, all-business Marine. General Greene was a Naval Academy graduate and a zealous protector of the Marine Corps concept of controlling its own air resources as a part of an integrated air-ground team. Last and by no means least was Admiral McDonald, a Georgia minister's son, also a Naval Academy graduate, and a naval aviator. While Admiral McDonald was a most capable leader, he was also a reluctant warrior. He did not like what he saw emerging as a national commitment. He did not really want the US to get involved with land warfare, believing as he did that the Navy could apply sea power against North Vietnam very effectively by mining, blockading, and assisting in a bombing campaign and in this way help to bring the war to a swift and satisfactory conclusion.

The Joint Chiefs intended that the prime topics of the meeting with the President would be naval matters—the mining and blockading of the port of Haiphong and naval support of a bombing campaign aimed at Hanoi. For that reason, the Navy was to furnish a briefing map, and that became my responsibility. We mounted a suitable map on a large piece of plywood, then coated it with clear acetate so that the chiefs could mark on it with greases pencils during the discussion. The whole thing weighed about 30 pounds.

The Military Office at the White House agreed to set up an easel in the Oval Office to hold the map. I would accompany Admiral McDonald to the White House with the map, put the map in place when the meeting started, then get out. There would be no strap-hangers at the military summit meeting with Lyndon Johnson. The map and I joined Admiral McDonald in his staff car for the short drive to the White House, a drive that was memorable only because of the silence. My admiral was totally preoccupied.

The chiefs' appointment with the President was for two o'clock, and Admiral McDonald and I arrived about 20 minutes early. The chiefs were ushered into a fairly large room across the hall from the Oval Office. I propped the map board on the arms of a fancy chair where all could view it, left two of the grease pencils in the tray attached to the bottom of the board, and stepped out into the corridor. One of the chiefs shut the door, and they conferred in private until someone on the White House staff interrupted them about fifteen minutes later. As they came out, I retrieved the map, then joined them in the corridor outside the President's office.

Precisely at two o'clock, President Johnson emerged from the Oval Office and greeted the chiefs. He was all charm. He was also big: at three or more inches over six feet tall and something on the order of 250 pounds, he was bigger than any of the chiefs. He personally ushered them into his office, all the while delivering gracious and solicitous comments with a Texas accent far more pronounced than the one that came through when he spoke on television. Holding the map board as the chiefs entered, I peered between them, trying to find the easel. There was none. The President looked at me, grasped the situation at once, and invited me in, adding, "You can stand right over here." I had become an easel—one with eyes and ears.

To the right of the door, not far inside the office, large windows framed evergreen bushes growing in a nearby garden. The President's desk and several chairs were farther in, diagonally across the room from the windows. The President positioned me near the windows, then arranged the chiefs in a semicircle in front of the map and its human easel. He did not offer them seats: they stood, with those who were to speak—Wheeler, McDonald, and McConnell— standing nearest the President. Paradoxically, the two whose services were most affected by a continuation of the ground buildup in Vietnam—Generals Johnson and Greene-stood farthest from the President. President Johnson stood nearest the door, about five feet from the map.

In retrospect, the setup—the failure to have an easel in place, the positioning of the chiefs on the outer fringe of the office, the lack of seating—did not augur well. The chiefs had expected the meeting to be a short one, and it met that expectation, too. Unfortunately, it also proved to be a meeting that was critical to the proper pursuit of what was to become the longest, most divisive, and least conclusive war in our nation's history—a war that almost tore the nation apart.

As General Wheeler started talking, President Johnson peered at the map. In five minutes or so, the general summarized our entry into Vietnam, the current status of forces, and the purpose of the meeting. Then he thanked the President for having given his senior military advisers the opportunity to present their opinions and recommendations. Finally, he noted that although Secretary McNamara did not subscribe to their views, he did agree that a presidential-level decision was required. President Johnson, arms crossed, seemed to be listening carefully.

The essence of General Wheeler's presentation was that we had come to an early moment of truth in our ever-increasing Vietnam involvement. We had to start using our principal strengths—air and naval power—to punish the North Vietnamese, or we would risk becoming involved in another protracted Asian ground war with no prospects of a satisfactory solution. Speaking for the chiefs, General Wheeler offered a bold course of action that would avoid protracted land warfare. He proposed that we isolate the major port of Haiphong through naval mining, blockade the rest of the North Vietnamese coastline and simultaneously start bombing Hanoi with B-52's.

General Wheeler then asked Admiral McDonald to describe how the Navy and Air Force would combine forces to mine the waters off Haiphong and establish a naval blockade. When Admiral McDonald finished, General McConnell added that speed of execution would be essential, and that we would have to make the North Vietnamese believe that we would increase the level of punishment if they did not sue for peace.

Normally, time dims our memories—but it hasn't dimmed this one. My memory of Lyndon Johnson on that day remains crystal clear. While General Wheeler, Admiral McDonald, and General McConnell spoke, he seemed to be listening closely, communicating only with an occasional nod. When General McConnell finished, General Wheeler asked the President if he had any questions. Johnson waited a moment or so, then turned to Generals Johnson and Green, who had remained silent during the briefing, and asked, "Do you fully support these ideas?" He followed with the thought that it was they who were providing the ground troops, in effect acknowledging that the Army and the Marines were the services that had most to gain or lose as a result of this discussion. Both generals indicated their agreement with the proposal. Seemingly deep in thought, President Johnson turned his back on them for a minute or so, then suddenly discarding the calm patient demeanor he had maintained throughout the meeting, whirled to face them and exploded. I almost dropped the map. He screamed obscenities, he cursed them personally, he ridiculed them for coming to his office with their "military advice." Noting that it was he who was carrying the weight of the free world on his shoulders, he called them filthy names—shitheads, dumb shits, pompous assholes –and used "the F-word" as an adjective more freely than a Marine in boot camp would use it. He then accused them of trying to pass the buck for World War III to him. It was unnerving, degrading. After the tantrum, he resumed the calm, relaxed manner he had displayed earlier and again folded his arms. It was as though he had punished them, cowed them, and would now control them. Using soft-spoken profanities, he said something to the effect that they all knew now that he did not care about their military advice. After disparaging their abilities, he added that he did expect their help.

He suggested that each one of them change places with him and assume that five incompetents had just made these "military recommendations." He told them that he was going to let them go through what he had to go through when idiots gave him stupid advice, adding that he had the whole damn world to worry about, and it was time to "see what kind of guts you have." He paused, as if to let it sink in. The silence was like a palpable solid, the tension like that in a drumhead. After thirty or forty seconds of this, he turned to General Wheeler and demanded that Wheeler say what he would do if he were the President of the United States.

General Wheeler took a deep breath before answering. He was not an easy man to shake: his calm response set the tone for the others. He had known coming in, as had the others, that Lyndon Johnson was an exceptionally strong personality and a venal and vindictive man as well. He had known that the stakes were high, and now realized that McNamara had prepared Johnson carefully for this meeting, which had been a charade.

Looking President Johnson squarely in the eye, General Wheeler told him that he understood the tremendous pressure and sense of responsibility Johnson felt. He added that probably no other President in history had had to make a decision of this importance, and further cushioned his remarks by saying that no matter how much about the presidency he did understand, there were many things about it that only one human being could ever understand. General Wheeler closed his remarks by saying something very close to this: "You, Mr. President, are that one human being. I cannot take your place, think your thoughts, know all you know, and tell you what I would do if I were you. I can't do it, Mr. President. No man can honestly do it. Respectfully, sir, it is your decision and yours alone."

Apparently unmoved, Johnson asked each of the other Chiefs the same question. One at a time, they supported General Wheeler and his rationale. By now, my arms felt as though they were about to break. The map seemed to weight a ton, but the end appeared to be near. General Greene was the last to speak.

When General Green finished, President Johnson, who was nothing if not a skilled actor, looked sad for a moment, then suddenly erupted again, yelling and cursing, again using language that even a Marine seldom hears. He told them he was disgusted with their naïve approach, and that he was not going to let some military idiots talk him into World War III. He ended the conference by shouting "Get the hell out of my office!"

The Joint Chiefs of Staff had done their duty. They knew that the nation was making a strategic military error, and despite the rebuffs of their civilian masters in the Pentagon, they had insisted on presenting the problem as they saw it to the highest authority and recommending solutions. They had done so, and they had been rebuffed. That authority had not only rejected their solutions, but had also insulted and demeaned them As Admiral McDonald and I drove back to the Pentagon, he turned to me and said that he had known tough days in his life, and sad ones as well ,but "…this has got to have been the worst experience I could ever imagine."

The US involvement in Vietnam lasted another ten years. The irony is that it began to end only when President Richard Nixon, after some backstage maneuvering on the international scene, did precisely what the Joint Chiefs of Staff had recommended to Present Johnson in 1965. Why had Johnson not only dismissed their recommendations, but also ridiculed them? It must have been that Johnson lacked something, Maybe it was foresight or boldness. Maybe it was the sophistication and understanding it took to deal with complex international issues. Or, since he was clearly a bully, maybe what he lacked was courage. We will never know. But had General Wheeler and the other received a fair hearing, and had their recommendations received serious study, the United States may well have saved the lives of most of its more than 55,000 sons who died in a war that its major architect, Robert Strange McNamara, now considers to have been a tragic mistake.

SOME GAVE SOME, SOME GAVE ALL
Ray Damaske

Even though it's been over forty-plus years ago, my recollection of this time still remains very clear in my memory. I guess maybe the close friends I said goodbye to makes me never forget. I write this memory by the request of Don Alsbro. He has listened to my perspective in the past years that we've known each other via *Lest We Forget* and he thought it would be appropriate for me to share my "non-military" account of my memory of the Vietnam war years.

Ray Damaske

In the spring of 1967, I was a senior in high school at Saint Joseph and looking forward to graduation. My desire was to attend Lake Michigan College in the fall. I was required to sign up in the Selective Service that summer.

My first meeting with the Selective Service Board on Wall Street in Benton Harbor was in the spring of 1968. They basically advised me that I would be allowed to finish my first year of college and that I would be eligible to be drafted. I continued my enrollment at LMC and in the fall of 1968 I was advised by the draft board that my "2-S" deferment would last until the following year. I enrolled for application at Western Michigan University. Lo and behold, in July of 1970 the Selective Service held their first draft lottery. My lucky number of "140" popped up and this designated me as fully eligible for the draft. My "2- S" status was still in effect until the fall of 1970.

I remember the tumultuous times during the months leading up to May of 1969. I recall very vividly the protests on the Western Michigan University campus and the wave of disdain for the local "ROTC" on campus. The "anti-war" sentiment was alive and well on the various campuses across the country. There was a nationwide protest originating in Washington DC in May against the war. Curiosity drew my friends and I to the large assembly of the student body of the campus at Western Michigan University. I was in the presence of the large demonstration at Milham Park in Kalamazoo. There were literally thousands of young students and other individuals [probably community organizers] waving peace flags, chanting, singing, yelling, etc. There was also local police, Michigan State police, and the National Guard, fending off the more activist protesters. I believe this movement called themselves "May Day" and it was directly related to the incident of the My Lai massacre and Lt. Calley.

I remember the National Guard marching up West Michigan Avenue, driving the crowds back and to restore as much order as possible. Rocks and debris were thrown everywhere—I remember well being hit with a rock! My 1963 Volkswagen also incurred minor damage.

As God as my witness, I was not in support of this calamity. My intrigue drew me to this unusual assembly on campus, and I wondered what it was all about. After listening to the anti-war "diatribe" against the United States and its military, I quickly knew what side of the fence I was on. I, in no way was in support of our involvement of this war, but I wasn't willing to sell my soul to the devil to denounce my birthright as a citizen of this great nation. I still considered myself a patriotic person. All of this is true, but the main reason for my humble "esprit de corps" feelings are because of some things that happened in my life.

I recall the pride of my uncles in their service in the military. I recall the effects it had on them after WWII. Both of them are gone now, but one of them fought on Omaha Beach at Normandy. He lost the use of his leg from a German sniper. The other uncle fought in the Philippines against

226

the Japanese. He killed more Japanese than he wanted to ever share in his memory. Both paid a heavy price—their health and quality of life for the remainder of their lives were cut short in their service to their country. Life was never quite the same for either one of them.

Back to 1970: I was called in to the Selective Service board and given the directive that stated I would be allowed to finish my semester. I was called one week after graduation and advised that I was re-classified as "1A" and that my physical exam papers were in the mail. That November, I gathered up my needed papers and headed to Detroit. All forty of us draftees met at the Selective Service street and got on that big ol' bus to Fort Shelby.

I knew it was my time and I guess I was ready. We arrived at Fort Shelby and were instructed to "do whatever we wanted" the night before, but be damned ready in the morning for Ft. Wayne! I didn't sleep too well that night…and I sure as heck didn't feel like partying in downtown Detroit that night. Morning came and I was there waiting for the bus.

We got to Ft. Wayne and we all lined up for registration. Our papers were reviewed as we were asked to strip and put on a makeshift worn-out hospital gown. We kept our socks on and stood in line staring at the hundreds of guys before us. I entered my appropriate line "D thru F" and the line seemed to pick up speed. We went through a medley of physical tests, questions, exams, shots, etc. We were then advised to go sit until our assigned number was called.

I went before a quiet, dark-eyed regimented doctor who reviewed my physical papers. He asked about an injury listed on my exam papers that I had on my wrist years before. I advised that it gave me occasional pain, but I could function and work. He examined it himself and paused. He looked in some big journal-type reference book and advised that "according to US Army regs, numbers, blah, blah" …. I was not acceptable. He then advised me to return to my family doctor at home and request a corrective operation surgery to restore full mobility. I was sent home along with 9 other guys and to my recollection, thirty were stamped "1A" and ready for the induction call. I was one of the "1-Y" deferments issued at that time. The military doctor, Dr. Holliday (I remember his name) gave me six months to have this corrective surgery done.

Six months to the day, I received a notification for a "pre-induction" physical review and made the same trip back to Detroit. There was no "night before" arrival for this group I was in. Arriving at Ft. Wayne, we gathered immediately in a different area, much like a Wal-Mart checkout lane with the review doctor behind a desk examining each of us. There were some twenty doctors in this area, and, believe it or not, the same "Doc Holliday" reviewed my status. Coincidence or fate?

When I returned home after the first physical, I went to my bone surgeon doctor and inquired on the corrective surgery needed as requested. Dr. Hudnutt and Dr. Brink advised against any surgery as they warned that the outcome could even further limit my usage of my wrist. I took their advisory in writing to the pre-induction and gave it to the military doctor. He reviewed and advised that he was sorry to tell me that I was not acceptable. Initially, this was great news to me, but to this day I have mixed emotions about not being able to serve and answer the call of duty.

A couple of months later, I was informed that a dear buddy and friend of mine was killed (July 2, 1970); it was very devastating to me. Sgt. Thomas Hayden Herndon was killed in a firefight. He was a ground casualty from enemy small arms fire. Tom was part of the 506th Infantry, 101st ABN Division. The real pain of his loss was when I was asked by his wonderful family to be a pall bearer for his funeral back home here. It was one of the most difficult things that I have ever done.

Ray Damaske

Years have come and gone since the Vietnam era, but to this day I am still confronted in my mind with the question of, "why Tommy?" Why didn't it happen to me? I was with Tommy the day before he shipped out and we said our farewell—little did I know it would be for keeps. When the LWF had the Traveling Vietnam Tribute Wall come here to Saint Joseph, I stood in front of that replica wall and in my peripheral view, I could see five names of our area heroes that had died in the war... some of them I knew..it could have been me!

Years have gone by. I was hired at the Berrien County Sheriff's Department in 1973 and served thirty years before retiring. I am proud of my service to the community in the area of law enforcement, but I still have as much pride in serving as a volunteer for the *Lest We Forget* veterans group. I have had the honor and privilege to meet and know the likes of Gail Cutler, Marv Fuller, Bob Heft, Al Rosinski, Mr. Frank Buckles, and the other patriot hero veterans who are no longer with us—may God be with them.

I still tear up when I hear the "*Battle Hymn of the Republic*" and "*God Bless the USA.*" I realize more and more as I get older that "some gave some...but some gave *all*!"

I want to meet them all again, someday...

WHERE IS THE HELP WHEN IT IS MOST NEEDED?
Douglas Dewey

Interview with wife Josephine R. Dewey, written by Robert Hatch

Sometimes early signs of a mental anomaly show up during the pre-pubescence period. Sometimes during the teen years and often they don't show up until stress is forced upon the individual. This is a situation in which all three occurred and ended fatally.

Douglas Dewey was born August 15, 1950. He was a young exuberant youth and was seemingly normal in every way. He did have his share of trouble in school, but not enough to have him expelled. After his Junior year, he dropped out from lack of interest.

After years of being a teen and an adult, he was drafted in the 1970s. It was not apparent to the draft board or its members that he was bi-polar. Signs of this were seen by his wife prior to his going into service, but since he was under control, it was not formally mentioned.

He joined the Army and was sent to Signal School at Fort Gordon, Georgia, where he was trained in teletype communications. His rating was SP4 E5. In 1973 he completed his GED and then was considered a high school graduate.

He was sent to Indochina, and then Vietnam. His letters home rarely mentioned his health, duties, friends or of course, location. He did mention that one of his company had put a bullet in his own foot to get out of there.

Douglas Dewey

He received medals for National Defense Service, Vietnam Service and Vietnam Campaign. Because of later revelations of his mental condition, he was released from service in a "Troop Program." This required his attending a 15-day annual training program (unless excused), complying with officer's orders, advising his unit commander of his current address at all times and complying with all officials' orders. He received his honorable discharge in April, 1974.

His wife had a lot of doubts regarding his ability to live in normal society considering the strange actions, either around others, or by himself, that she had experienced. Certainly there were good times, and other times, terrifying. Once during the Christmas season when her parents were in town shopping, he was with her and their son at home. Suddenly a loud backfire from a car propelled him and his family into the bathroom. Soon their was a knock on the door, he asked who was there, and refused to let her parents in—until later.

However the official records show that he was not free of the government's rehabilitative role. He was in and out of over 30 institutions in the following years, often escaping and walking away. He couldn't stand being cooped up. Claustrophobia was one of his many ailments. The medicines helped periodically, but he would go off them, and start his manic actions. He thought he was living in a three dimensional world and that he could stop his watch by his mental actions, or that he could move some bottles that were on the table (they weren't actually there). In his manic state, he frightened his wife, child, and friends. At a church meeting celebrating his return, he walked out in fear of the enclosed space and being surrounded by people.

In spite of his mental problems, he had a sense of humor that often showed up during his many incarcerations. In one of the many hospitals, he called his wife, lowering his voice dramatically, and pretending that he was an authority from the institution. He requested that she call Keller and Keller, Attorneys, and file the necessary papers to get him released. Another time he had one of his fellow inmates call her, pretending to be a therapist, to discuss her husband's problems. He often felt light-hearted in the hospital (possibly because of the meds) and came up with humorous thoughts and situations. Because of these activities, his wife is convinced that if it weren't for his basic mental problem, he would have been a productive member of society.

He worked as a janitor during these years and finally got bored. He decided he was going to jump the Blossomland bridge in an automobile, while it was open. He went to an auto dealership and took a car out for a test drive. .He contacted the bridge tender and requested he open it.

VIETNAM

When asked why, he said he wanted to jump over it. The tender called the Coast Guard and it was followed by a police chase. By the time he reached Roxies restaurant, he had shredded one tire. By the time he reached Maiden Lane, he had done $3,000 worth of damage. He was jailed and his license was suspended.

Much difficulty for family, friends, and hospital employees occurred. Finally he left the adult care home in Battle Creek, sought the nearest railroad track and watched a long 130 car train approaching him. Calmly he waited until it was about 30' away and stepped in front of it. Moving at about 25 miles per hour, they continually sounded their horn. He knelt down facing it, and just before it was upon him, he bowed his head toward it and waited for the eventual end.

Sadly, the Army had few experts to preview his mental condition, and whether they could have prevented his eventual suicide is a question that will go unanswered.

He left a sad family of three that still today, after more than two years, feel the pain of his suffering and wonder if there were more they could have done to help him.

Recalling some of the letters he wrote, his widow remembers he wouldn't talk about the war. Only things that happened, such as the personal relationships with the other fellows and the jokes they played on each other. He wrote about the rats in their hooch and how they paid *mommasan* to clean their hooch. He said if he ever got out of there, he would go one way, the right way, and he would point up to heaven. He talked about guard duty and how he had an encounter with a high ranking office who refused to halt. Considering his condition, it was resolved surprisingly peacefully.

To quote his wife: "I received a letter from the Army, saying that Doug was suicidal and had been honorably discharged. The Army stated in the letter that they would be de-programming him before he came home. I didn't know when he was coming home, or how. A high-ranking officer contacted his mother to let her know when he was coming home. She told my mom who told me because she did not want me to be shocked upon his arrival. The reason my mom told me he was coming was because I thought he was still in Vietnam.

He was sent to the National Guard to complete his duty. He never was the same after the war; he had many hospitalizations. He was unable to leave the war behind; it came back with him. He completed his life in Battle Creek, Michigan, on March 9, 2009, on the railroad tracks. The reason for sharing his story is because he was unable to share it. I pray that as others read this story, they will know there is help and hope available to them. All they have to do is ask."

TROPHY
Bruce C Dunzweiler

Self-portrait

Little boys are fascinated with their father's collections. Most dads keep mementos in a special place--items from their days of youth that they touch as if a talisman that propels them to the past. Secretly, sons find themselves eyeing their fathers as they go through these pieces of days long gone and wonder of their importance. I was no different.

When I was a young boy, my dad had the top right dresser drawer filled with his stuff. There were pocket knives, nail clippers, membership pins for Masons, Shriners and Boy Scouts, a state chauffeur's license pin (worn when driving trucks or anything for hire), a deck of cards with naked women, and many small items collected over his life. Among this treasure trove was an item that always caught my eye as I, often secretly and quietly, looked through the drawer. Small and grayish, this trophy was smaller than other trophies I had seen, but I could tell it was not a toy. Its heavy gray metal, possibly shiny when new, had dulled over time. A faint metallic odor wafted from the draw, posting notice of its aged importance and strength. The design was simple, a small emblem. Except for the words "Camp Perry," nothing else was described.

When I first asked Dad about the trophy, he said it had been given to him while he was in the Reserves. I had no idea what the Reserves were, but he told me it was when he first started in the Service as a young man. Part of his training had been at Camp Perry outside of Port Clinton, Ohio, on Lake Erie. Dad sat me down and explained that the camp held a marksmanship competition--shooting guns at targets--and he won over hundreds of others who had also competed. I could tell Dad was very proud he had earned this memento of the competition, but it was never openly displayed. His answers served to pique my curiosity even more over this piece of metal that represented a side of my father I did not at the time.

Dad did not talk much about his eventual enlistment in the Navy when war broke out in 1941, but his warm loving light blue eyes gave an extra gleam when he shared the story of the trophy. He explained how he had first learned to shoot at Boy Scout camp for a merit badge, but was never a hunter as he loved to see the beauty of the woods and its animals. We talked briefly about shooting, but except for my Roy Rogers six shooters, I had never touched a gun at that point of my life. Dad also talked of being on ship in the Pacific and, occasionally, on a slow day with calm glassy seas, his shipmates would hold a competition, shooting launched targets like clay pigeons or whatever expendable item they could spare, as it would not be recovered once it hit the water. Dad also won most of these contests on ship and the respect as the best shot on the ship. As a little guy, it was difficult for me to fathom my dad outshooting all of the other sailors on the ship. He was a large, but also a very gentle man, always warm and great to cuddle with when life's challenges fell on a little boy. My dad was my safe harbor, and him sharing his story of life in the Military made me look up to him even more. He was my hero; my dad--the best in the world!

Soon after our special conversation, we moved to the "country," two miles from Zanesville. There were few houses in our new subdivision and we enjoyed a double lot, along with a common wooded area. Our subdivision was built with a road running on the ridge of a hill, and there were no other housing developments nearby, only more farm fields in the more fertile lowland and woods on the hills. Our house, like most others in the area, had many windows at the rear, our living room overlooking the wooded area sloping to the bottom land below. Our basement was also exposed at the rear with more windows and glass for more view of the blue sky above and tops of the large trees and green below.

One special day I was given a BB gun as a present, and boy, oh boy, was I happy! I could not wait until I could shoot a gun. Dad taught me the proper method of shooting and how to maintain and care for a weapon. "You have to hold your breath and let it out slowly as you are slightly squeezing the trigger." I learned how to use it, maintain it, and safely shoot. Dad had me shoot at paper targets and instructed me on being able to tightly group my shots. After some practice, I managed not only to hit the target, but also to tighten my grouping. I still fondly recall shooting with my dad's friends and my Uncle Bobba. They even said some cuss words in front of me; it was real man-stuff.

Little did I know that the bonding with my father over target practice would be key during my tour in Vietnam.

After I entered the Army, my earlier shooting experience came in useful. During basic training, we had to qualify our marksmanship with the new M-16 where the rounds could be accurate over 300 meters. It was a light weapon, kind of like handling a toy. We were encouraged to compete in basic for our weapons qualifications. It was simple: just hit the targets. The better you did, the nicer the medal you could pin on your uniform for rifle qualification. At 300 meters you had to aim a little high. Just take a short breath, let it out slowly and gently, squeeze the trigger. Dad had taught me well. I could hit the targets as well as anyone, and demonstrated my prowess on the day we qualified with our weapons. I had not only scored the highest qualification in my company, but also in the battalion (about 500 men), and scored a weekend pass, an expert rifle medal, and a plaque to be presented at the end of basic. A trophy--just like my old man.

In addition to sharing top shooter of the unit, my dad and I were similar in that we did not relish the idea of shooting another man. My targets were in the shape of human beings. Every hit made caused the "man" to fall forward and be reset to be killed again. Because I had scored so high, I had just set myself up to be a "ground pounder," a "grunt," an infantryman. The last thing I wanted to do was die for my country. While some of the guys I was with were caught up on the idea of wanting to shoot a "gook," I did not. When you shoot a man, he doesn't re-set and pop back up. Instead, he lies there, dead, and a little bit of is lost in that moment.

In my struggles to come to terms with my pre-determined fate in Vietnam, I realized, too, that some in my country looked upon me with suspicion. Before leaving for the war, I took a weekend pass with two buddies. The three of us spent the weekend in Raleigh, N. Carolina, taking in the sights--but we spent much of the time in our room. Going to a bar or nightclub was not necessarily a good thing to do--we had shaved heads and were obviously in the service. And some people askance at us; others (mostly kids) yelled at us from their cars. It was all very uncomfortable for three young men contemplating their mortality. After all, we were in a war most people did not want.

Why did I feel like I was being shunned? I spent the weekend confused, scared, and not quite understanding what was happening. None of us had a very good time. We did not feel welcome or safe in our own country.

Suddenly, I better understood what it felt to be the target.

—READ MUCH MORE ABOUT DUNZWEILER'S EXPERIENCES ON OUR CD—

MY SECRET WAR
R.B. "Roddy" Glenn

I was born at midnight on May 13, 1938, at Hinsdale General Hospital, Hinsdale, Illinois. Mothers Day came on May 14 that year, so the doctor penned my birth certificate "May 14." In 1941, my mother and I returned to her childhood home in St. Joseph, Michigan. I enjoyed a good childhood during WWII. We had no money, but everyone had ration stamps for gasoline, shoes, and meat. We had family members with farms. They shared Sunday chickens, hams, and vegetables. Everyone had a Victory Garden on vacant plots of land or in backyards.

When a student of St. Joseph High School, I joined the Radio Club. Ed Zick, my Science teacher, was trustee for the club. Ed often told new members the following story about December 7, 1941. On that Sunday, he had attended church and enjoyed chicken dinner with his family. About 2:00pm (14:00 hrs EST), he was in his garage, operating the 10-meter amateur radio station W9PYP that he owned. Swinging the radio beam west, he called CQ-CQ-CQ 10 Meters (a general call for other hams to call him back). Almost immediately, a ham radio operator in the Hawaiian Islands responded. (It was 6:00am in Hawaii.) After exchanging the usual information--names/locations/radio gear info--the Hawaiian ham reported loud airplanes over his house. He knew it wasn't maneuvers, since it was a Sunday. Stepping outside, he saw a Japanese plane flying so low he felt the prop wash. He ran back to his radio and said, "I can almost touch them. The Japs are attacking Pearl Harbor. See you after the war." Astounded, Ed called the newspaper to report the conversation, but no one believed him, since AP had not reported it on the news wire. It would be 24 hours before they called Ed back and asked for his report on the attack.

Within minutes after this radio contact ended, the Japanese put a bomb down the stack of Naval Destroyer USS Downes, which was in dry dock for repairs. Chief Radio Operator George E Jones (W8SIO), a past president of the St. Joseph High School Radio Club, was killed in action. He was the area's first hero. Even though hearing about it years after the fact, this event became my first combat loss. Ed Zick made sure everyone understood their duties of citizenship. Since it was now my personal loss, too, I wanted to serve my country someday and make Ed Zick proud.

I graduated with the Class of 1956 and left home for work in Chicago, then journeyed on to become a student at Southern Methodist University in Dallas, Texas. I attended daytime classes and played nights as a drummer in a band at the Dallas Hilton. During the 1961 spring break, I returned to Chicago to visit my mom who now lived there; it had been several years since my last visit. My homecoming was short-lived. The FBI showed up to arrest me for a Selective Service violation (failure to report). I had no idea about my status. The agents demanded, "where have you been? Why did you not report?" Suddenly, my mom chimed in, "Oh! Is that what those papers were? I thought they were advertising." For over a year, the Government had sent papers to my family, and I was hearing about it for the first time!

After being arrested and held, I was asked, "Are you willing to serve in the US Army?" Remembering Ed Zick, I knew my duties. Yes, I would serve! I was inducted into the US Army two weeks later. Life moved on a fast-track train for Fort Leonard Wood, Missouri, also known as, Little Korea. I arrived in March 1961 for 16 weeks of Basic Training to become a trained soldier. The training is reinforced with constant vocal encouragement (yelling in your ears), causing your thought process to take the shape of your helmet. What is most amazing is that when you are in crisis/combat, you remember everything clear as a bell. The Drill Sergeant you learned to hate in Basic becomes the Drill Sergeant you love the most.

After checking my background, I was cleared for Top-Secret. When I graduated from Basic, I reported for Code & Cryptographic training at Fort Jackson, S. Carolina. Having earned several FCC licenses in high school (the equivalent of a college EE degree in 1960), I began training for the Army Security Agency (ASA). Communication School was not as hectic as basic training had been, but re-learning Morse code is like watching paint dry. (I can receive 30 words/minute now.)

Bored to tears, I decided to ask the class instructor if I could go ahead and just take the tests. The Sergeant said, "Captain Dowie will make that decision.

I felt the Army would be a fresh start. In basic training, the Drill Sergeant asked me to be a Squad Leader and a member of the Drill Team." I asked for an appointment, and he granted my request. I soon discovered that Captain Dowie was a soldier's hero. He was a leader and fun to be around. I was assigned to his fix-it team with Sergeant (E-5) Matthews. Besides fixing his appliances, I drove his jeep while he shot deer (out of season--the game warden was his friend). Once on bivouac, surrounded by mock-enemy soldiers, Captain Dowie said, "floor it, damn it; I will not become a prisoner." One mock-enemy soldier cracked our windshield with his rifle in his enthusiasm, but we got away and Captain Dowie treated his team to steaks in town that evening.

Life in the Army was good and I re-enlisted. During duty hours, the fix-it team built new projects for the school. I came up with a training tool to make the code instructor's roll more efficient. The school applied for a patent, which was approved after I had left on orders for Vietnam.

I traveled to Vietnam in civilian clothes with a passport. My orders read "Report to the American Embassy, Saigon." First, though, I had to report to San Francisco. I was provided with a fancy hotel room. Someone at the Presidio would leave messages at the hotel desk or call on the phone when they needed me to report. An envelope arrived with my orders, "Report to Hangar X, San Francisco International Airport, tonight, 20:00 hours. Bring your luggage and be prepared to depart CONUS."

Hangar X was remote and difficult to find, especially at night. The building was filled with 150 civilian-dressed people. There was a long line of tables and chairs. It appeared to be a production line that moved from station to station. I was informed that I would not depart SFO until my shot card and paperwork were in order. I wondered where we were all going, but knew nothing. My security clearance just said "Top Secret."

Four hours passed and I finally reached the last station: Passports. The agent asked personal questions (mother's maiden name, date of birth, etc.) while paging through my passport. Seeing a problem with my birth certificates (due to family issues, I actually had four certificates in both my real father (Glenn) and stepfather's (Schuhknecht) names, he said, "sorry, you will not ship on this lift. The official did not complete your approval process. Go back to your hotel and wait for new orders." By then, it was 5:00am. I was too tired to call my mother who assumed I was leaving on this flight. Instead, I slept all day and caught a movie at 7:00pm. The next morning, my eyes caught the San Francisco Examiner's headline: "PLANE DOWN - ALL LOST." That was my plane. When I called my mother, she was crying. She was sure I had died in the crash; the Chicago papers had run a similar report that morning. I wondered what was going on. Why did the plane go down without me? At the same time, a school classmate (Captain Gerald Miller) was refueling at a US Air Base in the Philippines. His destination was Ton Sun Knut Airport in Saigon. The same story circulated in the Far East bases. It was published one time, then never made the papers again. To my knowledge, the Pentagon still considers the matter Top Secret, for 50 years later, the records still remain classified and I've been unable to find my personnel and combat records from Vietnam to confirm the story. They do not believe that I need to know what I did or where I did it.

I finally landed in Saigon ten days later. The American Embassy told me to stand by, "we are working on Plan B." (Whatever Plan B replaced!) Booked into a luxury hotel with a swimming pool, I was told to enjoy Saigon's restaurants and clubs. I did attend orientation meetings. One meeting, in particular, sticks in my mind. It was held in a large auditorium with only a handful of people attending. We grouped towards the front center seats--a few Americans, a dozen Vietnamese women, and an assortment of foreign-looking Embassy types. A short Vietnam Army Corporal slipped through the swing doors and at the top of his lungs yelled, "FUK!" (I wondered what the ladies in the crowd would think.) Turns out, FUK is the Vietnamese word for ATTENTION. I asked myself, what has the American Army gotten me into?

In March 1962, America had up to 1000 people in Vietnam. After my flight crashed, the hurry-up was on. It grew to maybe 25,000 over the next year. Since I didn't need to know, my numbers do not exist. Call it a WAG (wild ass guess). One certain fact: once Americans show up with lots of money, BIG things start to happen!

I stayed on in Saigon for another week or so before I was ordered to Can Tho (in the Delta). The Delta command is renamed "Four Corp." The Army Security Agency established a Special Operations team in each province.

My first housing unit was new; it was built for two people. My first roommate was from the CIA; he delivered money in suitcases. Counting officers and civilians, we had 10 Americans. That was enough to organize a community mess. I had no idea what each person did, but it looked like an intelligent group. I was not offered an assignment or daily work for the first three weeks. Finally, the Four Corp Commander ordered me to Soc Trang Province (Lt. Colonel Hagen). A small airfield I called "Soc Trang International" would become the launch site for a US Army Helicopter Company, and later a Marine helicopter air wing.

I met America's last Flying Sergeant. He flew an aging C-47 (with a nose wheel). As I moved from my Can Tho digs, I wondered what the Soc Trang assignment would look like? Living in a tropical climate/jungle creates problems. The Army provided special built wardrobe closets for clothing and shoes. Everything would rot in days, unless you kept a small light bulb burning at the bottom of the closet. The Soc Trang detachment consisted of Lt. Colonel Hagen, Captain Larson (an Infantry Ranger), a young 2nd Lt. (he turned yellow overnight (liver), was retired within weeks of returning to Conus. There were two Infantry Sergeants (I forget their names) who worked with Captain Larson; and American Captain (I can see his face, but forget his name, too) who served as G-2 Officer; Staff Sergeant (E-6) Abe (was the Intelligence Clerk); and lastly, PFC. Rodney Bruce Schuhknecht (aka, R. Bryce Glenn) as the Chief Radio Operator, Code/Cryptologist, Electrical Engineer, and smiling Ambassador-at-large.

We designed and built new Communication Centers for the Army of Vietnam (ARVN), Province Civil Guard detachments, and US Special Operations groups. We installed RF radio antennas (cut to the operating frequencies), trooped on combat missions with senior American officers from Embassy headquarters, province detachments, and Special Warfare teams working in Four Corp.

Ironically, after 50 years, the ASA, Signal Corp, Pentagon, CIA, and other agencies continue to block access to personnel files and combat records (1961-64). PFC Rodney B. Schuhknecht (aka, R. Bryce Glenn) was inducted into the US Army under the name "Schuhknecht" (William E Schuhknecht was my stepfather). I never questioned serving my country (even in Vietnam). A relative of my stepfather's, Ronnie Schuhknecht, skipped out and went to Canada. I only mention his name so that people who know me do not confuse his untoward decisions as mine.

EYES IN THE SKY/RECKY BIRDS

Phil S. Manni

I was born, raised and educated in Rockford, Illinois. I can always remember having a love and interest of flying and, of airplanes. When I reached the age of 16, I began flight training. I was working as a Busboy at a very busy Country Club, and though only making $1.00 per hour plus tips, I was able to finance my Flight training, and these funds also allowed me to purchase my first car, a 1956 Oldsmobile. Throughout my high school years, the Vietnam War was always in the news and always managed to come up when I got together with friends. Many of my friends, as well as me, were concerned about the Draft Lottery, and as required by law, registered for the Draft following our graduation in 1967.

Phil Manni

I enrolled in College, carrying a full load, as well as, working and continuing to hone my skills in the cockpit. By the time I graduated from College, I had earned my Pilot's License, as well as, my Multi-engine rating, and was now the Assistant Manager of the Country Club where I was employed. I was now aware of the fact that I no longer had my College Draft Deferral and was now classified 1A, and knew that our "Uncle Sam" was very interested in me. With this in mind, I went down and enlisted in the United States Air Force, entering active duty on November 11th, 1969, Veteran's Day.

After passing my Enlistment physical, we were flown from Chicago's O'Hare Field, to Lackland Air Force Base, in San Antonio, Texas for Basic Training. Three weeks into Basic, my parents informed me that I was number 13 in the Draft Lottery system, so I was relieved that my timing to the join the Air Force was spot on.

As we continued through Basic, we were given the usual GI haircut and fatigues. I tried to figure out the necessity of all of us looking alike and then realized that this is what basic training is all about. We were leaving our individuality at the Front Gate and were now being programmed to work as a unit. I was chosen as the Catholic Chapel Guide, which allowed me to march my Catholic brethren to Mass on Sunday mornings.

We were informed by our Training Instructors (TI's) that with our 6 weeks being completed just before Christmas, if we kept our acts together, there is no reason why we shouldn't be able to go home for Christmas leave, before reporting to Technical School (Tech School). Keeping this in mind, we put our best feet forward and really applied ourselves. Uniform, shoes, beds, dorm, all impeccable, and always in inspection condition. We were up every day by 5 am and marched everywhere we went. We always sang songs as we marched, which help us keep in step, and our TI's informed us that we sounded quite good and that we might want to adapt a popular song to our marching. We decided that the song "California Dreaming", by the Mamas and Papas, was one we could adapt. We got so good, that we would stop cars and pedestrians on base as we marched by, singing OUR song. Now with all of this going for us, we certainly could plan on being home for Christmas, right? WRONG! The wants and needs of the Air Force always takes precedence and so on the 23rd of December, 1969, I flew to Lowry AFB to begin my Technical training. I had tested quite high in the Electronics field, so I entered training to become an Airborne Electronic Reconnaissance Systems Technician, AFSC (Air Force Specialty Code) 301X5A. In layman's terms, I was going to spend 48 weeks training on equipment used on Spy Planes (Reconnaissance Aircraft, or as we call them "Recky Birds"). This equipment was not cameras, but was in fact electronic sensors that took pictures using heat signatures (Infrared) and Doppler Frequency Shifts on aircraft that had the capabilities to fly low altitudes very fast, and also fast at altitudes so high that they were not visible to the human eye.

During our 48 weeks, we went to school throughout the week. We marched to and from school, and also marched in parades on base. In our free time, we had to study, keep our rooms and barracks in constant inspection condition, spit shine our boots and iron sharp creases in our uniforms. After graduation, I was informed that my AFSC was needed in Vietnam, but I would have to attend another school which would fine tune my Tech School training. I was transferred to Shaw AFB, in Sumpter, South Carolina, and began training on the Infrared Mapping Reconnaissance System on the McDonald RF4C Phantom II. This aircraft system took pictures using the temperature difference between those items in view. The photos were used by ground personnel to direct Air and Ground Strikes of potential targets.

I completed out processing and then, flying through Clark Air Base in the Philippine Islands, we landed at Tan Son Nhut AFB in Saigon, South Vietnam, my new home for the next 12-13 months. When the cabin door opened and the outside air hit me, it was very obvious that I was in for the environmental shock of my life. We landed around 10am and the temperature and humidity were both in excess of 95 degrees. Following in-processing, I was taken over to the shop that I would be assigned to and working out of for my tour in Vietnam. This was the Infrared Mapping Shop supporting the AAS-18 Infrared Reconnaissance System on the McDonnell RF4C Phantom II aircraft. Our mission was to provide Day and Night, high and low altitude photographic reconnaissance and mapping. At low altitude, the aircraft provided highly detailed pictures at altitudes of between 400-700 feet above the ground, at speeds approaching 500 miles per hour. Once our systems were downloaded and the pictures/maps were reviewed by photo interpreters, the acquired data for air strikes was then passed on to the Fighter Squadrons. After these air strikes, many times we would fly missions over the same area for the purpose of Battle Damage Assessment

During peak periods, we would fly 25 "sorties" (flights/missions) in a day. Many times, critical information was gathered, and perhaps because of mechanical problems, we had to perform "Hot Turns". The aircraft would be chocked on all landing gear and then would be serviced, repaired, re-crewed and refueled, all with the engines running, thereby minimizing down time. There were several periods, when the war was escalating, that we worked 12 hour days, 7 days per week. We were normally given 2 hours off on Sundays for church services and attending to other personal issues. Our unit was awarded the Presidential Unit Citation with 2 Oak Leaf Clusters for our performance in support of the war.

After I had served about 3 weeks in country, my eyes were opened to some of the horrors of war. I was out on the Flight Line when I noticed one of the revetment hangars was empty, with the exception of the Fire Bottle assigned to the aircraft that was out flying a mission. The Fire Bottle was situated right in the middle of the revetment and when I inquired about this position, I was told that this was the procedure used when the Aircraft, assigned to that revetment, was overdue or missing. I had gotten to know the crew of this aircraft during my short time in country and we had mutual respect for each other. This aircraft never returned and I never saw this crew again.

The Air Base was attacked by rockets on 3 occasions during my tour. We always knew when an attack was imminent because the number of Vietnamese locals that showed up to work on the base would drastically decrease on those days. These rockets were launched from near the center of Saigon. I found this very unnerving not knowing who, and exactly how close, the enemy was to us.

We began the Vietnamization process as I neared the end of my tour in Vietnam. The US commanders, and their Vietnamese counterparts, took part in the official ceremony and we began the process of deploying our unit and aircraft to Thailand and back to the United States.

I rotated back to the United States on a World Airways DC8. There was 200 GI's on board and a crew of 8. We processed through Travis Air Force Base and then departed for home out of San Francisco International Airport. I experienced the anti-war sentiment as I walked to my departure gate with unkind words spoken toward me and the fact that I was spit at, not spit upon, but spit at.

After spending my 30 days leave at home and purchasing my first brand new car, which I still own, I drove my new 1972 Pontiac LeMans GT to my next assignment. I processed on to Beale Air Force Base in Marysville, California and was now assigned to the most sophisticated aircraft in the Air Force inventory at that time. I was assigned to the Side Looking Radar Reconnaissance system on the SR71 Blackbird. This reconnaissance platform was the successor to the U2 spy plane after Francis Gary Powers was shot down and captured by the Soviet Union while conducting a reconnaissance flight over Russia. He was exchanged for a Russian spy after his trial.

The SR71 was the most advanced aircraft at that time. It routinely flew above 80,000 feet at more than Mach 3, or more than 3 times the speed of sound. To put this into laymen's terms, when the aircraft was on altitude and speed, it was more than 15 miles high and was capable of flying coast to coast in 67 minutes. This allowed the aircraft to fly high enough and fast enough to virtually eliminate the possibility of being shot down. The United States wanted an aircraft that would prevent another Gary Powers incident. The Slide Looking Radar, the system I was assigned to, could provide reconnaissance photos mapping 60,000 square miles per hour, and could do so without overflying a sensitive area.

Our squadron and Blackbirds supported the Vietnam War from the island of Okinawa. The Haiphong harbor was mined to prevent the North Vietnamese from operating out of this area and the SR71 flew flights to monitor the situation. On each flight, our Side Looking Radar cameras could always be counted on to provide 4 crucial bits of information. Photo interpreters would always be able to determine the number of ships in the harbor, the number of crew members on the decks of those ships, whether these individuals were male or female, and last but not least, whether the male personnel on the decks had mustaches. We were very proud of our accomplishments during our operations in support of the war. The SR71 was fired upon over 1000 times during operations and was never hit and, of course, never forced to make an emergency landing due to battle damage.

I was discharged and arrived home four years to the day that I entered the Air Force. I was able to use my Air Force training and was subsequently employed as a Research and Development

Engineer for 10 years following my Discharge. During these 10 years, I continued to fly and secure advanced licenses and ratings, including my Instructor Certificates. I was able to do this with the help of the GI Bill. I began flying Charter and through the contacts that I made in this venture, I interviewed and was hired by the Whirlpool Corporation in 1984 as a Corporate Pilot. I flew for 25 years with Whirlpool as an International Captain and retired in 2008, having traveled to nearly all of the Continents and having conducted six around-the-world trips.

I was married to my wife on December 28, 1974, and raised three boys who have blessed us with nine grandchildren, to date.

As I review the time I served in the United States Air Force, I can say that I was very proud to do so, and without question, I would do it again. I matured during this time and received some of the best training that I have ever had. This training has helped me immensely in civilian life and taught me the importance of what working as a team can truly accomplish.

BUCK'S HEROES: KELLY
Johnny Mayo & Kelly-819A

Scout Dog Team – 173rd Airborne Brig.

Dedication:

This book is dedicated to the loyal dogs and their handlers who served during the Vietnam War, and to the 58,469 men and women whose names are etched into the black granite surface of the Vietnam Memorial. Nearly 300 handlers are among this number. We also honor and remember the MIAs and POWs of the Vietnam War.

Over 10,000 handlers and 4,000 military working dogs heroically performed their duties saving the lives of soldiers, sailors, marines, and airmen who depended on the abilities of the canines. They performed their duties well.

Buck's heroes are the 4,000 War Dogs that served in the Vietnam War: only 204 are known to have survived and been deployed to other military assignments during the war. Buck's Heroes is dedicated to the 3,800 war dogs that did not survive and died as a result of combat, disease, and military standard operating procedure.

We, as dog handlers, will never forget them, and may our country never forget their undying loyalty and sacrifice.

My personal tribute is to my own two gallant Scout Dogs, Tiger-9A34 and Kelly-819A. They will forever be my heroes.

Johnny Mayo & Kelly

Excerpt:

Within three days after my first scout dog, Tiger, died from shrapnel wounds in October 1970, I was assigned Kelly-819A. Kelly would be my scout dog on point with the 173rd Airborne Brigade for my remaining tour of duty. The silver German Shepherd with the nipped left ear was a great scout dog. I knew of his history even before my Tiger died and was pleased when he was assigned to me.

Working dogs are channeled to hunt and detect what the training requires. Kelly was exceptional in picking up enemy scent, and very good on trip wires. Almost all our missions were in the central highlands inland from LZ English. As the point man, Kelly and I walked trails that had been used for years by the VC in their wars with the Americans and French before us.

Working Kelly off-leash required complete control without voice commands. I used a single and double click of my tongue and "shuh" giving commands needed for him to move down the trail, stay, or return to me. Working off leash required complete obedience. Kelly was not shy or afraid of combat. He became excited when contact was made with the enemy. He did not know fear.

Walking point is considered one of the most dangerous duties for an infantryman in Vietnam. All scout dog handlers were 11 Bravo—with a German Shepherd. My life and the lives of the squad or platoon behind us relied on Kelly's keen sense of smell detecting the enemy.

As I entered my first mission with Kelly, I knew he wanted and loved being on point—he wanted to hunt and find the enemy. Unlike some of Tiger's cautious traits on point, Kelly worked much like the classic hunter, hunting his prey with every sensor in his nose, eyes, and ears. He would search scanning all in front of him, and when he did alert, he stayed locked in position, sensing what I could not see and sniffing the air for scent I could not smell. As the handler, my job was to read the alert and make decisions to determine how far or how near the enemy were. Kelly could detect the VC better than any human but still it was the most dangerous place in the jungle—on point. The plan is simple: if all works according to plan, we find Charley before he opens up on us.

The mountains of the Central Highlands is hell to fight battles. It seems were were always walking point up a steep ridgeline or coming down them, not the most perfect footing for combat. Kelly was very protective of me when we were in the jungle. He did not like ANY Vietnamese, not one! I also had to give a short briefing to the platoon I would be working with, telling them to "let me know if you're coming near me day or night." He would also bite our guys if I did not give him his OK command. He needed his password, "OK, Kelly," to allow anyone near me.

Our missions were usually up to 5-6 days, but could be as short as one day. I carried his water and food (Gaines-burgers—7 per day). All he had to do was keep us safe and alive. Missions through the end of 1970 kept us busy as we worked out of LZ English and Uplift. In late January 1971, one of the most memorable of missions brought both of us close to death several times. In the 506 Valley, Kelly and I were working with one platoon in a valley below a ridgeline where my friend and his dog, Axel, were working with another platoon. We heard an explosion. Axel had detonated a booby trap and died several hours later...he and his handler were flown out by chopper as Kelly and I were called up to the platoon on the ridgeline to take point into what would be a moderate size VC base camp. Kelly was alerting on enemy scent everywhere as I attached his leash to the scouting harness. His look of alert when he detected a tripwire was very noticeable in that his line of sight was towards the ground in front of us and not on the surrounding forest and VC base camp. We had passed the spot where Axel had walked through the tripwire that killed him; Kelly was eyeing the second one about six feet down the trail. We pulled back and detonation team blew it in place. Kelly and I continued back on point into the base camp, inspecting living quarters, food cache, etc., as Kelly discovered a spider hole. The platoon sergeant asked if I would send Kelly into the tunnel. Part of our training and instructions back at Benning taught us we did not have to send our scout dogs into tunnels. I've heard of a few handlers that would not hesitate to send their dogs into a tunnel, but I would not sacrifice Kelly's life, knowing he would go after and fight to the death with any VC in the tunnel, if they were there.

As we left the base camp and worked our way down the ridgeline to my original platoon, a couple of explosions hit to our left and right as we reached an old rice paddy at the base of the ridgeline. The VC had bracketed our positions and started dropping in mortar rounds from two tubes. Kelly always was excited when the action started, which made it tough on the ME holding onto a 95-lb German Shepherd hauling ass and puling me as I carried full ruck running across calf deep water in the rice paddy. I followed the grunt in front of me and hearing each of the mortar tubes as they launched their ordinance, Kelly and I stopped at the edge of the rice paddy and I attempted to hunker down at the edge of the angled clay bank in front of us as the rounds were hitting close. Kelly was not ready to stop and as I lay prone in the muck, waiting for the last mortar round to hit, Kelly went up the bank to the end of his leash and pulled against my hand in the leash—he stood up on his back legs—twisted his body left and right as if he were trying to get me to move my ass further up the trail. NOTE: When remembering a combat situation and its description of a sequence of events, time seems to move much slower than it was in the real-life event. As I looked up from the muddy water at Kelly standing on his hind legs above me pulling, I jumped up and scrambled hand over hand up the clay bank another 12-15 feet. As the top of the clay bank leveled, I grabbed the end of the leash and pulled Kelly to me as the mortar round hit behind us at the base of the clay bank. If I had stayed where I had been in the rice paddy, the round would have landed just a few feet away. We were still close to the explosion, but as the slope of the bank at the top protected us from the shrapnel, only pelted with rocks and dirt. As I jumped up to move out again, the Herd paratrooper had come back to me, knowing I had taken a hit.

Before we would catch the chopper back to LZ English, the VC stormed the perimeter of the platoon we were with and lobbed in a couple of grenades in the quick raid before daylight. Kelly would walk point for two more days, finding another tripwire and having a close encounter with two surprised VC.

In February 1971, Kelly and I would go to the field on three more missions. The last, February 21, Kelly again had his strong alert on a dense trail, sensing something to our right. As both of us and our slack man focused to the right, he had missed something in front of us and I stepped into the edge of a punji pit, falling forward and taking punctures to my left hand and right leg. I jumped up and continued on with the mission as Kelly had alerted on several bunkers and a small base camp. By morning, the swelling from the hand had reached above the elbow, and the leg was about the same. We had heard through all the training at the range the range training back in the States that Charley used some of his body excrements to provide juicy little cocktails on the sharp tips of the junji stakes. I assume this is true, because it put me into the hospital for 10 days. Kelly stayed at my side at the hospital for the rest of the day until another handler came for him. This would be our last mission.

Sixteen days later, I would leave LZ English and my friend, brother, and warrior, Kelly. I would walk him the last time several days before leaving Vietnam and hand him over to his new handler. It was an honor to have served in combat as an infantryman with a dog. I thank both my dogs for giving me my long life. I regret Tiger's service and life was so short. Thank you, Tiger, for my life! Kelly was only one of thousands of military working dogs in Vietnam. I was only part of his tour of duty, even though all of us dog handlers always refer to them as "My Dog." They were all heroes that should have come home to their own parades and recognition from America.

Thank you, Kelly, for my life!

Buy the book at http://www.wardogwall.com / PO BOX 7396, West Columbia, SC 29171 / 803-767-6756

FIRE BASE TOMAHAWK
Tom Miller

At the beginning of 1968 I was enrolled in college eagerly waiting my student deferment. I also noted that there was a strike by the faculty starting. Simple math: 1968 need for troops at an all-time high and college kids not going to school. Lyndon Johnson immediately offered me a position I could not refuse and I was on my way to Fort Leonardwood MO. Amazingly five weeks later I re-enlisted in order to go to EOD (Explosive Ordnance Detachment) School commonly known as bomb squad or Every One Drinks. This is a very intense and long school with about a 50% washout rate. This was also very good training for finishing college when I got out of the service. It was also a multi-service school and had a mixture of enlisted and officers in the classes. All and all, a very good training ground to learn how to get along with just about anyone including the students from foreign militaries.

After school it was a desire of the US Army to have everyone spend at least one year working in the United States mainland to gain experience from veteran EOD personnel. I am not sure what the policy of the Navy, Marines or Air Force were. I got to spend my year less a few months in Virginia. The nice part of this is it was an election year and I spent a fair amount of time assigned to the Secret Service in providing security to the candidates, a nice job if you can get it. The exception might be doing the Democratic Convention of '68 in Chicago. Well, you can only live in la-la land for so long before reality catches you and says it is your turn to find out what living in the tropics is like, so off to the Republic of Vietnam I went.

It was the summer of 1970, hot and dusty and I was closing in on my first year in country. We had finished our nightly ritual of drinking beer until we were ready to pass out so we went to our bunks under the pretext that we were ready to go to sleep. Little did we know that it would be a short night.

We were the EOD team in central I Corp in Phu Bai located near the 101st Airborne Division's main base, Camp Eagle, and the old imperial capital of Hue City. This was a good place to be. Hue was off limits to American GIs and so still held on to some semblance of its former self. There were virtually no bars and you had to really know the city to find as the term was, number 1 girls. The area was filled with ancient temples and buildings, a University, Old Walled City and a large open air market by the river.

When the phone rang it was still dark and a glance at my Seiko watch let me know it was 4:00 AM (0400 back in those days). The call was from the 101st Airborne and all they said was to be at the helipad and a chopper would be waiting to take us to a firebase that had been hit hard and there were a lot of bodies, one with a live round in it.

Chuck and I grabbed our tool bag and went to the chopper pad. The bird was running and waiting for us when we got there. As we climbed aboard the Huey, I looked at the door gunner leaning on his M-60 machine gun, he didn't look real happy about this trip. Was it too early in the morning or did he know something we didn't? It would turn out that it was both.

I never liked flying at night, I thought we made too easy a target. Fortunately the pilot flew relatively high as we headed south along QL (highway) 1. It was very dark below, you had a hard time telling how far above the ground we were. No lights in the villages or traffic on the road. After about fifteen minutes I saw some flares and recognized the Thuy Wa Bridge where my old high school buddy ran a mortar support team. I hadn't seen Greg in four years and made a mental note to try and visit him someday soon.

During the day that highway was very busy and fairly safe to travel on. Before I had long to ponder this, the flares in the distance caught my attention. There were way too many. There were hand flares, mortar flares and flares dropped by aircraft. They lit up the hill like daylight and I recognized that hill, it was Fire Support Base Tomahawk. I had been there many times in the past but always by Jeep and in the daylight. As we came into land, I had an uneasy feeling. Why had we brought our pistols instead of M-16s? Why were we landing outside the perimeter? Why were we jumping out of this chopper instead of flying away with it? Why was the bird lifting off before our feet hit the ground? Why was there shooting?

I could hear the distinctive sound of AK-47s and also M-16s. As we walked toward the gate of 2x4s and concertina wire two guys swung the gate open and screamed at us to get down and run. Once inside we met a Captain and explained who we were and why we were there.

He then explained that Tomahawk was still under attack, the pilot was not supposed to land there and only an idiot would be here with no helmet or flak jacket on.

One of our duties after an attack was to check enemy bodies for booby traps. That was one of the reasons we had been sent; the live round inside a body was the other. Neither Chuck nor I relished that. Doctors get real nervous around live armed rounds and EOD people make lousy surgeons. With any luck it would be in a North Vietnamese body, which would make it easier to take. Chuck and I had never dealt with live rounds in human bodies. It happened before more than once—we had read the reports and even seen a film about it in EOD School. This was not going to be a good day.

As we made our way through the bunkers, we came across a Captain and a Chu Hoi (a North Vietnamese who had defected to our side) translator. They were yelling at a North Vietnamese Soldier that was in a dugout in the wire. The Chu Hoi was telling him to surrender, that he will be treated nice, given food and medical help. The sapper just smiled and shook his head no. After three or four tries, the Chu Hoi walks over, pulls out his pistol and shoots half of the sapper's head off. Wow! I was glad that Chu Hoi worked for our side.

All this time we could hear shooting on the other side of the hill. We finally met the Lieutenant who was going to show us around and he explained there were a lot of dead NVA on the hill and only one dead American. The American was the one with the live round in him. This day was getting very bad very fast.

The Lieutenant suggested we check on the American first, so we could get his body out as soon as the fighting stopped. Then we could start checking the NVA dead. As we walked to the south side of the hill, we could see the poncho covering the body. I also noticed that the closer Chuck and I got to the body the farther the others got away from us. When we pulled the poncho back we both froze. There was this young man that couldn't even be 20. His skin was smooth and childlike, probably hadn't even started shaving. He looked so calm and peaceful with an 81MM mortar tail fin assembly sticking out of his forehead like a unicorn. No blood, no swelling no nothing. This had to be the unluckiest person in Vietnam that day. He had grabbed his rifle, flak jacket and helmet to go to the perimeter to repel the attack. As he was running in the dark towards a fox hole, he had slipped onto his back and knocked his helmet off at the same time that an illumination mortar separated too soon and the tail fin came down inside the perimeter about 100 feet short of where it was supposed to go and into his head.

What happened next is not clear. First there was no explosive danger. This was only the tail fin from an illumination mortar round. My feeling was that a doctor should remove it surgically so there would be as little damage to the young man as possible. However you can't explain this very well to the Medevac Pilot who does not want a mortar going off in his helicopter. When the Medevac landed, we talked to the pilot and he agreed to fly the body if we guaranteed that one of our people would meet the bird at the Evac Hospital in Phu Bai.

It was now daylight and approaching 90 degrees. The fighting had stopped and it was time to check the NVA dead. The total for the night had been 29 NVA killed, 3 captured, 1 American lost and 0 wounded. Once the American had been evacuated the others on the hill started to relax and realize what a good job they had done. An interesting note is that Tomahawk had gained a reputation for laxity. Sleeping on guard duty and marijuana use was common. A new hill commander had taken over only a couple of days before and given an apparently persuasive lecture on alertness. Information from the prisoners indicated they had been watching the hill for over a month and there was a total of 80 NVA. If they had had the attack a week earlier, the results would have been horrific for the Americans.

POETRY TO REMEMBER
Richard "Murph" Murphy 1C3 (SS)

USS Lafayette SSBN 616

USS Tiru SS 416

I wrote the following poems about the four years I served in the US Navy Submarine Service. I joined the Navy straight out of high school in Virginia at the tender age of 17 in 1967. My dad had to sign for me to enlist and, even though I could have gone to college as my dad offered, I told him it would be a waste of his money and my time. I told him I wanted to go to Submarine School and serve my country on a submarine, and after my hitch was done, I would go to school on the GI Bill. I signed up on the 180-day delay plan and left for Boot Camp at Great Lakes, Illinois, just before Thanksgiving Day 1967. Coming from Virginia the winter weather at Great Lakes left something to be desired, but after graduating, I was cut orders to US Navy Submarine School, New London, Connecticut. I graduated Submarine School in May of 1968 and received orders to report to USS Lafayette SSBN 616 fleet ballistic submarine going through shipyard refit in Newport News Shipyard, Virginia. I did shipyard refit, sea trials, shakedown cruise and missile weapons test launches at Cape Kennedy, Florida, then on to Roosevelt Roads, Puerto Rico, for torpedo weapons firing exercises. Lafayette Gold crew then transported submarine to Rota, Spain, for deployment of first deterrent patrol cycle after refit. I was assigned to the Blue Crew for the next 90-day patrol rotation. I remember telling a man I was stationed on an atomic submarine during my time in the Navy. He asked me if I was on a fast-attack submarine. I told him, no, those were hunter killer submarines; they hunted other submarines. I told him I was stationed on a fleet ballistic missile submarine; we hunted continents. He got the idea.

I made five patrols on Lafayette Blue crew, then January '71 after making 3rd-Class Petty Officer, I was transferred to USS Tiru SS 416 Guppy, Illinois, Diesel Electric submarine. I made one med run and various other submarine operations and was discharged from service in September 1971 in Charleston, S. Carolina.

"*I Remember*" is a poem reflecting about my time and qualifying onboard the USS Lafayette SSBN 616 nuclear fleet ballistic submarine.

"*Once Upon a Time*" is about my service and time on a nuclear and conventional submarine and our submarine tradition and history.

I don't want these memories to just vanish away and never be told. When I was in service, we never thought of death or dying, we were all bulletproof, invincible, nothing bad happened to us. We were on the cutting edge of technology and the world was our apple for the taking. We lived with danger every day, but we blew it off and did our job no matter what was asked of us. So much submarine espionage happened during my time of service, and when I read about it or hear about it and the valuable intel we gathered during that time by my branch of service and so many cold war patrols that will never come to light, I can only smile and think about those submarine sailors who are out there at this present time upholding our traditions and heritage we were given from those guys who went to sea in steel submersible coffins during WWII and drew a line across the Pacific and told the Japanese, you'll come no further, then proceeded to unleash holy hell on those who tried.

ONCE UPON A TIME

We once rode under the seas in boats

And dazzled all the young ladies with all our quotes

We would stay out all night' till the cows came home

In every exotic port we would roam

We were wild and wooly, invincible young men

Bound into a Brotherhood by an odd looking little pin

Some sailed on smokeboats by diesel electric power

Some by nuclear propulsion which was their shining hour

I feel that I was doubly blessed to experience more than most

Because I got to serve my country on both types of undersea boats

A lot of you started out on diesel boats and ended up on boomers or a fast-attack

My lot was I started on an FBM and was allowed to turn the clock back

My first boat was a boomer, so squeaky and so clean

That it looked more like an hospital boiler room than a navy submarine

But she took me in and made me home

And filled me with awe and pride

And I'll never ever forget the honor I felt the day I qualified

Five patrols later and feeling pretty cocky

I had turned into a seasoned old salt, a veteran submarine jockey

I thought I had the world by the tail but my life was about to swerve

After I'd made 3rd Class, the Navy threw me a curve

I couldn't believe the orders that NavBuPers had wrote

I had been transferred off my boomer to a Guppy III diesel boat

Being full of shock and not quite knowing what to do or think

I sat down with my boomer crew for one last final drink

I was told by one of my shipmates that I would never forget this day

Because I was being transferred from a Cadillac to a worn-out old Model A

My old chief winked and shook my hand and said you're going to have some fun

You're going to experience the old fashion way of how we used to get 'er done

My first look at my new home was one I'll always remember

As I climbed onboard her and went down the hatch at old Sub Pier November

A new guy coming from a Nuke boat throws a diesel crew in quite a spin

Until they all saw that shiny reflection of that odd looking pin

It didn't take long to be accepted and we got along just fine

Because I'd earned all of their respect and they had surely earned all of mine

So another orphan gets a new family that will stick with him 'til the end

And he now has earned the right to call them all Shipmates, Brothers and Friends

We all lived for the moment and danced right out on the edge

We were all like modern day pirates who ruled the briny brink

We acted on dare and impulse without caring what others might think

Our submarines have stood the test of time clear back to '41

When we stemmed the terrible invading tide from the Land of the Rising Sun

Fifty-two boats and their crews were so great a price to pay

But that was our cost of Liberty when we sailed off into Harm's Way

But in truth, with time, we have slowed down, grown older, wiser and tame

And lost much of that craziness we proudly used to claim

The days of wild abandon have all been mellowed down

All the times and places we used to tear around and rip

Have now all been replaced by Geritol and tubes of Poly-grip

The old times I remember seems so much like it was a dream

That I really served my Navy hitch onboard a submarine

The things we did in secret and the missions, Oh so bold!

Many of these can never or ever will be told

We hunted the Bear in his watery lair

And learned all the tricks of his trade

We stalked our foe in depths below and whatever sounds he made

Our boats were like ghosts that haunted Ivan's coasts, keeping our enemy off guard

Our missions were trying, right out on the edge and sometimes really quite tough

But back then it was years before they came up with a name for them

And called it "Blind Man's Bluff"

When the Soviets threatened to turn up the heat as everybody knows

Our silent boats won us victory and brought the Cold War to a close

So now we'll hold fast to our history and gather together each year

To share tall tales of escapades mingled with laughter and beer

Then was then and now is now

And our deeds should be passed on and told somehow

It's our job to keep our stories true and pass our legacy on down to you

You, who now wear the Dolphins on your chest

To those who have qualified and passed the test

You, who have accepted our honored crown

You, who live by the phrase, "Take her down"

So to you young lads we pass the baton

It's up to you now to carry on

Make us proud and keep us free as you navigate the depths of the seas

So whenever we gather together and talk of boats and shipmates gone by

It's OK to get that misty feeling that wells up from deep in your eye

Get up and go look in the mirror and you'll fully understand why

That age has cone and caught up with us and technology has passed us on by

So now whenever I raise my glass and toast each boat and their crew

I drink from both sides of my cup to honor each and every one of you

I drink deep to toast the future and I taste to remember the past

And I let my drink rest upon my tongue so my memories will forever last

Of Cracker Jack hats and bell-bottom blues and all the good times I hold of my past

One by one we'll slip away and sail to another shore

Where we'll meet again our Brothers all, who have gone on ahead before

The noise we'll make and our welcome there will raise up quite a din

For St. Peter will announce over Heaven's 1MC,

there's another submariner checking in.

May 8 1968-January 31, 1971

Five Patrols

USS TIRU SS 416

February 1, 1971 – September 13, 1971

I REMEMBER

Here's to us, one and all who heard the message and answered the call

To break away from the old mainstream and live our lives on a submarine.

Sub school gave us the chance to pass the test

to declare to all that we were The Best of the Best.

When we left New London with orders in hand,

we all headed out on different courses for distant faraway lands

Some went east coast some went west,

but no matter where you ended up, your first boat's the best.

You reported on board not knowing what to think

but now you're known to all as a nub and a dink.

You learn about Tradition and learn about Pride,

you learn about Honor and the men who have died.

You learn about Heritage that's been passed on to you

because now you're considered one of the crew

You study that boat from bow to stern

From the conning tower to the bilges, it's your duty to learn

where and what makes that boat go, how it operates and in what direction it flows

How to charge those batteries and keep them alive or how to rig the boat for a dive

Draw those systems fore and aft, blow the shitters, check the draft.

These are the duties that you must glean when you live your life on a submarine

When you've learned all there is to know about your boat

You show 'em you know it, by your walk-through vote.

You go before the Qual Board, card in hand

where they question and grill you to beat the band

And when you think you can take no more
they tell you to wait just outside the door

For what seems like eons, time stands still
and when they call you in, you feel quite ill!
But they congratulate you for doing so good
And welcome you into their Brotherhood
Right of passage declares that you must drink your "fish"
And the tacking on process is not something you wish
But you wear those dolphins on your chest with pride
Because down deep in your heart, you know you're Qualified

It seems like yesterday, it seems like a dream
That I truly lived on a submarine
Most Boats are gone, a memory of time
I wonder what happened to that old crew of mine?
The Old Boats that are left, are all museums
And even if you rode 'em, you have to
pay admission now just to see 'em

So here's to us, those that remember
Who rode the boats out in all kinds of weather
To those past, present and even the future
To those young, hardy lads who still love adventure
So let's lift our glasses and have a toast
To the memory of those daring young sailors and their
undersea boats.

Given at the 1st USS Tiru SS 416 Reunion, Charleston , South Carolina, October 29,2003
Transcribed by Lila Megna

FROM WATERVLIET TO VIETNAM
Corky Openneer

Corky Openneer

272nd Signal Battalion

I was born September 1, 1945, in Watervliet, Michigan, the older of two children to Glenn and Doris Openneer. My younger sister was born in May of 1947. My father was a returning World War II veteran and my mother was employed with the local school district. I spent my youth growing up in Watervliet, graduating in 1963.

During my Junior year of high school, along with one or two others, I joined the Naval Reserves based in the Armory in Benton Harbor and attended drills there for the better part of the next year. At some point during this time, they determined that I had albumin (sugar) in my urine. Apparently that was enough to have the Navy decide I was not fit for active duty and I was released from the Reserves.

At that time, the military recruiting offices were in the old Post Office building on Territorial in Benton Harbor. By June 28, 1963, I had joined the Army and was sent to Ft. Wayne in Detroit for testing and physicals.

Having now been sworn in, I was soon placed on a bus with others and we were sent to Ft. Knox for basic training. I was homesick and miserable for the next three months. I spent many a late night/early morning sitting in the latrine, writing my parents and begging them to get me back home. That plan didn't work well and I endured basic, graduating in September of 1963.

Following basic I was sent to Ft. Gordon, Georgia, for 3 months of teletype and cryptology school. I hadn't requested this training, but apparently they thought I had some type of aptitude for communications. During the next nine years I spent in the Army, I never used that training again in any capacity.

Our graduation was slated for November of 1963. We had received our orders for our next duty assignments and two weeks leave when they placed us in formation to tell us President Kennedy had been assassinated in Dallas and all leaves were cancelled. We spent another week restricted to the base before things started to be cleared up and we were allowed to go home on leave.

Just before Christmas of 1963 I was assigned to the 272nd Signal Battalion, Ft. Wainwright in Fairbanks Alaska. One of my first assignments was helping to supply radio and telephone communications in the aftermath of the Good Friday earthquake in April 1964. For two months we traveled between Fairbanks, Valdez and Anchorage helping restore communications and whatever assistance was needed. Finally in the fall of 1994, I was transferred to another signal unit in Anchorage where the high spot in that assignment was spending almost three weeks on a peak in the Brooks Mountain Range constructing a radio relay site. The scenery was tremendous and the weather wasn't really bad, as I remember, except for some strong winds. I also learned how to play (and lose) the game of *Hearts*. In March of 1965, I had come to the conclusion that I rather enjoyed the military and decided to re-enlist. There weren't a lot of options back then in regards to re-enlistment. My benefit package for six more years was a total of $600.00 and a one year guarantee at the duty station of my choice.

After three weeks of leave at home, where I managed to blow my entire re-enlistment bonus, I reported to Homestead Air Force Base outside Miami, Florida. I was actually assigned to a missile unit which was scattered over south and central Florida. Homestead AFB was a SAC (strategic air command) base and there was a lot of security activity going on. I was also fortunate enough to be selected for the basketball team and actually spent a good portion of my year there traveling and playing ball. Not a bad way to start your re-enlistment.

Following my tour at Homestead AFB, I arrived at Ft. Dix, New Jersey in April of 1966. I was assigned to the 86th Engineer Battalion (Combat Bridge). This unit had received orders that it was being sent to a country called Vietnam (first time I had ever heard of Vietnam). The next few months were spent shuttling vehicles, equipment, etc. from Ft. Dix to Oakland Army Terminal where it was shipped to Nam. In September of 1966 personnel were loaded on a troop ship in Oakland and departed on a 30-day cruise to Vietnam. In spite of the cramped quarters and people being sea sick, I actually enjoyed the cruise. They tried to keep busy and I ended up working on the ship's newspaper, the main reason being I could type. We also had a chance to leave the ship for a few hours after reaching Okinawa. During a two-day stay in Naha, they let half the ship have liberty one night and the other half the following day. For most of us, it was our first adventure with Saki and most of us paid the price for our indiscretions.

We finally arrived in Cam Rahm Bay in early October and brought ashore in LSTs. We arrived on shore in full field pack carrying weapons with no ammunition. Our arrival in a war zone came with unloaded weapons and greeted by children selling Coca Cola and cigarettes. In short order we convoyed to Phu Loi which was to be our home for the next year. At some point Phu Loi was a small village surrounded by an abandoned rubber tree plantation. There were also a number of old French-styled villas in various stages of disrepair. The engineer's mission was to clear jungle and create base camps. There wasn't much need for teletype operators so I soon became a radio operator and on occasion helped string wire and operate a telephone switchboard once the base camp was constructed. We also learned the art of filling sand bags and hanging mosquito netting. With the exception of three or four rocket attacks and a few isolated incidents, I really enjoyed this tour of duty. I also had the opportunity to go to Singapore and to Taiwan on R & R. When I was growing up in Watervliet, I never thought I would have the chance to see places like these. The year passed rather quickly and in early September I boarded a Flying Tiger Airlines jet and returned to the States.

Prior to going to Nam on that first tour, I had become engaged to a girl from Wheaton, Illinois. Her parents owned a summer home on Paw Paw Lake and we were introduced by a mutual friend. Following my return from Nam we were married in Wheaton in late September and departed to Ft. Hood, Texas, for my next duty assignment with the 13" Support Group. This unit supported an Armor outfit and constantly was in the field training. Being newly-married I wasn't crazy about being in the field constantly and soon volunteered and was selected to serve on a team performing Military Rites for soldiers killed in Nam.

With the war having escalated, there was no shortage of burials and this soon became very depressing duty. In June or July of 1968 I volunteered to return to Vietnam for a second tour. I soon received my orders and in early September of 1968 landed at Tan Son Nhut Airport.

I quickly realized I had probably made a bad decision when we passed a hanger filled with bodies waiting to be returned to the States.

I was soon processed in and sent to Long Binh where I was again assigned to be a radio operator with a recon team based in Bear Cat. Its mission was both medium and long range recons in support of the various infantry units in the area. It was on a recon in May of 1969 and after spending the morning reaching our LZ, the chopper I was on was hit by ground fire shortly after it lifted off. The chopper was filling with black smoke and was rapidly losing altitude. The chopper was probably about 20-25 feet high when our interpreter and I bailed out. We were the only two to survive; the crew of three was killed on impact. While on the ground, I received shrapnel in my left leg caused by the exploding chopper. I never saw our interpreter again nor heard what happened to him. After what seemed like an eternity, another chopper was able to get in and evacuate two other wounded and myself and flew us to the 4th Field Hospital where we received treatment. The next few weeks were spent in therapy and rehab and me trying to drown my sorrows in whiskey in the Cholon district in Saigon. In late August I received my orders that I would be going to Germany and was soon on my way home.

After arriving home it was fairly easy to see that our marriage wasn't going to last long. I was drinking heavily and carrying a lot of baggage from the last tour in Nam. Actually the split was pretty easy. We had no kids, very little personal possessions and just decided we would go our separate ways.

In September of 1969 I arrived in Karlsruhe, Germany, and was again assigned to a VHF/UHF radio communications unit. One of my first duties was to go on Operation Reforger, a joint exercise with British and German troops where we set up a communications center in an old German WWII ammo bunker. Very dark, very damp and that was our home for the next two weeks. After returning to Karlsruhe following the joint exercise I was interviewed and selected for the best possible duty you could ever hope for: I was assigned to the United States Embassy in Paris, France, working with the ongoing peace talks between the US and Saigon. I had absolutely no knowledge of those talks; my only purpose was to make sure the communications link-up between Saigon and Paris was in order. Due to a prior agreement between the US and Charles DeGaulle, the only uniformed military presence in France was Marine Embassy Guards. I was then assigned to the American Red Cross, told to let my hair grow and blend in with the local populace. No problem there. That assignment lasted 90 days, I was returned to Karlsruhe for administrative and pay purposes (and get a haircut) for 30 days, then returned to Paris for another 90-day period. This sequence continued for roughly the next 15 months.

By this time I had been in the Army for almost 9 years and it was approaching the time to either re-enlist again or get out. By then I had been promoted to S/SGT and had given serious thought to making the service a career. I agreed to re-enlist if I could have a 3-year guarantee of my next assignment at either Lakehurst Naval Air Station in London or continue my assignment in Paris. They would only guarantee me two years at either place. Since this was only February of 1971 and the war in Nam was still going strong, I knew that third year would be back in Nam. No thank you!! So in March of 1971 I returned to Ft. Dix New Jersey and received my discharge and returned to my home town of Watervliet.

After returning home I joined the Benton Harbor Fire Dept. where I injured my left knee again and underwent a series of knee operations at Hines Veterans Hospital and the Ann Arbor Veterans Hospital. I also had been introduced to my future wife Susan on a blind date early that summer and we were married in December of 1971. The following summer, we became parents of twins, Steven and Stephanie who are now 40 years and still reside in Watervliet with their families. In 1977 I was employed in the Public Works Department for the City of Watervliet and was promoted to Director of Public Works in 1984 where I remained until my retirement in 2001. I then served a term as City Commissioner and two terms as Mayor. Since leaving local politics, I have remained active in the American Legion, Veterans of Foreign Wars and have served as a representative on the Berrien County Veterans Trust Fund for twenty years.

CHERRIES: EXCERPT
John Podlaski

Reprinted with permission by John Podlaski To order your own copy of <u>Cherries</u>, visit: http://cherrieswriter.wordpress.com or amazon.com.

John Podlaski served in Vietnam during 1970/71 as an infantryman with both the Wolfhounds of the 25th Division and the 501st Infantry Brigade of the 101st Airborne Division. He was awarded the Combat Infantry Badge, Bronze Star, two Air Medals, and a Vietnamese Cross of Gallantry. He has spent the years since Vietnam working in various management positions within the automotive industry and has recently received a Bachelor of Science degree in Business Administration. He now works in sales and logistics for a Belgium company that supplies gears and shafts for transmissions and diesel engines. John is a member of Vietnam Veterans of America Chapter 154 and lives with his wife, Janice, in Sterling Heights, Michigan. They own a 1997 Harley Davidson Heritage and are both members of the Great Lakes Chapter of Southeast Michigan Harley Owner's Group. *Cherries* is his first novel.

Ron Podlaski

CHAPTER ONE

Many U.S. Army personnel began their journey to South Vietnam from the Overseas Processing Terminal in Oakland, California. It was 1970, and just outside the compound, hundreds of hippies and former soldiers picketed and protested against the war. They targeted those soldiers who were dropped off by cabs and heading toward the main gate. Dozens of Military Police officers (MP's) were holding the protesters at bay and created a clear path through the mob. The crowd tossed flowers at the passing soldiers and chanted loudly for peace.

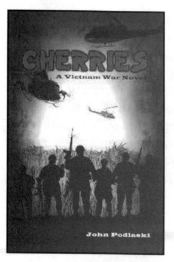

Some in the group pleaded with the new arrivals, trying to convince them to quit the military and refuse to fight in the war. Most soldiers passed through the gates without hesitation; however, a few did stop on occasion to seriously reconsider their options.

John Kowalski had passed through the main gate earlier in the day and was wandering through the massive facility, a converted airplane hangar, in search of friends from his Advanced Infantry Training (AIT) Platoon at Fort Polk, Louisiana. The entire training company had received orders for Vietnam, and each person was to report there after a thirty-day leave.

The PFC was maneuvering his six-foot frame through a maze of cubicles. The rubber soles of his newly acquired combat boots squeaked loudly as he crossed through these quiet sections. An earlier coat of wax on the red tile floor also made it appear wet and slippery; John stepped along cautiously as if walking on ice.

The twenty-foot-by-twenty-foot cubicles comprised of eight-foot high pieces of plywood and two-by-fours rose up toward the thirty-foot ceiling. Each of these enclosures held a dozen bunk beds; sleeping youths occupied many while awaiting their turn to fly off to war. His efforts to find a familiar face within the maze were unsuccessful, so he began a quarter-mile hike to the other side of the building, which was set aside for recreation.

He found the area to be quite active and noisy compared to the morgue-like atmosphere he had just left. Here, there were hundreds of highly enthused soldiers, all dressed in jungle fatigues – the green machine! Rows of pool and Ping-Pong tables cluttered the area, but were barely visible through the crowd. It was obvious that many of the players were having difficulty with their games, the close proximity of the many spectators inhibiting their movements. John stood on the outskirts looking in. He removed his olive green baseball cap and ran his hand over the light brown stubble length of hair. Satisfied that it was again growing, he replaced the cap and traced a line across the rough four-inch long scar on the left side of his neck - the consequence of a confrontation with some escaped felons during Basic Training.

His hazel eyes continued to scan the many faces, hoping to spot someone he knew. Suddenly, a player on a nearby Ping-Pong table backed up quickly to return a hard serve from his opponent. He tripped over a spectator, creating a domino effect on the group standing behind him. A young soldier, who looked fifteen at most, found himself sprawled out on top of the adjacent pool table. The remaining balls were scattered, some falling to the floor along with a stack of ten-dollar bills. All of this happened as an African-American soldier, twice the kid's size, was preparing to take an advantageous shot. He became enraged. "You dumb motherfucker! I had this game in the bag."

"It wasn't my fault," the kid cried out in a shaky voice, "I got pushed up here by those other guys," he pointed to those soldiers standing around the Ping-Ping table.

"Pushed, my ass," the black soldier challenged, "you just cost me a hundred bucks. So pay me what I lost, and I'll let you slide."

"I don't have that kind of money," the skinny kid replied, climbing down from the table.

"Let me see your wallet, and I'll take what I think is fair," the behemoth threatened, reaching behind the kid to snatch the wallet from his back pocket.

The kid pushed back into the crowd, attempting to escape the reach of the thoroughly pissed off Army private.

"It was an accident!" he hollered. You're not taking my wallet!"

The crowd tightened, everyone shifting to find the best-unobstructed view of the altercation. Trapped, the kid had no place to go.

"Come on brothers, are you with me?" The soldier called out to a group of black comrades standing nearby. "This white boy owes me some money!"

His supporters wielded cue sticks and pool balls and moved toward the petrified youth.

A group of white soldiers took a step forward, ushering the young kid behind the pack and quickly engulfing him. One of them stated in a southern drawl, "Why don't you boys pick on somebody your own size?"

Hearing this, the leader of the black group turned to his followers and said giddily, "I guess we have to kick a whole lot of white ass to get my money."

"Yeah, let's do it. We're with you!" his followers chanted.

Individuals within the black group were now beating the palms of their hands with the thick end of the cue sticks and lofting pool balls lightly into the air. Two of them broke ranks and moved toward the white group. Suddenly, a dozen MP's forced their way through the crowd before either of the two groups could strike a blow.

"Let's break this shit up!" The MP Sergeant ordered, separating soldiers, and shoving them out of his way. He stopped, facing the leader of the black group. "What is this all about?" he asked.

"That skinny white boy owes me a hundred bucks!" The black private protested, pointing out the alleged culprit. "All I want is to get my money back and these white boys want to come over and start some shit with us."

"That's bullshit, sarge," the southern soldier responded. "There was an accident. The kid fell on the pool table and fucked up their game. He doesn't owe him shit."

"Is that correct, private?" The sergeant fixed a deep, piercing stare at the kid.

"Yes, sergeant," he replied in a trembling voice, "there was a lot of shuffling and pushing behind me. I found myself sprawled out on top of the pool table. I couldn't help myself."

"That's a damn lie!" The black soldier protested. "I couldn't give a fuck about the game; I'm pissed because he pocketed my money during all the commotion."

"I don't think he has the balls to do something like that," the sergeant replied after sizing him up. "I'd be willing to forget this incident if everybody would just walk away and return to what they were doing."

"What are you going to do if we don't? Send us to Vietnam?" a voice called out from the crowd. The taunt was enough to change the atmosphere of the group and some began to laugh and snicker.

"Yeah, you'll still go to Vietnam, but you may spend a few weeks in our stockade first," the sergeant growled.

The crowd started to disperse, and soldiers moved away, resuming their activities from before the interruption. The black soldier shifted back and forth from one foot to the other, his expression changing as he tried to compose himself.

The MP Sergeant looked at him. "Well, what's it going to be?"

"I'll let it go, man. I don't need any bad time on my record. I want to serve my year and get back home."

"Then, do I have your word that you won't bother these guys anymore?"

"Yeah, man, you got my word." He turned and walked back to the pool table and his waiting friends. The kid had vanished.

Once everything was back to normal, John turned and moved toward yet another undiscovered part of the large building. After a few minutes, he heard a familiar voice call out, "Hey, Polack!"

He stopped and looked around for the source.

"Hey, Polack, over here," a tall, lanky soldier with red hair, freckles, and a broad, toothy grin called out again. He was pushing through the crowd and waving frantically.

John's face lit up in recognition, returning the man's wave with a wild one of his own.

"Bill," he called loudly after seeing his close friend from training.

They embraced warmly like long-lost relatives.

"Polack, you son of a bitch, am I ever glad to see you." Bill, as gaunt as a scarecrow, slapped John's back a few times.

"I am too, Bill. How the hell are you?"

"I'm good. When did you get here?"

"About four hours ago. What about you?"

"I got here yesterday."

"Why did you come so early, Bill? Didn't they have a flight available when you needed it?"

"I didn't fly. I took a train instead."

"You rode a train all the way here from Tennessee? Are you shitting me?"

"Nope, I've never been on a plane in my whole life, Bill admitted sheepishly. I was so afraid of the thought of flying that I checked into the train schedule and found that I had to leave a couple of days earlier to get here on time."

"How did you get home from Fort Polk?"

"I rode in by bus."

"Damn Bill, you missed out on three days of your leave just because you're afraid of flying?"

"Yeah, I know, I know. Don't remind me."

"Now you don't have a choice. There aren't any trains or buses that go to Vietnam."

"I know and thought hard about that on the way here. I've got a perfect solution – I'll get drunk and pass out. That way, somebody could carry me on board."

"Maybe they can just give you a shot or something to relax."

"No thanks. I've had enough shots for now! Once I got here, they gave me a worse physical than the one I had to take when the Army first called me up. Here, they move you along like an assembly line."

"I know what you mean. And that paper work was really a bummer - there must have been twenty-five forms to fill out!"

Bill produced a wide smile, "Yeah. That part took me almost an hour."

The two young men commiserated about the humiliating experience of having to strip down to their underwear and stand in long lines of strangers from all over the country–herded along like cattle.

"What did you think when you saw the ten doctors on each side of the line giving everyone shots with those air-powered guns?"

"I didn't have time to think. I just blindly followed everyone else and hoped for the best."

"A guy in front of me moved his arm just as the doctor pulled the trigger," Bill commented. "When the blood squirted out, I almost shit myself."

"The shots weren't too bad - kind of felt like a punch in the arm. But, as I'm standing here now, they're starting to ache pretty damn bad," John said.

"It'll feel better in a few hours. I feel fine today," Bill volunteered.

"The thing I didn't like was having to ship all our own clothes and stuff home. What a hassle! And these new jungle fatigues and boots we're in are just like those in basic training."

"Yeah, but it was all worth it. Don't we look good?" Bill asked, striking a pose.

John would not have been more surprised if Bill's ball cap came off his head and twirled in the air by itself. Bill flexed his arms and posed like a body builder in the final pose of a competition. His head quivered as he strained his muscles. Bill's face was stern and solemn as he concentrated on this show of strength.

John suddenly burst out laughing "Damn Bill, what was all that about? It looked like an advertisement for *Scarecrows Incorporated*." He stopped chuckling before continuing, "All you needed was a bit of hay sticking out in the right places, and you'd have nailed it." John pointed to Bill's face, "I especially like how you managed to cover your front teeth with your lower lip. You did look scary, but it also seemed like you had a mouth full of snuff."

"Okay. Okay. You've had your fun for the day, Polack." Bill looked more hurt than embarrassed. Bill Sayers, raised in the back woods of Tennessee, spoke with a heavy southern drawl. He was the third eldest of nine children who shared everything from chores to clothes while growing up on the family farm. He had never experienced the feeling of receiving new clothes–all he had ever worn were hand-me-downs from his older brothers. When the Army issued him the first five sets of new fatigues, he treated them as if they were made of gold.

"C'mon Bill. I'm just giving you a hard time and didn't mean anything by it." John wrapped his arm over his buddy's shoulder and pulled him tightly. "You have to admit - it was funny as hell!"

Both men shared a hearty laugh.

"Have you found a bunk yet?" Bill asked.

"Not yet."

"Great, then come with me, I have a cubicle all to myself."

"Lead the way."

John followed Bill to the other side of the building and then through the maze of cubicles for another ten minutes before reaching the smaller room with six bunk beds.

"Looks like it'll be nice and quiet here."

"Shit, it is now. Yesterday, you couldn't hear yourself think."

"And why was that?" John inquired.

"I had to share this cube with ten other guys who have been together since Basic Training. All they did was party the whole night."

"What happened to them?"

"They left on the first flight this morning. So I guess it's just you and me until new neighbors move in."

"I'm okay with that. Have you seen anyone else from our AIT Platoon yet?"

"Yeah, matter of fact, yesterday, I bumped into Joel McCray and Larry Nickels. Do you remember them?"

"I do. Where are they?"

"They left this morning with those other guys. And you'll never believe who else was with them."

"Who?"

"Sergeant Holmes."

"No shit? I thought he was returning to Fort Polk this week to start training a new platoon of recruits."

"That was his original plan, but he had his orders changed during his leave and volunteered for a second tour."

"Why did he do a fool thing like that?"

"He told me that he was fed up with the civilians and all the hippies. He said that while he was on leave, people spit on him and got into his face yelling that he was teaching soldiers to be baby killers and then sending them off to Vietnam. He said there was not a day gone by without somebody picking a fight with him. After the cops had jailed him for the second time for disorderly conduct, he went and signed the papers."

"The world is filled with jerks. Too bad, he had to volunteer for Nam to get away from it all. Did you know he was wounded during his first tour?" John asked.

"Yeah, I remember him telling the story about that big Tet offensive in '68. He got some shrapnel in his back from a mortar round, but also said that the fighting is not at the same level as it was in 1968 or earlier, so we all have a good chance of making it home in one piece."

"I hope that's true."

In the AIT Company, everyone liked Bill because he always had something good to say about others. Stories told about life in the big cities fascinated him to no end. It was difficult for him to imagine doing things that many city folks took for granted as part of their everyday lives.

He walked everywhere, including the three miles each way to school and back. In fact, the first time Bill had ever ridden a bike was in the Army.

Bill and John became very close while serving together in the Army. They had developed a friendship that made it easy to confide in one another on sensitive issues. John had promised to visit Bill in the hills of Tennessee one day, but only if Bill agreed to visit him in Detroit. Bill was ecstatic and could not wait; he continued to remind John periodically of this agreement.

All the excitement of the day was beginning to take its toll. Both were tired and struggling to stay awake.

"I had it rough last night." John began, "My mother gave me a going away party yesterday. All of my close friends and relatives were there. After dinner, we all sat in the living room and talked while the news was on TV. Everyone quieted down when a bulletin came on from Vietnam. It seems some outfit ran into an ambush. They showed helicopters burning. Dead and wounded soldiers were carried past the camera, and the commentator sounded so nervous. The women looked over at me and started crying. They all ran over and hugged me."

"Damn," Bill said with a sympathetic look upon his face.

"Well you know me." John continued, "I put on the brave act and told them that nothing was going to happen to me while I was in Vietnam. I told them that we'd all be back in this same living room in a year to laugh off those worries."

"What happened then?"

"Everyone started to leave for home before it got too emotional. When everyone left, I went up to my bedroom and tried to sleep, but just couldn't. I kept thinking about that news story and got all shaky and nervous."

"Polack, you aren't alone in that feeling. I'm scared too."

Both sat quietly for a few moments.

John lay back on his bunk and glanced to his watch. It was 3:30 in the morning. He thought about everything that had happened since leaving Detroit only fifteen hours earlier. Everything seemed to be "hurry-up-and-wait."

On the flight to California, he had been the only military passenger. The flight attendants and fellow passengers had made him feel special. When they heard he was en route to Vietnam, they bought him drinks, offered him magazines and candy, and wished him luck on his tour.

He was very proud and felt honored by the way he was treated. His fellow passengers respected him, and not one person had treated him as Sergeant Holmes had been treated.

"Hey Polack, get your lazy ass out of that bunk!" Bill shook him a few times.

Startled, John jumped up from the bed quickly, bumping his head on the frame of the upper bunk.

"Damn you, Bill, you scared the shit out of me," he grumbled, rubbing the top of his head.

John looked at his watch and noted that it was 1330 hours.

"Jesus, Bill, its one-thirty. When did you get up?"

Bill looked at his watch, "about six hours ago."

"Why didn't you get me up sooner?"

"Hell, I'd have been wasting my time. I know you city boys like your sleep. You would sleep all day long if somebody let you. Besides, it wasn't necessary for both of us to check the shipping manifest for today."

"What did you find out?"

"Both of our names are listed, and we're leaving for Vietnam at ten o'clock tonight."

—READ CHAPTER 2 ON OUR CD—

DONUT DOLLY: THE HOT LZ
Joann Puffer-Kotcher

From *Donut Dolly: An American Red Cross Girl's War in Vietnam* Permission to print: DONUT DOLLY: An American Red Cross Girl's War in Vietnam, copyright 2011, Joann Puffer Kotcher and published by the University of North Texas Press, www.unt.edu/untpress. To order your copy, visit http://untpress.unt.edu/node/3080 or amazon.com or call (940) 565-2142.

Saturday, August 6, 1966, Landing Zone Oasis, Pleiku, South Vietnam

That afternoon I traveled from An Khe to my assignment at Dong Ba Thin. I had an escort wherever I went. That day I had no escort. I raced out to the An Khe airfield at 1:30 to catch the 2:00 flight to Cam Ranh Bay. The Army dispatcher at flight operations told me, "That flight is full, but you can get on the regular 3:00 run." No need to hurry. I unloaded my luggage from the jeep.

For the next two hours the dispatcher bumped me off one flight and onto another. Finally he said. "I can schedule you on a flight that will come in at 4:00. It's a Caribou from Dong Ba Thin that's working for the Cavalry. It is taking troops to Oasis." That was a landing zone west of Pleiku near the Cambodian border. "When it's finished, it will go back to Dong Ba Thin, empty."

Later, the dispatcher made still another change. "We've discovered that there are so many troops going to Oasis that the Caribou will have to make an extra trip. You can ride with the last load of troops. The plane can go to Dong Ba Thin from there, instead of coming back to An Khe to pick you up."

The tent at An Khe. Sandra, Joann, and a friend compare the tan on their arms.

Operation Paul Revere II was five days old. That explained why so many planes were flying to Pleiku. The dispatcher had worked hard to get me on a flight; he had scheduled a plane to make a special trip to pick me up. It wasn't the first time someone had done something like that for the Red Cross girls. I suspected that it happened more than we knew. When I got to the runway, about 30 soldiers already waited. They didn't move around on the blazing-hot, empty runway. Standing near them, I overheard the movement control officer say to a mechanic, "One of our ships got hit at Oasis and isn't flyable."

The mechanic answered, "So that's why we keep getting behind. That landing zone must be hot."

The officer answered, "Must be. Help me with these bags." I thought, Oasis is a hot landing zone? When the dispatcher put me on the transport he told me it would make a stop at Oasis, and then go to Dong Ba Thin. "Hot" meant there was a war. I would fly into the war. I couldn't tell how many of the troops also heard the conversation. I thought, That must be part of the back up that has bumped me all afternoon. One of the ships has been shot down. That made me apprehensive, but there was nothing I could do. Besides, lots of ships had come and gone all day. Only one had been shot down. The odds looked good.

My plane came in, a half hour late. It was loaded with cargo. I watched to see what would come back from Oasis. First, the ground crew pulled off boxes of cigarettes. When troops were in the field the Army gave them free cigarettes. In base camp, soldiers had to buy them. Next, the workers unloaded duffle bags. That surprised me. Usually, soldiers carried their own duffels. Rain and mud had soaked the bags. Instead of Army green, they were red-chocolate brown. The wet bags contrasted with the crisp boxes of cigarettes. The tired crew inside the plane dragged the bags to the cargo door and heaved them to the edge of the runway, as if they were indestructible.

I remembered I had heard that a company of the 5th Cavalry had been wiped out the day before. Probably a rumor. The company more likely had been in a fight, but had not actually been wiped out. I wondered if these bags were the personal belongings of the men who had been killed. Some of the bags fell open. One spilled out some pieces of paper. Probably they were

263

Joann with her sister, Phyllis, just promoted to captain. Phyllis was stationed in Saigon and made a two-hour visit to An Khe on the 4th of July. \Army PIO photograph

pages from a letter. A crewman scooped the pages up, stuffed them back into the bag, yanked the top shut, and gave it a heave. One page blew away.

A bag full of baseball bats came off the plane. The fresh troops looked on in their clean fatigues and new helmet covers, though no one had spit-shined his boots. The men had packs on their backs; hand grenades hung around their bodies; mosquito repellent and gun oil stuck in helmet bands. Each man seemed to have glued his rifle to himself. The men stood, some with weapons slung by the strap over one shoulder. Others held their M-16s by the handle with one hand, down at their sides, or with the butt resting on the ground. They moved little, didn't talk, and their crisp posture had faded. They had been standing and waiting for some time in that heat.

I looked at the soldiers and then at the sad duffels that flew through the air. Did each bag represent someone who had stood here a day or two before? Had that man watched the bags come off another plane? Would some of these men follow him? Would their possessions be heaved off a plane tomorrow without care? I thought of the Chinook that landed near the hospital last month. A covered truck backed up to it; and men unloaded black canvass bags. It was hard to find dignity in death when there was so much of it. If we mourn the dead or think about them too much, we would be frozen. We had to harden ourselves, otherwise we would or break. Crewmen continued to heave the bags like sacks. The bags landed side by side, with military precision, in neat rows. At first it had looked like the crewmen threw the bags with disregard. After a while I saw it was with care and precision.

I looked at the faces of the soldiers who waited, and I wondered which ones would come back. I stopped myself. I remembered what Major Hayne had told me. "You assume you will come back. You have to."

I stood on the airstrip now. My thoughts shifted to watch men getting off another plane that had just landed. The soldiers looked like the duffle bags. From helmet to boot, mud had soaked them through. Even their faces and hands were brown. They looked tired. I was relieved.

These were the men who belonged with the bags I had seen earlier. To make it easier on the combat-worn soldiers, the Army had transported their bags on a different plane. The men sagged with a fatigue that comes when adrenalin is drained. They were safe. I felt myself quietly smile at how filthy they were. They were a contrast to my fresh memories of shined and buffed soldiers in the States and Korea. The difference between the exhausted and fresh soldiers was remarkable—these were two faces of warriors.

The crew finished unloading the plane. We scrambled aboard. Thirty of us sat against the sides facing center, and from the front, I could see everyone. The loaded Caribou took off. Every man on board lit up a cigarette at once, as if on cue. I watched. Every one was smoking, even though I knew that not everybody smoked regularly. They were nervous. Had some of them overheard the mechanic say that LZ Oasis was hot? They were young. I wondered which ones wouldn't return. I stopped myself. No good to think. That flight was the same as the bunker when I sat and listened to the shells fly overhead. I needed something to occupy my mind. In the bunker, it was a conversation. To these men, in an airplane too noisy to talk, it was a cigarette. Maybe the Army knew what it was doing, issuing cigarettes to men in combat.

The first thing I always did with a group of soldiers was smile. That was all it took to lighten them up. I smiled. Nothing happened. They didn't smile back. In training we had been taught how to catch a man's eye and smile. I tried that. One man gave me a half-hearted smile. No one else responded. They were stressed. That wasn't going to work.

I got out my diamond nail file and filed my nails, the feminine gesture that had delighted the door gunner on the way to Buon Blech. The magic failed. I put on some fresh lipstick, another gesture that men found endearing. Still no one responded. Nothing worked. Instead of smiling I realized that it would be better just to look pleasant. I settled back and tried to relax. They knew I appreciated how they felt.

The plane engines were too noisy for anyone to talk. But one man asked me where I was from. It was a question everyone asked each other. I was tired of it, but this time it didn't bother me. I gave him the answer that always got a laugh. Since so many men were from the South, I would answer, "I'm from the South, southern Michigan." He appreciated my joke.

Well into the flight, one of the more bold soldiers asked the Crew Chief, "The area we're going to. Is it hot?" I thought, Yes, they know.

The Crew Chief shook his head. "Naw, there's nothing much going on."

The boy couldn't believe his ears. "Nothing going on? Really?" It was too noisy to frame the obvious question, Then, why send all of us up there in such a rush? The answer was the crew chief had lied. Oasis itself may have been quiet. Only one plane had been hit, but near there, where the troops would go, the Viet Cong were waging a fierce battle. The weathered crew chief knew it was best to ease the tension. It seemed to work a little. Nobody needed to confirm that the troops had waited so long for a ride because their plane was shot down, at LZ Oasis.

One man asked me, "Are you going the same place we're going?" I gave him a pleasant smile and said, "No, I'm going on."

About half an hour into the flight, the crew chief sat down and strapped himself in. The drone of the engines changed to a deep growl, and the wing flaps whined to maximum drag. The nose of the aircraft dropped; we went into a steep dive. The plane shook. Gravity pulled me forward, out of my seat. We plunged toward the earth. The landing gear ground open and thumped into place. The pilot couldn't abort and try a second time if he came in wrong. He had to be right the first time, with a load of troops and their gear. He knew the VC were watching.

Finally we leveled off, then landed, fast and hard. The engines revved up to a scream, straining to stop the loaded caribou on a short runway. We had made a combat approach to a hot zone.

Cruising at altitude, we were safe. On the ground, no hostile fire in the zone threatened us. The danger lay when we descended into the range of fire from the ground. If the VC had shot at us, we hadn't heard it. If they had hit us, as long as we could still fly, the mechanics would only count the bullet holes. If this had been a helicopter drop with enemy fire, the aircraft would have stayed on the ground for a few seconds. Everyone would have had to dive out shooting, running for cover.

When we landed at LZ Oasis, no one hurried to get out of the aircraft. I spoke to the men as they got off, after some of the noise had stopped. "When you get back, come over to our recreation center. It's right next to 2nd Surgical Hospital, under the big yellow Cavalry patch." It was the right thing to say. Major Hayne's words helped several of them visibly relax and smile.

A handful of men commented, "I may do that." "I'll have to do that." I had assumed that they would come back. Major Hayne had told me never to lose my optimism. These boy-soldiers needed all the encouragement they could get. I didn't know if it lasted until they got out of the plane, but for a moment they smiled. I hoped that the soldiers knew what I was trying to do for them. I had learned from the doctors in the mess hall, that if a wounded man could get to the hospital, he had a 98% chance of survival. These men would be all right. Out of 30, a few might be wounded, but they would all make it back home.

The Caribou now empty, the pilot suggested, "Would you like to ride in the cockpit?" Pilots did that for Red Cross girls, even when the aircraft was full. I was sure the pilots kept me with the soldiers on the inbound flight because they knew the men would benefit. Take off repeated the hot landing in reverse: a short, fast sprint down the runway, a leap into the sky, a climb, engines racing, the plane straining, and then we leveled off and relaxed into the familiar cruise drone. Safe at altitude again, the pilot invited me to fly the plane. I was eager to try; I loved it. Those moments in the cockpit too, were part of my work. They gave the pilots reminders of home, as we cruised toward our base.

VIETNAM BATTLEFIELD EXPERIENCE & AGENT ORANGE
Ronald D. Robaska, Sr.
(Buck Sgt., Sgt. E-5)
U.S. Army: 1967 – 1970
Written by Ron Schadler

In January of 1966, I enlisted in the U.S. Navy for Submarine Service. The Navy did not have any openings for the Submarine Service at the time and put me on a delayed entry. This meant I would have to wait to enlist until an opening became available at Submarine School. The Vietnam War was going on at the time and, being young and impatient, I became tired

Ron Robaska

of waiting for the Navy to call me.

In March of 1967, I made my weekly trek to the Naval Recruiter Office in South Bend, Indiana. The Recruiter still had no idea when a Submarine class would become available, but he would indeed call me when he found out and had an enlistment date. When I left the Navy office, I passed by the Army Recruiting office. The Staff Sergeant Recruiter yelled at me as I passed by the office and he invited me to sit down. After 30 minutes, I had signed on the dotted line and had enlisted for three years in the U.S. Army. Ten days later, I was southbound on a troop train from Chicago headed to Fort Knox, Kentucky, for basic training. After Basic, I went to Airborne and Ranger training. I went through Ranger training at Ft. Gordon, Georgia. I spent most of my training in the Okefenokee swamp of southern Georgia and was trained in Long Range Recon Patrol.

After Ranger school, I got a 10-day leave and returned home to say goodbye to my friends and my Fiancée, Janey. At the end of that 10-day leave, Janey and I had a very emotional good bye and I boarded my flight to begin my trip into the unknown.

I arrived in Vietnam in mid-August at Cam Rahn Bay, Republic of South Vietnam. I expected to be assigned to the 173rd Airborne. Instead, I was sent to Pleiku in the Central Highlands of South Vietnam. I was assigned to Company A, 1st Battalion, 12th Infantry Regiment, 4th Infantry Division, or simply put, Co. A, 1/12th Inf., 4th Inf. Div. The 4th Division had just suffered heavy casualties just prior to my arrival in South Vietnam. Anyone with Infantry, Airborne, or Ranger training was being sent to them. Everyone I talked to said "the 4th Division never sends anyone out of the boonies for a rest unless they are dead or wounded." For the most part, I later found this to be amazingly factual.

Before I go any further, I would like to say that enemy soldiers were not the only enemies that frontline troops faced in South Vietnam. The troops faced such hardships as trench foot and Emersion foot from walking through rice paddies and mangrove swamps and swollen rivers and streams and monsoon rains for months on end. Drowning deaths were sometimes reported by troops in the central highlands trying to complete missions by crossing fast moving and swollen streams brought on by monsoon rains. The troops faced wounds and death from booby-traps. They suffered, and sometimes became fatalities, from jungle fever and malaria. Infections could cause sickness and death as Vietnamese rice farmers used both animal and human feces to fertilize their rice paddies.

I spent my tour in Vietnam in the Western and Northern Jungle Mountains where South Vietnam, Cambodia and Laos come together. We dealt with double and triple canopy jungles where sunlight rarely penetrated. The mountains were steep, razor-backed peaks with thick brush, heavy stands of thick growing bamboo, tanglefoot and wait-a-minute vines. In the monsoon season, the mountains presented precarious and very hazardous climbing. Slipping, sliding, and sometimes broken bones were common. Some of the leaves and plant vines offered the troops such things as unrelenting itching if touched, and also caused blisters filled with

VIETNAM

pus which would then turn into a very hard to cure skin problem, called 'Jungle Rot.' If not treated, it could become cancerous.

The mountain jungle was a dark, shadowy, secluded, and nearly impenetrable region. Visibility most of the time was limited to anywhere from one to six feet in front of you. As you forced your way through the jungle growth, dirt, leaves, twigs, leeches and other insects and sometimes Bamboo Vipers (green snakes) would fall from the underbrush. In the dry season, the jungle was hot, sticky and sweaty with 100% humidity. The temperatures usually averaged 100^0-120^0 in the daytime. Nighttime temperatures in the dry season were 60^0-$100.^0$ In the monsoon season it was not unusual to get anywhere from 2–6 inches of rain per day. During the monsoon season, the daytime temperatures would average 50^0-75^0 in the mountains. The night time temperatures could drop down to 40^0-70^0.

You would sweat heavily in the daytime while "moving" through the jungle. At night, when you stopped, you would shiver and shake uncontrollably. Your teeth would chatter, your skin was wrinkled, and when you thought the rain and wind would stop or let up, it would begin raining again so hard, visibility would be limited to 1-2 feet.

There was no where to hide from the lightning. We had one trooper killed by a lightning strike during our tour of duty. It rained constantly every hour of every day for months. Your skin was always wet and wrinkled, you were constantly wet, and rarely, if ever, dried out. Your clothing ripped, tore, and rotted off of you.

It was during the monsoons that the various types of fungi began growing on your clothing and on the troopers' bodies. The fungi contributed to the cracked skin, jungle rot, itching, and in many cases, if not caught early enough, caused the jungle rot to turn into cancerous pus-filled sores. Thus, you became a casualty and had to be medevac'd out of the bush until the jungle rot was healed.

Of course the wet weather would also bring out leeches. They would somehow work themselves under your clothing and attach themselves onto your blood. We often stopped during the day to make a "leech check." If you found them on you, the only way to get them to let go was to touch them with a lit cigarette or spray some bug juice on them. (Everyone carried a small bottle of Army-issued bug juice in their camouflage helmet cover band.)

An occasional drowning was not uncommon as you gave pursuit to enemy troops and had to cross rivers and streams that were overflowing their banks and running very fast. Crossing through open areas meant crossing through saw grass, which would cut your clothing and your skin to shreds.

There were two types of poisonous snakes we came across daily. The first was a beautiful lime green snake, known as the Bamboo Viper. These snakes lived mostly in the trees. They were also known by the troopers as "two steppers." The venom from the Bamboo Viper entered your blood stream so quickly that if you were unfortunate enough to be bitten, you would get two steps before dying from the snake bite. The second snake was the King Cobra. This snake mainly stayed on the ground and if you were bitten and medivac'd out quickly, you stood a chance of living, if you received the anti-venom in time.

Two other residents of the jungle floor that would try to crawl in with the troopers at night to keep warm were huge hairy spiders called, tarantulas. Many were as big as a man's hand.

All you had to do when you got up to stand guard was shake out your poncho and they would crawl away.

The second jungle floor resident was the jungle rat. These rats would reach lengths of 2 ½ feet and be as large around as your thigh. If cornered or rolled on during the night, they would bite chunks out of the trooper's skin and were impossible to catch. This meant a medevac trip to the nearest Evac Hospital where you had to undergo series of painful rabies shots. There was also a very good chance of getting jungle fever from the infections.

Malaria was very common, as the jungle swarmed with mosquitoes day and night. There were two types of malaria and I was unlucky enough to get both of them. The main concern with malaria was getting extremely high fevers which could damage the brain and/or kill you. I ran a 105° F fever with my first case of malaria. The cure: being dunked into a horse tank filled with ice water and drugs given by I.V. or shot form. Ice water treatments were dreaded by everyone who wasn't delirious from the fever. I spent 10 days in the Evac Hospital getting rid of the malaria.

The mountain areas I worked surrounded Dakto and all the Provinces surrounding Dakto. This area also included the area where South Vietnam, Laos, and Cambodia come together. This is where the North Vietnamese Army built and maintained a trail through the jungle. This trail is known as "The Ho Chi Minh Trail." There were huge supply depots all along the Ho Chi Minh Trail as well as truck and tank parks, troop rest areas, ammo and food depots, weapons storage, and artillery depots. Hospitals used by the North Vietnamese Army were created in caves and in a network of underground tunnel systems.

Another enemy of the foot soldier was his rucksack or pack. In the area I worked, we were re-supplied twice a week by helicopter re-supply. The weight of our packs varied from approximately 70 lbs. to over 110 lbs. Troops wore a web gear rig and carried at least 6-12 hand grenades, two colored smoke grenades, 12 magazines of ammo in two canvas ammo pouches hanging from the web gear, two canteens of water and a canteen cup on the web belt, two wound dressings and canvas covers, and one white phosphorous grenade. Over the web belt and harness, were two bandoliers containing 20 magazines of mig ammo. Over all this came the pack. The pack carried one nylon sleeping blanket wrapped in a waterproof poncho tied to the outside bottom of the pack. Inside the pack, the trooper carried his personal items in a waterproof bag like an ink pen, stationary, envelopes, shaving gear, toothbrush & tooth powder, and dry socks. Also inside were cans of c-rations to last for up to 10 days, extra hand grenades, pieces of rope and string, extra boot laces, four metal stakes, anything sent from home (letters, pictures, food package, Kool-Aid, etc.), extra bandages, one or two claymore mines, two trip flares and a small bale of trip wire to set booby traps and trip flares. On the outside of the pack, we carried another 20 magazines of M-16 ammo, stored extra c-rations in the pockets, and 100-200 round belt of M-60 machine gun ammo for the squad machine gun crew.

VIETNAM

Everyone carried a machete attached to his pack within easy reach. Squad leaders, such as me, also carried a law rocket launcher used to blow up bunkers, a map, and a compass. Each man also carried a bayonet somewhere within easy reach. Each platoon carried a chain saw, pick, axes and shovels, which were traded off to different squads daily to share the loads. Iodine tablets were used if we did not get re-supplied on schedule and had to get water from mountain streams and rivers. Malaria pills were also given out. One was a daily pill and one was taken weekly. No wonder the sound the men made as they hoisted their packs onto their backs resulted in their nickname, "Grunts."

The trees in the jungle reached a height of 200 feet and trying to get re-supplied by helicopter or in cases of making contact with the enemy and evacuating the wounded could pose a problem. This is where a plastic explosive called C-4 came into play. It came in a 2 lb. bar and could be molded into any shape desired. To clear the jungle away to make an LZ (landing zone), you would place enough C-4 at the base of the trees and blow the bottoms away. Some times, the jungle of tree tops were so thick, the trees failed to fall after being blown. Then the chain saws and axes were brought into use. At least a hole could be made for a helicopter to drop a sling load of ammo, water and rations. If enemy contact was made, medevac choppers could lift the wounded out on a sling and basket lowered through the tree tops. I could go further with these inconveniences, but there was a deadlier enemy, trooper faced.

This enemy was the North Vietnamese regular Army troops. These troops were determined, tough, well trained and well armed. They were highly trained by both Russian and Red Chinese advisors, who also supplied them with cheap, but very effective, weapons and ammunition. They would fight to the death! There were actually two types of troops in Vietnam. There were the ones I've already described and the second group was called Viet Cong, or V.C. These were part-time soldiers. During the day they were mothers and fathers, shop owners, Rice farmers, street vendors, businessmen and even Vietnamese employed at U.S. bases. At night, they would dig out their weapons from hiding places and harass or try to kill U.S. soldiers. I never came across or fought against the V.C. troops. I fought the hard core North Vietnamese Army troops who came down the Ho Chi Minh trail from North Vietnam.

I still to this day, break out in a cold sweat, shaking in a restless sleep and wake up yelling and screaming from the nightmares that still haunt me. One such incident occurred on March 20, 1968. We were on a search and destroy (ie., find & kill) mission. This occurred in the Province of Ban Me Thout (Ban Me To-It) Province near the Laos and Cambodian borders, just east of the Ho Chi Minh trail. As my unit was about to leave our night lager location, our Platoon leader, A 2nd Lt. with field experience and loved by everyone in the platoon, ordered my squad to walk point for the company. I assigned my best friend, a young 21-yr-old who came to Vietnam with me on the same day, to walk the lead point position. His back-up man was to follow him. His job was to watch the flanks for the point man while the point man watched both flanks as well as everything directly in front of him. Their objective was to keep us from walking into an ambush. After the back–up man, I followed and then another friend, and infantryman, and then my two man machine gun crew (M-60).

As we left the night lager area, we had gone only about 20 steps when George, on point, opened fire. An exchange of gunfire erupted, building into a steady roaring crescendo of noise. Small arms, hand grenades, machine gun fire and rockets shattered the early morning silence.

I ordered my squad to link up and form a perimeter with the other units of the company. At this time, the point back-up man ran towards me yelling. As he ran past me, I tripped him and asked where George, my friend and point man, was? He yelled into my ear something to the effect that George had been wounded and was laying out there. He then got up and ran to the middle of the company.

Our company Commander, a Captain, was very experienced in combat and North Vietnamese Army tactics, was already calling in artillery which was ringing our positions. I yelled and Boone, my squad member, I was going out after George. As I crawled forward, I spotted George about 10 yards in front of me moaning from the pain of his wounds. Squatting next to him on one knee, was a North Vietnamese Army soldier holding an AK-47 rifle against the crown of George's head. The North Vietnamese Army had a wide smile on his face as he spotted me in the brush. I was carrying an M-79 grenade launcher loaded with a double "oo" buck round. I sighted down the barrel aiming at the North Vietnamese Army soldier's head. He continued "smiling" at me! I quickly motioned for him to back away and had every intention to let him live if he didn't hurt or kill George. At this point, the North Vietnamese Army soldier smiled wider and pulled the trigger!

At this time, everything seemed to happen in slow motion. I was saying to myself "no, this didn't happen," but at the same time, my mind and body were in a rage that this animal called a human being, had murdered George and had smiled as he did it. I immediately pulled the trigger as the North Vietnamese Army soldier was trying to raise his rifle at me. I watched as his head exploded into a ball of mist. This smile was gone! I crawled up to George, hoping there was life left in him; there was none. I grabbed George by the shirt collar and crawling backwards, pulled George the 10-20 yards back into the company's perimeter. I wasn't going to leave him out there alone. Making sure to remember where he was located, I returned to the perimeter. I crawled behind a large fallen tree trunk.

As I peeked over the top of the log, I spotted what appeared to a North Vietnamese Army officer pointing and yelling orders at his troops. I loaded the M-79 with an H&E (highly explosive) round. I peeked over the log again, sighted in on the target and fired. The H&E round struck the North Vietnamese Army officer in the chest, but failed to detonate. The M-79 H&E round had to travel so many feet and/or turn so many revolutions before it armed and detonated. Apparently the North Vietnamese Army officer was closer than I thought. I know if he wasn't dead, he was very badly wounded because I saw blood and flesh fly from his chest when the round struck him. Still peering over the log for another target, I watched as two North Vietnamese Army soldiers ran to the officer. They grabbed him under the arms and began to drag him away when the M-79 round in his chest exploded. It killed all three of them!

Still lying next to the log, I rolled onto my back to get more ammo out of my pouches. As I lay on my back, I heard a "thunk." I looked skywards and saw an M-79 disappear downwards on the other side of the log. It then re-appeared over the top of the log and fired again. A North Vietnamese Army soldier had apparently taken the weapon and ammo off of a dead G.I. and was using it against us. Potato masher grenades began falling out of the sky on my side of the log. The North Vietnamese Army used the potato masher grenades against us.

Everything happens fast in combat, and at the same time, I was thinking about how I could eliminate the North Vietnamese Army on the other side of the log. Then, it struck me. I pulled a hand grenade from my web harness as I laid on my back. I pulled the pin and held the handle. When the North Vietnamese Army soldier stuck the barrel over the log again, I grabbed it as firmly as I could and jerked it right out of the North Vietnamese Army soldier's hands. I let the grenade handle fly as I got up to run away and heard it explode, followed by screaming.

The potato mashers were being thrown at me and as I took my 4th or 5th step to get away, one of them landed next to my left side and exploded. I received shrapnel wounds to the left side of my face, left shoulder, left side of the chest and upper arm.

I blacked out from the concussion and then remember being led to an LZ (landing zone) for a medi-vac. My friend John Boone was with me, having been shot in the arm. We both loaded George's body onto the same chopper with the two of us. George flew his last helicopter flight with John and I back to the 85th Evac. Hospital. We gave him one last hug at the 85th Evac and went to surgery with the nurses.

George was returned to his mother in Reading, Kansas, where he received a full military burial service. Boone was transferred from the 85th Evac to the Army hospital in Japan. I spent three weeks at the 85th Evac to heal my wounds. After I recovered, I returned to combat with a different type unit. John returned to our unit in the 4th division to finish his tour.

After completion of my Vietnam service, I returned to the States with 18 months of active duty left. I was assigned to Fort Hood, Texas. Janey and I married, and she came to live with me in a small apartment until my enlistment time ended. The Army offered me $10,000 in cash and a promotion to Staff Sergeant (E-6) to return to Vietnam for my last year of service. With Janey at my side at Fort Hood, I knew I couldn't return to Vietnam.

While stationed at Fort Hood, I began to break out with mysterious rashes and blisters. My joints and muscles ached strangely at times. The Army doctors insisted my body was re-adjusting itself to the healthful fresh air, environment, good food, and these issues would clear themselves up eventually. I thought, well, neither the Army nor the Government would lie to me. I was told by the Army doctors that this was a common occurrence of returning soldiers from Vietnam.

I found out a few years later that the Federal Government and the Vietnam Administration did, in fact, lie not only to me, but to every returning Vietnam veteran. The rashes continued off and on, my joints and muscles began aching for no known reasons to me. Finally, everything came to a head on December 23, 1983. That day I suffered a severe heart attack that almost killed me. Over the next 10 days, I suffered six more major heart attacks. I expired during one of them and had to be electrically shocked to be revived. I contacted the V.A. and indicated to them that I had been contaminated with Agent Orange exposure and when I saw a V.A. doctor, after much red tape and arguing, the V.A. doctor refused to admit I had been exposed to Agent Orange.

Agent Orange was an herbicide used in Vietnam that was sprayed on dense jungle from Air Force C-130s and other aircraft. It was used to defoliate jungle cover and expose enemy units, bunkers, storage areas, etc. along the Ho Chi Minh Trail. They sprayed mainly in the areas I just happened to be assigned to. Many times while on missions, aircraft would fly over us and dump tons of Agent Orange on the jungle we were in and it would cover our fatigue and exposed skin. On contact with the skin, it would burn the skin, soak into your pores, burn your eyes and blister your skin. It would get into your C-rations and would be ingested into your system when you ate.

Over the past several years, my teeth are breaking and falling out, and my dentist has said that the bones in my jaws are deteriorating. She said this is probably caused by the Agent Orange poisoning as she can't find any other reasons for them to deteriorate like they are. My second son was born with bone defects in his ankles and feet which were caused by my Agent Orange poisoning. This was backed up by reports from the Agent Orange Investigation Board. However, the V.A. denied all my claims when this occurred and special fitted shoes with braces and medical treatment and corrective shoes, devices and braces were paid out of my pocket (see following story).

"AGENT DEATH" (AGENT ORANGE) IS KILLING ME
Ron Robaska

Ronald D. Robaska, Sr.

My wife passed away on December 1, 2007. It was now mid-January. A heavy snow was falling as I walked into the empty house. I had just gotten home from the grocery story with a quart of milk and put it in the refrigerator. I walked into the living room and immediately had a strange sensation come over me. As the light began to leave my eyes and things started to go black, I could feel myself begin to die. Suddenly, I felt as though I had been kicked by a huge horse as my defibrillator sent a large burst of electricity to my heart. The shock had picked me up and literally threw me across the living room. My heart had gone into what is called "v-tach," where it just stops beating and weakens so that it cannot pump blood; it just lies in your chest and quivers. This is called "sudden death syndrome."

Had I not had the defibrillator, I would have died on the spot. In the next twenty minutes my defibrillator fired and delivered large shocks to my heart another 10-12 times, bringing me back from the dead each time.

As my defibrillator fired a third electrical charge to my heart that day in January 2008, the jolt threw me out of the living room. I landed next to the dining room table. I felt very weak but was able to pull myself to my feet, using the table for support. On top of the table, I found my portable phone. Finally! I could dial 911! As I picked up the phone, the defibrillator fired once again. When I came to I found I had been thrown against the entrance door of my home. I didn't have the strength to get off the floor--I was very weak and some of muscles didn't want to work--but I knew I would die all alone in my home if I did not force myself to do something. I could not locate the phone, and was sure it had been sent flying with the jolt. Reaching up to the door knob over my head, I turned the handle and pulled the door open, thinking that if I could fall out the front door, maybe a passerby would spot me and stop and call 911. It was snowing very hard as I dragged myself outside and down my snow-covered driveway. It was so cold! My bare hands began burning from the cold. After what seemed like hours (but I'm sure was just a few minutes), not one car or neighbor passed by.

Looking around, I saw my neighbor friend's truck in his driveway across the street, and I knew he was home. I tried to raise to my hands and knees, but the blackness returned and I got shocked again. As I became conscious for the fifth time, I saw that the heavy snow was sticking to me. My only hope now was to somehow get to my friend's house. I began to crawl. Halfway across the street, I stopped to rest, thinking, "I'm halfway there!" The snow continued to fall, soaking my clothes, but no cars came down the street. I continued to drag myself through the snow and slush until I pulled myself up the two steps to Ted's front door and began banging on the door until he came and helped me inside the home. I gasped out, "I need help; call 911," then the blackness returned and I felt myself shocked again.

When I came to, I was lying on his kitchen floor with his girlfriend giving me mouth-to-mouth resuscitation. When I was breathing on my own again, she covered me with a blanket, put a pillow under my head, and talked to me gently. I was like a limp rag and had no strength whatsoever. I remember saying "thank you" as my chest and heart burned from the defibrillator shocks. Even as I noticed the burning, the defibrillator fired up and shocked me again.

This time I found myself outside my body, looking down at myself and feeling an overwhelming warmth and peace and love. I felt my wife was there with me, looking down at my body. Once again, I felt an horrific shock and found myself back on the floor. My neighbor's girlfriend was holding me for comfort and telling me that everything would be okay. I had no more strength left--physically or psychologically--and only wanted to be with my wife. But then my son was kneeling over me, having hurried over at my neighbor's call. Everything went black again (I understand it was three more times), but I don't remember anything except the fire burning in my chest and being loaded into an ambulance.

When I awoke, I was in a bed at Lakeland Hospital, St. Joseph, Michigan. The doctor and nurses explained what had happened to me and that I was in the heart unit. After 2-3 days, two nurses ran into my room, saying the monitor I was wearing had alerted them that I was going into V-Tach again. At that moment, I felt a strange sensation in my chest and everything began to disappear into a deep, deep blackness.

The following was told to me by my sons and daughter 2-3 days later...They had been notified by hospital staff that things had gotten worse for me and they should come to the hospital as soon as possible. When they arrived at my room, the doctor and staff were attempting to revive me with chest compression, electrical shocks from paddles, and putting me into a drug-induced coma--all at the same time.

I was put on Life Support and kept in a drug coma until I became stable enough to be transported by life helicopter to the University of Chicago cardiac unit for experimental surgery. In the helicopter I was very aware of where I was, what was going on, and all that had happened. I laid back and enjoyed the flight from my stretcher, watching the shore of Lake Michigan below us.

I went through the surgery with just a few minor problems occurring, stayed for about a week, then returned home with follow-up checks as part of the surgical research group. The same problem returned and I was once again transported to the University of Chicago for more surgery under the research program. This time, the surgery was more successful and

I returned to Lakeland Hospital, then was sent to a rehabilitation center for two months to recover and regain strength.

Things are certainly not back to normal, but normal is what you make of it. I have approximately 17% of my heart left, but I'm making it. My balance, equilibrium, sight perception and a few other small problems remain. I have a cane, a walker, and a power chair which makes a lot of things easier to do. I am also on oxygen all of the time as a result of all the heart damage. My wife fought breast cancer for five years before she was taken from me. She had a lot of courage to fight for so long, and she has inspired me to fight back as well. I have had a few more bouts with the defibrillator, had angiograms and angioplasties, underwent a triple bypass, and was given a severe staph infection during surgery. As a result, I almost died from the MRSA staph. I had to wear a wound vac system over my heart wound, underwent chest muscle replacements to cover and protect my heart, and underwent six months of intense IV antibiotics daily to kill off the infection.

Some days I feel okay, others I have recurring chest pains. I sometimes get very painful headaches, lose balance and have had approximately fifteen TIAs, or minor strokes. The last stroke I had caused numbness to my hands and arms, as well as, drooling from the right side of my mouth. The nerve endings in my lower back are slowly deteriorating and cause severe burning and extreme pain to my lower back and hip areas. My feet and legs get very numb. I have a constant numbness around my nose and eyes due to my last mini-stroke…but I'm not alone.

Thousands of other Vietnam veterans are going through the same things. Many suffer from cancers or nerve damage, heart-related diseases or more. Neither they nor I seek pity or sympathy in any way. We are all leftovers of the Kennedy Presidency and felt obligated to defend our country against communism at that period of time in our lives and in history, emulating our fathers who had stormed the beaches on D-Day or planted the flag on Iwo Jima. We fought our war like our fathers and grandfathers fought theirs. All we seek is fair treatment for our wounds, be they from bullets or Agent Orange poisoning.

Lawsuits were filed against Dow Chemical (producer of Agent Orange); they were forced to reveal all of their scientific studies and the true facts of exactly what effects Agent Orange had on our veterans. I myself was part of an enormous class action suit against the company, and eventually, Dow was found responsible for its actions and ordered to compensate all those included in the suit. The settlement helped some pay for medical expenses and/or for funerals of those veterans who had died from Agent Orange poisoning. It would take another three decades before the Military, Federal Government, and the Veterans Administration would admit their guilt and began making settlements and take over the responsibility for veterans' health care. At first, Chloracne and several types of cancer were identified to be a result of Agent Orange, followed by bone and nerve deterioration. In 2010, Agent Orange poisoning was found to be the cause, or at least a contributing factor, to some forms of brain loss/brain damage, as well as some forms of heart disease and heart-related problems. Finally, in December of 2010, Agent Orange poisoning of Vietnam and Korean veterans is recognized by our government and Veterans Administration.

I urge you, the American people, to never again let the Military and our Government lie to our veterans as they did in the case of Agent Orange…"Agent Death."

AGENT ORANGE

Thousands of men and women of all races were killed in action during the Vietnam War; thousands more were wounded in action. When the troopers were pulled out of South Vietnam in 1973, everyone thought they would return home and forget about Vietnam and what happened there. Even though the war had changed many of them mentally and physically, they just wanted to return home and pick up life where they had left off before the war. It wasn't that easy. Thousands of those returning troops were unaware that an agent of the war had followed them home. It would take over their bodies, destroy their lives and families, extinguish their hopes and dreams, and even cheat them of life itself. I call it "Agent Death;" the Government, the Military and the Veteran's Administration call it "Agent Orange" poisoning.

I am a victim of Agent Orange poisoning. I am not going to go into the chemical ingredients of Agent Orange; suffice it to say that besides the two main ingredients--2, 4-D and 2,4, ST--Agent Orange contains 17 other contaminants harmful to plants, animals, and human life. Troops who questioned what effects Agent Orange might have on them at the time or in the future, all received the same answer: it was safe. Dow Chemical (who produced the herbicide), the Military, and the US Government all made statements that the herbicide was safe to use and would have absolutely no ill health effects on the troops then or in the future. This, of course, turned out to be an utter lie by all three entities. Eventually, the truth and seriousness of the health affects that Agent Orange was causing Vietnam veterans surfaced, as it began showing its effects on veterans in the 1970s.

Agent Orange poisoning has many faces and causes many diseases, including:

- Sudden outbursts of anger

- Damage to the cerebral cortex

- Continuous and irregular muscle contractions or convulsions

- Difficult, painful breathing

- Many types of cancers

- Emphysema

- Edema (ie., drowning in your own body fluids)

- Congestion of capillaries

- Fibrosis

- Masses of nerve tissues and cells--ganglionic

- Papilloma--tumors of the skin or mucus membrane

- Dilation or constriction of blood vessels

- Irregular heartbeats

- Racing or rapid heartbeats

- v-tachycardia--rapid heartbeat that causes sudden death

- Cardio sympathy--inability of heart to pump

If you have been exposed to Agent Orange, you can have any, or a surprisingly large number of, the above symptoms.

A WALK IN THE JUNGLE

Ron Springer

This stream is almost exactly like the one in the story. This man was in my friend, Joe Krestan's, squad, as I recall, and I got the photo from Joe Krestan. (Summer 1971, I Corp, Vietnam)

The following incident happened to me during the summer of 1970 while serving with the 101st Airborne Division in Northern I Corp, Vietnam. Incidents like this happened wherever men fought, from the mountains to the rice paddies sometimes with different results. I was a squad leader at the time when a change in our operating procedures came down from headquarters. We were switched from operating in Platoon- Company size elements (30/100 men) to five men teams. I believe the idea was to put as many resources over as wide an area as possible to prevent infiltration into the lowlands by NVA looking for food, etc. Needless to say, there were not a lot of "happy campers' with this new change.

Each five-man team had an RTO (radio man), M-60 machine gunner, M-79 grenadier, and three M-16 rifles (including the RTO). We would soon find out the ramifications of having only one radio. Of the four other members of our teams, I can only remember the M-60 machine gunner, Mike Carvalho. Carvalho was from California and looked it, kind of like a lean surfer, 150 pounds, dirty blonde hair and usually with a smile. During the middle of the monsoon (four to five months of mostly cold rain and overcast skies), he was known to stop and gaze up at the rain and clouds and say, "You know, I think it's going to blow over." This never failed to crack us up.

I believe we were operating in the vicinity of FSB Brick, a new area of operation (AO) to us. We'd been out several days, patrolling down a ridgeline near a shallow stream that flowed over the boulders and into the more flat terrain. We'd stopped for a break and to update our location. The jungle canopy was quite thick where we were. Try as I might, I couldn't shoot any azimuths with my compass to known landmarks that would give us our location. I considered myself good with a map and compass and I knew if I could break out into some semi-open terrain or find an opening through the heavy vegetation, I could find out where we were. I decided to take one rifleman and told the others I was going down the stream and try and pinpoint our location. None of us were particularly keen on breaking into even smaller groups, but I only planned on being gone for fifteen or twenty minutes. I left the RTO, M-60 gunner and the other man behind. We were nervous, going without a radio, but I didn't want to drag everyone along. Naturally, Murphy's Law was in full force and I could never get a fix on any identifiable terrain features. I kept going "just another few minutes". As the minutes ticked on, I realized I had exceeded my estimate of fifteen to twenty minutes as we'd been gone almost an hour. I knew the others would be worrying so we turned around and headed back. Back at our small base camp, the RTO had received a call from our LT telling us to be at new coordinates in two hours. The RTO said that would be a problem as one, we didn't know where we were and two, the Squad Leader and another man weren't there. The LT was not "overly pleased" to hear this and said: "Go find them"! Well, the RTO and the other members were not "overly pleased" to receive this order and they argued to no avail with the LT before reluctantly starting out down the stream knowing full well that I had no idea they were coming. Carvalho was walking point with the M-60; the RTO was next followed by the M-79 man. Slowly they walked through the knee deep water trying not to make any noise. Meanwhile, we were also moving slowly through the same knee deep water, trying to be as quiet as can be without any idea that we were both heading toward each other.

I still don't know for sure who saw who first. I think I saw the barrel of Carvalho's machine gun come around a bend in the stream. This next part probably occurred in less than a second although it seemed like a lifetime (especially to Carvalho). I was walking with my M-16 rifle at waist height, pointed to the front and on full automatic, finger on the trigger in case I had to spray the area should we run into the enemy. As our eyes locked, I froze and Carvalho saw the wide-eyed blank look in my eyes. He could see that part of me wanted to pull the trigger because my rifle was pointed straight at him with my finger still on the trigger. Part of my brain was screaming that person should be the enemy, shoot him. The other part said, no wait, you recognize him. Carvalho yelled: "Springer, it's me, it's me," my shoulders relaxed, and Carvalho started to breathe again. After getting our wits back, we all headed back to our base camp.

Why didn't either of us shoot? Carvalho, of course had the advantage in knowing he was looking for me. I on the other hand, had no such knowledge. Although we'll never know for sure, my best guess is that as we weren't in a "high contact" AO, we weren't as conditioned as some units were to react swiftly to an incident such as this and blast everything in sight. And maybe, I just didn't want to shoot anyone that day.

Upon getting back to our base camp, the LT had to fly over in a helicopter while we taped a smoke grenade to a tree limb and waved it as high as we could. He finally located us and we made it to the proper LZ. One of the reasons I had a tough time finding our location was because the stream we were walking in was not shown on the map which was common due to the irregular terrain.

BETTER LATE THAN NEVER

Denny Swanson
US Army, 1967-69

After serving in the US Army in Vietnam, one of the most difficult things for me was to re-engage with any military organization. Upon returning in 1969, we soldiers were vilified by America's liberals, called "baby killers," and spat upon. In order to use a two-thirds priced airline ticket from San Francisco to Chicago, I had to wear my dress green uniform during the trip—a big mistake at the San Francisco airport. I wanted my rifle and bayonet back!

Denny Swanson

Upon arriving home, the dress greens and all but one set of fatigues and boots were promptly trashed. I had no intention of being involved with anything military again in my life. A few months later when I surprisingly received orders to attend summer camp with the Reserves, I had nothing from the Army to wear. They happily took care of that need. The men I camped with were well trained and fine military people, but almost none of the higher ranking officers and enlisted men had any active duty experience. After those two weeks, the last thing I could think of was to admit to any military experience, and I stayed far away from military organizations. That lasted many, many years.

I had been within two months of completing my Master's Degree at Michigan State University in the fall of 1966 when our local draft board changed my status to 1A. I asked them to please let me graduate, and they accommodated that request. Meanwhile I visited an Army recruiter and asked, since I was recently married, what I needed to do so that my wife could accompany me during some of my assignments. They told me I had to be "an E4 over 4." That meant nothing to me, and when it was explained, I was not sure that four years was what I wanted to do. The other possibility was "you could become an officer." I said that sounded fine, and I signed up. While I was not certain how a war in such a small country that far from home would have any significance to me, I did not attempt to escape my responsibility (two of my best friends had joined the National Guard, which was a reasonably safe option). My decision was primarily based upon the fact that my father missed WWII due to being a critical maintenance engineer at an airplane manufacturing company. One of us needed to represent our country in the military service, so I guessed that would be me.

Unfortunately, a few years earlier I had voted for Lyndon Johnson for president. One of his campaign promises was that "If elected president, I will not send another American boy to Vietnam." Of course this turned out to be another Johnson lie as he sent 3.5 million to Vietnam, and as a young American, I personally experienced the validity of a campaign promise quickly forgotten by an elected president. I also discovered that a huge number of fellow soldiers could give Johnson's speech from memory. During my active duty, I believe that, after Jane Fonda, Johnson was the most despised person by the men I served with.

I was raised in Grand Rapids, Michigan, many miles from any military base. The only uniforms I had ever seen were on television. Consequently, at first, it was a joke for me to correctly apply the brass, insignia and patches to my uniform and not be chewed out by the drill sergeant. Fortunately, a New England National Guard unit was having their basic training within our training company, so those guys helped me with the uniform work, saluting, and learning to avoid KP. Basic training was in Ft. Dix, New Jersey, beginning in January, 1967. What a place to start – cold and ugly. Bivouac at minus 14 degrees became a dangerous exercise, and was called off after one day and night. We all felt that, if Ft. Dix was not the end of the world, at least you could see it from there.

After earning a college degree prior to joining the Army, I was among the older guys in our training unit. That helped me with the mental side, adjusting to the amusing things the DI would do to the trainees. During our nearly two weeks on the rifle range, I started something myself that was innovative. We always double-timed the four miles to the range carrying our pack, M-14, and were warmly dressed. Once there, our underclothing was soaked with sweat, and until noon (when we finally dried off) we froze while lying in the snow shooting at targets. (Remember, this was January and February at Ft. Dix.) On the third day I brought a second set of underclothes, and when we arrived at the range, the DI, as usual, gave the unit a smoking break. I stripped (out in the snow in front of everyone) and put on my dry underwear. Many laughed, but I was now warm as toast. The following day, another twenty joined me, and we maxed out with about half the company joining in. Even our hardnosed platoon DI gave me credit for using my head—he ran along with us and probably would have liked to do the same, but pride would never allow that!

Advanced Individual Training was in Ft. Ord, California, a much different climate, reasonably good food, and good training. We were now treated like soldiers, had some time off, and actually visited San Francisco a few weekends. It was there in Ft. Ord that I found out about a great decision I had made back while joining the Army. The first weekend we were eligible for leave, our DI told us that if we had not signed up for the Savings Bond program, there would be a required movie and discussion about the value of buying bonds to support America. This program would take place Saturday evening around 1900 hours. Of course if you had to attend that meeting your opportunity for a weekend pass anywhere but near the base was over. Thank goodness I already was in the bond program. A small voice had told me that somehow agreeing to purchase bonds would pay off. The meeting was extremely effective, because there were many guys who signed up immediately. What a beautiful and subtle way to sell bonds!

It was at Ft. Ord that we had an opportunity to fire many different weapons our Army used, as well as an AK-47—the bad guy's choice of rifle. It was cheaply made, shot reasonably straight, and was one of the most reliable rifles in the world. Covered with wet mud the weapon would still shoot, quite unlike the M-16 we used that required lots of tender loving, care and cleaning. The M-60 machine gun was our favorite when it came to reliability and accuracy, a great weapon!

My next assignment was Officer Candidate School, class 61, at Ft. Benning, Georgia. Lots of red clay, constant harassment by senior OCS candidates and TAC officers, and some of the finest leadership training I have ever been exposed to. We had thought that basic training was tough—it was nothing compared to OCS. While the physical side was where most of the punishment occurred, it was really the mental part that defined success. I had no plans to quit no matter what they did to me. I left there in the best physical condition of my life. (Then I found out later from military friends that OCS was nothing compared to the Navy Seal training.) No matter what you do, someone always has it more difficult— and that is also a life lesson.

Overnight field exercises were common in OCS. Normal procedure before we left was a threat by the TAC officers concerning candy (pogey bait). If you had any, they said to leave it in the center of the formation—if you were caught in the field with it, you would pay. On most exercises I would be eating Hershey candy bars with my C-rations in the field, and my buddies would wonder where I was able to hide them. Someone turned me in, and I was subject to several searches, but no pogey bait was ever found, and no TAC officers ever saw me eat any. As it turned out, an empty clip for the M-14 rifle would hold two candy bars perfectly – and we always carried several filled with blanks for our "pretend firefights."

We began with approximately 235 candidates, and graduated 120. Physical training, mental challenges, and the honor code did in the drop outs. Due to my having a master's degree I applied for and received an Adjutant General assignment, as opposed to being an infantry platoon leader, and automatically off to fight in Vietnam. I believe all of our graduates went to Vietnam in one capacity or another, many of them happy to go and lead men into combat.

Ft. Benjamin Harrison in Indianapolis was next, a short five-week stay, then off to Ft. Lewis, Washington for nearly a year. What a beautiful part of our country. I worked in a training battalion as a platoon leader for most of that year. My largest challenge was with the younger guys who had such a difficult time adjusting to the orders, the rules, and everything having to be the same. I was appointed Trial Counsel (prosecutor) for approximately eight months in military court. It was a nice break from my normal job, and the Colonel in charge was sad to see me go to Vietnam because I had won all my cases. One case had an interesting end. A private had hit his Commanding Officer, and was easily convicted due to witnesses. When I got to Vietnam, one day I was reading the "Stars and Stripes" newspaper and an article described a soldier from Ft. Lewis flying in a military plane to Leavenworth to serve his sentence. He refused to board the airplane without a parachute, and was finally given one. When the plane achieved proper altitude, he opened a door and jumped. Two days later he was apprehended walking on a highway in Nebraska. He was one I had convicted.

Our time in Ft. Lewis was wonderful. It was a great base, with so much to do outdoors. Fishing was available everywhere, Mt. Rainier was fun to visit; my wife and I hoped to return to Washington once the Army was done with me.

Orders for Vietnam were received in time for me to have just over a year in the country. My orders changed several times from the first issue, and finally they said "just go there and they will find a job for you." I worked in many locations: Vinh Long, Soc Trang, My Tho, Vung Tau and Can Tho, mostly in the Delta region. I ran a postal unit and served in some staff positions. Travel was common, on anything that flew. Sometimes the travel resulted in ambushes and other live fire situations, but my time was safe compared to the endless firefights my OCS friends experienced. Many of those friends did not return from Vietnam, and I have found their names on the memorial in Washington DC.

Two events happened to me that, while not life-threatening, gave me an opportunity to witness the firepower of the US military. One was a B-52 raid that was very close, and the other a napalm drop within 500 yards that radiated enormous heat and enemy loss of life.

281

I was lucky. Some people told me that if I had gone to the military first, they would have paid for my education. Instead, I paid for my education, and it likely saved my life in Vietnam. The life of a platoon leader was a most dangerous job, and with my background I was assigned other work. Doing the things our fighting troops (about 30% of the total men and women in Vietnam when I was there) had to do, not just against the VC and North Vietnamese, but also the leeches, snakes, insects, and issues at home, for a lousy $65/month combat pay was very difficult. I was proud of the Army troops that I served with, and was very pleased with the leadership training that was part of OCS. It was something I could actually apply later in my business career.

Was our family able to return to the wonderful state of Washington after I left the military? No. Boeing Corporation had just lost an opportunity to build the supersonic transport plane, and after they downsized, there were no jobs to be had. We landed in my home state of Michigan instead.

Finally, a few years ago I purchased a State of Michigan "Vietnam Veteran" license plate, my first admission since 1969 that I had military/Vietnam experience—other than telling friends and relatives. Then, this summer while on a family vacation to Mt. Rushmore and the Badlands, a proud moment occurred. We attended the night light show at Mt. Rushmore, and during that event, the Park Ranger gave a moving speech about our country. At the end he had all veterans come to the front while everyone sang "God Bless America." When we were all assembled, he asked the Vietnam veterans to come further to the front because we were the most poorly treated by our own country, and he wanted to help correct that affront. Wow, that was first class. Our country has changed how it views military service since 1970, and it feels a lot better. Programs like _Lest We Forget_ are also making American veterans feel proud.

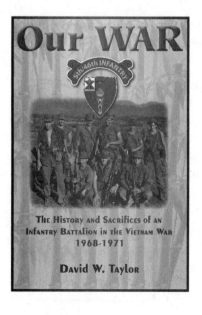

OUR WAR: BATTLE OF PINKVILLE
Dave Taylor

Excerpt from Our War, reprinted with permission by Dave Taylor.

To order your copy of the book, contact Dave Taylor at dwtaylor@ohio.net, 330-722-7455, www.warjournalpub.com or War Journal Publishing, P.O. Box 10, Medina, Ohio 44258-0010.

At 11:00AM on July 4, 1968, the 198th Brigade Commander's attention was drawn to a report from an American ARVN advisor, flying in a helicopter up the coast to Chu Lai, who observed a large group of Vietcong in uniform just north of a coastal enclave known as "Pinkville" - My Lai (1).

Although the 5th/46th Infantry Battalion, recently arrived on LZ Dottie, was exhausted from the Burlington Trail and Vance Canyon missions, an operation was quickly organized. Air strikes, artillery and helicopter gunships were laid on and LTC David Lyon, commander of the 5th/46th was told to stand by. Alpha Company had just arrived from the Ha Thanh Special Forces Camp and was the only unit not strung out on patrols on the coastal plain near Dottie. Although its strength was down to eighty-four grunts, Lyon told Alpha's commander, Captain Herbert Erb to get ready as a reactionary force. Erb's troops were bone-tired from the trek in the mountains. What Alpha desperately needed was some rest. What they got was an air assault into one of the deadliest hamlets in the Americal Divisions AO.

At 6:30PM on July 5 Erb's troops were air assaulted to the beach just north of the Pinkville hamlet, near where the VC formation had been spotted. Gunships prepared the LZ with heavy rocket fire, and then shifted fire to the west and south. Erb's troopers were carried in on five slicks in three lifts. His soldiers found enough light in the waning day-time hours to see the enemy bullets reaching up to their helicopters, looking for blood. Yet it was dark enough to see the muzzle flashes across the ground below them.

Sergeant Bob Cummings, a squad leader in the 2nd platoon turned to one of his men, Bob Salter, and asked, "How can a chopper tell if it is being fired at with all this noise?" At that instant they heard loud "cracks" of bullets zinging by. They also saw tracers that seemed to be curving up to meet them. Cummings turned to Salter, "Oh, so that's how you tell!"

Cummings thought Salter, sitting in the open doorway, was getting "edgy" as he began firing down on the enemy. So intent was Salter at answering the enemy fire that Cummings held the straps on Salter's rucksack to keep him from falling out. They landed on a narrow peninsula running north from Pinkville, a beach enclave with the South China Sea on the east and the My Khe River on the west.

The river ran south through Pinkville, creating a canal between the beach and the hamlet. During the air assault, gunships protecting the slicks killed eight Vietcong and set off a total of seven secondary explosions in the area, indicating caches of enemy ammunition were hit. Jet air strikes were added to the gunships, killing more insurgents. Alpha would later find bodies everywhere.

LTC Lyon in his command & control bird flew low to survey the area where the gunships were hitting their targets and his bird took hits from automatic weapons fire. The chopper lost oil pressure and emergency lights came on, followed by a loss of power. Lyon's pilot landed the bird by autorotation, essentially guiding it to the ground with dead engines, onto the beach near Alpha's troops.

By this time Erb had placed his 2nd platoon five hundred yards south on the sandy beach, only five hundred yards from the north edge of Pinkville. After Lyon's bird crash-landed the 2nd platoon received heavy machinegun fire from Pinkville. Lyon's Huey crew removed the two M-60 machineguns from the chopper and prepared a defensive position. Within twenty minutes another bird arrived to take Lyon and his crew back to LZ Dottie and Erb was tasked to guard the aircraft until the next day.

Sergeant Cummings soon learned that shit falls downhill quickly. Erb tasked the 2nd platoon leader, Richard Horne Jr., to secure the ditched chopper. Horne in turn ordered Cummings' squad to get it done. Noting that the downed helicopter was not within the defensive lines of the rest of Alpha, Cumming's squad dug deep holes and remained awake all night, their position completely exposed.

At midnight Alpha's commander received a warning from the brigade headquarters at LZ Bayonet, "You are in a heavily booby-trapped area. Expect to find yourselves completely encircled. This comes from a commander who worked in your area before".

By 7:30AM on July 6 Erb moved his headquarters element and 2nd platoon into the hamlet of Ky Xuyen (1) which was close to where he landed on the beach. His 3rd platoon was more than one half mile south on the beach-like peninsula. The 1st platoon was tasked to move north from the 3rd to link up with Erb. The troops with the headquarters element were busy in the hamlet finding tunnels, bunkers and munitions. An Explosive Ordnance Demolition (EOD) team was choppered in from LZ Gator to help out. Crater charges were used to destroy the enemy munitions but there was so much destruction lying on the ground that logs and trees were blown sky high, the soldier's eyes following the timber going up, then dodging the logs when they fell to the ground. There was simply no place to take cover on the sandy beach.

Dead bodies were everywhere. The battalion had initially reported the eight dead VC from the gunships which prepped the landing zone but Alpha's grunts were finding many more bodies with weapons. No one was interested in reporting body counts beyond the original eight previously reported because no one asked for them.

By 2:30PM the engineers destroyed a cesspool of bombs and bomb-making equipment, including an unexploded five hundred pound bomb from a previous air strike. Thousands of flies were everywhere amidst the carnage, the dead bodies now rotting in the sun. If a soldier opened his mouth for any reason, flies flew in. Before soldiers could get their canteens to their mouths to drink much-needed water, flies flew inside the canteens. If they tried to open a can of C-rations, two layers of flies were on the food instantly. They were everywhere, landing on their sweat-soaked bodies and crawling into their eyes and ears.

The next day Erb moved his troops farther south on the sandy beach to the northeast corner of Pinkville. The canal separating the beach from the hamlet was only thirty yards wide and a small footbridge connected both sides. At 10:05AM Alpha came under heavy fire from Pinkville (My Lai 1) again. After establishing a base of fire from the beach, Erb was ordered to attack the hamlet. He sent small groups of grunts by leaps and bounds over the footbridge to establish a position on the other side at the edge of the hamlet. Gunships were requested to help in the attack but none were available.

Alpha had little choice but to press the fight forward since its position on the beach left it too exposed. Once soldiers on the Pinkville side of the foot bridge gained a foothold, Erb and a larger group of grunts dashed over the bridge to add weight to the fight. The Vietcong got what they wanted. Their trap was set and the bridge exploded from a command-detonated mine. In an instant, bodies were lying in the water and on the beach, seventeen grunts wounded in all, including Richard Horne the platoon leader and Erb, the company commander. Alpha's grunts received a shocking blow that traumatized everyone. Then loyalty to one another, and guts and determination took over in the midst of disaster.

Although SP/4 Donald Hess's face was bleeding from shrapnel he grabbed another injured soldier and carried him back to the beach while under heavy fire. He went forward to bring another grunt back and treated both, giving comfort to his traumatized buddies. SP/5 Jon

Kester was a medic who caught shrapnel in the right eye and over most of his upper body. Ignoring his wounds he organized a medical treatment effort on the beach while under fire, advising the other grunts on the use of field dressings, morphine syrettes, splints and tourniquets. His direction provided order and comfort amidst the chaos.

PFC Stephen Richards, another medic was unable to move because of serious wounds but yelled out instructions for other grunts to efficiently use his supplies. He was able to hang on long enough until a dustoff took him back to the hospital in Chu Lai but he succumbed to his wounds twenty-one days later. He was posthumously awarded the Silver Star.

Sp/4 Carl Roegner, an RTO, had been hit in the face but waved off any medical aid while calling in dustoff support. PFC Kenneth Steele, another RTO was wounded in the face and foot. Under the heavy automatic weapons fire coming from the hamlet, he made two trips, carrying two wounded grunts fifty-five yards away from the demolished bridge back to the beach. SP/4 John Bridges had not been wounded but exposed himself repeatedly under the heavy fire to get off effective shots with his M-79 grenade launcher. He crawled thirty yards to grab an aid kit left in the open and brought it back to treat the wounded.

Staff Sergeant William Weber was in the first group that had crossed the bridge. When the bridge exploded he directed fire on the enemy positions. Realizing more effective action was needed, he led his team to assault a gun position in the hamlet. SP/4 Charles Bennett was up with him, firing his M-79 grenade launcher. Both soldiers were cut down by enemy fire.

Those on the hamlet side of the canal were now supported by jet aircraft, which dropped five hundred-pound bombs on the hamlet. By 1:30PM the balance of Alpha was consolidated back on the beach-side of the canal in preparation for a counterattack and to secure the dustoffs for their wounded. Another air strike was made west of the canal at 1:48PM, to suppress the fire still coming from that direction. Clearly Alpha, and by extension the battalion, had hit a hornets nest in Pinkville. It was only the beginning of what would be three days of hell.

A RENDEZVOUS WITH DESTINY

Theodore N. Tees, SSG, Army US, 101st Airborne Division

Before the Army

Ted Tees

I grew up in Buchanan, Michigan, during the 1950/60s, the oldest of three kids. We lived in a nice house in a town with enough industry to support many middle-class families, good schools, and a community that had much to offer.

My mother did not work outside our home until all of us were at least in high school. My father worked as a machinist at Clark Equipment Company, retiring after over 40 years. Buchanan was a great place to grow up and could have easily been the hometown of Wally and the Beaver from the TV show, "*Leave it to Beaver.*"

My introduction to military service was a result of my own actions. After graduating from Buchanan High School at 17 years old, I entered Lake Michigan College in the fall of 1965 at the old campus on Britain Avenue. Classes went fairly well, yet a new set of friends, new experiences, new-found freedom, and a level of immaturity all contributed to my focus shifting from academic pursuits to socially available activities.

I feel obligated to clarify early on in this story that despite the reputation of the sixties, my friends and I were not engaged in the drug culture or any form of the so-called counterculture. We did, however, consume our fair share of cold beer on the weekends. This was a great time with groovy music and there were always dances within a short driving distance, often with first-rate live bands. Virtually every weekend we would congregate, dance, make new friends, and sometimes find someone special.

The first semester of my sophomore year I enrolled in a five credit hour Analytic Geometry and Calculus class that included differential equations. Those familiar with these "Diffie Q's" know that this is not a class in which you want to fall behind. Due to my extensive social calendar, I did in fact fall behind and ended up failing the class.

I was called into the registrar's office and notified that I was being placed on academic suspension for one semester due to my GPA falling below 2.0. To my dismay, he also mentioned he was obligated to notify the draft board that I would not be returning next semester. As I sat there wishing I could melt into the chair, he mentioned that my student deferment would be in jeopardy.

I was drafted and inducted into the Army on 28 May, 1968. I got on a bus at Local Board #11 in Benton Harbor, and was off to begin my military career. They took us to Detroit for a physical and in-processing and then dashed most of us off to Fort Knox, Kentucky where the intent was to make Government Issue soldiers (GIs) out of us.

During basic training, we learned fundamental military courtesy, physical training, and knowledge needed to become a productive soldier. Training also included weapons initiation. Here we learned everything that every soldier needed to know, no matter if you were to be the battalion surgeon or the toilet attendant.

Each morning began quite early for our basic training company, starting with Master Sergeant Webb calling everyone to attention, asking, "give me my sick, lame, and lazy," for sick call. This was followed by a nice, refreshing run, a cool-down period, and, finally, breakfast. On a personal note, I feel I benefited from being rather tall, as when our platoon "fell in" (aligned ourselves in a formation, specific width and four men deep) I was assigned a position in the back row, as the height arrangement had been shortest to tallest, front to back. This put three rows of other trainees between me and our Drill Sergeant.

Our platoon was made up of individuals from all over the country, draftees and volunteers, all with various levels of education. Before moving on, I should explain that becoming a "Drill Instructor" or "Drill Sergeant" brings with it the right to wear a drill sergeant hat, often called a "Smokey the Bear" hat. Not everyone who attempts to qualify as a drill sergeant is successful, and the hat is worn with pride and garners respect from others. This leads me to one particular situation where Drill Sergeant Carlisle announced that he had an important yet difficult task and would need someone who was well educated. He had everyone who had at least attended high school raise our hand. He then began an elimination based on education (graduated high school, attended college, graduated college, etc.). I was surprised by the level of education among us, noting that many held four year degrees. Ultimately, the "winner" was a guy by the name of Tom Masters, who coincidently held a master's degree. By now, we were sure that Tom had certainly escaped running or physical training that day to take on some difficult administrative task, perhaps in an office.

It was at this point Sergeant Carlisle called Tom up front (the first of many times throughout our basic training), turned to him and carefully handed Tom his hat saying, "Hold my cover, and if you drop it, you will NOT have a good day!"

Philosophical note: I would not be surprised if told that not much had changed since WWII as far as the Army's basic training. New weapons and lessons learned, of course, but the fundamentals of military courtesy, processes and the required adjustments to basic human behavior had not changed. Many of us were sons of the Greatest Generation and the strategies were the same. One thing for sure, the system and methodology worked!

Marching, running, fighting, shooting – all were taught and learned as a unit as opposed to individual. In many cases, if one failed, all would fail. This outcome was avoided as trainees began to understand individual strengths and weaknesses then took measures to help others succeed. These tactics resulted in unit success (and maybe a little less running). Our training continued, and though it did not become any easier, it became more manageable. We learned to deal with the unexpected as our bodies and minds adjusted to this new, regulated world of military life. Though many of us did not "want" to be there, our moral and ethical principles would not allow us to quit or run away. We finished our basic training, graduated, and were granted a weekend pass before moving on to our next destination, where our newfound, basic military skills would be combined with a specialized set of military skills that we would learn in an advanced training setting.

Having a year and a half of college and a strong, rural work ethic behind me, I knew that I would most likely end up with an assignment requiring strong thinking, writing and math skills, attention to detail, all combined with strong interpersonal skills. My assignment would become an opportunity perhaps dealing with the public, or possibly preparing important governmental documents, never landing in the. . .

Infantry

It had to be a mistake! Why would the Army want to waste a skilled and charming fellow such as me in the infantry as a rifleman? I eventually found out, but it took many, many months.

In reflection, I can only compliment the infantry for how it selects, trains, and uses the best and the brightest of this nation to accomplish the designated mission.

After Advanced Individual Training for the Infantry (Military Occupational Specialty MOS 11B) at Ft. Polk, Louisiana, I was sent to the Non-Commissioned Officers Candidate Course at Ft. Benning, Georgia.

The standard tour of duty in Vietnam was 12 months in-country. As troop deployment numbers rose, many of those deployed were draftees, and many chose not to re-enlist after returning from Vietnam, knowing that jobs and/or educational opportunities seemed a better choice than a military career. This contributed to a growing shortage of Non-Commissioned Officers (NCOs, or sergeants) to fill the role of squad and fire-team leaders. Thus was born the Noncommissioned Officer Candidate Course at Fort Benning, Georgia, operating 1967-1972, and graduating over 26,000 who served valiantly in Vietnam and around the world. It was an honor to be offered the opportunity to attend, and I took it.

Perhaps the most notable aspect of our training was being put into difficult, near impossible situations with resources depleted and more being taken away. It was then that our trainers would issue that unforgiving question: "Whattaya gonna do now, Patrol Leader?" They taught us that "impossible" is relative. We received an abundance of harassment both day and night. Obedience to orders had to be blind at times. I don't know how OCS (Officers Candidate School) could have been much tougher: low crawling, the bars, and, of course, more running came at all hours of the day and night—not to exclude surprise inspections.

I thought the Army was trying to break us at times during NCOC training, especially during Ranger Week, where the challenges and difficulties became too much for some guys. NCOC School lasted 13 weeks and the last week was called "Ranger Week." We carried 60 pound rucksacks everywhere we went and the week culminated by dropping (while hanging at the position of attention) from 30 feet up in the air into 12 feet of water at "Victory Pond." The intent of that exercise was to help us overcome two of man's most natural fears—heights and water! My personal issue was that it was January and there was a thin crust of ice on the pond when we arrived. We got a bonus that morning, "ice cold water in Victory Pond!" Many of the training days were long and hard, sometimes boring and sometimes very interesting. They kept us awake by telling us that our training and learning to stay alert might keep us alive in Vietnam.

The training was good but it was a lot to digest in such a short time frame. To be at NCOC School at Fort Benning was indeed a privilege. We felt we were different, some of the best, but it was a whirlwind for body and soul. The two most memorable parts of training for me were the rappelling and the tower at the pond (heights and natural fears again).

Compass courses, map reading, artillery missions, adjusting fire, and honing basic leadership skills would be the most used courses once we arrived in Vietnam. Our job was to follow orders, accomplish the mission, lead the men, kill the enemy, and be a parent to our squad, all while aiming towards the underlying mission of getting us all home safely. Our job was a little more difficult because of our rank. Consider the first line supervisor in industry, the foreman, or the high school principal. My training gave me leadership skills, made me competent, and caused me to realize that I could do anything if I put my mind to it. This has helped out time and time again in my post-military life.

I graduated in January, 1969, and Col John Glenn (USMC Retired) was the keynote speaker at our graduation. Virtually all of us knew our destiny, which was to spend a single stint with trainees fresh out of Basic Training and assigned to the Infantry. The time we spent with these trainees allowed us to practice the skills and apply the knowledge we had acquired while at Fort Benning NCOC School.

Somewhere during this period of time, I realized I had become an adult and had responsibilities, not only to myself, but to others as well!

Off to the Republic of Vietnam

I arrived in the Republic of Vietnam on 15 May, 1969, at Ton Son Nhut airbase in Saigon. Knowing the army practice of "hurry up and wait" would surely continue here, I was amazed to find out how fast and effective the staff there were at checking me in and getting me off to my next destination of Camp Evans, northwest of Hue. Upon arrival, we were picked up and delivered to our respective destinations; mine was an assignment with Bravo Company, 1st of the 506th Airborne Infantry, 101st Airborne Division. Ah, home sweet home. I could settle in, put away my personal items, get a little rest, write a letter or two, and find out what was next. Little did I know...

The company clerk, armory NCO, and "everything that needs to be done" guy came and told me to bring my "stuff" over to Company HQ and he would get me ready. "Ready for what?" I was thinking as I followed him. He asked me to dump out my duffel bag. I did and he helped me repack it with those things I would need when I returned for "Rest & Recuperation," or "R&R" (a one-week leave similar to a vacation). Or when it was time to go home. He matter-of-factly asked if there was anything in my duffel bag that would embarrass me or my family if its contents (personal, non-military) were returned to my family. *Oh my!*

He then told me that the Captain I came in with was "Viking," whose real name was Captain Harold Erickson. He had been on R&R with his wife in Honolulu at the time the battle of the year had unfolded. Bravo Company, along with three other companies from the 1/506th were among the US troops attempting to drive off a fixed enemy force occupying Ap Bia mountain, Hill 937, later known as, "Hamburger Hill."

I have the original first letter I wrote from Vietnam to my parents (actually, I have all of them, because my mother kept them, arranged chronologically with a note on the front recording when they arrived). Reading what you wrote to your parents 40 years in the past can be entertaining and puzzling, as it is a reflection of what and who you were as opposed to who you are today. In this letter, I talked about how hot it was and noted, "this 101st Airborne Division has a lot of spirit behind it. They are the only division in Vietnam that doesn't wear a subdued or camouflaged shoulder patch. This is because of their reputation. Higher enemy headquarters have sent out memoranda to their smaller units saying, 'do not engage in close combat with the American GIs bearing the patch with the chicken on it. They don't know what an eagle is here.'"

We continued my preparation to go to the field and join up with my company. The NCO (I think his name was Tim Coder) was very deliberate about preparing my rucksack and everything else. We put together three bandoleers holding six magazines each of M-16 ammunition. A box of ammunition holds 20 rounds of ammo, but he emphasized I should only put 19 rounds in each magazine in order to prevent a jam initiated by a magazine packed too tightly. I have spoken to several other infantrymen that practiced our trade in Vietnam and almost all never loaded more than 19 rounds in a magazine.

He continued to prepare me, packed my rucksack with C-Rations, canteens of water, iodine tablets for disinfecting water gathered on the trails from streams or bomb craters, and then he gave me a steel "ammo box." This was a latchable, waterproof container for mail, cigarettes, writing materials, and anything I did not want to get wet. Next, I was given a poncho, jungle

blanket, claymore mine, clacker (electrical detonation device), and a length of wire to connect the two. This was all followed by his generous donation of three or four pounds of C-4 (composition C-4, a plastic explosive) which he indicated was sometimes needed to blow trees for a Landing Zone (LZ). He also explained that C-4 was a much quicker means than the "heat tabs" we were given to heat water for coffee. C-4 was indeed quicker and hotter, and could burn a hole right through a dry canteen cup.

I was then outfitted with the rest of my needs. He felt that four frags (fragmentation grenades) and two smoke grenades would be all I needed initially. He said they didn't carry any "Willie Petes" (White Phosphorous) grenades in the field, but kept them in the bunkers on the fire bases. It was then that he presented me with an item which remained with me the rest of my tour: my M-16A1 rifle, which he claimed to have meticulously checked over the previous day. The serial number was 996131. My son makes fun of me because I can remember my Army serial number and the serial number from my M-16, but may have forgotten what someone told me half an hour ago!

It was late in the day and I was told that I would be going out in the morning with Viking. I was

Pictured above are Specialist Gordon Roberts and Sergeant Ted Tees. Both were awarded the Silver Star for Gallantry in Action. Roberts was later upgraded to Medal of Honor.

introduced to him and he spoke with a little bit of a southern accent. That was comforting. He also reiterated I NEVER salute him again until he told me it was ok. If a group is being targeted by a sniper, the one he wants to kill is the one in charge.

Bravo Company would move after daybreak to a Landing Zone for re-supply and a turnover between Viking and the temporary Company Commander. I wrote a couple of letters and went to bed on a cot, wondering if I was up to carrying that rucksack and all the other items in and attached to it (hand grenades, ammunition, water, and food all weigh up pretty fast). I was told that I would soon figure out what I really needed

Out to the A Shau Valley- the Breeze, the View, and then Reality

We flew out at daybreak and it was great—it is about 25 degrees cooler once you get above 1000 feet. I will talk about helicopters quite a bit in this story and will often refer to them as "birds." That's what we called them. The Bell UH-1 was in the service of the US Army during the Vietnam War. The original designation of HU-1 led to the helicopter's nickname of Huey. Another term often heard was "slicks," which were nothing more than a Huey with the seats removed (we sat on the floor with our feet hanging out). In September 1962, the designation was changed to UH-1, but Huey remained in common use. Approximately 7,000 UH-1 aircraft saw service in Vietnam.

Our training back in the States was very complete, as far as preparing for what was in store for us. Though I had been on helicopters many times before, I now realized a few things had gone overlooked. The trip to join up with Bravo Company ended at what was not really a Landing Zone, but rather a patch of six to eight foot tall elephant grass. They hovered over the grass and the door gunner indicated I should jump! A six or eight foot jump into soft soil and elephant grass by a 20 year old in prime physical condition should not be an issue, right? We had done this numerous times in training back in the States and it went well.

What they didn't necessarily tell us is that you don't do it with a sixty pound rucksack on your back—which would have rotated me into a slamming fall on my back, possibly injuring me badly. The door gunner helped me remove my rucksack, dropped it down, and I jumped with no consequences. I noted Viking was gone and undoubtedly well into his turnover with the temporary company commander.

I was introduced to my Platoon Leader, a first lieutenant who was from Idaho, ergo his name was "Super Spud" or "Spud" for short. Smart guy, seasoned, competent – everything you wanted in a Platoon Leader. I later learned that competency was valued as much or more than bravery. We were roughly 2000 meters from Dong Ap Bia (Hill 937). The battle for this little piece of real estate has been well documented in the history books as well as Hollywood. I remember my thoughts based on my first week in the boonies (a term used for any time you are not in a secure area), "it is going to be a long year." After all, I was engaged in my first fire fight the first day I was in the boonies!

We moved up the hill until we made "contact" with the North Vietnamese Army (NVA), exchange fire, pull back and call in an air strike or ARA – Aerial Rocket Artillery. We were supported that summer by our good friends from "C" Battery, 4/77 Aerial Rocket Artillery.

They would fly their Cobra Gunships into the heat of any battle and fire rockets and mini-guns with pinpoint accuracy. These pilots went by the call sign of "Griffin," aptly named as they seemed to be part lion and part eagle! We would then move back up the hill and do it again. It was all about real estate and who owned it. Our wounded would be moved back to an LZ and a medevac would pick them up.

I was new (the slang term used was "cherry") and was not thrust into a situation for which I was not prepared. My duties were "administrative" in nature for the first week. Spud had me watch the map and track our movements, ensuring I knew exactly where we were at all times. This sounded easy enough, but I soon found that even though we had been "moving" for a half hour or more, we may not have covered much distance on the jungle trails.

It was 20 May, 1969, when we made the final assault up the hill. Three Companies from our Battalion and numerous other units from the 101st along with a battalion from the Army of the Republic of Vietnam (ARVN) marched up the hill, driving the NVA back into Laos. It was then that I realized something important about the NVA: they were well trained, well fed, well equipped, and well motivated. They were fighting us from bunkers constructed of reinforced concrete, deep in the ground and had plenty of rice and water, plenty of ammunition, communication devices, medical supplies, clothing, and many other supplies too numerous to list. I watched the 1987 film Hamburger Hill and found the most memorable and accurate moment was when the medic (Doc) said, "We've been up on that hill ten times, and they still don't think we're serious." That statement, purposely full of sarcasm and cynicism, is clearly the most insightful line in the film.

A and C Companies, 3rd of the 187th had taken many casualties and were airlifted to a secure area on the Gulf of Tonkin called "Eagle Beach" where they were afforded a brief R&R and did some reorganizing due to the losses at Hamburger. Other units involved coordinated the organizational and logistical tasks necessary after the ten day battle to take possession of Dong Ap Bia.

Over the next few weeks, we continued patrols in the area, locating dead NVA and continued to make minor contact with NVA. The casualties we ("B" Company) took on Hamburger were enough to put us in line for a trip to Eagle Beach. We were there for almost two days and I even had an opportunity to water ski in the Gulf of Tonkin! I remembered writing a letter to my parents where I mentioned a hill we called "Hamburger Hill" and wondered if there had been anything in the paper about it. Evidently there had been and continued to be, as I still have the June 17, 1969 Headline from the Niles Daily Star: "North Viets Back on Ap Bia Mountain." We kept chasing them away and they kept coming back.

Esprit de Corps

While at Eagle Beach, after casualties were considered, Viking determined that 3-6 (our Third Platoon) had taken enough casualties to warrant reorganization. The lieutenant leading the third platoon had been wounded and would not be returning. With other casualties and numbers down, they disseminated the remaining men among the first, second, and fourth platoons. This re-org gave me a full squad (pictured) to lead instead of the three men with whom I had started.

What happened next was somewhat revealing as to the nature of unit mentality. When we reorganized, the third platoon, whose numbers were down and the lieutenant had been wounded, was dispersed into the first, second, and forth platoons as I mentioned. A short time after that, we were told that Battalion Headquarters knew that "B" company had three platoons, but found it confusing that they were identified as First, Second, and Fourth Platoons. This cannot be! When they monitored our radio traffic and we reported locations, it caused confusion for the REMFs (Rear Echelon MFs—the polite term could be "Motivational Forces"). Viking was directed to have the fourth platoon assume the designation of Third Platoon. It turned out this was more difficult than one might expect. The fourth platoon wanted to remain the fourth platoon and the guys from the third platoon wanted no part of a "new" third platoon. This went on for several days until Viking convinced the right Colonel that we would be more effective with no third platoon. When I left ten months later, there was still no third platoon in Bravo Company. The Third Platoon was a casualty of Ap Bia Mountain, Hill 937 – better known as "Hamburger Hill."

Over the course of my tour, I became well aware of how our enemy had learned that they could no longer expect to defeat us in conventional warfare practices. In WWII and Korea, there were often battle lines and the military would focus on controlling real estate. Once defeating

or "pushing back" the enemy, the victor would continue on, gaining ground and controlling the land behind them. However, both the NVA and Viet Cong had adopted "hit and run" practices which could be characterized as early versions of terrorist tactics.

Our days were made up of patrols, rotating on point, hours and days of boredom complicated with moments of terror. Always on guard, alert, and quiet when in boonies, we were "boonierats" or "11 bush" (slang terms associated with our Military Occupational Specialty of 11B Infantry). The following link provides further insight: http://www.youtube.com/watch?v=58vQ7_4I2P4.

In the "boonies" we needed to be quiet, stealthy, and "ready" while moving up and down the trails and paths. Humans are a social animal and being asked to constantly be quiet and not interact presented its own challenges. Often written on the back of the camouflaged cover of a boonierat's helmet were the words, "IF YOU CAN READ THIS – YOU ARE TOO F***ING CLOSE." This was rooted in understanding the basic psychology that says that a combatant (your enemy) will instinctively shoot at one in a group of enemy before shooting at a lone enemy. People have a natural desire to congregate, talk, and socialize. But in the boonies, we avoided these "crowds" to save our own lives and the lives of others in our platoon. For many of us, these habits returned home with us. I can state honestly that one of the most challenging experiences in my adult life was entering a subway car during a morning rush hour. It was not terrifying, but terrifying was one of the adjectives I considered using to describe it.

Another outcome of my time spent in the boonies was the need to sleep very quietly. Upon my return from Vietnam, my wife noted that she would sometimes need to reach over and touch me to see if I was even in bed, as I made no noise and rarely moved while sleeping.

There were countless things I continued to learn as a new guy. A couple of important lessons I learned in the first couple of weeks were related to water. You can only carry so much water and you need to ration it. Drink what you need and not necessarily what you want! Another lesson was related to eating a LRRP meal. LRRP (Long Range Reconnaissance Patrol) meals were lightweight, dehydrated meals to which you added hot water, allowed soaking and swelling, and it would turn into a nice warm stew, chili, or other delicacy. Often we would eat very late in the day with little to no daylight left, and sometimes I needed to heat my water under my poncho in order to avoid detection from the light of the heat tab or C-4 burn. I would be extremely hungry. So hungry that I sometimes did not allow adequate time for the LRRP to completely "soak and swell." If this process finishes in one's stomach, it can wreak havoc and up it comes. I soon learned to wait until the meal was ready. We would often locate our NDP (night defensive position), but stay back several hundred meters and not enter it until right at dark. We would usually eat our evening meal during this wait, then quietly enter our NDP, establish a perimeter, deploy claymore mines and trip flares, and finally settle in for the night, rotating on guard duty throughout the night. We would wake everyone before daylight, telling them, "Stand 2" and be prepared. This strategy and the phrase "Stand 2" is rooted in the hour in which the French and Indians attacked, therefore you are up on watch an hour before dawn and an hour after dusk. After daybreak, we would accommodate our personal needs, i.e. shaving (using precious water!), coffee, breakfast, visit the "restroom," repack our rucksack and do the same thing all over again. You would have been impressed how 60 to 80 men could do so much so quietly!

Though I cannot put a date stamp on it, it was not too long before I realized that I was no longer a new guy. I had seen battle, had been on several CAs (Combat Assaults) – where they "insert" you in a new location via helicopter. What a beautiful country from a couple of thousand feet! Problem was that they kept putting us back down on the ground! We would do this on a regular basis, moving here and there within our Area of Operation (AO). But along with being moved came the most important things we needed. Mail was delivered for our mental health, water and meals (C-Rations) were provided for our physical well-being. Ammunition and grenades were provided on request and would be delivered anytime we needed them, as long as the helicopters could fly.

About ten years ago I had an opportunity so speak with a guy who I had gotten to know while in Vietnam. We spoke just once, but we talked at length about kids, careers, etc. Recently, we have been exchanging emails and he told me that the most memorable part of our earlier conversation was my reply to a question he had asked me: "What do you tell people who ask about Vietnam?" My answer was, "I tell people that I served in an exotic place 10,000 miles from home and I don't remember a thing about the flora or fauna of the country." As a person who grew up outdoors and close to nature, that was so true and yet, so profound; a true indication of our intense state of mind at the time.

Over the course of my tour in Vietnam, I was impressed as to how effective the defoliant was in the jungle (weed control for us farm boys). The trails and crude pathways coming from the North and from Laos were not overgrown and could be easily observed from the air. "Crude pathways" may be a misnomer, as many of the well-worn trails had bamboo steps constructed on the steeper hillsides, facilitating the constant flow of ammunition and supplies being brought from the North day and night. It was a number of years later when we began to learn the long-term consequences of what was done to preclude growth of vegetation in the rain forest.

A Long and Deadly Summer in the A Shau Valley

We continued to pursue the NVA that summer. Many combat assaults resulted in contact with the NVA on a regular basis. Given the choice, I thought it would be safer to be on the second or third bird in on the LZ, as we assumed that the NVA would start shooting right away as we put the first six or seven guys on the ground. NOT TRUE! The NVA had figured out that if they started shooting right away, the helicopter would not put the guys on the ground and would just pull off and call in a firestorm of various types of shelling on the whole area. As it turned out, they learned to wait until we had committed six, twelve, or more troops to the ground before they started firing. We were committed at that point, with boots on the ground. I only saw red smoke once during my tour, and once is enough. A "hot" landing zone is designated with red smoke (taking fire—get in and get out) as opposed to yellow or purple (called on the radio banana or grape). My platoon was fortunate enough to make more than enough Combat Assaults and we were awarded the Air Medal "for meritorious achievement while participating in aerial flight."

My mother saved a newspaper article written by a journalist/soldier published June 29, 1969 in the Minneapolis Tribune. The article was titled, *"Boredom Is Real Vietnam Enemy, State Soldier Says."* He goes on to write, *"in nearly every division except the war-weary 101st Airborne and 25th Infantry, the foot soldier's main foes are trench foot, blisters, heat exhaustion, and the damnable boredom that comes from having nothing to do but slap mosquitoes...."*

There was a great deal of fact in the private's article as we (units of the 101st) were making contact every two-three days at least, with NVA and often with elements of Ho Chi Minh's best, the 29th NVA Regiment, well trained, well equipped, and well motivated. The area of operation assigned to the 1/506th—mostly in the A Shau Valley, up to and into Laos—was a hotbed of activity.

In a July letter to my parents, I described a long day with my squad on point, as "tense, but uneventful." We were dug in for the night and about 2000 meters from the Laotian border. I told them that tomorrow's official objective was a point about 200 meters from the border, looking for large bridges camouflaged from above that are part of an important supply link from the north into RVN. I told them we would either be extracted or we may slip into Laos and look around. I followed this statement with a request that they, "don't write your congressman! We need to find those bridges." We found them, pinpointed their location and I think it was the Air Force who disassembled them.

Sometime during the summer, Spud rotated back home and my new Platoon Leader was 1st Lt. Steve Bowman (West Point, 1968). Lieutenant Bowman was an Airborne Ranger and a fine officer. With him in charge we continued our patrols, dealt with jungle rot, mosquitoes, personnel matters, the constant heat, and routine contact with the NVA. I was older than many of the guys in my squad—20 turning 21—and along with being their leader I had to do my part to keep them on task, ready to do what they were trained. I had to listen, discipline fairly, counsel, and sometimes just be there for them. I believe I even heard a couple of confessions in an unceremonious fashion.

We routinely found psy-ops flyers on & near the trails in the A Shau near Laos. I thought, "how ridiculous!" I, for one, knew that these things would not work on the sophisticated, well rounded US soldier. But then again, I can still remember the name on one of the flyers explaining how to surrender to the North. No one would have considered crossing over, but the flyers did seem to have an impact, however slight.

The psy-ops leaflets left out on the trails by the US and South Vietnam targeting the NVA were also routinely found on the trails—I kept one, not knowing what it said, but clearly understanding the message that went with the picture of the B-52s and the firepower they delivered when bombing the trails from the North. It was a given that the bombers and the devastation they delivered so accurately were both hated and feared by the North.

Over the course of my tour, people in my squad, platoon, and company were rotating out and being replaced with new men. This helped me become established and accepted as an "experienced" squad leader. Other events contributed to my credibility in our platoon and Company. Times were never boring in the A Shau. On 21 July, 1969, during combat operations in the A Shau Valley, approximately 700 meters from Ap Bia Mountain, the following events occurred (verbatim from general orders number 14788):

SGT Tees awarded for distinguishing himself while serving as squad leader

"For gallantry in action in the Republic of Vietnam on 21 July, 1969. Sergeant Tees distinguished himself while serving as a squad leader in Company B, 1st Battalion (Airmobile), 506th Infantry, during combat operations near the A Shau Valley, Republic of Vietnam. As Company B began to ascend the slope of a ridge north of Dong Ap Bia Mountain, the lead element came under intense enemy small arms, rocket propelled grenade, and automatic weapons fire from an unknown size enemy force situated in well-constructed bunkers. In the initial encounter, the lead man was critically wounded and subjected to further enemy fire. Realizing the gravity of the situation, Sergeant Tees quickly began to maneuver his way toward the wounded soldier. As he approached the wounded man's position, the enemy force began directing a heavy volume of fire toward him. Sergeant Tees immediately began leveling a heavy base of suppressive fire, killing one of the insurgents. He then placed the wounded man on his shoulders and began carrying him to safety in spite of the constant enemy automatic weapons fire. Due to his courageous efforts, the life of one comrade was saved and friendly casualties were kept to a minimum. Sergeant Tees' personal bravery and devotion to duty were in keeping with the highest traditions of the military service and reflect great credit upon himself, his unit, and the Unites States Army.

Authority: By direction of the President of the United States under the provisions of the Act of Congress approved 25 July, 1963."

Described above was the first event in a long day's battle. Our platoon, my squad had the lead for the Company that day. I had assigned the man who was wounded as the "point" man that day and I was walking third, behind his "slack" man. My guy was down, they continued to fire on him, and I went out and carried him back. I had positioned the rest of my squad —machine gun, two guys to keep the ammo coming, a couple riflemen and an M-79 grenade launcher— to cover me. I got to him, carried him back and Viking already had a medivac coming. We eventually loaded him and he went home. The most important part of this story is that his name did not end up on the wall.

The story does not end here. When I got back into the clear with the wounded guy, I noted that a guy named Roberts from the Second Platoon had been up helping cover me. I distinctly remember looking him in the eye and saying, "What the hell are you doing up here, Roberts?" Gordy Roberts could not stay out of the fight. He did not break ranks or abandon his post, but recognized the need for additional firepower at the moment. What happened after that is a matter of record, as shortly after I got back with the wounded man, Gordon Roberts maneuvered his way around and assaulted the NVA in their bunkers, killing several of them and causing the rest to run. His assault allowed the medevac to come into a crude and marginal LZ to pick up the badly-wounded man and remove him from harm's way. Both Gordon Roberts and I were awarded the Silver Star for Gallantry in Action. In March of 1971, Gordon Ray Roberts was awarded the Medal of Honor for his "conspicuous gallantry and intrepidity in action at the risk of his life above and beyond the call of duty" on 21 July, 1969. Gordy and I became good friends for the balance of our tours.

At some point in the July – August timeframe, I was asked if I would be interested in any of the rear jobs that came open from time to time. Recommendations combined with personal approval were required in order to be added to a list of those to be considered for "rear" jobs. The candidate list was long and the opportunities were short, but this was the process used for assignments in these rear jobs. Our records were reviewed and short lists were made for jobs that came up where they wanted an experienced individual (someone who had seen combat) for specific jobs. I was excited when I was considered for a job as a FAC liaison. What this entailed was riding in a plane with a Forward Air Controller (controls and directs fire from the fast movers – Jets). The duties of the infantry NCO would be to communicate with the infantry units on the ground, ensuring that nothing was lost or overlooked due to communication styles, acronyms, slang, and any other factors that could cause errors in the placement of firepower. As it turned out, I was considered, but someone else landed the job. It was rewarding to even have been considered.

Each of the companies assigned to a particular AO (area of operation) would rotate into duty protecting the perimeter of firebases. Firebases, usually positioned on a hill or mountaintop, were strategically located throughout the AO, and were available 24/7 to provide firepower in support of activities throughout the area. Firebase duty was a refreshing break for the units that had been in the boonies for a while, as you typically received mail and one hot meal a day. There was potable water available at all times. Other luxuries included two sit-down outhouses - perhaps a misnomer, as there were no walls, doors or roof, but it was a "sit down" facility. In early June, I wrote my parents that we were at Fire Base Berchtesgaden, noting that we had, "two outhouses, with no doors, and the view from either one is really great!"

While on the firebases, the Battalion Surgeon would visit and help with physical problems that anyone was having; what we called "jungle rot" on areas of our bodies was the most frequent issue and we were all encouraged to use the standard issue foot powder and various antiseptic creams to help us heal. These firebases also sported a shower, constructed of 2x4s, a little plywood for structural integrity, and a roof framework that held a five gallon container for the water you would carry and fill. Not very private, but functional – and besides, it was just us guys, right? Not always. One hot July afternoon, with our company once again assigned for a week of duty at Fire Base Berchtesgaden, I decided to take a shower. I went up to a supply bunker and retrieved a set of clean jungle fatigues, clean socks, and a towel. I went to the water supply and carried a full bucket of water to the shower and dumped it. Then I went back to my nearby bunker, stripped, grabbed my M 16, a bandoleer of magazines, soap, and towel and proceeded to the shower wearing only my boots and the bandolier of M-16 ammunition. I had only begun to wash up when several Cobra Helicopter Gunships arrived and began circling the perimeter of the Firebase. This was unusual, as they were circulating as if perhaps enemy combatants had been spotted. I continued to finish my short shower when a Huey helicopter circled the perimeter. This time I spotted what all the fuss was about – there were seats in the Huey, and there was a blonde woman waving to everyone! As it turned out, it was Judith Ann Ford, Miss Illinois and Miss America 1969. She had insisted on visiting some of the troops in the field along with the more secure areas that had been planned for her tour. I hustled back to my bunker and sent the two men who were on guard at two adjacent bunkers. I took up a position between the bunkers and remained on guard. Judy and I had seen enough of each other for the day! As a follow up, I remain a fan of the long-ago Miss America Judith Anne Ford. She was a champion gymnast, beauty queen, and now a retired educator. She has always been a patriot.

Administrative matters were more easily handled at the firebases as mail came every day and we could be in routine contact with Battalion Headquarters. Administrative matters would include scheduling R&R, health concerns, an opportunity to visit with the Battalion Chaplain and/or attend brief Church services that he would make possible. Squad and platoon leaders would have security briefings along with lessons learned and strategy briefings. One of these briefings (June, 1969) included a recommendation that the 90mm Recoilless Rifle be considered as a viable weapon for defensive measures at a firebase. The anti-personnel canister flechette round (we called them "beehive" rounds) was recommended as a means to repel personnel attacks in some situations. It was much more convenient to handle these and other relevant matters while stationed at a firebase.

Being 'fixed' forward positions, established in the enemy's territory by forced entry, Fire Support Bases were beacons and quickly became targets for enemy artillery and sapper units. At night, the infantry on the perimeter of the fire support base would hold "mad minutes" several times throughout the night. We would preplan these, and everyone would be up and ready to fire, initiated by a flare and ended approximately one minute later with another flare. The objective was to catch the enemy during an attempt to penetrate our concertina wire and defensive positions.

"Sappers" were very specialized and well trained infiltrators who would penetrate a fire base (or other perimeters). Sometimes wearing very little clothing, they would thread their way through concertina wire and other defensive measures; some would disable mortar and artillery on the way through using satchel charges, with a target of disabling bunkers and night defensive positions on the other side from behind. Then, a main attack force would come in and overrun from the disabled sector of the perimeter. These satchel charges were explosive devices, not sophisticated, and did damage by concussion.

Fire support bases would hold "mad minutes" several times throughout the night where everyone would fire all at once. Three or four mad minutes would be scheduled for each night and the perimeter would be saturated with rifle, machine gun, and M-79 grenade launcher fire. We would often change the location of the machine gun prior to firing, so as to not compromise its location for our enemy. The M-60 machine gun is a formidable weapon and was a high priority target for any attacking force.

On August 24, 1969, my company was once again providing perimeter defense for Fire Base Berchtesgaden. We were settled in and the mad minutes had been scheduled. There was something different about the scheduling that night though, as Viking had his radio operator (RTO), a guy named Sutton, pick the times. Sutton thought we had become predictable with our times, often spacing them about two hours apart. That night, he picked a time for a fourth and final "mad minute" for 3:40 am, just 15 minutes after the third scheduled "mad minute." We started shooting at 3:40 and did not stop until daylight. A large force of NVA had been staged to overrun our firebase that night, and their scheduled time to begin the attack was when the shooting stopped after the third "mad minute." When the 3:40 am shooting started, it did not stop until daylight about two hours later. Their skilled sappers had penetrated our concertina wire, avoided our trip flares, disabled many of our claymore mines, and entered our firebase. The sappers were about to penetrate the perimeter, disable another part of the perimeter, and allow the main force to overrun Firebase Berchtesgaden. We held our own, but it was not easy, as we were up against a skilled, determined, and well trained force. Their intent was to overrun the firebase, blow up the artillery, and kill as many Americans as possible before daylight, when reinforcements might show up and helicopter gunships would be very effective on their ground troops.

We held our own, but after the first hour, ammunition began running low in several of the defensive positions. The lighting provided by flares released by helicopters was good, but not good enough for the pinpoint accuracy needed. At some point, I maneuvered my way through the bunker areas, gathered and redistributed ammunition, took more ammunition to my machine gunner, and then went to the ammunition bunker and brought out a 90mm Recoilless Rifle and some flechette rounds ("beehive" rounds). I made my way over to a bunker where we could see NVA working their way up the hill. To be effective, this is a two man weapon, one to aim and shoot and the other man to spot, load, and unload the weapon. I loaded the Rifle, and we waited until we could see several NVA working their way up the slope again. The time came and we fired several rounds, raining tens of thousands of steel wire flechettes at them. This removed all motivation from them at that point. I left my man with the 90 mm, several flechette rounds and instructions to watch over that same ridge. He still had his M-16 and plenty of ammunition. I then went and retrieved more hand grenades and determined that our M-60 machine gun still had plenty of ammunition. None of my men received more than superficial wounds that night. We had repelled a determined force and daylight was near.

The enemy departed with their wounded and disappeared into the jungle. We gathered 31 dead NVA and suspected many others may have escaped with fatal wounds. The spooks arrived at daylight (we called them spooks – really army intelligence – they arrive with cameras, take pictures of the dead, gather anything in their pockets, don't say much, and then leave). Our impression of them was that they had no sense of humor. A helicopter arrived with a sling with a webbed net and we placed their dead bodies in the net. The helicopter then removed the sling with the dead and dropped it on trails where enemy activity was suspected. They were allowed to retrieve their dead this way. This served three purposes: a potential bio-type hazard was removed from the area, the enemy was allowed to collect their dead, and the psychological impact on the enemy was obvious. Reciprocal behavior was expected.

For the actions I took during the battle that night, I was again awarded the Silver Star for Gallantry in Action. The award was based on the evenings events, "….quick thinking and sound judgment minimized friendly casualties and resulted in the rout of the enemy force. Sergeant Tees' personal bravery and devotion to duty were in keeping with the highest traditions of the military service and reflects great credit upon himself, his unit, and the United States Army.

Authority: By direction of the President of the United States under the provision of the Act of Congress approved 25 July, 1963."

Opportunity Knocks Again

During late August, I had a brief interview for job opening in the Battalion Tactical Operations Center (TOC). The TOC was maintained operational at Camp Evans and sometimes out at Fire Bases in the Valley. Each line company submits candidates for the upcoming opening and I was one of four who were interviewed. On September ninth, I wrote home telling of the good news about my new job, working eight hour days, seven days a week. My responsibilities included coordinating with the four infantry companies and one reconnaissance platoon in our area of operation. I reported to a duty officer and supervised two RTOs and an artillery liaison. I maintained a logbook as well as a large map with the location of all friendlies as well as suspected enemy locations. Key to my job was to know all that was going on within the Battalion, where they were, where they were going, what they were doing, and what was needed. This information was always ready for the duty officer, Battalion Commander and his staff members. Coordination with Brigade Headquarters (next higher unit level) was also part of the job. Attention to detail, accurate reporting and record keeping, all combined with accurate plotting on our clear vinyl covered operational map were essential. I did have to begin shaving every day, shining my boots, and getting regular haircuts. I did not, however, have to deal with AK-47s or RPGs on a regular basis. I obviously had some emotions about leaving the boonies and my line company. Ho Chi Minh had just died and we were unsure on how this was going to affect the fighting. I had to get over the thought that I was abandoning them. I had paid my dues, and perhaps I had earned this opportunity. The guys in my squad and platoon appeared happy for me and outside of a little razzing, they wished me well.

The job was challenging, yet rewarding. The time spent in the boonies was tremendously valuable in that I understood what was being reported, could anticipate the needs of the line companies, and be prepared to respond to their requests in an efficient manner. Because I had "done my time," there was no hazing and everyone was very supportive while I learned my new job. It seemed that there was always some sort of activity going on and there was plenty to do, report, plot, and call. The job was administrative in nature and my understanding of what happens in the field helped me learn my new job quickly. I learned to enjoy it as well as the people I worked with. Gordy Roberts had been promoted to Sergeant and was moved to the rear as a "Combat Photographer," largely because of his nomination for the Congressional Medal of Honor. We had as much fun as the situation would allow and all of the guys in the Battalion Support Staff were great to work with. The Colonel had the good sense to surround himself and his Battalion Headquarters with very effective, quality people.

One of the tasks handled at the Battalion TOC was to maintain a manifest of Battalion personnel. We referred to "line numbers" on the current manifest and the real names of personnel were never used over unscrambled radio. When personnel arrived or when they left, the company and battalion manifests were corrected. I was reviewing updates on new arrivals in December when I saw a name that I recognized. Sergeant Terry Handley had arrived and was assigned to "D" Company. I wondered if it could possibly be the same Terry Handley that I knew growing up in Buchanan. I caught up with Terry before he went out to his Company and we talked at length. He too, had become a Sergeant through the NCOC program. It was great to talk to someone from home.

In early 1970, Terry's grandmother passed away and notifications were being made via the normal military methods. Terry's mother wanted him home for the funeral, a difficult, yet achievable undertaking. Though the system did work, it was not nearly as efficient as things are today with the internet and other electronic mechanisms. The first obstacle was getting the Battalion Commander's authorization. I took it upon myself to notify the Colonel, explaining that I knew Sergeant Handley's family, they were very close, and that they were prepared to wait for Sergeant Handley's return before holding the funeral. The Colonel stared straight into my eyes for somewhere between four seconds and four minutes, waiting for me to blink. I did not blink and he said, "get him in and get him home." We did just that. Terry went home for his grandmother's funeral and then returned to finish his tour. Since our return from Vietnam, Terry and I have gotten together just one time; we had a few beers, a few laughs, and went on our way.

Over twenty years after that, I received a call from Terry's mother, who still lived in Buchanan. In a very emotional voice, she thanked me for helping get her son home from Vietnam for his grandmother's funeral. She shared with me something that Terry had not told me. While Terry was home for the funeral, Delta Company had been involved in some fierce fighting and his platoon had taken numerous casualties. Terry may very well feel that he could have made a difference and he may be fighting demons over his absence during those critical times. We call it survivor's guilt.

Early in December, I was promoted to Staff Sergeant E-6. In a war zone, the celebration and related festivities were minimal, but the sincere and genuine congratulations were abundant. The promotion came with words of Army wisdom from the Colonel and First Sergeant, along with suggestions related to making the army a career. I responded respectfully, indicating that I would consider the military as part of my future.

Every soldier in Vietnam was offered the opportunity for a week of R&R (Rest and Recuperation). There were many destinations available but I chose Australia in late December of 1969. I had a great time for one week in Sydney and aside from meeting a number of interesting characters, my R&R was uneventful. I rested emotionally and had a chance to catch my breath. The most notable and memorable story came at the end of my week in Sydney, when I took a cab and arrived at the airport. I pulled out my wallet to pay for my ride and the driver held up his palm and said, "nope, this one's on me mate, where you're goin', you could use a break!" The sincerity in his voice and in his gesture was genuine. I did not expect that, and I will never forget it.

Working in the Tactical Operations Center held its own rewards; personal satisfaction came about when you felt that you had done something extra for the units in the boonies or at a firebase. The logging, reporting, and anticipating the activities of the Battalion Units did not ever become so routine that we became bored with it. Just when you thought you had seen it all, something new or unexpected would come about. In our free time, once mail had been read and letters had been written, we made attempts to fill our time productively. I became friends with a Light Observation Helicopter pilot who, like most of his counterparts, loved to fly! A Light Observation Helicopter (LOH) – often referred to as a "Loach," is a two or four seat helicopter and is very fast and agile. I often volunteered to go with him on special missions, mail delivery, and out to the fire bases. I would like to think that my presence provided some comfort – having an armed infantry NCO with you while flying over unsecured areas. Our flight path just outside of Camp Evans usually took us over a small farm where we noticed six or seven little kids running around. They would often run out, look up at us, and wave as we went over. I thought "nice kids – what can we do to make things a little better for them?" I began going to the supply depot before a mail run and retrieving a case or two of C-Rations (for one of our companies in the boonies, of course!). We would fly over to our adopted family and kick the C-Rations out for them. Somewhere in amongst my "stuff," I have a picture or a slide of them waving as we flew away.

US strategic policy changes

Vietnamization became a policy of the administration of President Richard M. Nixon after he was elected in the 1968 election. The intent was to "expand, equip, and train South Vietnam's forces and assign to them an ever-increasing combat role, at the same time steadily reducing the number of US combat troops." Vietnamization led to what we referred to as "early-outs" which would shorten our tour from one year to ten or eleven months. I was the beneficiary of this policy and my tour in Southeast Asia was reduced by approximately 49 days, returning me back to the US on 27 March, 1970. I must admit that I experienced troubling feelings about leaving, similar to the feelings I had when leaving my line company for the rear job. I got over it once I realized that I would be replaced by someone who would perform the job just as well or better than I did. I had served my time and I needed to let go. Out processing at Fort Lewis, Washington was very efficient and thorough. The Army must have felt they could get along without me at that point, as they gave me an Honorable Discharge from active service and immediately placed me in the United States Army Reserve. I had spent 10 months and 17 days (less seven days R&R) in Vietnam and was glad to be home.

Upon returning from Vietnam, I did not necessarily get spit on or suffer any demeaning treatment. Because I understood the times and had observed the unpopularity of the war in Vietnam, I began growing my hair back out (it was 1970, after all) and made every effort to disappear back into society. I had the good fortune to reestablish the relationship with the love of my life, got married, raised two great kids and held several rewarding jobs. At the time of this writing, I am contemplating a new career traditionally called "retirement." Retirement holds many possibilities, and Jo Ann and I plan to explore many of them.

SSG Tees is awarded second Silver Star

Some things stay with you for a long time. For me, confirmation of this occurred in 2007 at the Ruzyne Airport in Prague. I arrived early in the morning, had cleared the first security check, and my luggage had been checked in. I arrived early so that I would have time to resolve any problems encountered with luggage and flights. While walking around, observing the people, obviously from all around the world, something much unexpected happened. There were two men, with families in tow, waiting in line at a food court. My reaction is best described as somewhere between "going on alert" and being "drawn" to them! Something was, according to my subconscious, wrong and I wanted to understand what it was. I casually walked over near where they stood and immediately noticed that their carry-on luggage was tagged for "Hanoi." I just continued to walk and found the whole experience amusing as much as unsettling.

My military career, however short in duration, has had a huge factor in defining my character and personality. Consider entering the army post puberty, in the midst of your formal education, before choosing a career, during the dynamic and exciting times of the late '60s, and being dashed halfway around the world to fight a war that isn't very popular.

In retrospect, knowing how things have turned out, I do not think I would trade it in for anything different. My life with Jo Ann has been great and I love her and our two kids. What saddens me is that I waited over 35 years before openly talking about one of the most significant emotional events in my life that had occurred halfway around the world.

Ted Tees was on active duty in the United States Army 28 May, 1968 -14 April, 1970, when he entered the inactive Reserves. After training, he served a tour of duty in the Republic of Vietnam, serving initially as an infantry squad leader, sometimes platoon sergeant, and finishing the last six months of his tour of duty as a Staff Noncommissioned Officer at the Battalion Tactical Operations Center. During his time in Vietnam, Ted was awarded the Air Medal, the Army Commendation Medal, the Bronze Star Medal, the Vietnam Service Medal, the Combat Infantryman's Badge, and was twice awarded the Silver Star for gallantry in action.

Ted is of the opinion that many of these awards may be a matter of opportunity: an assignment with the 101st Airborne Infantry, operating in the A Shau Valley in the summer of 1969 offered much opportunity for bold actions and valor.

Of all the awards earned, Ted is most proud of the Combat Infantryman's Badge. He was an infantryman, a miserable, dirty, and underpaid job. But it was his job and it needed doing.

303

Pictured is a memorial at the National Infantry Museum at Fort Benning, GA.

"To Brothers In Heaven"

by Gary Higgins – NCOC Class 15-69

A Soldier boy, a Shake 'n Bake,
Our unique name, we had to take,
Young and scared, tested and dared,
A.I.T. to Benning, NCOC always winning,
Weapons, grenades, we made the grade,
Tested and proven, grunts always movin',
We come and go, at times Gung Ho,
So glad to be,
From the home of the Free.
"Follow Me" We did our best,
Your C.I.B., proud on your Chest.

MISSING IN ACTION
Cheryl Lane Walberg

Chuck & Cheryl Lane

It had been a warm day on the plains of South Dakota on August 23, 1967. The small grain harvest was close to being done. Harvest had been very late that year. I was living on a farm with my parents. My husband, 1st Lt. Charles Lane, was an Air Force pilot. He was stationed at Ubon RTAFB in Thailand and was the back seat pilot of an F-4D phantom fighter. It was Chuck's childhood dream to be a pilot and fly fighters. Chuck had wanted me to live with my parents while he was in Thailand because I was pregnant with our second child.

After Chuck left South Dakota, he first went to survival school in the States, then to jungle survival in the Philippines. On that day in August, he had flown 94 missions over North Vietnam and was expecting to complete the next six in less than two weeks and then he would be home.

That night in August it was reported on the "Nightly News with Huntley and Brinkley" that three F4s had been shot down that day. Two planes were brought down by air-to-air missiles and the other one by a SAM. A weird feeling came over me. The rest of the evening I just waited.

Around 11:45pm there was a knock on the door. There wasn't a whole lot of doubt about who was there. My father answered the door. It was the priest from the Catholic Church that I attended and two Air Force Officers. They confirmed what I seemed to already know. The plane that Chuck had been flying in was shot down by an air-to-air missile from a MIG 21. Two planes out of his formation of four were lost. There were four pilots in those two planes. The other pilots in the formation reported seeing three parachutes. Three strong and one weak emergency signal was received when the four pilots were asked to respond after they were on the ground. The weak signal had come after they had asked Chuck to respond.

The big question always has been whether that response they heard was truly a response from Chuck or something else. We were told that although people reported seeing only three parachutes, there could have been more. On one of the reports I was given it said that when the other pilots from the formation were interviewed, one man said that he had seen Chuck eject. The area was too far north for any chance at a search-and-rescue mission. The pilots were "on their own."

Chuck was flying with a new front seat pilot named Larry Carrigan. Within two weeks, I saw Larry listed as a POW in the *Air Force Times*. After the initial report of Chuck being reported as MIA, I was assigned a Casualty Officer. He met with me several times. The Air Force made certain that my daughters and I were taken care of. My husband's pay and benefits would continue while he was missing. He would be promoted when the time came. In a letter that I received from him after he was shot down (that had been written and mailed before he was shot down), he told me that he had changed his mind about being captured. He had decided that all that mattered was to get out of the plane and survive. That gave me some hope.

305

Chuck Lane

I moved out of my parent's house into my own apartment. I settled into a routine of every once in awhile getting a phone call from the Casualty Office telling me that someone had been allowed into the prison in Hanoi and they were going to televise footage from it on the six o'clock news. This happened intermittently, but especially at Christmas. North Vietnam was ingenious at playing with our emotions. We would sit in front of the television and watch to see if we would see anyone we recognized. We had friends in the other two planes that had gone down the same day as Chuck's did. We also had a friend that was shot down 10 days prior. There were many people we may be able to recognize. But for the next seven-and-a-half years, I did not see anyone that I knew on any of the films that were brought back.

One of our former pilot friends did report that he thought he had seen Chuck on one of the films. I went to one of the television stations and reviewed the film. At that time, I felt that it could possibly be Chuck. More hope. A few months later the Air Force informed us that it was not Chuck. The person had been identified as another pilot.

All of the families of the missing and captured men were told not to discuss our plight. On a farm in South Dakota that was impossible. The neighbors were all very sympathetic. Across the United States information was leaking out about the inhumane treatment that our POWs were being subjected to. Finally the wives and families formed "*The National League of Families.*" We started speaking out. The treatment of the POWs improved. We were allowed to mail packages once a month to our family member that was MIA or POW in North Vietnam. I mailed packages faithfully for years. The North Vietnamese must have enjoyed everything I sent.

In May of 1970, I attended the National League's Convention in Washington DC. We were flown to DC on Air Force planes. The plane I was on had been assigned to General Curtis LeMay when he was at Offit AFB in Omaha, Nebraska. Needless, to say, we went first class. They even cooked us steaks on the way to DC. The conference was wonderful. I met so many people that were in the same situation that I was in. *The National League of Families* stayed active, even after the POWs came home. However, there was major disagreement among factions of that organization, so there was much in-fighting.

Once the POWs were released, I agreed with the determination of a change in status from MIA to KIA/BNR for my husband. The front seat pilot, Larry Carrigan, came to visit me and presented me with a flag that had once flown over the White House. He told me all he knew. While in the POW camp, he never heard of a Charles Lane being captured. They had a fabulous communication network and knew about almost everything that was going on. I purchased many books written by the freed POWs and learned just how excellent that communication system was.

It has now been over 40 years. They have had teams in, searching for any information on Chuck, nearly 20 times. We have been given reports each time. Some have been very disturbing, such as the possibility he was taken by the Chinese. Of the six pilots that were shot down that day, four came home. Chuck and our friend, Ron Sittner, did not. In 1998 they found a tooth embedded in part of Ron's flight suit. He was identified that way. The family finally knew for certain that he had died on that hillside in North Vietnam.

In 2006 we were notified that Chuck's remains had been found. We saw a picture of the mini coffin with the remains in it when it was unloaded at Hickam AFB in Hawaii. We waited to hear more, but it was over a year before one of my daughters went to JPAC (Joint POW-MIA Accounting Command) at Hickam AFB in Hawaii and asked about the remains. The result was that, although many articles from the crash site were found, there were no human remains. One of the items found was the ejection seat buckle. It had never been opened. Consequently, he never ejected from the plane. The area that the remains were found in has been burned many times. The heat of the aircraft exploding would also make it nearly impossible for there to be human remains.

As recently as December of 2010 a JPAC team has been investigating the crash site. In that investigation they believe that parts of the plane are now in a museum in Vietnam.

Our oldest daughter was 19-months-old when he was shot down. Our youngest was one month. Chuck knew I had had the baby and that it was a girl. He even had a chance to see a picture of her, even though at that time there was not the technology that there is today. My daughters have had some hard times dealing with the fact that there has never been any remains found. If some were found, it would certainly bring closure for them. I do feel there is enough evidence to determine that he went down with the plane. With that, there is closure, but it would be nice to have his remains.

We will continue to live wondering what really happened. I tell people that it is so much better to know the truth, than it is to have to wonder for the rest of one's life.

Although I am not a veteran, I feel like one. I have gone through the war experience from a different perspective. I also have my wounds.

MY VIETNAM EXPERIENCE
David F Walberg

In May, 1968, several of us from Aberdeen, and other South Dakota locations were inducted into the army at Sioux Falls, SD. We were sent to Basic Training in Ft. Lewis, Washington and upon completion sent to Ft. Sill, Oklahoma for Advanced Infantry Training in artillery. At the end of A.I.T. training, we spent an additional week on Self Propelled artillery. After than we were sent home for 10 days of leave before being shipped to Vietnam.

I consider my 'war stories' rather mundane in that I did not see combat style 'blood and guts.' That in itself is rather interesting because of the million folks sent to Vietnam, there will be about a million different stories. Of course, movies and news clips don't show the mundane side of serving in Vietnam or any other war.

Upon arriving in Vietnam, one of the memories that stay with me is the smell. The smell of the humidity, foliage, odor of burning kerosene (part of latrine disposal), and the heat, became immediately obvious. About 8-10 of us were sent to Chu Lai to spend time with the Americal Division. On our first day we found ourselves in the First Sergeant's office and one of the questions he asked was, "has anyone here had any training in math?" One rule in the Army is to never volunteer for anything. When I considered that I could be humping 'pro-jos' or doing something math-related, I volunteered that I had a college degree in math. As a result I was sent to Headquarters of Battalion Fire Direction. I stayed right there on 'Cherry Hill' for the next 14½ months, working in a bunker for 12 hours a day. We switched hours with the other shift monthly. Coincidently, most of the other guys I was initially with also wound up in Fire Direction but at one of three of the Firing Battery outposts. Our job at Battalion FDC consisted of verifying artillery firing data that was computed by the Fire Direction folks at the firing batteries, located up to 30 miles away. We used land line, as well as secure and non-secure radio, to make sure firing data was correct. Once it was verified, and clearances obtained, we gave them the go-ahead to fire. Just for information, there were three artillery batteries, each consisting of six 155mm howitzers. These firing batteries were generally stationed in the same location. but. occasionally. would move to another location and support various operations of ground troops and/or the First Cav.

Some of the names that occasionally cross my mind from Headquarters Battery of the 3rd Battalion, 16th Artillery, are: Jose Padilla (Don Juan), David Smith (Spoon), Emanuel Mamakos (Zorba the Greek), Penny Cardona (Poncho), Don Timm, Tom Hammond, Fred Ledbetter, Lou Denisen (Big Lou from Detroit), (Red), Capt. Gladfelter, Capt. Ford, Lt. Achentheller, Major/Colonel Durbin. I was called "Wally." Many of the guys I got to know pretty well were those stationed out in the boonies at the firing batteries. We were not restricted on the use of the land lines and could talk for hours on end if we were so inclined and the firing missions were at a lull.

The place we were located was across highway #1 from the Americal Division Headquarters and Marine Air Group #13. The place we were at was called "Cherry Hill" since there was no strategic importance for the Viet Cong or NVA. They normally left us alone, other than a few incoming rockets that we assumed fell short of their target of the MAG 13 group about ¾ of a mile away. The only deaths for the whole battalion during the time I was there included an accident (stepping in front of a 50 cal), one murder (when a drunk was rudely awakened by another drunk late at night) and one instance of a fellow watching for incoming rounds while standing in the door of the bunker, instead of being inside the bunker.

The previous description is pretty much the 'nuts and bolts' of my experience from October 1968 to December 1969. I extended 72 days to be eligible for a 150-day 'early out' that was offered to folks in 'the Nam.' As a result, I got out of Vietnam and out of the Army just in time for Christmas of 1969.

Some of the incidental observations and memories include going to the beautiful beach in Chu Lai, Vietnam. The coast was a virtual highway for Hueys going north and south. As we were in swimming one day, a helicopter opened up with its 50 caliber firing into the ocean not far from where some of the guys were swimming. We thought something was just a bit strange. Lifeguards ordered everyone out of the water since a shark had been spotted. After closer examination and waiting a few minutes, everyone got back in the water and continued on with whatever they were doing. The whole thing might just have been some guys in the Huey screwing around but the lifeguard said that he did see a shark fin. The beach at Chu Lai was as beautiful as any beach that I have ever seen anywhere. Miles and miles of beautiful white sand made it an inviting place to run and swim and I have probably never been in better shape as I was then.

Pot smoking was generally frowned upon and in the Fire Direction group we stayed pretty straight. However, it was generally available for many of the guys. When you hear of guys that are screwed up or watch movies of the era, you might think that pot smoking was all the guys did.

Unpleasant memories include incidents like getting emergency clearance after-the-fact for a howitzer that shot 155mm artillery shells in the wrong direction. One of the worst incidents involved a Fire Direction Officer in the field calling for first round "Firecracker." (a vicious artillery shell with a timed fuse). While flying through the air and still about 600 meters high, about 90 small hand grenades were ejected from the rear of the artillery shell. When these small grenades hit the ground, they would jump up and explode. He didn't want to zero in on the target with a smoke round since the 'gooks in the open' would not stand around waiting to see what happened next. The last we heard was a desperate cry for "cease fire" since hundreds of little grenades were coming in right on top of his location. I never did hear if he survived or not.

The real story might not even be my story, but that of two very similar but very different stories with two very different endings. One is mine which precedes this annotation. The other is the story of one of my fellow draftees and a guy who lived in the same part of town. I'll not use his real name, but rather call him Bob. Bob and I lived in the same neighborhood, and vaguely knew of each other, but I knew his older brothers. He was a recent high school graduate and I was a recent college graduate when we were both drafted. We went through similar experiences together; basic training, AIT, a 10-day leave, then to Vietnam together. There we parted ways, but left Vietnam at the same time. My story is rather uneventful and I went on with my life with the proverbial million-dollar-experience-that-I-wouldn't-give-a-nickel-for. His was a bit different.

His firing battery was attacked by the Viet Cong and things got very hectic. One of his friends who was right beside him during the melee and confusion was separated from him. Bob did not know for about 25 years what happened to him. Even worse, Bob was exposed to Agent Orange and had numerous symptoms that he attributed to Agent Orange. Try as he might, the Government would never admit that there was a real problem. He watched his children grow up with several symptoms that were common to children of vets who were exposed to Agent Orange such as Obsessive Compulsive Disorder. In other words, he lived with constant reminders of his war experience.

These and other problems led to his losing his job, struggling to get government disability, drinking heavily, and many other adjustment problems. He once shared a book with me that explained his predicament and other

Dave Walberg

Vietnam Veterans. According to this book, his symptoms were all very common such as, PTSD, alcoholism, divorce, children with Agent Orange problems, etc. He had read this book five or six times. I must add that this book was full of lies and distortions, but he believed what he wanted to believe. He had given copies to myself and several of his veteran friends. He obsessed over what the book was telling him and it became his life focus. It was all he seemed to think about and all he wanted to talk about. The last I heard, he finally achieved his goal of total disability payment from the government and has turned almost vegetative.

Sometimes it is our experiences and sometimes it is how we handle our experiences. Our post-Vietnam experiences could not be more different even though they were similar in many regards.

HEROES OF THE VIETNAM GENERATION
US Senator (VA) James Webb

Reprinted with permission by James Webb

The rapidly disappearing cohort of Americans that endured the Great Depression and then fought World War II is receiving quite a send-off from the leading lights of the so-called 60s generation. Tom Brokaw has published two oral histories of *"The Greatest Generation"* that feature ordinary people doing their duty and suggest that such conduct was historically unique.

Chris Matthews of *"Hardball"* is fond of writing columns praising the Navy service of his father while castigating his own baby boomer generation for its alleged softness and lack of

Senator James Webb

struggle. William Bennett gave a startling condescending speech at the Naval Academy a few years ago, comparing the heroism of the "D-Day Generation" to the drugs-and-sex nihilism of the "Woodstock Generation." And Steven Spielberg, in promoting his film *Saving Private Ryan*, was careful to justify his portrayals of soldiers in action based on the supposedly unique nature of World War II.

An irony is at work here. Lest we forget, the World War II generation now being lionized also brought us the Vietnam War, a conflict which today's most conspicuous voices by and large opposed, and in which few of them served. The "best and brightest" of the Vietnam age group once made headlines by castigating their parents for bringing about the war in which they would not fight, which has become the war they refuse to remember. Pundits back then invented a term for this animus: the "generation gap."

Long, plaintive articles and even books were written examining its manifestations. Campus leaders, who claimed precocious wisdom through the magical process of reading a few controversial books, urged fellow baby boomers not to trust anyone over 30. Their elders who had survived the Depression and fought the largest war in history were looked down upon as shallow, materialistic, and out of touch.

Those of us who grew up, on the other side of the picket line from that era's counter-culture can't help but feel a little leery of this sudden gush of appreciation for our elders from the leading lights of the old counter-culture. Then and now, the national conversation has proceeded from the dubious assumption that those who came of age during Vietnam are a unified generation in the same sense as their parents were, and thus are capable of being spoken for through these fickle elites.

In truth, the "Vietnam generation" is a misnomer. Those who came of age during that war are permanently divided by different reactions to a whole range of counter-cultural agendas, and nothing divides them more deeply than the personal ramifications of the war itself. **The sizable portion of the Vietnam age group who declined to support the counter-cultural agenda, and especially the men and women who opted to serve in the military during the Vietnam War, are quite different from their peers who for decades have claimed to speak for them. In fact, they are much like the World War II generation itself.** For them, Woodstock was a side show, college protestors were spoiled brats who would have benefited from having to work a few jobs in order to pay their tuition, and Vietnam represented not an intellectual exercise in draft avoidance, or protest marches but a battlefield that was just as brutal as those their fathers faced in World War II and Korea.

Few who served during Vietnam ever complained of a generation gap. The men who fought World War II were their heroes and role models. They honored their father's service by emulating it, and largely agreed with their father's wisdom in attempting to stop Communism's reach in Southeast Asia.

The most accurate poll of their attitudes (Harris, 1980) showed that 91 percent were glad they'd served their country, 74 percent enjoyed their time in the service, and 89 percent agreed with the statement that "our troops were asked to fight in a war which our political leaders in Washington would not let them win."

And most importantly, the castigation they received upon returning home was not from the World War II generation, but from the very elites in their age group who supposedly spoke for them. Nine million men served in the military during Vietnam War, three million of whom went to the Vietnam Theater. Contrary to popular mythology, two-thirds of these were volunteers, and 73 percent of those who died were volunteers.

While some attention has been paid recently to the plight of our prisoners of war, most of whom were pilots, there has been little recognition of how brutal the war was for those who fought it on the ground. Dropped onto the enemy's terrain 12,000 miles away from home, America's citizen-soldiers performed with a tenacity and quality that may never be truly understood. Those who believe the war was fought incompletely on a tactical level should consider Hanoi's recent admission that 1.4 million of its soldiers died on the battlefield, compared to 58,000 total U.S. dead.

Those who believe that it was a "dirty little war" where the bombs did all the work might contemplate that it is was the most costly war the U.S. Marine Corps has ever fought—five times as many dead as World War I, three times as many dead as in Korea, and more total killed and wounded than in all of World War II.

Significantly, these sacrifices were being made at a time the United States was deeply divided over our effort in Vietnam. The baby-boom generation had cracked apart along class lines as America's young men were making difficult, life-or-death choices about serving. The better academic institutions became focal points for vitriolic protest against the war, with few of their graduates going into the military. Harvard College, which had lost 691 alumni in World War II, lost a total of 12 men in Vietnam from the classes of 1962 through 1972 combined. Those classes at Princeton lost six, at MIT two.

The media turned ever more hostile. And frequently the reward for a young man's having gone through the trauma of combat was to be greeted by **his peers with studied indifference or outright hostility.**

What is a hero? My heroes are the young men who faced the issues of war and possible death, and then weighed those concerns against obligations to their country. Citizen-soldiers who interrupted their personal and professional lives at their most formative stage, in the timeless phrase of the Confederate Memorial in Arlington National Cemetery, "not for fame of reward, not for place or for rank, but in simple obedience to duty, as they understood it." Who suffered loneliness, disease, and wounds with an often-contagious elan. And who deserve a far better place in history than that now offered them by the so-called spokesman of our so-called generation.

Mr. Brokaw, Mr. Matthews, Mr. Bennett, Mr. Spielberg, meet my Marines. 1969 was an odd year to be in Vietnam. Second only to 1968 in terms of American casualties, it was the year made famous by Hamburger Hill, as well as the gut-wrenching Life cover story showing pictures of 242 Americans who had been killed in one average week of fighting. Back home, it was the year of Woodstock, and of numerous anti-war rallies that culminated in the Moratorium march on Washington.

The My Lai massacre hit the papers and was seized upon the anti-war movement as the emblematic moment of the war. Lyndon Johnson left Washington in utter humiliation. Richard Nixon entered the scene, destined for an even worse fate. In the An Hoa Basin southwest of Danang, the Fifth Marine Regiment was in its third year of continuous comb at operations.

Combat is an unpredicatable and inexact environment, but we were well led. As a rifle platoon and company commander, I served under a succession of three regimental commanders who had cut their teeth on World War II, and four different battalion commanders—three of whom had seen combat in Korea. The company commanders were typically captains on their second combat tour in Vietnam, or young first-lieutenants like myself who were given companies after many months of "bush time" as platoon commanders in the Basin's tough and unforgiving environs.

The Basin was one of the most heavily contested areas in Vietnam, its torn, cratered earth offering every sort of wartime possibility. In the mountains just to the west, not far from the Ho Chi Minh Trail, the North Vietnamese Army operated an infantry division from an area called Base Area 112. In the valleys of the Basin, main-force Viet Cong battalions whose ranks were 80 percent North Vietnamese Army regulars moved against the Americans every day. Local Viet Cong units sniped and harassed. Ridgelines and paddy dikes were laced with sophisticated booby traps of every size, from a hand grenade to a 250-pound bomb. The villages sat in the rice paddies and tree lines like individual fortresses, crisscrossed with the trenches and spider holes, their homes sporting bunkers capable of surviving direct hits from large-caliber artillery shells. The Viet Cong infrastructure was intricate and permeating. Except for the old and the very young, villagers who did not side with the Communists had either been killed or driven out to the government controlled enclaves near Danang.

In the rifle companies, we spent the endless months patrolling ridgelines and villages and mountains, far away from any notion of tents, barbed wire, hot food, or electricity. Luxuries were limited to what would fit inside one's pack, which after a few "humps" usually boiled down to letter-writing material, towel, soap, toothbrush, poncho liner, and a small transistor radio.

We moved through the boiling heat with 60 pounds of weapons and gear, causing a typical Marine to drop 20 percent of his body weight while in the bush. When we stopped we dug chest-deep fighting holes and slit trenches for toilets. We slept on the ground under makeshift poncho hootches, and when it rained we usually took our hootches down because wet ponchos shined under illumination flares, making great targets. Sleep itself was fitful, never more than an hour or two at a stretch for months at a time as we mixed daytime patrolling with night-time ambushes, listening posts, foxhole duty, and radio watches. Ringworm, hookworm, malaria, and dysentery were common, as was trench foot when the monsoons came.

Respite was rotating back to the mud-filled regimental combat base at An Hoa for four or five days, where rocket and mortar attacks were frequent and our troops manned defensive bunkers at night. Which makes it kind of hard to get excited about tales of Woodstock, or camping at the Vineyard during summer break.

We had been told while training that Marine officers in the rifle companies had an 85 percent probability of being killed or wounded, and the experience of "Dying Delta," as our company was known bore that out. Of the officers in the bush when I arrived, our company commander was wounded, the weapons platoon commander wounded, the first platoon commander was killed, the second platoon commander was wounded twice, and I, commanding the third platoons fared no better. Two of my original three-squad leaders were killed, and the third shot in the stomach. My platoon sergeant was severely wounded, as was my right guide. By the time I left, my platoon I had gone through six radio operators, five of them casualties.

These figures were hardly unique; in fact, they were typical. Many other units; for instance, those who fought the hill battles around Khe Sanh, or were with the famed Walking Dead of the Ninth Marine Regiment, or were in the battle of Hue City or at Dai Do, had it far worse.

When I remember those days and the very young men who spent them with me, I am continually amazed, for these were mostly recent civilians barely out of high school, called up from the cities and the farms to do their year in hell and he return. Visions haunt me every day, not of the nightmares of war but of the steady consistency with which my Marines faced their responsibilities, and of how uncomplaining most of them were in the face of constant danger.

The salty, battle-hardened 20-year-olds teaching green 19-year-olds the intricate lessons of the hostile battlefield. The unerring skill of the young squad leaders as we moved through unfamiliar villages and weed-choked trails in the black of night. The quick certainty when

313

a fellow Marine was wounded and needed help. Their willingness to risk their lives to save other Marines in peril. To this day it stuns me that their own countrymen have so completely missed the story of their service, lost in the bitter confusion of the war itself.

Like every military unit throughout history we had occasional laggards, cowards, and complainers. But in the aggregate, these Marines were the finest people I have ever been around. It has been my privilege to keep up with many of them over the years since we all came home. One finds in them very little bitterness about the war in which they fought. The most common regret, almost to a man, is that they were not able to do more for each other and for the people they came to help.

It would be redundant to say that I would trust my life to these men. Because I already have, in more ways than I can ever recount. **I am alive today because of their quiet, unaffected heroism. Such valor epitomizes the conduct of Americans at war from the first days of our existence That the boomer elites can canonize this sort of conduct in our fathers' generation while ignoring it in our own is more than simple oversight. It is a conscious, continuing travesty.**

NOTE: Former Secretary of the Navy James Webb was awarded the Navy Cross, Silver Star, and Bronze Star medals for heroism as a Marine in Vietnam. His novels include _The Emperor's General_ and _Fields of Fire_.

STORIES FROM MIDDLE EAST

1990 – 2012

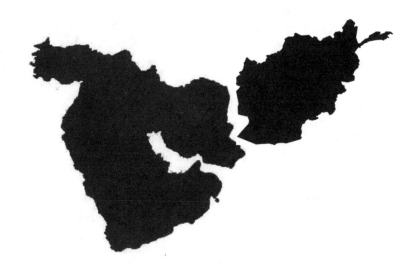

Territories involved:

Iraq

Kuwait

Afghanistan

CCATT: ER IN THE SKY

Brian Dykestra, MD

DISCLAIMER: This story is not intended to represent the Air National Guard, US Air Force, or Department of Defense. The viewpoints in this story are those of the author.

Brian J Dykstra is a Pulmonary (Lung) Medicine and ICU specialist. He is CCATT Physician, Senior Flight Surgeon, and a Colonel in the Air National Guard. He has been deployed as a CCATT physician to Iraq, Afghanistan, and Germany in support of Operations Iraqi Freedom, Enduring Freedom, and New Dawn. He has more that 400 flight hours in a number of different aircraft and has more than 25 combat sorties and 140 combat flying hours in support of these missions.

CCATT: Critical Care Air Transport (CCAT) team

A routine patrol outside the wire 20 miles from their Forward Operating Base (FOB), somewhere, in Afghanistan has just begun. Intel notes that this should be uneventful since a patrol of the area a few days earlier had revealed no insurgents. Because of this seemingly low risk mission, a number of Marines dismount from their vehicles. Despite being vigilant, an IED blast occurs at 1800 hours local.

Brian Dykestra, MD

Time (T) – 0: A 23-yr-old Marine sustains the full force of an IED blast: 70% burns, both legs appear to have significant injuries, major bleeding is occurring.

T + 5 minutes: The unit secures the area and begins self aid and buddy care—tourniquet placements on both legs, quick clot in the wounds to stop the bleeding, immediate call for a medevac dust off.

T + 15 mins: UH60 taking off from the FOB for pickup of the injured Marine.

T + 30 mins: Casualty evacuation from the blast site via army medical UH60 (Blackhawk) to the combat surgical hospital (CSH) in Kandahar. The army medics begin immediate resuscitation—airway control with intubation with an emergency breathing tube, IVs, pain control…

T + 60 mins: Arrival at the CSH where he is taken directly to the OR for damage control surgery and continued resuscitation. He is placed on life support, emergent amputations of his legs, chest tubes, abdominal surgery to control bleeding, blood transfusions. A Critical Care Air Transport (CCAT) team is alerted for a mission – to transport this critically injured Marine to Joint Base Bagram and the level 1 trauma team. A C130 cargo plane is put on alert for this emergency mission. The plane is reconfigured from its cargo layout to a medevac layout.

T + 90 mins: The CCAT team arrives at the CSH to evaluate and prepare the Marine for flight. Once the Marine is out of the Operating Room (OR), the CCAT team assesses him, switches his life support equipment for smaller, portable, flight worthy equipment and "packages" him onto a transport litter, attaching all of his life support equipment to the litter for quick access and adjustment during flight.

T + 2.5 hours: The Marine is loaded on a C-130 cargo plane now configured for medical evacuation; a flying Intensive Care Unit (ICU).

T + 4.5 hrs: Arrival at Craig Theater Hospital, Bagram; taken immediately back to the OR for re-evaluation, continued resuscitation, and damage control/life saving surgery. Given the severity of injuries, immediate transfer to Germany was felt necessary. A second CCAT team is alerted for this mission while the first CCAT team returns back down range. A KC135 Tanker configured not for refueling but for medevac is already airborne from Ramstein, Germany, heading for Bagram. Its mission is to take this Marine back to Germany Landstuhl Regional Medical Center (LRMC) – the second leg in a journey back to the US.

T + 7 hrs: The Marine is out of surgery and is transferred to the ICU. He is stable but still critical and remains on life support. The second CCAT team arrives at the hospital to assess the Marine and prepare for the next flight to Germany. In addition to the more than 500 pounds of equipment and supplies the CCAT team already has, extra supplies are added and blood is requested in case a transfusion is needed during flight. The Marine is again packaged for flight.

T + 10 hrs: The Marine is transferred from the hospital to the flight line, loaded on the KC135 that will act as another ICU for the next 8 hours. A night time takeoff is scheduled.

T + 20 hrs: Arrival at Ramstein Air Base, Germany. He is unloaded onto an ambus for a 20 minute ride to LRMC. He is again taken back to the OR for revaluation and continued treatment of injuries. Due to the extent of injuries it is felt necessary to get him to Walter Reed National Military Medical Center (WRNMMC) for continued management once he is stabilized. While he may be stable, he still remains in critical condition on life support. A third CCAT team is now put on alert for a mission – this time in a C17.

T + 48 hrs: After the CCAT team readied the Marine for flight at LRMC and he was transported back to Ramstein Air Base, he is loaded onto the waiting C17, again with all the life support equipment and supplies for a 10 hour flight over the Atlantic Ocean.

T + 58 hrs: The plane lands at Joint Base Andrews, and he is immediately transferred to Walter Reed NMMC for definitive care.

From the time of injury in Afghanistan to definitive care in the US —transported across three continents, on three different aircraft, having had multiple surgeries—is less than three days. During Desert Storm, the same injury would take up to 15 days and in Vietnam it took up to three weeks to move the most severely injured. Because of this, the survival rate has dramatically increased: greater than 96%. This allows for a lean and smaller medical footprint in the war zone and the ability for far forward lifesaving medical treatment.

Aeromedical transport of wounded soldiers and marines have been going on since World War I. In 1909, Capt George H.R. Grosman, during a conference with the War Department, stated, "I clearly see that thousands of hours and ultimately thousands of patients can be saved through the use of airplanes in air evacuation." While the use of air ambulances was minimal during and after WWI, they were being used. In 1942, the first medical air ambulance squadron was formed at Ft Benning. These air-evacuation squadrons were made up of nurses and medical technicians to transport stable patients. This continued through Desert Storm

Emergency care in the air

In the mid 1990s it became apparent that the future of air-evacuation needed to include not just the stable patient, but stabilized patients that may still be on life support and still very critical. This philosophical change changed the face of medical care in the US military across all branches, not just the Air Force. While there has always been far forward medical care for the wounded, the severely wounded generally remained in the war zone for days, if not weeks, until stable enough to be transported to the next higher level of care. The Air Force developed a plan to transport critically wounded out of the war zone to definitive care in a matter of hours. The Critical Care Transport (CCAT) team was born.

The Air Force's CCAT team is a three person team made up of a specialized critical care physician (ER physician, Anesthesiologist, Trauma Surgeon, or Pulmonologist/Intensivist), a critical care nurse, and a cardiopulmonary technician (a respiratory therapist). The equipment that the CCAT team uses is state of the art, about 700 pounds and worth close to $400,000. The equipment includes ventilators, cardiac monitors, IV machines, surgical equipment, medications, IV solutions, and everything else that is needed to treat critically wounded people. The equipment and supplies that are used allows the CCAT team to manage them without resupply for up to three days. In addition, medically ill patients such as those with heart attacks, pneumonias, and severe infections can also be treated. The team's capability is equal to that of a medical or surgical ICU team at any level 1 trauma center.

The goal of the CCAT team is not just to watch the patient during transport, but to treat and improve the patient from the time they take responsibility to the time they deliver the patient to the next hospital. Many missions are up to 12 hours long from the time the patient leaves the hospital until they are in the next hospital which includes 10 hours on board the aircraft during flight. Treatment occurs during the entire flight including takeoff and landing with all of the challenges of flight – pressure changes, vibration, and loud noise.

CCAT teams are deployed around the world in both low risk and high risk locations. They are stationed at US military hospitals in the U.S. and friendly countries but on the other extreme may also be deployed with Special Forces. CCAT teams were deployed with US Special Forces within days of the 9/11 terrorist attack. They are used to transport patients under fire and are used for transporting military personnel even between military hospitals in the US.

Treatment of battlefield wounds has dramatically changed over the years. In Korea and Vietnam the wounded were first treated at a Battalion Aid Station then on to a Field Hospital, a Theater Hospital and finally to definitive care in Japan or the U.S. taking up to 23 days or longer. Now treatment starts at the point of injury with three stages of far forward battlefield care: care under fire known as self aid and buddy care (SABC); tactical care at the combat surgical hospital; and evacuation care such as done with a CCAT team. To perform SABC, all of the soldiers and marines are supplied with an Individual First Aid Kit (IFAK) which includes, among other things, tourniquets and combat or quick clot gauze. These two items have the incredible ability to stop massive bleeding and save lives. By keeping the wounded alive during the "golden hour," it allows for the time to get the injured to a forward surgical team or combat surgical hospital for damage control and resuscitative surgery – tactical care. Evacuation care begins when they are transported to a level 3 hospital still within the war zone. Continued resuscitation occurs and within hours the critically wounded can be on their way to Germany. In some unique instances there have been direct flights to the US from Iraq or Afghanistan with multiple in-flight refuelings in order to get the wounded to definitive care without having to have multiple landings, take-offs, loadings & unloadings.

The CCAT team is a unique, highly specialized medical asset that can create and operate a portable intensive care unit (ICU) in flight on board any available transport aircraft in the Air Force inventory: C-130s, C-17s, KC-135s, C-21s, C-5s, KC-10s and even reconfigured commercial aircraft if necessary. No longer are there any dedicated medical planes. This allows for more rapid and efficient use of air assets. The CCAT team has been designed to be flexible in response and operate across the spectrum of potential scenarios from humanitarian and relief operations through small-scale contingencies to major theater war in times of peace, war, and covert operations.

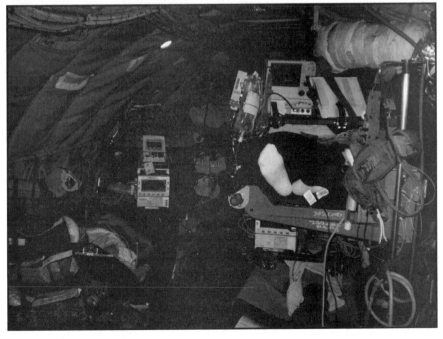

ONE SOLDIER'S TALE
Sean Fitzgerald

Sean Fitzgerald

On June 26, 2000, I made the most significant choice of my life, the choice to join the Michigan Army National Guard. I joined on a six-year active two-year inactive term and received the usual song and dance of the local recruiter. You know the one where they say, you will never leave the continental United States and absolutely never see an all out war. Well we all know how that works. September 11, 2001 changed our lives and our country forever. The reality of my guard unit possibly going overseas was coming true. As we all watched the third Infantry Division (ID) tear its way from Kuwait to downtown Baghdad, I realized I could be the next to go. A few weeks later my number was up.

As we prepared for the long journey ahead, we went through many classes teaching us to be mentally ready for the things we might see: dead bodies, demolished buildings, families living out of their cars and begging us for food, among other things. At the time it seemed just a precautionary measure to scare us; later we would understand why. We were then sent from our home unit in Kalamazoo to Fort Riley, Kansas, for more mobilization classes and what seemed like hundreds of medical shots including anthrax, small pox, and malaria all hurting equally and making push-ups even harder than before. On our second week at Riley we began weapons qualification and field training. While my unit had the pleasure of being in the field for a week, I had the privilege of getting five of my teeth pulled and being on light duty while they were gone. I am not sure why, but for some reason, I wasn't fit for war unless I was bleeding from the mouth. Looking back, I should be thankful because 1 hear getting your wisdom teeth pulled is expensive.

I was issued an SAW (squad automatic weapon) which replaced the M-60 a few years ago and was capable of firing a thousand rounds a minute and is just as accurate as the M-16. Fully loaded, it weighed around 30 pounds, mostly in the 200-round drum. If you've ever wondered why soldiers are always sweating, it is because we, on average, have to carry 40-50 pounds of equipment every day, everywhere. On qualification day, a.k.a the longest day of the deployment, we get to get up at 5:00am, get chow in the field and begin the hurry up and wait process. Our unit only had 16 SAWs and around 60 M-16s. Those of us with SAWS got to do range duty for the M-16ers. The reason it's the longest day is because people forget everything they have learned about shooting a weapon and have to be taught all over again how to do the slightest things. (Not very re-assuring when you are getting ready to go to a war zone). By nightfall it was too dark for the SAW people to shoot, so we were on again for the next day.

The week before leaving for Kuwait we had to railload all of our equipment on a train to be taken to the Gulf of Mexico where it was loaded on a container ship and set sail. For those of you keeping track, it takes the ship six weeks to get to Kuwait and a week later it took us 22 hours on a 747.

Long story short, it was a long wait in Kuwait. The only up side to that long flight was that my motor sergeant volunteered me and my battle buddy for the loading and unloading of the plane and therefore got to ride in first class with reclining chairs and personal DVD players the whole trip. Reality met us as soon as we landed, on the first step off of the plane—3:00 in the morning and 105 degrees. It was like a slap in the face with a hot wet towel. After unloading the plane, it was chow time and quite possibly the first of the worst meals of my life.

We spent five weeks in Kuwait to acclimate to the heat and surroundings. Duties included sweating and occasional classes on convoy techniques (at that time we still had no vehicles). At around the end of week four, our vehicles finally floated to the dock in Kuwait city. After a very thorough cleaning we finally started to pack for the great voyage north to Baghdad.

On the first day of our voyage we managed to lose five soldiers to heat stroke and heat exhaustion. Which for those of you doing the math was two and a half vehicles worth of drivers. So command, being what it was, decided that there didn't need to be any support and radio operators in those vehicles on this voyage. One of those drivers fell asleep at the wheel and flipped both the Humvee and the tailored generator it was towing. Yippee for me I now have some work to do. Being that I was the wrecker operator, I now had to flip both Humvee and trailer back on its wheels and tow them the rest of the way to Baghdad, about another 200 miles of so.

With the first day of our voyage behind us, we rested at a road side camp about the size of the average grocery store. It was hard to sleep with all the excitement of the day mixed with the fact that it was still 95 degrees out, oh and anybody that could pick up a grenade could hit me in the face with it in our miniscule camp.

The next morning brought a whole new exciting experience to our lives. Our very first sand storm! Did I mention that we couldn't wait it out because the "camp" was expecting another group, and there wasn't enough room for all of us. So, on we went with Humvee and trailer in tow, on a sand blasting voyage. About 75 miles in on MSR Tampa (Main Supply Route) as I was riding shotgun and beginning to understand why the locals wear the headgear or hattah that they do, and me doing my best American impression of trying to keep sand out of my eyes and mouth. We had begun to be passed by another convoy of newer faster military vehicles. Then as my luck would have it we came upon a narrow bridge that maybe my truck alone could barely fit on. As my driver prepared to squeeze through, a fuel truck suddenly appeared on our left, forcing my driver to cut right and go off of the main road.

After the dust kind of settled and I radioed ahead to stop, the convoy looked ahead and saw a rather large drop-off and us about 10 feet from it.

After realizing my first near death experience came from fellow troops, I exited the wrecker and tried to access the damage. Remember the Humvee and trailer we were towing? Both on their sides again, Damnit. The good news: I have already done this once so I know how to do it again. The bad news: we are still in a sand storm and I can't see the people helping. About an hour into the goat rodeo in a sand storm, the skies cleared. Finally we can get going again. That is, until we look on the horizon, and see a small farming village about a half mile from us. I think ignorance took all of our common sense from us as well took up fighting positions to defend ourselves. We had been training for so long that we actually thought every person in

Iraq had AK-47s and wanted to use them on us. After a few minutes of pointing our weapons at mud huts I decided to go back to work and stop something horrible from happening. As we got back on the MSR, all vehicles with all four tires on the ground heading north, we finally get to our overnight camp as the sun was setting.

Day three was the final leg of our journey to BIAP (Baghdad International Airport). About 50 miles south of Baghdad we finally found paved roads, and could go faster than 45 MPH. At about the 30-mile mark we began to see the carnage of air raids and gun fights: tanks and vehicles still smoldering, the unforgettable smell of burning flesh, and locals rummaging through the remains of what was once their homes. The most sobering day of my life. To think that a day ago we were saying "I can't wait to get there and set up camp." I wish we could have waited.

The next thirty miles was more of the same, everyone on edge wondering if we were going to have to squeeze our triggers at another human being, trying not to imagine this day getting any worse. We finally made it to BIAP, and to what was going to be our command headquarters.

Looking back I would say we were among the lucky ones with our HQ location. Somehow we landed in the resort area of BIAP. Our command set up in huge marble buildings that were almost cold compared to outside. We were in B Company and the only group from Michigan with the rest from Iowa. As the Big Ten feud would have it, we got to sleep in what was once the BIAP Zoo. No real buildings, lots of animal excrement, and far from Battalion HQ. as we laid out under the stars that night, we came to realize that where there are animals, there are fleas. The next morning looked as if a chicken pox outbreak had occurred. A few trips to the medic and a few bottles of 100 percent deet later, we were able to actually sleep.

After a few weeks of living like an animal, our battalion started receiving orders to disperse units to remote locations all across Iraq. Our first mission was at a place called Camp Dogwood. If you went to the middle of the desert and looked left, you would have seen Camp Dogwood. Not a dogwood tree in sight, it actually got its name from the unusual amount of wild dogs roaming the grounds. The camp had two parts, one was the main camp, and the other was more towards the middle of nowhere. That is where we were. The good news was we had a firm building over our heads, the bad news it was overrun with pigeons and rats. A few packs of fireworks and the pigeons were gone, and a few weeks of at least five rats a night in traps and the rats were gone...mostly.

Being that we were the National Guard, we had soldiers that had expertise in plumbing, electrical and culinary fields. So, we had lights, air conditioners, plumbed showers, and a half descent meal every day. Considering where we were, life wasn't so bad. We were a signal company, so I called home almost every night.

In the beginning of our camp Dogwood experience, we were mortared almost every day, and every time we would grab our weapons like we were going to shoot the mortars out of the sky. After a while we got used to it and made a game out of guessing the size and trajectory of the shell. One day the game wasn't fun anymore. A mortar of which I'm guessing to be about 80mm in size went off just outside our building. As I lay on the ground in shock, trying to get my eyes to focus, hearing shouts for the medic, wanting to get up to help, I come to realize the shouts are coming from the sergeant looking over me.

It was about four hours before I finally came back to reality. I was in the camp hospital, with IVs and an oxygen tube in my nose. The concussion from the mortar, threw me a few hundred feet from what I've been told. Which is impressive, seeing as I am 6 foot 4, and was 250 pounds at the time. A few different doctors came in to see me, all doing the same tests on me, and all seeming to be focusing on my back. With no proper equipment like an x-ray machine, they guessed that I possibly fractured a vertebra or slipped a disc. "Time will tell" they said. Well, they were right; time told us that it was a slipped disk and I was to be on a 10-pound lifting profile for the next month, to help it heal.

When you are on a ten-pound lifting profile there are just a few things you can do, like guard duty and KP. I got to know the kitchen crew pretty well over the following weeks. As it turned out, they, too, were not from Iowa. Just four good ol' boys from Nebraska. Apparently if you let potatoes ferment, you will get the most disgusting alcohol imaginable, but it will get the job done if you want to let loose.

We lived and became a community at Camp Dogwood for three months before our next mission came. Over the course of the war, the military acquired a significant amount of Iraqui equipment. The powers that were at the time decided to put all of this equipment in one camp, known as Camp Taji. This new camp needed a communications unit to be the voice of the center of the military in Iraq. As you've probably guessed, we were that unit.

Camp Taji was at one time the Iraqi army training facility. As we explored the grounds of our new home we came across both the armory and the general issue buildings. So not only are we housing all of their heavy equipment, but also the weapons cache. The point I'm trying to make is Camp Taji is the most attacked camp in all of Iraq. We made it our home nonetheless.

On December 14, 2003, as I was sitting in the chow hall, a voice came over the intercom saying "We found him. We found Saddam Husain" a roar of applause, high fives, and hugging followed. It was almost surreal, to think that the mission we set out to do, was finally achieved. The following three months Taji was only attacked twice.

Once again we made small communities at our camp, and under the circumstances, life was good. While at Taji, we logged more convoy hours than any other National Guard unit had so far, averaging, three trips to BIAP every day for supplies and support of other units.

Since Taji was between Baghdad and Mosul, our unit was in charge of maintaining every signal unit between the two. About every twenty miles there was a node to keep the signal strong across the country. Every week or so we would have to go and do any maintenance needed to the nodes to keep things running smoothly.

After four months at Taji, battalion saw how comfortable we had gotten and decided to move us again. This time as far as they could get us from them, Mosul to support the 101" Airborne Division.

Mosul was by far the best living situation while in the country. There was both a Bob Hope dining facility and workout facility. The only real difference was that of all the units we had supported, the 101" was the only one that required us to be a part of their lifestyle, the hardcore ARMY lifestyle. It was by far the most fun for me to see some of the old dogs try to remember how to be a true active duty soldier. In the two months we were in Mosul it snowed twice and we weren't attacked once.

Our next call from battalion HQ was the best one yet. "We are going home." I think we packed up faster and more efficiently than ever before. I'm not sure if it was because of the training or because we knew we were going home. Either way we could see the light at the end of the tunnel.

We spent another month in BIAP packing up the rest of the battalion and were slotted to start our journey home on Monday after Easter 2004. Easter Sunday was set up to go to the range to qualify with our weapons before we head back. As I got in the prone position to squeeze off the first shots since I had been in Iraq, all hell broke loose. Mortars came in from all directions, small arms fire in the distance, a strategic planned attack on the US forces in Baghdad. We hurried to our vehicles, hit the gas and started for camp. Mortars landing all around us, the unmistakable zip of bullets flying by, and the unforgettable sound of my weapon, a M-249 SAW firing rounds at anything that moved and wasn't on our side.

My commander shouted "this is what we were trained for" as we pulled into our camp. A mortar hit one of our buildings, and I could hear shouts of terror. It's strange what goes through your head in a moment like that: *What do I do? Where are my friends? I was getting ready to go home.* Then just as suddenly as it started, it stopped. A whole new noise was heading this way, a group of Apache helicopters in attack formation moving swiftly our way. I've never been happier in my life. In the aftermath of the day's attack, not one single soldier from my battalion was injured, physically. Emotionally, I don't think any of us will get past that day. We did what we had to do to survive.

The next day as scheduled, we began our journey home. The feeling when we crossed the Iraq/Kuwait border was a flood of emotions. Every man and woman cried and hugged. Every person we began our journey with crossed that line together. I know now that we are among the few that can say that and it breaks my heart to imagine their loss.

We were in Kuwait for another month cleaning our equipment and going over inventory before we were cleared to fly home. Another 22 hour flight, but this time the air was electric with positive emotions. We finally touched down in Kansas, got to our barracks, and called home to tell my fiancée, "baby, I'm almost home." We were at Fort Riley for a week for psyche evaluations, and de-briefings.

Mothers Day 2004, the C-130 takes off from Kansas heading for Kalamazoo, Michigan, and all of our families. We were supposed to have a final formation before being released to our families. Lucky for us, our command was outnumbered by family members, and a mob of loved ones took over. I was finally home, back where I was meant to be. I'll never regret what I did while in Iraq because I know as long as our flag flies, it was worth it.

NO TIME FOR SNOWMEN
Zoltan "Z" Krompecher

LTC Zoltan "Z" Krompecher enlisted in the Army in 1985 as a cannon crewman and joined the Special Forces in 1989. Following service in the Green Berets, he graduated from Ohio University ROTC with a bachelor's degree in secondary education, commissioning in Military Intelligence, and Michigan State University with a Master of Arts. His assignments have included: Korea, Fort Campbell, West Point, Fort Huachuca, Fort Gordon, Fort Leavenworth, Western Michigan University, Fort Bragg, and Fort Lewis.

LTC Z Krompecher

Following an assignment at the United States Military Academy in West Point, where he taught English, LTC Krompecher reported to the 1st Special Forces Group (Airborne) before serving as an instructor at the U.S. Army's Command and General Staff College in Fort Leavenworth. He served with Special Operations Task Forces in Iraq and Afghanistan. He feels his greatest accomplishment is being the husband of Tina and the daddy of Leah, Annie, and Jack.

Letter written on the eve of deploying to Iraq in 2004:

Dear Leah and Annie,

My precious little girls. I write this letter to you because soon I will leave for Iraq. Your mommy and I just tucked you both into bed, read your books, and said our prayers together. I've been watching the news and am worried that there could be the off-chance that I might never get to watch you board the school bus for the first time, place a Band-Aid on a scraped knee, or walk you down the aisle of your wedding. So if you are reading this years from now, I want you to know how very much your daddy loved you and that I am also watching over you and protecting you. You are my everything, and now I must say goodbye to you. I cannot express adequately how much you mean to me, but I will try.

While I was your father, I was not always a good daddy. I failed in balancing the life of a soldier with the awesome responsibility of being a daddy. Even now I talk about, almost brag, to my fellow soldiers about going over—many of them are not deploying—but I suppose I do this to convince myself that I'll be fine and to hide my fear and worry about what could happen. I am a soldier, and going to war is something few American soldiers, at least those I know, want to miss. Fighting our nation's war is what we train, sweat, and prepare for our whole careers.

Still, I am worried. When I was a young, single Green Beret, I was so full of bravado that little would faze me. But now, I have you two, my little princesses, and your brother and mother to think of. I don't want this to be our last goodbye, but I realize that thousands of others

MIDDLE EAST

have left their families to go to the sound of the guns: I am going to, and I am proud of the fine men who give much of themselves who I'll be serving with over there, but I am scared about not coming home alive. I worry that the next time you see me will be when you stand in front of my coffin wearing your Sunday best to say goodbye to a daddy you hardly knew. I'm scared, but I'm a soldier...I can't make sense of it either.

Leah when you were two, we went sledding for the first time, just the two of us—daddy and daughter-- out enjoying the Michigan snow. After each ride down the hill, I would tow you back up while you sat on the sled. During one of our treks up, I overheard you crying and looked back to see that one of your snow boots had fallen off at the bottom of the hill. I picked you up, placed your foot in my jacket and headed down the hill to retrieve your boot. Little did I know that you would forever remember that incident as a pleasurable one because it was a moment in which we bonded. Now, any mention of snow and you respond happily with, "Daddy, remember when we went sledding and my boot 'felled' off?" quickly following with, "Daddy, when can we go sledding again?" That was two years ago, and you still remember it as if it were yesterday.

One night during this past December, I read you girls The Snowy Day before bedtime. The next morning revealed 3 inches of fresh powder. That morning you greeted me with the plea, "Daddy, can we go outside and play like Peter did in his book?" I replied that I had to get to work but maybe we could build a snowman after I returned home. Unfortunately, it was so dark by the time I returned from work that there was no time for snowmen...or anything else.

In the mornings, I would walk outside to kick the icicles hanging off my jeep before driving to work through the slush-covered roads. In January, it snowed again, and you (Leah) came running up to me with your pull-on boots on the wrong feet and wearing an unzipped jacket and mittens. At the same time you, Annie, pointed excitedly at the blanket of snow which covered our backyard. You both stood in front of me: smiling eagerly in hopes of playing in the snow. Sadly, my response was not so soothing. Put simply, I felt that I had no time to play games in the snow with my daughters. I was preparing to go to war. Eventually, you both stopped asking me to play in the snow and would instead sit quietly in your reading chairs while I called Fort Bragg. Your silence rang in my ears.

During one of the unseasonably warm days we had just a few weeks ago, I arrived home late but just in time to witness you (Leah) attempting to play kickball with the neighborhood children while Annie looked on from her plastic picnic table in the front yard. In the middle of the field was another father from across the street. He moved towards you, Leah, and gently rolled the ball as you stood uncertainly at home plate. You responded with a kick and laughed hysterically while attempting to run the bases. Annie clapped and cheered you on.

"It" hit me. Sitting in my car wearing my uniform, the thought of how I had wasted so many precious moments with my little darlings slammed into me. I realized how that should be me out on that plate. That should be me guiding my daughter to first base and then deliberately miss tagging her out as she rounded third for a homerun. That should be me enjoying a tea party with my daughter at her plastic picnic table. I suddenly understood how I should have taken you both sledding to see if perhaps we could make it down a hill without her boot falling off.

Later that week, I saw you, Leah, ride your bike for the very first time. I asked mommy who had fastened your bicycle helmet and helped you move the bike from our backyard to the front of the house. Mommy explained that you had found your helmet, dragged your bike to the front of the house, and proceeded to ride (with no one walking at your side). This was the first time she did not have anybody walking by her side ensuring that she would not fall: this time you rode alone. I knew then that you were growing up and would not always need me.

When we were stationed in Georgia, my friend, Sergeant First Class James Smith sent me an email that ended with the quotation, "To the world, I am an individual. To an individual, I am the world." Unfortunately, I never understood that line until recently receiving orders for this deployment.

Last night, as I was putting you both to bed, Leah looked up at me and said, "Daddy, I have tears in my eyes because you will be leaving." Annie, you must have realized something was wrong because you started crying, too. With that statement, I resolved to take SFC Smith's advice to heart and decided to "be the world" to you all. Years from now, I do not want to be the guy who sits alone sifting through a box of pictures trying to recapture fading memories because he left his children clinging to unfulfilled promises.

April has arrived, and there is little evidence of the long winter. I have put the sled away until next year. Winter is over, and I leave for Iraq next month. You are growing. Man, I wish it would snow just one more time.

Love,

Your Daddy

It snowed ten days after CPT Krompecher wrote this letter. He and his girls spent a wonderful afternoon sledding and topped it all off with rounds of hot chocolate. He left for Iraq and returned safely.

This letter appeared in the book <u>Operation Homecoming: Iraq, Afghanistan, and the Home Front, in the Words of U.S. Troops and Their Families</u>, a Washington Post "Book of the Year." The author was invited to read it at the Library of Congress.

HERO OF THE DAY
LTC Z. Krompecher

In his off time, LTC Krompecher spends time with his family and writes. He enjoys capturing the moment through writing and has been fortunate enough to have his works published in the book "Operation Homecoming" and a number of newspapers and periodicals. He was invited to speak at the Library of Congress to read his letter "No Time for Snowmen" and was a guest speaker at the Army Learning Summit in 2011. LTC Krompecher is married to Tina (Gallo) of Westlake, Ohio, and they have three children.

MIDDLE EAST

Tales of war usually include a soldier, bloody and bleeding, who rises up to overrun a position, take a hill, or kill large number of the enemy against withering fire. All wars have their heroes, and I've known a few, but the one who stands out in my mind is the furthest thing one could imagine.

The Special Operations units I served with in Afghanistan and Iraq were full of courageous Americans who volunteered to serve and fight: wherever our nation deemed necessary. Most of us have served multiple combat tours, but few complain too loudly—we still complain, like soldiers do—about the conditions in which we currently exist because this is our chosen profession. Still, it's good to be remembered.

Among the plains and mountains of Afghanistan, we fight mostly for each other. And sometimes—amid the frenetic pace of missions, memorial services for fallen brothers, the noise and the dust—we temporarily lose ourselves. For short durations, we become myopic because our focus is concentrated on the fight, and the idea of home gets pushed to the fringes of our minds...but only temporarily, because home occasionally arrives in the form of mail.

I came in one night, crawled into my sleeping bag and was soon asleep, only to be awakened soon after with the announcement that I had received three boxes of mail. My buddy handed me the goods, and then I rolled over and fell back to sleep for a few hours. The next day was hot, dusty, and unpleasant.

News came that we had lost another comrade in arms. I sat in my hooch and offered a prayer, then looked to my side and noticed the care packages with a return address from Ms. Phyllis Leach of Catawba, Ohio.

Opening them up, I found a treasure trove of food, hygiene items and pencil, paper, rulers and crayons for a local Afghan school for which we were collecting needed supplies. I hate to admit it, but I had missed chow and greedily nourished myself on some of the snacks while sifting through this cache from home. And here is where Phyllis Leach made a difference in the war that day.

I was down to my last bit of toothpaste, so that found its way into my pocket. I needed soap, and the ten bars she sent would keep me relatively clean (maybe not enough for a formal event, but passable by Afghanistan standards). I carried the rest of the goods to my truck, which has earned dubious admiration for the fact that, despite five bullet holes, no air conditioning and a questionable chassis still ran. (I hang two stale pine-tree fresheners in it, just for kicks.) I started the truck and rolled out to enjoy the compassion of Phyllis Leach.

It was hot that day, and dusty, and the news of our fallen comrade weighed heavily on us. Going through a checkpoint, I couldn't help but notice the sun beating down on the young soldiers manning the gate. I went through and then pulled over. Turning off the engine, I sighed before getting out and carrying a box of goodies to the group.

"Here, have some love from Ohio," I offered. Those words did the trick, and it did not take any prompting for them to grab some of the delights. One of the soldiers was from Mansfield, Ohio and his pride in the Buckeye State was noticeable on his face when I explained that Phyllis Leach used to watch me and her son run sprints on the football field and roll around on wrestling mats many years ago. Too many years.

Looking around, I noticed a group of Airmen (I'm Army, and there is an unspoken rivalry) standing nearby. I called them over and shared the wealth. Within seconds, that precious trove was gone, gathered up by soldiers hungry for the comforts of home.

I drove a little farther and came across five locals digging a ditch in the heat. My muscles were not responding to my brain, which said, "Keep driving, fool. Keep driving. You don't even know these guys!" But what I did know was that they probably felt hot, dirty, and tired.

Sighing again, I pulled over, grabbed my second box of love and made my way towards them

"Assalamu alaikum"—peace be upon you—I said.

"Walaikum assalam—and may peace be with you—was their response.

I replied, "I brought you gifts from America," and gave the one I guessed to be the informal leader the box. The men looked inside and then looked back at me, as if they did not understand. I explained that I was offering a gift to ease their labor. They placed their hands on their hearts and thanked me, after which I placed my hand on my heart and told them the thanks went to a kind woman in Ohio.

They put down their shovels and commenced eating.

Earlier in the week, I had been talking with some of my Afghan counterparts when a little boy ventured towards us. One of my Afghan friends noticed me looking at him and explained the boy was from a local village and should be in schools, but the village was poor. I told him how a group of Knights of Columbus had launched a drive to collect supplies for the nearby schools. My friend explained how good this was, because education offered an alternative to the gun. Remembering our conversation, I took the final box to our post chapel in hopes the new weapon of choice for young Afghans would be a crayon instead of a rifle, and then made my way back to my hooch to think of my friend who had left his legs on a dusty hilltop after being hit with an IED..

Though most of the snacks were gone, I somehow felt fuller inside and let a smile drift across my face.

Some people call us heroes, but that's not entirely true; we volunteered and are proud to serve our country. On that day, among the smiles, handshakes and greetings of peace—against the backdrop of war—the real hero was Ms. Phyllis Leach of Ohio.

NOTE: Krompecher is a Green Beret and intelligence officer who served as the Professor of Military of Science at Western Michigan University, 2011-12. He is presently stationed in San Antonio, Texas. He hopes to retire one day and teach at a high school or community college. These views are his own.

CANDLES & CORDITE
LTC. Z. Krompecher

Afghanistan 2010

This morning was another Groundhog Day
Stirring, I looked around my hooch
Put on my dirty uniform
Andwalked outside to greet Afghanistan

Back home, my daughter woke to her
10th birthday

Last night involved another mission
Tracers, burned like candles
And cordite filled noses
I remember sharing my water
With a local suffering a gunshot wound
That night, I checked my weapon
And magazines
In the Midwest, my other children
Laughed with the birthday girl

Tonight there will be another
Celebration. Deliberate in planning.
And tonight, another well-planned
party will occur
With candles alight
Like tracers
And the smoke from them
Exciting the celebrants
Like cordite

123 Pleasant St., Anywhere U.S.A.
Same planet, different worlds.
Happy Birthday, Sweetheart

MY SON'S HANDS
LTC Zoltan Krompecher

I came home from Iraq to see my baby son
And watched while he held his hands in front of him
Holding them one way, switching their position
gazing some more, I do not know who is
more fascinated: him or I

I reach out, and little fingers clench my pinky
My mind drifts backwards and accelerates,
and I think
Will my son have the hands of his father?

Will he know what it is like to grip a bat
and feel
the sensation of hitting his first double
(on an error)
after striking out time and time again?
Perhaps he will proudly march across the
playground
holding a little girl's hand,
or experience the joy of
cradling a newborn,
maybe he will touch the gravestones
of his own and contemplate those before him?

Hopefully, he will spend time in manual labor.
I want him to feel the power of the
earth as he turns it with a shovel
while appreciating the humility and strength of
honest men.

I pray he won't grip a drink so hard as if the bottle
contains
life's answers. I hope not, but our family has a history
of seeking solutions in a brown bag.

If I know anything, and it's not much
I hope he never has to wrap his hands around the
receiver of a gun
hoisting it and burying the stock in his shoulder,
during a fleeting moment,
a moment which seems like forever,
and then finds himself unsure about his next move
Squeeze and the doubts stay for eternity,
hesitate and tomorrow might never arrive.

One day, I hope my son is there to squeeze my hand
again,
but this time I will be the feeble one, and he will be the
man.
I watch as my son inspects his hands, and I wonder.

Zoltan Krompecher
Written soon after returning from Iraq
zkrompecher@hotmail.com

PATRIOTISM

MEMORIAL DAY SPEECH: 2011

Blake Baiers

Good morning and thank you. I am humbled, and deeply honored to be here.

In the eighth grade, I traveled to Washington D.C. with the Honor Club. While visiting Arlington National Cemetery I received the great honor of laying a wreath on the tomb of the Unknown Soldier. Today, I have been given the great honor of addressing you, my friends and neighbors. Reflecting on the nature of the tomb, I realize that not just the soldiers buried there are unknown to me. In fact, many of the veterans here today are strangers to me. Before I begin, I would like to take this moment to thank all of the veterans gathered here for their service, and commitment to this great nation.

Every final Monday in May, we celebrate Memorial Day, traditionally marking the beginning of summer. Even though it will be another three weeks until the true natural

Blake Baiers

beginning of summer, today is seen as the day where all summer events may officially begin. This is a day where communities like Watervliet hold parades and ceremonies such as this, where families have barbeques or picnics, and when car dealerships mark down their prices. But today there is a feeling of solemnity knowing that some families may not be going on a picnic, (pause) that a young child may not be able to hold the hand of his father or mother as the parade passes. (Pause) Or that a mother may look upon the flag, at half-staff, and remember the folded flag in her home. To these individuals, this day holds special meaning, and I stand here today, empathizing with your grief that a loved one may not be here to celebrate with us. So today, let us set down our forks, look away from the parade, and forget about the car sitting in the lot, and remember the true reason we gather today, to honor the sacrifices our military has made, and continues to make, to ensure we have the freedom to meet back here next year, and celebrate Memorial Day once more.

To be human is to be mortal. We are given only one life, a life that may last a century or that may end in just an instant. It has been said that in order to truly know the value of life, we must experience the loss of another. The fact that death is so certain is why we place such a high value on it. Another thing valued very highly is our freedom, but that freedom comes at the greatest cost, the cost of life. It is the job of the Armed Forces to pay the bill of freedom so that we civilians don't have to. They fight for our freedom, fight for our way of life, and fight to maintain all aspects of this great nation put into place by our founding fathers. They fight to uphold all things good and virtuous, and to defeat the tyranny that plagues this world. Every day, soldiers step foot on the field of battle knowing that they are putting their life on the line in order to ensure that the American way of life is maintained, and that the American dream is left attainable for future generations.

In the 1960's, one-hundred years after its creation, Memorial-Day was moved from the traditional date of May, 30th, to the final Monday in May, turning Memorial Day into a relaxing three-day weekend. This extension of weekend leisure seems to have affected the way we celebrate Memorial Day. I see fewer and fewer people of my own age that have much of any concern for the true reason we celebrate this day, our veterans. I find it so profound that many young people, not all, give little reverence to those who gave so much in order for them to live a free and bountiful life. I am proud to stand here and say that I am not like many others of my generation. I had a grandfather, a veteran of the Second World War, who passed before I was able to truly get to know him. He flew cargo planes carrying supplies into combat and the wounded out. I know now that even had I gotten to know him I would have probably never heard any of his war stories; he was very reluctant to share any of his horrific experiences. None the less, the fact that I never had the chance to hear of those experiences drove me to dig into history and learn as much about World War Two as I could. This soon fueled my passion for learning about all of history. Learning about the suffering endured by the soldiers of all conflicts has taught me the true meaning of this holiday, and I truly honor each and every veteran for their service. I can remember being a cub scout in elementary school, before I really embraced the meaning of Memorial Day, and waking up at 6:00 in the morning to go and place flags at the graves of veterans at North Shore Memorial Gardens. It was a cold morning, and a dense fog coated the vast sea of stone and grass. At the time... I did not understand the significance of each and every tiny flag I stuck into the ground. For all I knew, I was only putting the flags up for decoration as the Memorial Day weekend approached. I now understand that I placed those flags to remind each and every passerby that they owed their life, freedom, and happiness to each and every person whose grave a flag sat beside.

Now as we all know, Life is a fragile thing, taken away just as easily as it is given. Knowing that life is so fragile, why do soldiers travel so far from home to risk everything? The answer comes down to a commitment to two things: Honor and Duty.

When a person dons the uniform of any branch of the United States military, he is no longer defined by his race, religion, or political affiliations. All he or she is left with is the title of being an "American Soldier." I can think of no title that demands more respect, not doctor, lawyer, or politician. All of the proceeding fall short of the honor a soldier in uniform carries. Whenever I see a man or women in uniform, I immediately hold them to the highest esteem. It is undeniable that as you pass a soldier in your daily life, you must feel some sense of admiration in some way or another. Children stare in awe and veterans salute. Their wearing of their uniform in their daily life is not simply for show. It is not to flaunt ribbons and medals. It holds a higher symbolism showing that persons commitment to upholding freedom, a freedom shared by each and everyone one of us here. The American soldier does not fight only for this nation; he or she fights for each and every individual citizen. Before receiving the title of American soldier one must swear an oath to protect the Constitution, the land, and the peoples of America from any and all enemies. In order to uphold this oath, American soldiers protect us with guns, with tanks, with airplanes and artillery. But most importantly, they protect us with their lives. This oath is a heavy weight to be put on any individual; still, many feel the call of duty and put on the uniform of the American soldier and advance into battle.

PATRIOTISM

Throughout its history, the United States has waged war all across the globe, and done so very successfully. American soldiers have traversed desert sands, tropical jungles, and the European countryside to combat oppression and tyranny, and to ensure that personal freedom is upheld. The victories we have celebrated came at a great cost of human life. This is the reason we gather here, to recognize and praise the bravery of the hundreds of thousands of servicemen and women who have put their lives on hold to put the wellbeing of this country in front of their own.

Our nation has done a fantastic job of building beautiful landmarks, commemorating the actions of our veterans. These monuments are no praise of battlefield success; they have been built in honor of individual service, and sacrifice. Memorial Day should be celebrated in the same manner. As former Senator Bob Dole once said on the topic of Memorial Day, "Today we do not pay tribute to war, rather, a tribute to the physical and moral courage that makes heroes out of farm and city boys, that inspires Americans of every generation to lay down their lives for people they'll never meet."

Each and everyday we feel the full effects of the sacrifices made by so many veterans on our behalf. As you look out into this open and hollow ground, you see many small American flags. Each flag represents not only that individual's service to the military, but also that person's service to each individual gathered here. Our veterans have given to us all they possibly can. Let us repay them all we owe by living the lives they ensured us to the very fullest; being

Virtuous (pause)

Reverent (pause)

And proud (pause)

ROBERT "BOB" HEFT:
Designer of America's Current National Flag
January 19, 1942- December 12, 2009

Don Alsbro, President of 'Lest We Forget' and friend of Bob Heft

Foreword

Bob Heft was a "TRUE PATRIOT" and a strong supporter of Lest We Forget. Bob made his first appearance at our Lest We Forget Patriotic Tribute, Nov 5-9, 2006. From that date to his death on Dec 12, 2009 he made at least eight appearances at LWF events. I think the following letter to the editor of the Herald Palladium, Benton Harbor MI that Bob wrote on Dec 1, 2006 expresses his feelings the best. I will not repeat the entire letter, but relate only a couple of paragraphs from the letter.

Editor:

I had the distinct pleasure of participating in the Berrien County tribute to all veterans Nov 5-9, 2006 in St Joseph. Since designing America's current national flag of 50 stars almost half a century ago, I have made more than 9,000 appearances at schools, community events, veteran's celebrations, Scout groups, conventions, churches and chamber of commerce banquets. I have spoken in all 50 states and in 57 countries.

I must say that the Lest We Forget tribute to honor veterans in the St Joseph area was without question the most memorable such event I have ever

Bob Heft

participated in. I hope and pray that the St Joseph community and surrounding area keeps this program going for years to come. Our veterans deserve it, our youth need it, and we as proud Americans should be proud to honor those who have kept and are keeping our nation safe. God Bless our veterans and our great and grateful nation.

Robert G. Heft, Designer, America's 50 star flag

Saginaw, MI

NOTE: If Bob was living today he would be proud of Lest We Forget and the patriotic role that we are playing in the community. We have tried to follow his guidance.

I've probably heard Bob tell his story at least a dozen times to school classes, community groups, and LWF functions. I will try and recount the story as I remember it. NOTE: Much of the information in this story comes from three sources: 1. Personal talks with Bob and listening to him tell his story to groups. 2. A pamphlet that he gave me, "The Amazing Story Behind the Design of the 50 Star Flag." This pamphlet was written by Bob and I never saw it in circulation and 3. newspaper articles.

—Don Alsbro

Bob Heft's Life Story

Subtitle: "I get no respect! and The Modern Day Betsy Ross"

January 19, 1942-December 12,2009

The subtitle should be explained. Rodney Dangerfield, well known comedian in the l980's and 90's became known for his "I get no respect" witticism and it certainly could be applied to Bob Heft. A few years ago there was a question on the TV quiz show, "Jeopardy." The question was "who designed the current American flag?" and none of the contestants could answer it. I attended many presentations Bob gave and he always talked in the beginning of his presentation about the fact that when people are asked who designed the American flag, most people can come up with Betsy Ross as the designer of the First Flag, but very few know who designed the current flag.

Bob was born on January 19,1942 in Saginaw MI, but grew up in Lancaster, OH being raised by his grandparents. Bob's dad died at Pearl Harbor, Dec 7, 1941 so he never had a chance to see Bob. There were 11 kids in the Heft family which probably was the reason that he went to Ohio to be raised by his grandparents, Mr. and Mrs. William Schromme. Bob always referred to them as his parents and I will do likewise.

Bob was very active in the Boy Scouts of America and that is where his interest and study of flags got started. As a 17 year old high school junior in the fall of 1958, Bob was in a history class when the teacher, Stanley F. Pratt told the class that every student would have an outside class project for the six week period. As most high school students do, Bob procrastinated to the very end and it came down to the last weekend before the marking period ended.

Bob was very astute when it came to politics and world affairs. There was talk of the territory of Alaska becoming our 49th state. He knew that Alaska was heavily Democratic, and knowing that the US Senate (Republican leaning) had to ratify statehood, he had a hunch. He felt that if the Republican administration under Republican President Dwight D. Eisenhower and the Republican Senate was set to admit the Democratic territory of Alaska, they might want to admit another state to give the Republicans more political power for the upcoming 1960 election. At that time the territory of Hawaii was Republican leaning. It is interesting that in the 50 years since, both states have reversed their political leanings. It is interesting to note that the election of 1960 was an extremely close contest between John F. Kennedy and Richard M. Nixon.

Bob was active in Boy Scouts and had studied flags for a merit badge. Knowing that the country would have to have a new flag, he decided to play a hunch and he would not make a 49 star flag, but rather a 50 star flag for his class project.

Bob's mother (grandmother) had an old foot operated treadle Singer sewing machine. While she wasn't a professional seamstress, she made clothing for the family and the neighbors. Bob loved to talk about the fact that he had never tried to operate the sewing machine, but had watched her many times and he said that she always had a way with the sewing machine. Whenever, something went wrong she would say her magic words and things would suddenly get better. Course those were words that weren't supposed to be used by children.

Bob had watched her sew on the sewing machine many times and he tried to get her assistance in the project of designing a new flag. She flatly turned him down. I don't think she realized how serious he was about the project. Not wanting to start from scratch, he decided to use the family 48 star flag that his grandparents received as a wedding present nineteen years earlier. Without asking, he took that flag downstairs and set out to make a new flag, using the red and white stripes and placing a new blue field in place of the forty-eight stars that adorned the family flag.

He went to the store and purchased a piece of blue cotton broadcloth and some iron on white fabric for the stars. The cloth and the Bond-X material cost him $2.87 in 1958. He used a seam ripper and a pair of scissors to separate the old blue field (48 stars) from the stripes, and then needed to join the new blank blue field with the thirteen stripes.

Since he'd never sewn before, he tried to get help from his grandmother. She was very upset about his plan to ruin their wedding flag and refused to have anything to do with it. She told Bob, "Wait until your dad comes home and sees what you've done!" Since she refused to help and the fact that the class project was due Monday, he decided to sew the flag himself. He ended up spending twelve and a half hours on this project. Bob always told how when his father came home from work, she told her husband to "go downstairs and see how Bob has ruined our family flag."

He cut one hundred stars (50 for either side) and then had to make a decision on the arrangement of the stars. He decided to alternate the rows by having six stars in the first row and five in the second row. He continued alternating the remaining rows, thus having five rows with six stars per row (30 stars) and four rows having five stars per row (20 stars), thus having the fifty stars required for his newly created fifty star flag.

Anyways, Bob always talked about the Monday morning bus ride to school. He asked his best friend, Dave what he'd done for his history project. He said that he'd forgotten about it until that morning, so he'd gone outside his house and picked five leafs from five different trees. He then proceeded to glue the leaves on a sheet of paper and write a short description of where they came from. He told Bob that he'd spent just a few minutes on the project.

That day in the History class, Stanley Pratt asked each student to describe their project. His friend got up and spent a long time talking about how beautiful the leaves were and that he'd spent a long time on the project. The class bell rang before Bob had a chance to talk about his flag project. However, when the projects were returned to the students , Bob's friend had received an A and Bob's grade was a B-.

Bob was furious. He was an A student and after spending twelve hours on his project he was given a B- and his friend only spent a few minutes and received a much higher grade. Bob approached the teacher, Stanley Pratt and asked why he received such a low grade. While a B- is not really a low grade, for Bob it was as he was an A student in the History class. His teacher said that he received a B- because it lacked originality, besides the US wasn't looking for a 50 star flag, but a 49 star flag. He further challenged the youthful Heft to "get the flag accepted in Washington and then he would consider changing the grade."

Bob took up the challenge. He sent the flag to the governor of Ohio with a note saying he made the flag in anticipation of the nation admitting two states. It was returned. He then got on his bicycle and rode cross town to the home of Ohio U.S. Representative Walter Moeller who lived in his hometown of Lancaster. He arrived at the home during dinner time and he handed the 50 star flag to Moeller, asking him to take the flag to Washington DC and submit it to the National Contest. Rep Moeller asked why there was 50 stars and not 49 and Bob told him his reasoning. Bob recalled Moeller responding "Why would anyone do that?" History proved Heft correct. Alaska gained statehood on Jan 3, 1959 and Hawaii on Aug 21, 1959.

While statehood can be granted anytime, a star can be added only on July 4, according to federal law. The 49 star flag had been used just one year, when a 50 star flag was needed, as Heft predicted. Moeller remembered the determined kid and entered the flag for consideration by Congress.

There were 1.500 flag entries submitted to Congress to commemorate Alaska and Hawaii. Many of them had alternating rows of five and six stars and at least three designs were identical to Heft's, but he was the only to stitch together a flag.

PATRIOTISM

After graduation June 1, 1960, Bob started a summertime job working at a local factory as a draftsman. The factory had 842 employees with 40 of them being draftsmen. On June 11 in the morning, Bob received an advance call from President Eisenhower's office notifying him that President Eisenhower would be calling him later in the day and to stay around the phone.

Bob likes to joke about how lunch hour came and he had a short debate with himself about whether to go out to lunch or stay at the job waiting for the phone call. Bob said that based upon his build (Bob was quite portly) you can tell what his decision was. He went out to lunch and when he came back, he asked the president's secretary, Mrs. Smith who had snow white hair, if anyone from the White House had called. She thought he was kidding. However, at

Bob Hope & Bob Heft

3:15 pm, she came back to his desk and in a shaking voice said, "Mr Heft, the President of the United States would like to talk to you."

Bob said that she went back and the plant supervisor had the call put on speaker phone so that all of the employees could hear it. Bob was very nervous. President Dwight "Ike" Eisenhower said, "Is this Robert G. Heft?" Bob replied, "Yes, but you can call me Bob." Do you have any idea why I'm calling?" Bob answered, "No sir," but he really did know. Ike said, "Do you remember sending in a 50 star flag to Washington DC, 2 years ago? I want to be the first to tell you that your flag has been selected as our national flag. Is there a possibility you can come to DC over the 4th of July?"

Bob replied, "Let me check. I've only been working here for 8 days." Bob put Ike on hold and asked his fellow draftsmen if they thought he could get off. They told him that would not be a problem and to get back on the phone. Bob got back on the phone and said, "Dwight, are you still there?" Bob said that President Eisenhower chuckled and said "Yes, Bob."

Bob ended up spending 4 days and 3 nights at the Capitol. He really can't remember what he said, but he did say that he was so nervous, "that my legs were like Hershey bars." Bob was more concerned about getting home and having his grade changed. The only thing he can recall saying was "I hope that this flag will last a long time."

After the ceremony, Bob drove all night, arriving in Lancaster at 4:30 am. He asked his mother to wake him at 6:30 am as he had to be to the high school by 7 am to talk to Mr. Pratt. When he got to the school, there were TV trucks from NBC and ABC as the word had been spread. Bob walked into the school and proceeded to Mr. Pratt's room. He walked up to Mr. Pratt's desk and after exchanging a few words, Stanley Pratt agreed to change the grade from a B- to an A. Bob had always received A's in history and Mr. Pratt had told him that he was one of his best students.

Bob never parted with his high school history project. Bob kept it in a safe deposit box but carried it with him on special occasions. Visiting Lest We Forget was always a special occasion and he always brought it with him. Bob told me several times that he wanted to sell the flag and provide the money received from the sale of this historic piece of history to his nieces and nephews for their college educations. Bob told me that he had the flag listed on Ebay and that it had brought in a bid of half a million dollars, but the bid was from a foreign country and he was hoping that it would go to an American bidder.

On December 9, 2009, Bob called me and said that he was looking forward to Lest We Forget's tribute to Vietnam veterans in June 2010, and he was very excited as the White House had just called and wanted him to come to DC on July 4, 2010, to honor his flag, as it is the longest flying flag in American history. On December 12, 2009, his nephew called me to say that Bob had had a massive heart attack.

Sadly, when Bob passed away, this flag has disappeared and its whereabouts are unknown. This flag which has flown over our country for 51 years, the longest flying flag in the history of the country, should be on display at the Smithsonian Institute in Washington DC. It is an American Treasure!

Bob attended Ohio University and Ohio State University. He went on to become a high school and college teacher, teaching what else, but the fields of history, government. business, economics and even art. He taught from 1966 to 1998. In addition, Bob is a former seven term Mayor of Napoleon, OH and served as State President of the Ohio Mayor's Association in 1988, representing Ohio's 973 communities. He returned to the Saginaw area in 1998 after retiring from Northwest State Community College in Archbold OH where he was a professor.

Never married, Bob traveled the world for decades. Along with teaching and politics, Bob managed to participate in over 9,000 patriotic events. He became one of America's most sought after speakers, having spoken in all 50 states and 57 foreign countries. Before Bob had his medical problems of diabetes, he traveled over 130,000 miles a year, making 225 speeches annually.

Bob was a White House visitor 14 times under 9 United States Presidents and flew on Air Force One nine times with six presidents. He toured and was on the TV shows of such notables as Bob Hope, Johnny Carson, James Brown, Johnny Cash, Dolly Parton, Regis Philbin, and Lee Greenwood. He appeared with Generals, William Westmoreland and Norman Schwarzkopf. However, Bob enjoyed talking to Mr. or Mrs. John Q Public just as much as the stars listed above. I always marveled at how when Bob came to our Lest We Forget events he was willing to sign his name and talk to the people, regardless what their station in life was.

Bob was a true server! In addition to being a high school and college teacher, seven time mayor, he served in a myriad of other organizations. He was member of the Resurrection Lutheran Church in Saginaw, past president of the Saginaw Lions Club, District governor of Lions International, active in Habitat for Humanity, America's Promise, Junior Achievement, 4H, former member of the Masons and an Eagle Boy Scout.

Bob took a special interest in children, especially disadvantaged children. He was active in the Lions Bear Lake Camp and the Special Needs Vision Clinic, both of which serve disadvantaged children. A friend and fellow Lion officer from Saginaw, Wil Hufton said Heft's interest in children with challenges stemmed from his own family. Imitating the kindness of his grandparents, Bob raised a nephew.

Bob died of congestive heart failure at the age of 67. His will according to Mr. Hufton, who filed his will, stipulated that a grand nephew receive the proceeds of his assets and his four grand nephews and grand nieces get the cash from the sale of the flag he designed, as long as they remain drug free. Unfortunately, as mentioned earlier in this story, it appears that the flag has disappeared. It is a piece of history that should be tracked down and recovered.

What Others Said About Bob Heft

"Bob Heft has been a friend of mine and Annie for over forty years. He stands for everything that is good about America. As a young boy, he answered a challenged that forever changed his life and the face of American history. A true American icon." – John H. Glenn, US Senator and Astronaut

"I am deeply proud to be considered a good friend of Bob Heft. He truly turned a history class project into a history making event. Annie and I share his enthusiasm for what Old Glory stands for. His efforts in speaking to groups around the world and his special emphasis to our school children is certainly a refreshing story that needs to be heard by every American." –John H. Glenn, US Senator and Astronaut

"He's a true American Patriot. His enthusiasm and love for America and the values we hold so high are many of the virtues that have kept this blessed land so great." –Bob Hope, Entertainer

"You have truly touched the hearts of our great Nation, by giving America its current flag of 50 stars. Your tours to bases around the world have brought appreciation and new meaning to patriotism." –Bob Hope, Entertainer (Bob traveled to Vietnam to appear with Hope.)

"Bob Heft gave us the flag that we salute for a land that we love so dearly. He demonstrates in his daily life, that it can be fashionable to be a proud American." – Ronald Reagan, President

"Thank you for your thoughtfulness and standing squarely behind America." –H. Norman Schwarzkopf, General, US Army

"Bob Heft took a dream and turned into it into an American success story that every young person should emulate and admire. He certainly demonstrated what persistence can do." – Jimmy Carter, President

"When I gave Bob his original grade of a B-, I had hoped that he would step up to the challenge and pursue a goal for improving his grade on his flag project. I really never thought that he would pursue that dream to the extent of actually getting it accepted as America's official banner.

"His untiring efforts certainly secured his place in history and made my life worthwhile place in history and made my life worthwhile and interesting. I am so proud of the part I played in his life and in our nation's history." – Stanley F. Pratt, Bob Heft's History class teacher

Bob's Humor and Philosophy

Despite his fame, Bob didn't take himself too seriously. He loved to tell jokes, especially about himself. In his introduction, he'd say, "My name is Heft. Just look at me. But you can call me Bob."

He liked to joke about his love for eating. He'd say, "You can tell that I haven't missed too many meals." He usually told that line when he was talking about making a decision to miss his lunch hour in anticipation of receiving President Eisenhower's call notifying him about the selection of his flag or to go to lunch. He chose lunch.

Some of his favorite sayings were:

"If you believe in what you're doing, don't give up!"

"Follow your dream!"

"Take action to make it happen."

I've heard him say these phrases so many times that as I write them, I can visualize him saying them. OH HOW LEST WE FORGET MISSES BOB!!!!!!

Lest We Forget's Obituary Tribute to Bob Heft

By WWII veteran Raymond Sreboth / December 14, 2009

Members of the *Lest We Forget* organization of Southwestern Michigan wish to express our condolences and our heartfelt sense of loss on the passing of a true patriot and our respected friend. Bob Heft gave much to our avowed mission of "Brightening the future by illuminating the past" through his many appearances at various public functions sponsored by our organization. His humorous presentations describing the events leading to the design and the adoption of our fifty star flag, enthralled countless numbers of children and adults in our area. His very presence, as a person of note in contemporary American History, brought a sense of appreciation for his efforts and a greater understanding of the meaning of our flag as a national symbol of unity.

Mr. Robert G. Heft
January 19, 1942 - December 12, 2009

PATRIOTISM

Rest assured that his contributions, good humor, and willingness to give of his time and talents, will long be remembered. Know, too, that we felt honored and greatly privileged, to have known this fine educator, gentleman and true patriot and we are grateful for his many contributions to our community and country.

Signed: Colonel Don Alsbro (US Army ret), President of Lest We Forget. On behalf of the members of Lest We Forget of Southwestern Michigan

HONORING AMERICA'S FALLEN HEROES ON MEMORIAL DAY
Robert B. Robeson, Lincoln, Nebraska

Permission to reprint was granted by Miitary Magazine, May 2012 issue (www.milmag.com)

War is a dirty, smelly, fearful and mean-spirited business. It's a grotesque funeral that often lasts for years. All combat soldiers have walked into this dark night of terror and dared death to have the last word. Sadly, and much to our sorrow, sometimes it did. Memorial Day is a time to remember these who stood tall for this country during our military campaigns and had their lives snatched from them while doing their part to end these conflicts and preserve liberty for millions around our world.

This year's Memorial Day observance spans a timeline extending from our War of Independence through America's involvement in the Iraq and Afghanistan Wars. These military actions have silenced approximately 1,317,804 voices forever. (This does not include those still missing in action.) But the true essence of this day involves individual human beings, not a compilation of assorted statistics.

As a helicopter medical evacuation pilot, who flew nearly 1,000 missions in Vietnam, I've been front-row-center for a lot of devastating action. I've often had an unrestricted close-up view of unspeakable battlefield carnage where unexpected, life-changing events swirled around everyone like fog in

(L-R) Captain Robert B. Robeson goes over details with CW2 Tim Yost (at Red Beach in Da Nang, South Vietnam) of a medevac mission for a captured and critically wounded North Vietnamese Army (enemy) officer—that they just flew under fire from the officer's own men—in time to save his life on March 7, 1970. (Photo by Bild am Sonntag, a West German newspaper that has given the author permission to use all photos taken that day.)

a rainstorm. That is where a soldier realizes in a flash that harm and death don't befall just the wicked. It's a place where I've heard my medics tell critically wounded comrades, time and again, "Hang on, buddy, you're going to be all right." A lot of the time we, and perhaps even those wounded, realized that this was undoubtedly a well-intentioned lie. These visions of violence are not cherished highlights in anyone's memory bank.

The real champions of our nation's wars have been those men and women who innately understood the horrendous risks and still left their safe havens in an attempt to preserve freedoms for others. These were freedoms that so many of them would never get to experience or enjoy much past their teen years, once they raised their right hands and took their enlistment oaths. The first things that had to be discarded in combat were any rose-colored glasses. These soldiers knew there would be little glory, no glamour, only darkness, destruction, disease, dismemberment and death. But still they went, willing to swim into piranha-infested waters or no-holds-barred confrontations to do their duty.

That's why the chalky-white tombstones stretching from Arlington to Gettysburg and across the Pacific Ocean to Omaha Beach, in addition to hundreds of other once violent places around our planet, speak so eloquently of America's military personnel over the course of its illustrious martial history. They voluntarily risked death to provide peace for the rest of us. And we must learn to live for it, too. Our fallen heroes have found their peace. Those of us fortunate enough to remain must continue to grope for ours in a world that still appears as dangerous and uncertain as ever. But even for we who remain, haunting memories and often nightmares may still persist long after the guns on distant shores have fallen silent.

Memorial Day is a time of solemnity and remembrance. We honor the dedication of those who were seized from us by the ravages of war and relive the pain of their loss. Armed conflict has always proven that not everyone survives these confrontational situations. Our fallen realized that the enemy was always lurking in the shadows with a goal to terminate their existence. They also accepted the fact that the odds were often stacked against them. When everything in close vicinity had descended into havoc and potential disaster, they all failed to be whiners, cowards or quitters. And they were intimately aware that in battle you can't call a time-out because you're tired, beat-up or outnumbered. It's an undeniable truth that rivers of warrior DNA flowed through each of them.

The soldiers I recall most vividly from combat were anonymous to all but their friends, families and those they served with. I witnessed too many of them die month after weary month. Some volunteered to crawl alone into dangerous and claustrophobic, enemy tunnel systems using only guts, a pistol and flashlight. They walked an exposed point while "humping the boonies" as grunts on the ground. Many flew through intense anti-aircraft fire over enemy strongholds. Others fought off massive human wave attacks in the dead of night on remote landing zones and artillery bases. Each morning, despite the unknowns, they forced their bodies to move out and do it all again. They persisted. They didn't back off. Fear, courage, close and final calls were a way of life to them in these tempestuous moments.

The legacy of our war dead is like summoning the legend of the Trojans who vowed never to come home without their shields. In every conflict this country has been engaged in, America's warriors came home with them...or on them. Their goal was never to betray themselves or act in ways unworthy of a great homeland.

Every war and battlefield in this nation's history has been unique, yet all of our fallen are connected by the strong threads of soldier commitment, determination and acts of valor. It wasn't a person's size, sex, age or race that mattered in the final analysis, because courage has always been defined by the individual act itself. That's why it's not appropriate to recount their countless heroic deeds with verbose and flashy rhetoric. The documented facts concerning their actions require no further elaboration or additional justification.

Each new soldier generation is required to take up the banner of safeguarding our nation and to derive the necessary sense of obligation from memories, stories and records of those who have gone before. That's why David's encounter with Goliath will never be forgotten, because it's recorded in the Bible. The legendary deeds of Odysseus in the Trojan War are remembered because of Homer's writings. So it's essential and obligatory that America's fallen warriors be honored in speeches and articles on this special and significant day. In this way, their manifestation of love, duty, discipline and gallant courage will never be allowed to be forgotten by those whom they protected and served to their fullest measure of devotion.

America's war dead have always been this nation's most precious resource because we would not have been able to appreciate or enjoy any of our other resources without their sacrifices. All of us, our children and everyone who will come hereafter, walk in their shadow and their debt. It's a debt we can never repay and must never forget.

One of the simplest, yet most profound, eulogies ever written for our combat veterans who never returned—this side of the Gettysburg Address by President Abraham Lincoln—was penned by combat journalist, extraordinaire, Ernie Pyle in 1943 in his WWII book Here Is Your War.

Pyle wrote, "Medals and speeches and victories are nothing to them any more. They died and others lived and nobody knows why it is so. They died and thereby the rest of us can go on and on. When we leave here for the next shore, there is nothing we can do for the ones beneath the wooden crosses, except perhaps to pause and murmur, 'Thanks, pal.'"

Pyle, a noncombatant civilian, was himself killed, on April 18, 1945, by Japanese machine-gun fire on Ie Shima, an island off Okinawa.

Like Ernie Pyle, war veterans have our own memories of fallen comrades that have been stored, like squirrels store their nuts, somewhere for safekeeping in the cache of our hearts. We reflect on their smiles in faded combat photographs we've stashed in dresser drawers, a box under our bed or

The uniform arrangement of headstones and American flags, at the Ft. Logan National Cemetery in Denver, Colorado on Memorial Day 2011, suggests that even in death these service members maintain their military discipline. (Photo by Rod Chandler, a professional photographer and former five-term U.S. Congressman from the state of Washington.)

dusty closets. Their smiles are frozen in time during moments of better days…before they were no more. These were times when what lay ahead was not yet known and couldn't be known, although we heard many of them provide unsettling and accurate premonitions long before these mental forewarnings became reality.

In today's society, it appears that many of the protected have short memories when it comes to understanding and appreciating the sacrifices of our war dead. Combat forces a soldier to take personal responsibility for representing his country, protecting himself and those around him. This is something that a large portion of Americans now appear comfortable letting others do for them. With the All-Volunteer Army, why not let someone else endure the risks and pain?

Some are even offended that anyone might suggest that they should have to "pay any personal dues" for the privilege of living in a free country, other than paying taxes. And many of their perceptions about the reality of war are based on the often skewed views of news and entertainment media or politicians who've never donned a military uniform or heard a shot fired in anger. One wonders what our Founding Fathers would think about the current path we find ourselves on as a nation.

Observing the deaths of Americans, foreign civilians and even the enemy, from close range, touches the very core of the human condition. It's something you can never dismiss or forget as long as you live. Each of the deaths of those I carried in my helicopter cargo compartment had its own strangeness and sorrow. I recall so many distinctive youthful faces tilted toward the light with open and unseeing eyes. This was a common sight and experience for medevac crews and also soldiers fighting on the ground. These fallen were the "heaviest" portion of all that we carried. They were the ones each of us did what we could to save, yet ultimately failed in the attempt.

Untimely death in war reminds us that life is fleeting but that any time spent defending freedom is time well spent, whether it's for our country or someone else's. And, on this special day, we can't forget warriors' age-old fear that their sacrifices might be forgotten. It is the obligation of those who survive, no matter which war it is, to see that this fear is never realized and to relate the stories of those who didn't, like Ishmael in Moby Dick.

Memorial Day can carry combat veterans back to WWII, Korea, Vietnam, Iraq or whatever war we fought in, as effectively as any time machine. It reinforces our grief of lost relatives, friends or comrades and continues to haunt us, hitching a ride on our thoughts and emotions by creating persistent aches in our souls. The memories of these silenced warriors will forever be etched in our minds.

This nation's main line of defense is not, and never has been, state-of-the-art defense systems destined for land, sea or space. Rather, it is the American men and women whose own lives have defended besieged foreigners and the rest of their fellow citizens for as long as we've been a nation.

So on this 2012 Memorial Day—regardless of where these fallen fought, what era military uniform they wore or whether they volunteered or were drafted—Ernie Pyle's memorable words are meant especially for them. "Thanks, pal." The democracy, peace and safety we experience today wouldn't be a reality without the selfless gift of their collective efforts.

FRANKLIN ROOSEVELT'S D-DAY PRAYER
June 6, 1944

My fellow Americans: Last night, when I spoke with you about the fall of Rome, I knew at that moment that troops of the United States and our allies were crossing the Channel in another and greater operation. It has come to pass with success thus far. And so, in this poignant hour, I ask you to join with me in prayer:

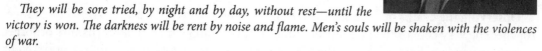

Almighty God: Our sons, pride of our Nation, this day have set upon a mighty endeavor, a struggle to preserve our Republic, our religion, and our civilization, and to set free a suffering humanity. Lead them straight and true; give strength to their arms, stoutness to their hearts, steadfastness in their faith.

They will need Thy blessings. Their road will be long and hard. For the enemy is strong. He may hurl back our forces. Success may not come with rushing speed, but we shall return again and again; and we know that by Thy grace, and by the righteousness of our cases, our sons will triumph.

They will be sore tried, by night and by day, without rest—until the victory is won. The darkness will be rent by noise and flame. Men's souls will be shaken with the violences of war.

For these men are lately drawn from the ways of peace. They fight to let justice arise and tolerance and good will among all Thy people. They yearn but for the end of battle, for their return to the haven of home. Some will never return. Embrace these, Father, and receive them, Thy heroic servants, into Thy kingdom.

And for us at home—fathers, mothers, children, wives, sisters and brothers of brave men overseas, whose thoughts and prayers are ever with them—help us, Almighty God, to rededicate ourselves in renewed faith in Thee in this hour of great sacrifice.

Many people have urged that I call the nation into a single day of special prayer. But because the road is long and the desire is great, I ask that our people devote themselves in a continuance of prayer. As we rise to each new day, and again when each day is spent, let words of prayer be on our lips, invoking Thy help to our efforts.

Give us strength, too—strength in our daily tasks, to redouble the contributions we make in the physical and the material support of our armed forces. And let our hearts be stout, to wait out the long travail, to bear sorrows that may come, to impart our courage unto our sons wheresoever they may be.

And, O Lord, give us Faith. Give us Faith in Thee; Faith in our sons; Faith in each other; Faith in our united crusade. Let not the keenness of our spirit ever be dulled. Let not the impacts of temporary events, of temporal matters of but fleeting moment—let not these deter us in our unconquerable purpose.

With Thy blessing, we shall prevail over the unholy forces of our enemy. Help us to conquer the apostles of greed and racial arrogances. Lead us to the saving of our country, and with our sister Nations into a world unity that will spell a sure peace, a peace invulnerable to the scheming's of unworthy men. And a peace that will let all of men live in freedom, reaping the just rewards of their honest toil.

They will be done, Almighty God.

Amen.

PATRIOTISM